The volume is a refreshing departure from the well-worn paths followed in many discussions of distributive justice since Rawls. While not neglecting standard arguments, the contributors provide a much broader, and welcome, perspective on fair shares, including views of justice from Southern Africa, discussions of less familiar figures in this context, for example, Herbert Spencer and Johann Fichte, and less familiar topics, such as the importance of territory in global distributive justice.

Carole Pateman, *University of California, Los Angeles*

This book is a thoroughly welcome addition to a burgeoning literature on distributive justice. Boisen and Murray have assembled an impressive group of contributors, with wide but mutually supportive interests. Together they highlight the crucial role that discussions of classic issues in history of political thought have had in framing debate in our contemporary (global) context. European, Anglo-American and African perspectives are brought to bear on issues that must concern us in a deeply unequal world. The book is sure to spark interest and debate among students, activists and academics with interests in distributive justice.

Bruce Haddock, *Cardiff University, UK*

Distributive Justice Debates in Political and Social Thought

Who has what and why in our societies is a pressing issue that has prompted explanation and exposition by philosophers, politicians and jurists for as long as societies and intellectuals have existed. It is a primary issue for a society to tackle this and these answers have been diverse.

This collection of essays approaches some of these questions and answers to shed light on neglected approaches to issues of distribution and how these issues have been dealt with historically, socially, conceptually and practically. The volume moves away from the more dominating and traditionally cast understandings of distributive justice and shows novel and unique ways to approach distributive issues and how these can help enlighten our course of action and thought today by creating new pathways of understanding. The editors and contributors challenge readers by exploring the role and importance of restorative justice within distributive justice, exploring the concepts of social and individual rights and obligations in welfare and economic systems, social protection/provision schemes, egalitarian practices and post-colonial African political thought.

Distributive Justice Debates in Political and Social Thought empowers the reader to cast a more critical and historically complete light on the idea of a fair share and the implications it has on societies and the individuals who comprise them.

Camilla Boisen is Postdoctoral Research Fellow in Political Theory at the University of the Witwatersrand, Johannesburg. Her area of research is on colonial political thought in relation to the development of ideas of property rights, trusteeship and humanitarian intervention and their influence on contemporary problems such as post-colonial restitution.

Matthew C. Murray is the Senior Project Advisor for the Growthpolicy.org project at the Mossavar-Rahmani Center for Business and Government at the Harvard Kennedy School of Government and serves as Special Lecturer of Philosophy at Providence College. Matthew is actively researching and publishing in the areas of critical theories of justice (subaltern, race, culture, gender and disability) and their effects on the ideas of and applications of distributive and social justice.

Routledge Studies in Social and Political Thought

1 **Hayek and After**
Hayekian Liberalism as a Research Programme
Jeremy Shearmur

2 **Conflicts in Social Science**
Edited by Anton van Harskamp

3 **Political Thought of André Gorz**
Adrian Little

4 **Corruption, Capitalism and Democracy**
John Girling

5 **Freedom and Culture in Western Society**
Hans Blokland

6 **Freedom in Economics**
New Perspectives in Normative Analysis
Edited by Jean-François Laslier, Marc Fleurbaey, Nicolas Gravel and Alain Trannoy

7 **Against Politics**
On Government, Anarchy and Order
Anthony de Jasay

8 **Max Weber and Michel Foucault**
Parallel Life Works
Arpad Szakolczai

9 **The Political Economy of Civil Society and Human Rights**
G. B. Madison

10 **On Durkheim's *Elementary Forms of Religious Life***
Edited by W. S. F. Pickering, W. Watts Miller and N. J. Allen

11 **Classical Individualism**
The Supreme Importance of Each Human Being
Tibor R. Machan

12 **The Age of Reasons**
Quixotism, Sentimentalism and Political Economy in Eighteenth-Century Britain
Wendy Motooka

13 **Individualism in Modern Thought**
From Adam Smith to Hayek
Lorenzo Infantino

14 **Property and Power in Social Theory**
A Study in Intellectual Rivalry
Dick Pels

15 **Wittgenstein and the Idea of a Critical Social Theory**
A Critique of Giddens, Habermas and Bhaskar
Nigel Pleasants

16 **Marxism and Human Nature**
Sean Sayers

17 **Goffman and Social Organization**
Studies in a Sociological Legacy
Edited by Greg Smith

18 **Situating Hayek**
Phenomenology and the Neo-Liberal Project
Mark J. Smith

19 **The Reading of Theoretical Texts**
Peter Ekegren

20 **The Nature of Capital**
Marx after Foucault
Richard Marsden

21 **The Age of Chance**
Gambling in Western Culture
Gerda Reith

22 **Reflexive Historical Sociology**
Arpad Szakolczai

23 **Durkheim and Representations**
Edited by W. S. F. Pickering

24 **The Social and Political Thought of Noam Chomsky**
Alison Edgley

25 **Hayek's Liberalism and Its Origins**
His Idea of Spontaneous Order and the Scottish Enlightenment
Christina Petsoulas

26 **Metaphor and the Dynamics of Knowledge**
Sabine Maasen and Peter Weingart

27 **Living with Markets**
Jeremy Shearmur

28 **Durkheim's Suicide**
A Century of Research and Debate
Edited by W. S. F. Pickering and Geoffrey Walford

29 **Post-Marxism**
An Intellectual History
Stuart Sim

30 **The Intellectual as Stranger**
Studies in Spokespersonship
Dick Pels

31 **Hermeneutic Dialogue and Social Science**
A Critique of Gadamer and Habermas
Austin Harrington

32 **Methodological Individualism**
Background, History and Meaning
Lars Udehn

33 **John Stuart Mill and Freedom of Expression**
The Genesis of a Theory
K. C. O'Rourke

34 **The Politics of Atrocity and Reconciliation**
From Terror to Trauma
Michael Humphrey

35 **Marx and Wittgenstein**
Knowledge, Morality, Politics
Edited by Gavin Kitching and Nigel Pleasants

36 **The Genesis of Modernity**
Arpad Szakolczai

37 **Ignorance and Liberty**
Lorenzo Infantino

38 **Deleuze, Marx and Politics**
Nicholas Thoburn

39 **The Structure of Social Theory**
Anthony King

40 **Adorno, Habermas and the Search for a Rational Society**
Deborah Cook

41 **Tocqueville's Moral and Political Thought**
New Liberalism
M. R. R. Ossewaarde

42 **Adam Smith's Political Philosophy**
The Invisible Hand and Spontaneous Order
Craig Smith

43 **Social and Political Ideas of Mahatma Gandhi**
Bidyut Chakrabarty

44 **Counter-Enlightenments**
From the Eighteenth Century to the Present
Graeme Garrard

45 **The Social and Political Thought of George Orwell**
A Reassessment
Stephen Ingle

46 **Habermas**
Rescuing the Public Sphere
Pauline Johnson

47 **The Politics and Philosophy of Michael Oakeshott**
Stuart Isaacs

48 **Pareto and Political Theory**
Joseph Femia

49 **German Political Philosophy**
The Metaphysics of Law
Chris Thornhill

50 **The Sociology of Elites**
Michael Hartmann

51 **Deconstructing Habermas**
Lasse Thomassen

52 **Young Citizens and New Media**
Learning for Democratic Participation
Edited by Peter Dahlgren

53 **Gambling, Freedom and Democracy**
Peter J. Adams

54 **The Quest for Jewish Assimilation in Modern Social Science**
Amos Morris-Reich

55 **Frankfurt School Perspectives on Globalization, Democracy, and the Law**
William E. Scheuerman

56 **Hegemony**
Studies in Consensus and Coercion
Edited by Richard Howson and Kylie Smith

57 **Governmentality, Biopower, and Everyday Life**
Majia Holmer Nadesan

58 **Sustainability and Security within Liberal Societies**
Learning to Live with the Future
Edited by Stephen Gough and Andrew Stables

59 **The Mythological State and its Empire**
David Grant

60 **Globalizing Dissent**
Essays on Arundhati Roy
Edited by Ranjan Ghosh and Antonia Navarro-Tejero

61 **The Political Philosophy of Michel Foucault**
Mark G. E. Kelly

62 **Democratic Legitimacy**
Fabienne Peter

63 **Edward Said and the Literary, Social, and Political World**
Edited by Ranjan Ghosh

64 **Perspectives on Gramsci**
Politics, Culture and Social Theory
Edited by Joseph Francese

65 **Enlightenment Political Thought and Non-Western Societies**
Sultans and Savages
Frederick G. Whelan

66 **Liberalism, Neoliberalism, Social Democracy**
Thin Communitarian Perspectives on Political Philosophy and Education
Mark Olssen

67 **Oppositional Discourses and Democracies**
Edited by Michael Huspek

68 **The Contemporary Goffman**
Edited by Michael Hviid Jacobsen

69 **Hemingway on Politics and Rebellion**
Edited by Lauretta Conklin Frederking

70 **Social Theory in Contemporary Asia**
Ann Brooks

71 **Governmentality**
Current Issues and Future Challenges
Edited by Ulrich Bröckling, Susanne Krasmann and Thomas Lemke

72 **Gender, Emotions and Labour Markets**
Asian and Western Perspectives
Ann Brooks and Theresa Devasahayam

73 **Alienation and the Carnivalization of Society**
Edited by Jerome Braun and Lauren Langman

74 **The Post-Colonial State in the Era of Capitalist Globalization**
Historical, Political and Theoretical Approaches to State Formation
Tariq Amin-Khan

75 **The Psychology and Politics of the Collective**
Groups, Crowds and Mass Identifications
Edited by Ruth Parkin-Gounelas

76 **Environmental Solidarity**
How Religions Can Sustain Sustainability
Pablo Martínez de Anguita

77 **Comedy and the Public Sphere**
The Rebirth of Theatre as Comedy and the Genealogy of the Modern Public Arena
Arpad Szakolczai

78 **Culture, Class, and Critical Theory**
Between Bourdieu and the Frankfurt School
David Gartman

79 **Environmental Apocalypse in Science and Art**
Designing Nightmares
Sergio Fava

80 **Conspicuous and Inconspicuous Discriminations in Everyday Life**
Victor N. Shaw

81 **Understanding the Tacit**
Stephen P. Turner

82 **The Politics of Expertise**
Stephen P. Turner

83 **Globalized Knowledge Flows and Chinese Social Theory**
Xiaoying Qi

84 **Reconstructing Social Justice**
Lauretta Conklin Frederking

85 **The Dialectics of Inquiry across the Historical Social Sciences**
David Baronov

86 **How Groups Matter**
Challenges of Toleration in Pluralistic Societies
Edited by Gideon Calder, Magali Bessone and Federico Zuolo

87 **The Politics of Rationality**
Reason through Occidental History
Charles P. Webel

88 **Gramsci, Materialism, and Philosophy**
Esteve Morera

89 **Emotions and Social Change**
Historical and Sociological Perspectives
Edited by David Lemmings and Ann Brooks

90 **John Rawls and the History of Political Thought**
The Rousseauvian and Hegelian Heritage of Justice as Fairness
Jeffrey Bercuson

91 **What Holism Can Do for Social Theory**
Barbara Hanson

92 **The Sociology of Knowledge in a Time of Crisis**
Challenging the Phantom of Liberty
Onofrio Romano

93 **Cosmopolitanism and the Legacies of Dissent**
Tamara Caraus and Camil-Alexandru Parvu

94 **The Metaphysics of Technology**
David Skrbina

95 **The Political Thought of Hume and His Contemporaries**
Enlightenment Projects Vol. 1
Frederick G. Whelan

96 **The Political Thought of Hume and His Contemporaries**
Enlightenment Projects Vol. 2
Frederick G. Whelan

97 **Rosa Luxemburg in Action**
For Revolution and Democracy
Rosemary H. T. O'Kane

98 **Innovation Contested**
The Idea of Innovation over the Centuries
Benoît Godin

99 **Phenomenology of Youth Cultures and Globalization**
Lifeworlds and Surplus Meaning in Changing Times
Edited by Stuart R. Poyntz and Jacqueline Kennelly

100 **Hannah Arendt and the Limits of Total Domination**
The Holocaust, Plurality, and Resistance
Michal Aharony

101 **The History of Compulsory Voting in Europe**
Democracy's Duty?
Anthoula Malkopoulou

102 **The New Materialism**
Althusser, Badiou, and Žižek
Geoff Pfeifer

103 **Authenticity, Autonomy and Multiculturalism**
Geoffrey Brahm Levey

104 **Marxism, Religion and Ideology**
Themes from David McLellan
Edited by David Bates, Iain MacKenzie and Sean Sayers

105 **Distributive Justice Debates in Political and Social Thought**
Perspectives on Finding a Fair Share
Edited by Camilla Boisen and Matthew C. Murray

106 **Re-Grounding Cosmopolitanism**
Towards a Post-Foundational Cosmopolitanism
Edited by Tamara Caraus and Elena Paris

Distributive Justice Debates in Political and Social Thought

Perspectives on Finding a Fair Share

Edited by Camilla Boisen and
Matthew C. Murray

Routledge
Taylor & Francis Group
LONDON AND NEW YORK

First published 2016 by Routledge

2 Park Square, Milton Park, Abingdon, Oxfordshire OX14 4RN
711 Third Avenue, New York, NY 10017

Routledge is an imprint of the Taylor & Francis Group, an informa business

First issued in paperback 2017

Library of Congress Cataloging in Publication Data
A catalog record for this book has been requested

ISBN: 978-1-138-82976-3 (hbk)
ISBN: 978-0-8153-7050-5 (pbk)

Typeset in Sabon
by Wearset Ltd, Boldon, Tyne and Wear

We dedicate this volume to David, Carole, Pete, Peri, Bruce, Graeme, Sarah, Gavin, Junichi, Steve, Kerstin, Wendy, Natalie, Claire and the many talented individuals in the Politics and International Relations Department at Cardiff University who enkindled and nurtured our passion for political thought as teachers and fellow students and forged our understanding of the paradigm's importance in understanding our world. We couldn't have done it without you.

Contents

Contributors

Editors

Camilla Boisen is a Postdoctoral Research Fellow in Political Theory at the University of the Witwatersrand, Johannesburg, South Africa. She did her PhD in history of political thought on the historical exemplars of humanitarian intervention in early modern just war theory at Cardiff University. Following her PhD she took up a research fellowship at the National History Museum, Frederiksborg Castle, Denmark before moving to South Africa in 2011. She has since embarked on exploring ideas of colonisation in Africa, and is currently working on a research monograph on trusteeship in South Africa. She is published in *History of European Ideas* and *Theoria*.

Matthew C. Murray is the Senior Project Advisor for the Growthpolicy.org project at the Mossavar-Rahmani Center for Business and Government at the Harvard Kennedy School of Government and serves as Special Lecturer of Philosophy at Providence College. Matthew received his MSc Econ and PhD in Politics from Cardiff University where he was affiliated with the School of European Studies (now, the School of Politics and Law) Political Theory Research Unit and served as an Associate Lecturer in the Politics Department. Matthew's research interests and ongoing scholarly contributions are focused on the development of accounts of distributive justice and the policies these accounts motivate comparatively and internationally. He has a particular interest in immerging treatments of inequalities, including physical inequalities (disabilities and talents), social inequalities and economic inequalities. Aside from his work in political and social thought, Matthew is actively publishing in the areas of disability studies and basic income systems respectively. Matthew co-edited *Basic Income Worldwide: Horizons of Reform* (Palgrave, 2012) with Carole Pateman.

Contributors

Christopher Allsobrook is director of CLEA (Center for Leadership Ethics Africa) at the University of Fort Hare. He previously taught Philosophy and Politics at the University of Johannesburg, at St Augustine College, Johannesburg, and at the University of Sussex, in the UK, where he completed his DPhil degree in Philosophy, in 2011, on genealogy and ideology criticism. His thesis focused on the ideology of determinate negation as a normative basis for social criticism. His current research is in critical theory and intellectual history, looking at historical patterns of political and epistemic imperial legitimation in southern Africa.

Kim Angell is a Post-Doctoral Research Fellow at the Department of Political Science, University of Oslo. He works mainly within political philosophy, with a particular focus on theories of distributive justice, nationalism, property and territorial rights. Angell has published on problems of territorial justice from a contemporary Lockean perspective, and will further his research on rights over land and territory as a partner in the project 'Who owns it? – Land claims in Latin America'. Angell is an Affiliate Member of the Centre for the Study of Mind in Nature (University of Oslo), and will be Departmental Guest at the Department of Politics, Princeton University (2015–2016).

David Boucher is Professor of Political Philosophy and International Relations at the School of Law and Politics, at Cardiff University, UK, and is the Director for the Collingwood and British Idealism Centre, on which he has published extensively. He is also a Distinguished Visiting Professor, University of Johannesburg. David Boucher is one of the foremost scholars in field of the political theory of international relations and rights theories and its subfield, the history of colonial political thought. He is the author of numerous articles on this topic and two major works, the most recent *The Limits of Ethics in International Relations – Natural Law, Natural Rights* and *Human Rights in Transition* (OUP, 2009). David is currently working on a research monograph on Hobbes and international political thought (forthcoming with OUP).

Daniel Engster is an Associate Professor of Political Science at the University of Texas at San Antonio. His work focuses on care ethics, contemporary theories of justice, public policy and the family. He is the author of *The Heart of Justice: Care Ethics and Political Theory* (OUP, 2007) and *Justice, Care, and the Welfare State* (OUP, forthcoming), and co-editor (with Tamara Metz) of *Justice, Politics, and the Family* (Paradigm, 2013).

Samuel Fleischacker is a Professor of Philosophy at the University of Illinois, Chicago. His publications include *The Ethics of Culture* (Cornell, 1994), *A Third Concept of Liberty: Judgment and Freedom in Kant and Adam Smith* (Princeton, 1999), *On Adam Smith's* Wealth of Nations*: A Philosophical Companion* (Princeton, 2003), *A Short History of Distributive Justice* (Harvard, 2004), *Divine Teaching and the Way of the World* (Oxford, 2011) and the forthcoming *What is Enlightenment? The Legacy of a Kantian Question* (Routledge, 2012). Professor Fleischacker has been a Fellow of the University Center for Human Values at Princeton, the Institute for Advanced Study in the Humanities at Edinburgh University and the Institute for the Humanities at UIC.

Lawrence Hamilton is a Professor of Politics at University of the Witwatersrand and Affiliated Lecturer in Political Theory, Department of Politics and International Studies (POLIS), Cambridge University. He is an elected Member of the Academy of Science of South Africa (ASSAf) and Editor-in-Chief of *Theoria: A Journal of Social and Political Theory*. In 2007 the South African National Research Foundation (NRF) awarded him their President's Award and in 2012 a Blue Skies Award for his research achievements. He is a leading scholar in his field on the political philosophy of needs. His research focuses on democracy, freedom, political judgement, needs, rights, states, power, public debt and representative government. He has published extensively on this, including *The Political Philosophy of Needs* (CUP, 2003) and *Freedom is Power: Liberty through Political Representation* (CUP, 2014).

Tessa Hochfeld is a researcher at the Centre for Social Development in Africa at the University of Johannesburg. Her research includes work on social work and social welfare, poverty and inequality, social policy, social protection, social justice and gender and development.

David James is Associate Professor of Philosophy at the University of Warwick. His main research interests are in the tradition of social and political philosophy associated with Rousseau, Fichte, Hegel and Marx. He is the author of *Fichte's Social and Political Philosophy: Property and Virtue* (CUP, 2011) and *Rousseau and German Idealism: Freedom, Dependence and Necessity* (CUP, 2013).

Carl Knight is Lecturer in Political Theory at the University of Glasgow and Senior Research Associate at the University of Johannesburg. His main area of research is contemporary political philosophy, with a particular focus on distributive justice. He has published numerous articles on this topic as well as *Luck Egalitarianism* (Edinburgh University Press, 2009) and *Responsibility and Distributive Justice* (co-edited with Zofia Stemplowska, OUP, 2011).

Thaddeus Metz is Research Professor of Philosophy at the University of Johannesburg, where he writes on four major topics: developing and evaluating theories of the meaning of life; addressing normative debates in higher education; resolving social controversies by appealing to Kantian values; and interpreting sub-Saharan morality analytically and applying it to contemporary ethical and political issues. About three dozen of his approximately 100 publications are on the latter topic, with recent articles including: 'The Western ethic of care or an Afro-Communitarian ethic?' *Journal of Global Ethics*; 'Developing African political philosophy', *Philosophia Africana*; and 'African conceptions of dignity', *Human Rights Review*.

Sophie Plagerson is a research fellow at the Centre for Social Development in Africa, University of Johannesburg. Her PhD on 'Child Support Grants and common mental disorders' was awarded by the London School of Hygiene and Tropical Medicine. Current projects include research on mental health, social protection, social justice, state–citizen relations, frameworks for rights and responsibilities.

Peri Roberts is Senior Lecturer in Political Theory at Cardiff University. His teaching and research interests are predominantly in contemporary political theory and focus on liberal justifications in a number of contexts. He has published widely on the justifiable liberal responses to the challenges posed by an increasing recognition of the extent and importance of pluralism and multiculturalism. He is the author of the book *Political Constructivism* (Routledge, 2007). Together with Bruce Haddock and Peter Sutch, he edited volumes *Principles and Political Order: The Challenge of Diversity* (Routledge, 2006) and *Evil in Contemporary Political Theory* (Edinburgh University Press, 2011). He is currently working on a book on John Rawls and the Law of Peoples.

Peter Sutch is Professor of Political and International Theory at Cardiff University in the School of Law and Politics. He teaches and publishes on normative IR theory and the politics of international law. He has explored questions of international justice, in particular questions relating to just war and humanitarian intervention, global governance, human rights and international law. He is the author of, among others, *Ethics, Justice and International Relations: Constructing an International Community* (Routledge, 2006); *The Politics of International Law and International Justice* (Edinburgh University Press, 2013) co-authored with Edwin Egede; *An Introduction to Political Thought: A Conceptual Toolkit* (Edinburgh University Press, 2012 2nd edn) co-authored with Peri Roberts.

Marianne S. Ulriksen is affiliated to the Centre for Social Development in Africa, University of Johannesburg, South Africa, as a Senior Research Fellow. Marianne currently resides in Tanzania and her research includes: comparative politics, political economy of welfare policy development, social protection, poverty and inequality, mineral wealth and resource mobilisation, and state–citizen relations, on which she is published widely.

Matt Zwolinski is an Associate Professor of Philosophy at the University of San Diego, and Co-Director of USD's Institute for Law and Philosophy. He is the author of numerous articles focusing on various theoretical and applied aspects of exploitation, the editor of *Arguing about Political Philosophy*, currently in its second edition with Routledge, and, with John Tomasi, the author of *A Brief History of Libertarianism*, forthcoming with Princeton University Press.

Preface

The Limits of Distributive Justice: A Brief Exploration of Restorative Justice

David Boucher

Collections of facts about social inequalities do not tell us about what would count as a just redistribution of resources. Indeed, they do not even establish that inequality, even vast inequalities, are unjust. For that there must be principles and values, sustained within a theoretical framework, in which social responsibility and shared resources are fundamental values which contribute to our self-identification and identity as persons, and in which others, although separated in many other ways, are conceived to be part of the community – local, national, international – sufficiently solidarist to sustain such principles, not only with rational argument, but also with passionate commitment. Whatever else this book is, it is a collection of essays that attempts to establish what these principles ought to be, in a variety of different contexts, and under widely differing considerations. The authors, in their different ways, bring to the surface the key issues as viewed from a broad range of perspectives.

It is nearly two and half millennia, as the introduction to this volume reminds us, since Plato, through the person of Socrates, posed the famous question, 'What is Justice' and gave the most unlikely answer in response. To such suggestions as that of Thrasymachus – justice is that which is in the interests of the stronger – Plato presents a more noble vision, positing an identity between justice in the individual person and in the polis. For Plato justice is a relationship based on the principles of order, harmony, specialisation and subordination. It is a hierarchical relationship between the three aspects of the psyche, wisdom, courage and appetite with their exact equivalents in the body politic, the philosopher king, the guardians or auxiliaries, and the workers, or economic class. Knowing one's place is essential to the harmony that is justice. Plato identified, even if his answer may remain unsatisfactory, the central problem of justice in general, and of social justice in particular: that is, what is the right relationship that should pertain among individuals and groups within society, and externally between societies, so that each may claim to be a just society in a just world.

The whole Platonic tradition has emphasised the necessity to control appetites, passions and emotions, by the exercise of right reason, excluding those from enjoying full rights of participation in the public sphere if they fell somewhat short of reaching the threshold where reason is in control. Non-Europeans such as American Indians, Australian Aboriginals and black Africans, including their slave ancestors, wherever they may be scattered throughout the world, and women of whatever creed or colour, fell short of the criterion of rational beings in the eyes of numberless philosophers and statesmen. Although all of these peoples may not be excluded to the same extent and on the same grounds as they once were, the disadvantage from which they started, and the knock-on effect on subsequent generations, perpetuates and accentuates contemporary injustices. Conceiving of justice in terms of equal opportunities, while condoning unequal unconstrained outcomes, that is, the ever-widening gap between rich and poor within and between nations, fails to capture intergenerational social justice, and the inherent disadvantages with which historic injustice has burdened certain peoples. As Charles Mills suggests, it is not only that European states and their former white settler colonies are globally dominant, but within those with a significant non-white element, including indigenous people, the descendants of imported slaves and voluntary non-white immigrants, whites remain privileged in relation to non-whites. Opportunities for such groups have expanded, but remain below those of whites (Mills, 1999, 2007: 106–133). Even if opportunities are ostensibly equal, the ability and capacity of individuals from such backgrounds to seize these opportunities remains impaired by the intergenerational inheritance, such as feelings of low esteem, insufficient valuing of such opportunities or the stark inability to escape the social and cultural constraints that surround these opportunities. The obstacles are not merely economic, but also psychological, social, religious and cultural, resulting from the relationships in which each group stands to others as a consequence of the burden of the past. Providing opportunities for education, where education is not valued as a means to advancement, is no opportunity at all in a society where the purchase of the expensive private education facilitates unequal access into privileged and elite positions, based not on educational attainment alone, but on historic privilege.

A great deal of discussion of social justice operates with a threshold criterion which affords people equal opportunities, while condoning unequal outcomes. Even the idea of basic income reflects this deeply ingrained idea. Once people are helped to the starting line they take personal responsibility for the choices they make which may lead to differing degrees of achievement, and ultimately considerable differentials between the relatively poor and the relatively rich. The degree to which choices are socially constrained is simply ignored by those who elevate the role of personal and moral responsibility in discussing the issue of welfare entitlements. The idea of a living wage does nothing to address the absolute inequality, but merely raises certain people to a threshold, and even if paid for by a tax on the rich does not necessarily reduce the income gap, but may simply retard the rate at which that gap widens. It is not self-evident that the gap should be reduced, and if people agree that it would be desirable, they disagree on what the threshold should be, the means by which it may be achieved, and upon the degree by which it should be reduced.

Social welfare, the means by which Western societies attempt to deliver better life chances by assisting people to cross the threshold at which greater opportunities are presumed to be attainable, is conditional upon something more fundamental than ideas about the desirability of top-down – the so-called cascade model of social benefit – or the bottom-up model of economic growth, that is, by increasing the purchasing power of the poor economic growth will be stimulated. In both cases the rationale is instrumental, and the question addressed is by what means the maximum of economic growth can be attained, delivering the maximum benefit for the greatest number of people, at the minimum cost in social welfare. On both models the aim is to transform economic liabilities, the poor, into economic assets, in the name of modernisation, and it is this principle that also underpins foreign aid, except for humanitarian relief from natural disasters.

The upheaval of industrialisation particularly in France and Britain in the 1840s, and later in Germany and elsewhere, forced upon modern societies a reconceptualisation of the relationship in which individuals stood to each other. It was not so much the arguments of Marx and Engels, but the unacceptable levels of contagious diseases, poor nutrition, deterioration in levels of fitness and debilitating poverty endangering not only the productivity of the workforce but also the viability of the army that generated social welfare programmes including the National Insurance Act in Britain, and the more social democratic programmes of the post-1945 era.

If there is to be social justice, and not just the eradication of injustices (something with which no one would disagree), there must be compelling reasons which establish principles of redistribution that override the default position that has persisted since Adam Smith, that of *laissez-faire* entitlement economics – each person is entitled to the fruits of his or her labour, or Herbert Spencer's desert principle where everyone is entitled to both the good and bad results of their endeavours. It is a default position that requires justification for redistribution, and rests upon an individualism antithetical to the presumption that the accumulation of wealth is a social resource, to which we are all entitled, albeit to differing degrees according to what principles the shares are allocated, perhaps, for example, on the basis of a basic income plus credits for acts of good citizenship.

There has been a remarkable proliferation of justifications of 'just' economic outcomes since the publication of Rawls's *A Theory of Justice* in 1971, even extending his principles to international redistribution, so much so that for modern political theorists social justice, and the concomitant reliance on some version of a social contract theory, became almost the only game in town. Principles of fairness, impartiality and entitlement competed for pre-eminence in how to redistribute the cooperative surplus.

A parallel development in the field of legal theory and practice, which overlaps with the interests of some political theorists, and in response to the perceived failure of retributivist and deterrent theories of punishment, and humanitarian atrocities on a nauseating scale, is the demand for restorative justice. The idea of restorative justice has almost completely been appropriated by those interested in criminal law, where the victim of a crime is central to the legal process, and restitution or reparations for loss, the restoration of equilibrium, are the desired outcomes (Braithwaite, 2002; Walgrave, 2002; Weitekamp and Kerner, 2003; Cunneen and Hoyle, 2010). International criminal justice is similarly focused on restorative justice, generated by the International Criminal Tribunal for the Former Yugoslavia, the International Criminal Tribunal for Rwanda, and to a lesser extent the International Criminal Court, whose exclusive focus on Africa has somewhat detracted from its potential for restitution. The mere titles of recent books indicate the degree of dissatisfaction; for example, *Rough Justice: The International Criminal Court in a World of Power Politics* and *Justice Denied: The Reality of the International Criminal Court.* (Bosco, 2014; see also Hoile, 2014; Sorensen, 2010).

Restorations or reparations are of course central principles in the idea of *jus post bellum*, and are extensively discussed by the classic and modern international jurists, but restorative justice is increasingly important in conceptualising and responding to the plight of refugees, one of the most pressing humanitarian crises of our times. Durable solutions to the unjust harms suffered by refugees are conceived in terms of reparations, or restorations for their displacement and loss, where voluntary repatriation, local integration and third-country resettlement are the principal responses (Souter, 2013).

Restorative justice cannot be conceived in isolation from social justice, and in my view it adds a dimension that is rarely to the fore in theories of social justice. Social justice focuses upon the present and the future, establishing principles by which unjustifiable inequalities may be identified, rectified and transformed for future good. Restorative justice focuses on the past, present and future. In principle, it determines how particular injustices have arisen, identifies their historic generation and restores, or gives reparations for, what has been lost. It has the propensity to conceive of justice in transgenerational and intergenerational terms, attributing responsibility for present inequalities and deprivations to past relations of power, subjection and subordination. Truth and reconciliation commissions are also closely allied to the idea of a comprehensive portrayal of restorative or reparative justice, and in this respect may identify past injustices and determine ongoing disadvantage and exploitation consequent upon those injustices, in order to contribute to an understanding of what restorative justice requires, including the redistribution of the proceeds accrued through past unjust relations between the exploited and the exploiters.

The complexities to such an approach are considerable, and we should not underestimate the enormity of the problems of establishing the 'facts' about past injustices, even with respect to the relatively recent past. Establishing the 'truth', however, is different from establishing guilt, and where responsibility and injustices are concerned there need not be such high standards of evidence as are required for a prosecution in an International Criminal Tribunal. Recent criminal tribunals, such as the International Criminal Tribunal for Rwanda, the Special Court for Sierra Leone, and Timor-Leste's Special Panels for Serious Crimes, unlike Nuremberg which relied largely on documentary evidence, rely on witness testimony to establish the basic facts. Findlay and Henham, for example, suggest that 'truth' rather than guilt should be an objective of justice with respect the International Criminal Court (Findlay and Henham, 2012). Indeed, even in relation to these International Tribunals and the International Criminal Court, Nancy Combs advocates a 'close-enough' approach to fact-finding (2010). Where neither documentary nor testimonial evidence is in abundance for specific injustices, as is the case with historic societal injustice, establishing the relations in which groups stood to each other, and their social and economic consequences, may be sufficient to determine the long-term harm.

For example, in the case of Mauritius, a small island nation in the southwest of the Indian Ocean, 500 miles off the east coast of Madagascar and uninhabited until 375 years ago, slavery was abolished almost 200 years ago, but the repercussions are still intensely felt despite the fact it is a relatively thriving country which has been a functioning democracy since 1968. Successive colonisers – the Dutch, French and English – have occupied the island, and the ethnic and cultural complexity makes it very difficult to deliver transitional and restorative justice without untangling those complexities. When France took possession of the island in 1721, renaming it Ile de France, Napoleon's Code Noir was enforced to control the slave population. Slaves, as was usual, were defined as property, prohibited from marriage, forbidden relocation, denied freedom of worship and outlawed from freedom of assembly. They suffered unspeakable brutality on the island's plantations. In 2009, Mauritius established the first Truth and Justice Commission to investigate the long-term implications of slavery and indentured labour over a period of 370 years. The conclusions of its report, released in 2011, indicate that the contemporary descendants of slaves and indentured labourers suffer discrimination, marginalisation and poverty as a result of the perpetuation of racism which emanated from the condition of their ancestors (Boswell, 2014).

Restorative justice, which necessarily includes a compensatory element, is not just about reparations for past wrongs. The Truth and Reconciliation Commission in South Africa, for example, was in the view of some commenters meant to heal psychological and emotional damage leading to national catharsis and forgiveness (de Gruchy, 2000). Restorative justice is also about restoring identity and self-worth which has been damaged or destroyed by colonial and imperialist attitudes to culture. Museums around the world are stuffed with sacred and ceremonial artefacts which are not only of historical interest, but more importantly have a contemporary value for cultural renewal among indigenous peoples who were forcibly deprived of their heritage, who now demand their repatriation as part of the healing process of post-colonial trauma. The re-socialisation of cultural icons in the contemporary practices of peoples is a vital aspect of cultural renewal and the transmission of intergenerational knowledge, which contributes towards the restoration of distinct identities and cultures stripped away by colonisation (Simpson, 2009: 122). Recent research in British Columbia, Canada, has indicated that the loss of cultural continuity jeopardises the well-being of whole cultural groups, and that collective endeavours to re-establish and preserve cultural continuities have contributed towards improvements in health and self-esteem, and lower suicide rates among First Nations communities (Chandler et al., 2003).

Perhaps, just as importantly, restorative justice is a homage to one's ancestors whose stories have been repressed and replaced with those of the coloniser, the aggressor, the victor, dominant culture or class. Restorative justice, in taking the past as its focus of fact-finding, acknowledges the injustices perpetrated against those who suffered from unequal and exploitative relationships, retells their stories in contemporary contexts, identifies the legacy and implications, and seeks to influence the establishment of different relations among peoples and groups, in order to achieve a just outcome. It is necessarily anachronistic in that it does not attempt to understand past unequal relations in their own terms, but instead looks at the consequences of those relationships in terms of their outcomes: their inhumanity, brutality, depravity, economic exploitation and much more.

References

Bosco, David (2014), *Rough Justice: The International Criminal Court in a World of Power Politics*, Oxford: Oxford University Press.

Boswell, Rosabelle (2014), 'Can justice be achieved for slave descendants in Mauritius?', *The International Journal of Law, Crime and Justice*, 42: 146–161.

Braithwaite, John (2002), *Restorative Justice and Responsive Regulation*, New York: Oxford University Press.

Chandler, M. J., Lalonde, C. E., Sokol, B. and Hallett, D. (2003), 'Personal persistence, identity development, and suicide: a study of Native and non-Native North American adolescents', *Monographs of the Society for Research in Child Development*, 68 (2, Serial No. 273).

Combs, Nancy A. (2010), *Fact-Finding Without Facts: The Uncertain Evidentiary Foundations of International Criminal Convictions*, Cambridge: Cambridge University Press.

Cunneen, Chris and Hoyle, Carolyn (2010), *Debating Restorative Justice*, Oxford: Hart Publishing.

de Gruchy, J. (2000), 'The TRC and the building of a moral culture', in W. James and L. van de Vijver (eds), *After the TRC: Reflections of Truth and Reconciliation in South Africa*, Cape Town: Rustica, pp. 161–171.

Findlay, Mark and Henham, Ralph (2012), *Transforming International Criminal Justice: Retributive and Restorative Justice in the Trial Process*, London: Routledge.

Hoile, David (2014), *Justice Denied: The Reality of the International Criminal Court*, London: African Research Centre.

Mills, Charles W. (1999), *The Racial Contract*, Ithica and London: Cornell University Press, pp. 37–40.

Mills, Charles W. (2007), 'Contract of breach: repairing the racial contract', in Carole Pateman and Charles W. Mills, *Contract and Domination*, Cambridge: Polity Press, pp. 106–133.

Pateman, Carole, and Mills, Charles W. (2007), *Contract and Domination*, Cambridge: Polity Press, 2007.

Simpson, Moira (2009), 'Museums and restorative justice: heritage, repatriation and cultural education', *Museum International*, 61: 121–129.

Sorensen, Juliet S. (2010), 'Restorative justice for victims of war crimes', *The Journal of Criminal Law and Criminology*, 100: 1689–1698.

Souter, James (2013), 'Durable solutions as reparation for unjust harms of displacement: who owes what to refugees', *Journal of Refugee Studies*, 27: 171–190.

Walgrave, Lode(ed.) (2002), *Restorative Justice and the Law*, Uffculme, Devon: Willan.

Weitekamp, Elmar and Kerner, Hans-Jurgen (eds) (2003), *Restorative Justice: Theoretical Foundations*, Uffculme, Devon: Willan.

Acknowledgements

This volume reflects the shared value we have as academic professionals, teachers, authors and now as editors that political thought has an underexposed role in understanding and analysing political behaviour. In our result-and-answer driven society, the tough and recurring issues of our political existence play roles worryingly near the periphery of our political understanding. This volume is our contribution to a particularly troubling aspect of political ideas and the fingerprints they have left on our understandings, concepts and the policies these ideas have motivated. We wanted to give the reader a set of critical tools that they can use to deepen their understanding, defence and development of their positions and the policies they motivate no matter what those positions may be.

We aim to encourage a broad range of intellectuals to engage with the ideas within, related to and beyond this text and to begin bridging the disciplinary gaps within politics and between political study and other fields that may be contributing to present political issues. We aim to serve academic professionals but equally the student, the advocate or even just the individual with a passing interest by producing a volume that is accessible to readers from many backgrounds and with many distinct skill sets. This is a volume of and for the people inside and outside of the ivory tower. The volume will allow readers to grasp the practical applications and approaches to political thought that exist, their tangible reflections through the example of African and global experiences and to gain insight into under-represented arguments and critics within the frequently closed canon of Western political and social thought.

We want to extend our deepest and sincerest gratitude to our many talented contributors. We have been honoured to work with such amiable and capable individuals on a work of shared interest. Your exuberance for the project and contributions to it are deeply appreciated. We want especially to show our gratitude to Sarah Gallimore, whose steadfast, nuanced and comprehensive knowledge of Grotius led to our rigorous approach to his political thought. We also want to thank Peri Roberts and Bruce Haddock whose post-graduate close-reading course (to which they were kind enough to extend an invitation for us) on the then recent release of *Frontiers of Justice* was inspirational in our chapter collaboration. We would also like to express our sincere gratitude to Natalja Mortensen, Lillian Rand and those on the editorial staff at Routledge/Taylor & Francis for helping bring this project to fruition.

Camilla would like to thank her family, especially Lucas and Felix, her partner Robert, her twin sister Nadia and her mother. She would like to extend a special gratitude to David Boucher for his continued support and mentoring in her academic endeavours. She would also like to give thanks to friends and colleagues at the University of Johannesburg and the Witwatersrand, and to Matt, for all his hard work on the completion of this volume. It is with gratitude that she acknowledges that Matt kept her (reasonably) sane whenever the ivory tower of academia threatened to discourage her.

Matt would like to give many thanks to his family for supporting him through this process, to Camilla for all of her hard work on this project and her tenacity in seeing the project through to completion, to Carole Pateman for her continued support and sympathetic ear, and to his friends and colleagues at Providence College (particularly Licia Carlson) and Harvard University (particularly Scott Leland and Jennifer Nash at the MRCBG at HKS) who have supported him through the process of producing this volume. He would also like to thank the Massachusetts Commission for the Blind for the adaptive equipment and solutions they have furnished that have made completing this volume possible.

Introduction

Distributing Distributive Justice

Camilla Boisen and Matthew C. Murray

As the reader of a volume of collected works on specific debates in political and social thought, there is a high if almost absolute likelihood that you were exposed to the works of Plato and their representation of Socrates' political and social thought early on in your foray into this field of study. It may not be the first, the best or the only piece of ancient thought that exists, but it is an undeniable part of the political philosopher's lexicon. These works are such a part of our collective experience as individuals with an interest in this field that it has become a part of collective understanding, even if we as a collective paradigm waiver on the importance, credence, meaning or even interpretation of these texts. It is a two-millennia-old touchstone that serves equally to illuminate why the study of the past is seminal in understanding the unfolding of history, our position in the present but equally our ability to forge a new path through the practice of asking new and better questions as we move towards the future and the policies, institutions and practices these ideas motivate.

Equally, these texts, written in a format intended to be accessible to the individuals of the polis, understood and articulated the power of ideas in observing political actions but also how the observation of these actions through contemporary and historical lenses chips the detail into the philosophic stone that makes the statue of our political and social lives when viewed in totality. In this sense, these works stand for something more than its words, foundational understandings and assumptions, meanings and prescriptions. *The Republic*, in particular, is a work that defines, for better or worse, what it is to be a political philosopher, not through what it says as a text but what it is, a comprehensive viewing of political life and conflict.

Plato, as many political philosophers and theorists have historically, felt the need to address a contemporary social injustice by addressing its root cause and the concepts that justified it happening. In this regard, one can see much symmetry between himself and the Western philosophers to follow, but also those outside of the Western canon. This is a characteristic that perhaps draws most political philosophers together, the realisation of injustice and the task presented to defend establishment or embrace change based upon some deeper understanding built up or out into a far larger social structure, action or institution.

As a seminal text in the field, it is concerned to a large degree with the question of what is a just state, which is argued for through specific state structures that are needed to ensure justice based upon many metaphysical, normative and even descriptive philosophic arguments. It is the basis of justice, the nature of this justice, the structure of it and the kinds of institutions that are needed to fulfil these commitments that ultimately give the work much of the character we so commonly associate with it. Though many of these specific ideas and prescriptions may seem dated or foreign to us, the questions and practices of asking them is not. The world has turned and left Plato where he stood, and though that highlights one of the conclusions of this volume, that ideas are formative and reactive to observation and practice, this does not undermine the practice of the work, if seen as a formative part of understanding political life.

One of these points which still raises much philosophic debate is the question of who has what and why in a just state. There are distributive elements to the composition of the people who make up Plato's state and their nature, to the goods, roles and basic services that individuals enjoy and undertake. One of the lasting qualities of this work is the ability of it to speak to reconstitutable problems and issues we still see governments struggle with today, issues of who has what and why being one of them. The nature of a just distribution, how to structure society to ensure such distributive understandings and how, when and why we restore or eliminate problems that exist in distributive areas of society are questions present in all societies and have a direct and undeniable effect on the lives of the individuals who comprise them. Plato, as many have before and since, saw this as a primary consideration of a just state, and with good reason. The things we have, naturally and socially, make up much of the composition of our lives as human citizens.

Yet, between the dominant forces in our field, the parochial nature of how it is approached in introduction, simply the academic artefact of how themes and questions are approached, or just the sheer impact this text has and had in our field of study, it is works like these that send political thought down a specific path. The existence of touchstones in thought that mark the progression of thought are a blessing to the political philosopher in that they cause a sense of siblinghood where the issues that pique our minds, spirits and wills are shared. The footprints can be sherpas up an unending mountain of questions and make our lonely road less so. However, they equally keep us from looking for a new way to climb. As such, the company these footsteps bring also divides, separates and even alienates us from one another as political philosophers, a feeling most if not all have had in attending a conference or other peer gathering where the act of exchanging ideas and perspectives frequently erodes into a competition between perspectives and traditions and how they are presented in keeping with academic practice.

All of those, it would seem are in opposition to what the practice of political thought is supposed to do as a field of study but it is a phenomenon even the most passive reader of this book can relate to over a dinner table, with friends or even watching 'news' networks, a concept of thought carved, defended and assumed which colours all the practices and perceptions that follow. To this end, this experience highlights how, in some degree, everyone is a political philosopher in some sense. It also highlights the great dichotomy of being a political philosopher: to be accepted as a passionate practitioner and alienated as a professional peer all at the same time, as the embrace of the practice of argument rarely aligns with those who have accepted one as a foundational assumption of their political observation or practice. Arguments do not come with a warning label that they are be consumed with caution and may cause the troubling side effects of anger, dissolution, political fervency, pedagogical prescriptions or, perhaps most importantly, a sense of certainty.

However, it is in this competition of ideas that we see how questions, concepts and ideas can fall into the dusty bin of time, even those from luminaries in the practice of political thought, in spite of their merit or importance contextually or perennially. This is sadly nothing new; and it may be that many of our current problems, issues and conflicts are informed by ideas that have been passed by or overlooked, or have been given new life in the face of changing context. Socrates' defence of an 'examined life' as recalled by Plato (Plato, 1997: 38a 5–6) may be the highest calling of the philosopher, but for the political philosopher we are asked equally to examine our life, the lives of others and our world, and to also examine our examination. This volume is a move to enlighten one of the primary issues of this consideration in exploring distributive justice not through the typical and time-honoured lens of 'the canon' nor in the derivative and craft-oriented approach of toiling deep within the footprint of a giant. Instead, we aim through this volume to accomplish two major objectives:

1 To bring to light under-represented perspectives on distributive justice in the history of political thought that question the direction, scope, totality, complexities and even the limitations of the practice of distributive justice in historical and emerging debates.

In light of economic events of the past decade, arguments about distributive justice and how perspectives, approaches and policies they motivate have succeeded or failed have become a point of increasing focus. However, as Carmen M. Reinhart and Kenneth Rogoff explain in *This Time is Different: Eight Centuries of Financial Folly* (2011), crises of economic disaster are not new. Humanity has long faced the spectre of economic justice and how best to work to ensure that our governments and societies do what they must for people. Economic crises are so troubling because of the effects they have on people. Without the ability to acquire and dispose of things, people lack a fundamental interaction with the world that is at least inconvenient, perhaps inefficient, frequently consequential and, at worst, deadly. Economic systems exist to do something far more fundamental to society. They are a mechanism of practice and procedure, yes, but one of purpose in the foremost case. It is the question of what this purpose is that lies at the heart of distributive justice.

2 To go beyond the typical volumised presentation of such work by giving these perspectives contextual relevancy through discursive illustrations of framing through an African and global lens as these particular areas exemplify many of the conflicts and factors which make distributive justice arguments contentious, difficult, pertinent and important. In doing so, we wish to show the need for a comprehensive approach to discussions in this area that use this intersectionality as a touchstone for the ideas of justice, how best to theoretically achieve them and the specific policy and institutional choices that result from these motivational ideas and frameworks.

It is one thing to talk about ideas and their impact, it is another to look at the real work being done or discussed by people related to situations in which the thought is pertinent. Ultimately, bridging this gap through 'non-ideal' theory which we would rather refer to as applied political thought, is perhaps the great *terra nullius* of our own discipline and a chasm that has increasingly placed political philosophy in a secondary role in the social sciences and even the humanities due to this under-explored intersectionality. We intend to not only raise the understanding of under-represented ideas (ideal, grand, applied and non-ideal) and their impacts in a specific frame of reference, we intend to show how this historical schism permeates beyond the examples here and how exploring many areas is the only real way forward in political discourse.

To accomplish this, the volume will first deal with specific historical debates and ideas as they inform recurring themes, issues and debates in distributive justice. The historical angle helps draw attention to the distinctiveness of earlier formulations in comparison to the modern and contemporary formulations. It helps illuminate the degree of their historical contingency. We highlight the different and under-explored perspectives on distributive justice historically to highlight their relevance to contemporary debates without being prescriptive of what this impact is for you, the reader. A historical approach to issues of distributive justice is necessary to critically understand and assess its contemporary breadth. This helps to draw attention to the distinctiveness of earlier formulations of what we today would term 'distributive justice' in comparison with the modern and demonstrates, ultimately, how ideas are historically contingent. Issues pertaining to distributive justice are historically bound but are not so easily transferable to the contemporary concepts we recognise today. Such historical sensitivity enables us to avoid comparisons and conclusions that assume that issues are perennial and that modern-day conceptions are related in some fundamental sense to the old. We can therefore avoid the 'anachronistic shorthand', which is often used to make broad assumptions about a concept to lend further legitimacy through its longevity.

Samuel Fleischacker illustrates this point in Chapter 1, in noting the anachronism with which Adam Smith's commentators have asserted his supposed rejection of 'distributive justice'. This historicist approach to philosophical interrogation allows us to be critical in considering, constructing and conceptualising new thinking about distributive justice. Some 'contextualists' – especially represented by Skinner and the 'Cambridge School' (see for instance Skinner, 1978; Dunn, 1982; although the contextual method is by no means a uniform school of thought) – might object to the claim of historicism we use in this volume's first section, that is of using a later term, 'distributive justice' to describe an earlier practice. The very academic undertaking of doing 'history of political thought' divides historians and normative political theorists on the very question of how to approach 'classical' texts and for what intentions. Do we analyse texts for their perennial relevance or in order to survey them in the context of their actual historical circumstances? We can acknowledge the Skinnerian claim that the historical context of the text is inescapable, demanding great sensitivity to the text's linguistic and social context. By including chapters that approach issues of justice in a particular historical context, we also want to avow that historical texts go beyond the recovery of historical meanings (which is certainly a worthwhile and important pursuit on its own), and that we can (and should) read them in relation to current problems. It is true that our view today from the white cliffs of Dover is rooted in our context, time and understandings of what we gaze upon which makes recovering them for those who follow vital, but we cannot in the same breath claim that we are the first and only ones to have stood there to gaze upon them and ignore the potential commonality we have with the eyes of our predecessors and successors.

An additional strength and novelty of how this volume approaches considerations of distributive justice is that it also includes perspectives of the Global South, more in particular southern Africa. The very habitual approach to distributive justice that we want to challenge here is also conspicuous in its not only Western attitudes to conceptions of justice, but also the hegemonic Western production of knowledge. Surely, if we are to overcome the hurdles of finding a fair share we need to be much more encompassing and inclusive to also recognise and consider African, regionalised, larger global and other non-Western perspectives to justice. Our chapters are not exhaustive in this scope, but they do exemplify the need and value of these approaches in our pursuit of understanding distributive justice. One important first step to rectify this is to acknowledge that the Global South and the resources, interests and claims that extend beyond our constructed languages of States, 'peoples' and societies, do not just serve as grounds for empirical surveys of political and social issues, but also serve as a worthwhile source of normative political reflection.

We will take forward this larger narrative, which will consist of many moving parts presented in our chapters, and conclude by challenging the reader to understand their role as active and not passive in moving their paradigms, the necessary intersectionality between paradigms and the inclusiveness needed in the creation and propagation of knowledge to accomplish both. We aim to enlighten the reader both in the issues and perspectives presented in the chapters, but also, and equally, to empower the reader to understand what they can do as practitioners, professionals or even just interested citizens in broadening our dialogue about distributive issues, studies of justice and the policies we use these ideas to motivate. We place these pieces together to show the larger challenges and narrative of how we comprehensively approach distributive justice in thought and practice of bridging this gap. We must not lose sight of the very real effects our ideas and the practices of talking about, developing and understanding them have on individuals and how we can help facilitate a more just world.

References

Dunn, John (1982), *The Political Thought of John Locke: An Historical Account of the Argument of the 'Two Treatises of Government'*, Cambridge: Cambridge University Press.

Plato (1997), *Complete Works: Plato*, edited by John M. Cooper, Cambridge, MA: Hackett Publishing Company, Inc.

Reinhart, Carmen M. and Rogoff, Kenneth (2011), *This Time is Different: Eight Centuries of Financial Folly*, Princeton: Princeton University Press.

Skinner, Quentin (1978), *The Foundations of Modern Political Thought: Volumes I and II*, Cambridge: Cambridge University Press.

Part I

Historical Approaches to Distributive Justice

The focus in this section is on specific historical debates and ideas of distributive justice. In dealing with the context of historical debates, the chapters presented here recover ignored and even lost aspects of justice in the history of political thought, whether it be in the political thought of a specific thinker or identifying specific concerns of justice that have been recurrent themes at different times and places. By approaching the contentiousness of ideas pertaining to 'distributive justice' as historically grounded and contingently conceived, these chapters create new pathways of understanding and conceptualisation, first by recognising the contingent nature of ideas and, second, identifying their historical locality and genesis. As we move forward to Parts II and III, this section demonstrates how neglected historical aspects of distributive justice that our authors explore in their respective chapters can enlighten present issues, arguments and approaches. To paraphrase one contributor in the volume, Samuel Fleischacker, good normative work in political theory is enriched by a firm grip on the history of the concepts used in our normative arguments. Indeed, interesting normative conclusions can sometimes be drawn fairly directly from that history. Only by doing this can we clarify our normative beliefs, and therefore more readily see their implications, when we understand better from where they came.

Fleischacker works on this very assumption as he inspects the notion of what a right to welfare has historically meant in coming to terms with its modern conceptual recurrence of what it should mean. Carl Knight carves a space for exploring the historical incidents of a key, but often underserved, aspect of contemporary debates in 'distributive justice', namely luck egalitarianism. David James writes about Fichte's *Closed Commercial State* to show it takes many conceptual turns that we take for granted in contemporary liberal theories of distributive justice. Finally, Matt Zwolinski shows how representatives of the Social Darwinist traditions might suggest closer proximity to contemporary liberal theories of social justice than has typically been assumed when considering core issues of justice such as luck and personal responsibility.

1 A Right to Welfare

Historical and Philosophical Reflections

Samuel Fleischacker

I explore here both what the right to welfare historically has meant, and what it should mean: inquiries that are not sharply separable, in my opinion. More specifically, I attempt to do two things. First I explain the origins of the notion of a 'right to welfare' and why it is a useful term by which to understand debates over the nature of distributive justice (sections I–III). I then argue, on normative grounds, that this right is best conceived as what eighteenth-century theorists and activists would call a 'natural right', not merely a legal right (sections IV and V).[1] I proceed throughout on the assumption that good normative work in political theory is enriched by a grip on the history of the concepts we use, and indeed that interesting normative conclusions can sometimes be drawn directly *from* that history: we clarify our normative beliefs, and therefore more readily see their implications, when we understand better whence they arose.

I

I developed much of the historical account I use here in my 2004 book, *A Short History of Distributive Justice* (Fleischacker, 2004), and would therefore like to begin by summarising my argument there. The book grew out of conversations sparked by two sentences in a review I wrote of Charles Griswold's study of Adam Smith. I complained in the review that there is something confused about saying, as Griswold and many other commentators do, that Smith 'rejects' the idea of distributive justice.[2] How can he reject that idea, I asked, given that it didn't come into existence, in its modern sense, until the 1790s, after Smith died.

As regards Smith's writings, it seemed to me that the point was fairly obvious. Smith does say that distributive justice 'cannot be extorted by force' (Smith, 1976), but he also makes clear that he is using the phrase 'distributive justice' in its traditional natural law sense, in which it 'comprehends all the social virtues', including charity and generosity but also such qualities as a disposition to serve and honour 'men of merit' (Smith, 1976, *TMS*: 269–270). Nobody, in Smith's time or since, has thought that all social virtues should be enforced, that people should be forced to show respect to 'men of merit' or indeed that people should be forced to give charity, on a one-to-one, interpersonal basis. Smith was reporting a commonplace of the natural law tradition, according to which some interpersonal obligations can be enforced while others cannot be, and 'distributive justice' is the name for the ones that cannot be.[3] He was not primarily talking about duties to the poor at all, and he was not, by any means, rejecting a tradition that had used 'distributive justice' for *enforceable* obligations that society might have to the poor.

So far, so obvious, I thought, but to my claim that the idea of distributive justice was invented in the 1790s, I heard a lot of 'what abouts?'. 'What about Jesus's teachings in the Gospels', I was asked, 'or Acts 4:35, which describes a community in which "distribution was made unto every man according as he had need"?' 'What about Plato, and the utopian tradition?' other people asked, and some brought up the English Poor Laws, or the 'right of necessity' in Thomas Aquinas.

Well, each of these 'what abouts?' had a ready response, but when I sat down to write up the responses, I found it took me over seventy pages to do so. It then occurred to me that I might have a book here, if I added in a little on what led the concept of distributive justice to arise in the eighteenth century, and a summary of the more familiar developments of that concept in the nineteenth and twentieth centuries. The result was a short history of the idea of distributive justice, among philosophers and political theorists from Aristotle to Rawls.

The main argument of my book is fairly simple. First, I lay out a set of criteria for what we call 'distributive justice' today. This takes the form of the following five premises, all of which are presupposed, I maintain, by the modern notion of distributive justice:

1 *Individuality*: Each individual, and not just societies or the human species as a whole, has a good that deserves respect, and each individual is due certain rights and protections in order to pursue that good.
2 *Material desert*: A share of material goods sufficient to cover basic human needs is part of every individual's due, part of the rights and protections that everyone deserves.
3 *Rationality*: The fact that individuals deserve this can be justified rationally, in terms to which people of any religion and no religion can agree.
4 *Practicability*: The distribution of this share of goods is practicable: attempting consciously to achieve it is not a fool's project.
5 *State as guarantor*: The state, and not merely private individuals or organisations, ought to be guaranteeing the distribution.

I then try to show how each of the pre-modern ideas and practices that looks somewhat like what we call distributive justice in fact rejects or ignores one of these crucial premises.

Thus Aristotle, who coined the phrase, meant by 'distributive justice' the virtue of giving goods to people in accord with merit, but merit was something that needed to be earned and it couldn't possibly be true that *all* people 'merit' any set of goods. That contradicts our second premise. Moreover, Aristotelian 'distributive justice' was primarily concerned with political, not material, goods – the distribution of a role in government is his main example. The early Christian emphasis on helping the poor, on the other hand, was largely part of a commitment to humbling oneself before God, not an attempt to eradicate poverty. Jesus and his apostles tried to *live with* the poor, not to end poverty. And the paradigm Christian mode of giving to the poor, until the end of the eighteenth century, was one in which giver and recipient alike saw the gifts as *undeserved*, as a reflection of God's grace to man in Christ. The poor *deserve* nothing from the rich, but receive something anyway, out of the rich person's grace. This, again, runs up against our second premise. In its reliance on religious rather than secular arguments, it also offends against our third premise, and (relatedly) it leads to views that conflict with our fifth premise, according to which the state, not private individuals or the church, ought to be the primary agent for helping the poor. We see here the sharp difference between justice and charity. Justice imposes a duty on the agent and a right on the recipient, while charity expresses a benevolence above and beyond duty in the agent, and bestows no right on the recipient. Justice is thus required of us, but is satisfied with an act, regardless of our motivations, while charity is supererogatory, but is satisfied only if we have a certain kind of motivation. And because justice is required of us, and satisfied by an act, it can be enforced by law, while the corresponding features of charity mean that it cannot be legally enforced. Moving aid to the poor out of the domain of charity and into the domain of justice thus has enormous implications for its relevance to the politics. Modern distributive justice depends on that move.

Something similar goes for the other 'what abouts'. Aquinas's 'right of necessity' is a stop-gap measure by which a person may take what she needs for immediate survival if it would endanger her life to go through normal legal processes; it is not, cannot be, a *part* of any normal legal process. But that means, contrary to our fifth premise, that it is not something provided by the state. The utopians, from Plato onwards, are collectivists who recoil from the individualism of our first premise and promote equality out of an interest in strong bonds across the polis, not out of a concern for what the poor deserve. Collectivists, from Plato through Marx, tend not to be enthusiastic about justice in any form, which they see as concerned to protect individuals against the will of the body politic as a whole. Pre-modern utopians, in addition, do not present their visions as practicable, offering them instead as a fictional device for enlarging our moral imaginations; our fourth premise is thus no part of their project. Finally, the various European Poor Laws that get formulated in the sixteenth century or so, including the English Poor Laws, are concerned far more to *control* the poor than to give them rights (Fleischacker, 2004: 151, fn. 86). It was at least as important a part of these laws that they inflicted severe punishments on able-bodied beggars as that they granted relief to the poor who could not work. Moreover, they were justified on grounds of societal *charity* towards the poor, not of justice (ibid.: 50–52).

Only at the end of the eighteenth century, with the rise of a social science that made a lot of things seem practicable that had never seemed so before, the decline of traditional beliefs in a natural human hierarchy in which poor people belonged at the bottom of society, and the first hints of the idea that the poor are equal in virtue and capacity with all other human beings – many of those first hints to be found in the work of Adam Smith – do the premises that allow for the modern concept of distributive justice begin to circulate. And only with the political programme of 'Gracchus' Babeuf, at the end of the French Revolution, and the writings of Tom Paine and Condorcet and Kant and Fichte, does that concept get expressly articulated and enter mainstream political discourse. Indeed, it takes a while for the idea to become really accepted even then, since neither utilitarians nor Marxists were fully comfortable with its basic terms, and the idea was bitterly rejected by conservatives and libertarians, such as Burke and Spencer (Fleischacker, 2004: 75–80).

II

That's the short version of my book. Since writing it, I've altered my views a bit. In particular, I've been influenced by Gareth Stedman Jones's *An End to Poverty?* Stedman Jones has a similar view of the role of Smith, and the French Revolution, in bringing about modern attitudes towards poverty, but understands those attitudes under a somewhat different rubric. Stedman Jones argues, as I do, that the notion that states should attempt to end poverty first arises in the late eighteenth century, but maintains that the central point of that notion was to provide the conditions for a properly educated and independent democratic citizenry rather than to help individuals lead private lives – that it was primarily part of a programme for radical *democracy* rather than part of a conception of *justice*.

The distinction between a concern for justice and a concern for democracy is interesting, and I'm not quite sure what to say about its place in eighteenth-century debates over poverty. It seems to me that *some* late eighteenth-century authors were primarily interested in fostering a democratic citizenry, while others saw aid to the poor as more a matter of giving people what they deserve in the pursuit of their individual lives: more a matter of justice, strictly speaking. Paine's writings, and the excerpts Stedman Jones brings from the report of the Comité de Mendicité, suggest that a concern for the poor as fellow citizens rather than (just) fellow human beings is the main consideration behind their proposals. Smith and Kant, to the extent that they contribute to this discussion, both imply that aid to the poor should be required of people as a duty to fellow human beings, more than to fellow citizens. Babeuf and Fichte understand duties to the poor as something that should *become part* of everyone's citizenly obligations, but only in virtue of the fact that states are supposed to protect natural rights: rights we have as human beings independently of our participation in a state. Babeuf declared that nature gives everyone 'an equal right to the enjoyment of all wealth', and that 'The *aim of society* is to defend this equality, often attacked by the strong and the wicked in the state of nature' (cited in Thomson, 1947: 33). Fichte argued that a right to maintenance follows immediately from the same principles that justify a right to property:

> To be able to live is the absolute, inalienable property of all human beings. We have seen that a certain sphere of objects is granted to the individual solely for a certain use. But the final end of this use is to be able to live ... [Hence a] principle of all rational state constitutions is that everyone ought to be able to live from his labor, ... and the state must make arrangements to insure this.
>
> (Fichte, 2000: 185)

So the writings we have from these initial defenders of what today we call 'distributive justice' anticipate our contemporary debate over whether our duties to the poor arise properly out of our relationship to them as fellow citizens or our relationship to them simply as fellow human beings.

There may, however, be less to this distinction than meets the eye. On the one hand, it seems that grounding duties of aid in fellow citizenship is a very different thing from grounding them in demands of justice. If duties of aid are rooted in citizenship, they go out just to those who are our fellow citizens, not (necessarily, at least) to those who live transiently among us, or immigrants who have yet to become part of our body politic, let alone strangers far across the globe. Moreover, the point of such duties seems in that case to have more to do with building a harmonious and mutually respectful society than with the rights that individuals have independently of their relationship to society. The right to aid, on this view, may indeed be linked to a duty to contribute in some way to our society, may even be made contingent on the poor person's willingness to contribute. A right to aid rooted in justice would seem to entail no such reciprocal obligation; its point would have to do with the obligation we have to foster or preserve certain basic features of the lives of all other human beings, not with our interest in building any sort of society; and it would go out to human beings everywhere, at least in principle, not just to those with whom we share a society.

On the other hand, it is quite difficult to separate issues of citizenship from issues of justice. The kind of society we want to build with our fellow citizens is a just society, for one thing: without justice, it will hardly consist of people who respect one another. Nor can we expect our fellow citizens to contribute to building such a society unless we treat them justly. If we look in the other direction, we find that all duties of justice are to some extent limited by fellow citizenship, and to some extent entail reciprocal obligations, on the part of those who benefit from them. We do not normally go out to protect people even against rape or murder, or to punish their assailants, in countries other than our own, nor can they appeal to our courts to restore their rights against an oppressive government. And while we do not make the protection of our fellow citizens against violence contingent on their doing anything to safeguard or enhance our country, we expect the protection of those rights to instil in them some sense of obligation to pay taxes, serve on juries and otherwise protect and support the institutions that grant them a space of freedom and security. We also tend to understand, if not fully excuse, people who lack this level of patriotism because their rights have regularly gone unprotected, or been violated, by the government. In this way, even duties of 'commutative' or 'strict' justice are linked to citizenship.

It follows that if a guarantee of a certain level of material goods belongs to our basic rights, it will not be easy to tell whether it is our status as citizens or as human beings that gives us a claim on this right. A difference between these grounds may still show in some cases – as regards immigrants who are not yet citizens, or our duties of aid to other countries – but will not necessarily affect the basic idea of a welfare right.

The main implication of the debate over whether a right to welfare is tied to justice or to citizenship has to do, I think, with the *scope* of our duties to the poor. Whether or not we have global obligations of distributive justice – whether or not people who live in rich countries have an obligation to help poor people worldwide – will depend a great deal on whether such obligations are owed to fellow human beings or just to fellow citizens. I shall, however, not pursue this issue further here.

III

Another thing that has become clearer to me since writing the book is that the initial debate over poverty in the 1790s did not make use of either the phrase 'distributive justice' or the phrase 'social justice'. Rather, most writers talked about whether the poor have a 'right to subsistence' or a 'right to maintenance'. The late eighteenth century was of course the heyday of talk about 'the rights of man', and its debate over poverty was couched in terms of whether being lifted out of poverty – being relieved of great need – belongs to those basic rights or not.

I therefore now think that the best way to trace the conceptual origin of the debates we have today over the state's role in alleviating poverty is to use the concept of 'rights' rather than of 'justice', to ask whether the poor were seen, at a particular time or by a particular figure, as having a 'right' to relief or maintenance or welfare, rather than asking whether a particular group or person believed in social or distributive justice. Rights-talk and justice-talk are closely related, of course, and if we can establish that people at a certain time believed in a right to welfare – what people in the eighteenth century would have called a 'natural' right to welfare, at least – there will be good reason to suppose that they believed in distributive or social justice.

Putting the matter this way allows us to formulate two useful questions. First, an historical question: *when* do people begin to speak widely of a 'right to maintenance' or to 'welfare'? And second – a more philosophical question – what exactly *goes into* a 'right to maintenance' or 'right to welfare'? What conditions need to be met if we are to say that a government or political movement upholds such a right?

To the first question, I suggest that a belief in a right to maintenance does not clearly appear even in England before the 1790s, that the old English Poor Law, in particular, was not originally understood in those terms.[4]

Stedman Jones points out that several writers in the 1790s seem themselves to have believed that the Tudor Poor Laws contained a right to relief.[5] This may be due, however, to their reading the polemics of their own time back into an earlier legal tradition. Or it may represent a *transformation* of the Tudor laws, by which they *became* a symbol of the rights of the poor, in or around the 1790s, without having been that before. The issue deserves close attention: the relation between the rhetoric of the 1790s and the practice of the old English Poor Law sheds a very interesting light, it turns out, on the history of ideas in general, as well as on the particular idea – distributive justice – we are considering.

By the early 1790s, there were major figures proclaiming a right to maintenance in both England and France. Stedman Jones quotes a passage from the 1792 report of the Comité de Mendicité according to which 'every man has a right to subsistence through work, if he is able-bodied; and to free assistance if he is unable to work'. He quotes Thomas Ruggles, in 1793, to much the same effect (Jones, 2004: 61, 74–75). He notes that William Pitt (the Younger),[6] in his proposed Poor Law Bill of 1796, called for England to 'make relief, in cases where there are a number of children, a matter of right, and an honour'. And he quotes Malthus, in 1803, as believing that English law had long granted people 'a right to subsistence' when they could not work, although Malthus himself thought there could and should be no such right:

> there is one right which man has generally been thought to possess, which I am confident he neither does, nor can possess – a right to subsistence when his labour will not fairly purchase it. Our laws indeed say that he has this right, and bind the society to furnish employment and food to those who cannot get them in the regular market, but in so doing, they attempt to reverse the laws of nature.
>
> (Ibid.: 104–105)

So the idea that the poor had a right to 'relief' or 'subsistence' or 'maintenance' was clearly in circulation by the early 1790s. But there is also evidence, in some of the very passages Stedman Jones cites and in other writings, that the 1790s witnessed the *first* recognition of any such right. Arthur Young noted ominously in 1797 that 'That relief which formerly was and still ought to be petitioned for as a favour, is now frequently demanded as a right' (cited in Peacock, 1965: 35; see also Lees, 1998: 77). Pitt, in the passage Stedman Jones cites, called for England to '*make* relief ... a matter of right', (Jones, 2004: 77) – believing, presumably, that it was not already such. Tom Paine was very restrained about grounding any sort of welfare on rights in his 1792 *Rights of Man*, moving in that direction only in his later, more radical, *Agrarian Justice* (see Fruchtman, 1994: 355–356).[7]

Malthus, as we have seen, denied that there should be any such right, and agreed in this with Frederick Eden, who wrote in his highly influential 1797 *State of the Poor* that 'It is one, and not the least, of the mistaken principles on which' laws for the relief of the poor are based 'that every individual ... has not only a claim, but a right ... [to be supplied with] employment when able to work, and with a maintenance when incapacitated from labor' (Eden, 1966: 447). So when some of these same writers claim that the old English Poor Law, for better or worse, had always contained a right to maintenance, I am inclined to think that they did not grasp the significance of their own arguments over the existence of such a right. The fact that they were arguing over it suggests that the idea of a right to maintenance was something *new*, something that had *not* been a part of the English legal tradition until that point.

Accordingly, I continue to believe that the Tudor Poor Laws were not intended to embody a 'right to relief' or 'maintenance'. As originally formulated, these laws imposed a duty of relief on the government, without granting a corresponding right to the poor who were supposed to receive that relief. Nevertheless, what the Tudor Poor Laws said and how they operated in practice are two very different things, and I now think the question about whether they granted a right of relief in practice is more vexed than I did when I wrote my book.[8] On the one hand, many people managed to claim assistance under the old Poor Law, the assistance could be quite generous – sometimes amounting to a pension or disability plan, a gift of tools or animals, or training in a trade – and those wrongly denied assistance, or who felt they had been inadequately aided, could appeal to higher authorities to correct the situation. On the other hand, for many the aid came with a price, in humiliation or in freedom. The young were bound over to apprenticeships, able-bodied adults could be forced into workhouses, and those permanently 'on the parish' had to wear a badge with the letter 'P' on it and observe conditions for receiving relief laid down by their parish (see Hindle, 2004: 381–398). Moreover, relief was not given out in accordance with clear, impartially administered procedures. Rather, applicants for it had to develop personal relationships with overseers and members of the vestry, making a case to them in obsequious terms, and could never be sure they would receive it, whatever the law might say.

For these reasons, one recent author doubts that in the seventeenth century, at least, 'the poor, even the aged poor, believed they had a "right" to relief', and maintains that those who see such a right in the old Poor Law are taking evidence from the eighteenth century and reading it backwards into earlier history (Botelho, 2004: 71).[9] The same author notes that one's ability to claim relief was often tied to whether one had a 'religious affinity' with the local elites. Until the late eighteenth century, relief was officially disbursed under the supervision of churchwardens, who often used their power to try to coerce church attendance (along with other kinds of approved behaviour). And where the local elites came from outside the established church, religious affinity with *them* often made the difference between being subsidised and being destitute (ibid.: 15–16; see also Hindle, 2004: 382).[10] But if that is true, then the aid was being disbursed to the poor as fellow *Christians*, of some variety or other, not as fellow citizens or fellow human beings. In the terms I have laid out, that means that we are not dealing with a proper right here.

So there is some reason to think that the old Poor Law did grant a right of relief, and some reason to think it did not. The reasons to think that it did get stronger as one moves towards the late eighteenth century: the punitive aspects of the Poor Law fade or become milder, the types and amounts of aid become more generous, fewer strings are attached to it, the dispersal of aid is tied less and less to the church, and people come to have a firmer expectation of being able to receive aid (see Lees, 1998).[11] Perhaps the best thing to say is that the old Poor Law was not instituted in the name of justice, nor seen, when instituted, as expressing a right to relief or maintenance, but increasingly came in practice to embody such a right (ibid.: 163; King, 2000: 52).[12] Paul Slack suggests that the regular encounter with parish officers under the old Poor Law 'taught the poor their rights'; Steve Hindle modifies that claim, arguing that it was the intervention of magistrates to protect the poor *against* lazy or ill-willed parish officers that taught the poor their rights (Slack, 1998: 192; Hindle, 2004: 420). On either view, but especially Hindle's, the operation of the law may have gradually worked against the earlier, purely church-based, distribution of aid to begin to establish a view of that aid as grounded in justice rather than charity. Poor people, who saw officers of the law step in to correct for arbitrariness in the actions of churchwardens, began to see the aid they received as part of their legal rights, rather than as something the church might disburse at its own discretion. The process was slow, and the fact that church officials for a long time continued to have final say over who got aid and who didn't made it difficult for the move from charity to justice to take place fully, but the workings of the old Poor Law may well have initiated that move. That would mean that when late eighteenth-century activists and thinkers came to argue for a proper right to relief, they had a set of practices already in place to guide them.

As with many other ethical matters, practice would then precede theory; theory would articulate norms that are already implicit in the way people live.[13] But theory clarifies the meaning of practice, and when an idea that lurks implicitly in a set of practices comes to the fore, those who now have to decide what they think of that idea may well resist it rather than endorse it. It is therefore at this point that I think we can properly identify whether people, as individuals or as a group, really believe in the idea or not. Just as we determine what an individual really believes when she consciously chooses whether or not to endorse something she has been doing subconsciously, so we can determine what a group really believes when it confronts the articulation of its practices in theory, or explicit political rhetoric. I am therefore still inclined to see the real birth of the idea of a right to welfare – of modern distributive justice – in the 1790s. But I think it makes better sense to understand that birth as a matter of tacit norms and attitudes becoming consciously recognised than as a creation *ex nihilo*, springing forth full-grown from the heads of the great Enlighteners.

IV

Let's turn now to the second, more philosophical question I mentioned earlier: What exactly is a right to welfare? What do people need to think in order to believe in a right to welfare, or for others reasonably to attribute such a belief to them?

There are at least two different clusters of issues here, one centred around the word 'right' and one centred around the word 'welfare'. To begin with the second group: I have spoken pretty indiscriminately thus far of rights to 'relief', 'subsistence', 'maintenance' and 'welfare', but of course these are quite different things. One of the points of my book was that a right merely to *relief* – a right against starvation, say – is very far from what a modern proponent of social or distributive justice believes that governments should do for the poor. A right against starvation is consistent, after all, with the belief that it is a good thing for poor people to remain poor: to remain, indeed, needy enough that they are always on the *verge* of starvation. Only a right to 'maintenance' sounds even approximately like a right to 'welfare' – to the education, health care and the like that might enable one to rise out of poverty (of need) itself, or at least to have a reasonable chance of doing that.

What about the word 'right'? Well, first, it is essential, for a right to be in place at all, that there be a remedy for its violation. Second, it is important, if a right is to capture an element of justice, that it be construed as a *moral* right, or what was called in the eighteenth century a 'natural right', as opposed to a mere legal right. To see the point of the first condition, consider the laws providing aid to the poor in nineteenth-century America, which were justified on the ground that poor people 'have claims upon the sympathy … of society' or that 'the impulses of common humanity' lead us to care for them (Abbott, 1940: 5, 74; Marshall, 1981: 84). In practice, an effect of this rooting of the law in 'sympathy' or 'humanity' ('charity', essentially) was that no poor person could effectively sue for the relief they were supposedly guaranteed even when it was wrongly denied to them. In one infamous case, a man suffering from frozen feet was wrongly denied aid in county after county until he reached the point at which his feet had to be amputated. The Iowa Supreme Court roundly condemned the agencies that had failed this man for not living up to their humanitarian duties (it even cited the story of the Good Samaritan to make this point), but refused to grant damages to the victim, on the principle that there could be 'no liability … to a pauper for failure to furnish relief, no matter how grievous the consequences, or for the negligence of [the government's] officers in furnishing relief' (cites Abbott, 1940: 20–22).[14] We are very far from a proper right here. The law in question established a duty for the state to care, but no corresponding right for anyone to receive that care.[15] Laws of this sort express a commitment to charity rather than justice, and recipients of the benefits they offer are not seen as deserving what they get. Outside of England,[16] most legal structures granting aid to the poor were similarly justified and kept similarly distant from rights and justice, throughout Europe as well as the United States before the twentieth century.[17]

We have moved a significant step beyond such structures today, even in the United States; people legally entitled to welfare can sue for damages if they do not receive it (Glendon, 1992). But this is not enough to show that a true right to welfare has yet entered American law. For the terms under which poor people can sue for relief are strictly limited to the terms of the welfare laws that actually happen to be on the books. There is no right to sue either a state legislature or the Federal government for the failure to pass adequate welfare legislation in the first place. A homeless person, no matter how 'deserving', cannot sue anyone in the United States for a home to be made available to her: no right to a home, or to health care, or to education, has yet been put into our Constitution. (In his 1944 State of the Union address, President Roosevelt called for a 'Second Bill of Rights' to guarantee welfare in this way, but the proposal went nowhere.) I am not sure exactly how the United States compares with other developed countries in this regard, but I am not aware of a country in which a poor person can effectively sue for the *installation of adequate welfare programmes* if they do not exist. In eighteenth-century terms, we may say that to this day countries do not recognise welfare as a *natural* right.

Why should they? What is the advantage of conceiving welfare as a natural right? Well, natural rights doctrines provide an excellent language in which to counter the evils of legal positivism, in which to couch standards to which all actual laws can be held up. To say that free speech is a natural right is to say that the laws permitting it are not merely the expression of the will of the majority at one particular time, much less of some absolute ruler's will, but an essential element of the entire *structure* of government by which we regard the law-making process in our country as legitimate. By calling free speech a natural right we say that no group of legislators, however overwhelmingly elected, can set it aside without calling into question the very process by which they were elected – without shattering the sense of shared citizenship leading us to abide by the results of elections.

Similarly, to describe some standard of welfare – say, housing, health care, enough food to survive and a decent education – as a 'natural right' would be to declare that a guarantee of that welfare is based on something more than the will of the electorate at one particular time. A citizenry thereby declares that guarantee to belong, rather, to the very underpinnings of its government's legitimacy, to what allows the government legitimately to command their allegiance. And the idea that a minimal standard of welfare is indeed a basic condition for legitimacy like free speech can be defended in a number of ways: because people without education, and people who live without adequate food or shelter, or in constant fear of losing their access to food and shelter, do not have the skills or the time to participate in the political process; because people in that desperate a condition have no reason for the most basic loyalty to their governmental system, cannot regard it as concerned about even their most fundamental interests; or because people in this condition are not truly free, do not have the basic liberty that government is supposed to protect – because, as Locke might say, living under government is for these people in some ways worse than the state of nature (Locke, 1988). It is not implausible that a minimal level of welfare belongs, for some or all of these reasons, to our natural rights.

I'd like to close with a four-step scale along which we might see nations as approximating a right to welfare. The lowest level on the scale would be one in which there are no political institutions aiding the poor at all, or in which such aid is merely part of a programme to control the poor, to restrict their rights and keep them from threatening the better-off. Call this 'welfare as private charity'. Above this is a condition in which state agencies are supposed to aid the poor, but the poor themselves have no remedy if the agencies fail in that obligation: we might call this 'welfare as state charity'. A step above that is the one we've currently reached – 'welfare as a legal right' – in which there are welfare programmes and those eligible for aid under such programmes have a legal remedy if the relevant agencies fail in their duties, but no constitutional principle is recognised according to which governments *ought* to have such programmes. The highest, fullest realisation of a right to welfare would come when and if it were taken to be a full-fledged natural right, not merely a legal one, and transformed for that reason into a constitutional right, a supra-legal principle to which the ordinary laws of a nation can be held responsible.

To clarify the reasons for this scale, compare, again, the right to free speech. At the lowest level, we might have a government that simply prohibits free speech, or free speech on certain issues – speech critical of itself, perhaps. A step above that is a government that officially permits free speech, but does not allow citizens to file for relief against attempts to proscribe their speech, even when those attempts flagrantly violate the law.

(An agency of the government itself, perhaps, is given exclusive power to determine the scope of free speech and to decide how to handle violations of the government's own rules on the matter.) A notch higher, and closer to the recognition of true freedom of speech, would be a condition in which there are laws and policies protecting speech, but one's right to speak is fully determined by those laws and policies. Here if a law declared that, say, criticising military policies lies beyond the limits of protected speech, there would be no publicly recognised grounds for calling that law itself unjust. The final stage – and the only one most people would accept as demonstrating a true right to speak freely – is one in which a constitutional right to free speech is recognised in addition to whatever legal rights there might be on the subject. Here, laws restricting speech can be scrutinised in the light of a higher standard defining the right they are supposed to be protecting, and perhaps struck down in the name of that right. Some such laws might survive the scrutiny, of course: free speech does not necessarily mean that anyone can say anything anywhere and at any time. But the idea that the right of free speech stands beyond all existing laws attempting to protect it needs to be in play if a state is truly to recognise free speech as required by justice. And the right to welfare will similarly truly be recognised as such only once it comes to be seen as transcending positive law.

Which is to say that few if any countries in the world even today have yet truly recognised a right to welfare. Certainly the United States has not done so. But we are much closer to it than we have been in the past. All the major universal human rights declarations include a right to welfare, which suggests that it is now recognised, to some degree, as a natural right. They are not justiciable, but their proclamation at least suggests some public belief in a natural right to welfare. If my account of natural rights is correct, however, they are properly understood as a call for the establishment of constitutional rights. So no country can truly claim that it recognises the natural right to welfare until it incorporates a right of that sort into its constitutional principles. This seems to me a reasonable extension of the thinking about welfare and justice that has gone on, if fitfully, from the 1790s to the present day.

Notes

1 Natural rights are supposed to inhere in people independently of government, and their protection is supposed to be the prime purpose of government (Locke's *Second Treatise*, widely read in the eighteenth century, is the classic source of this idea). On this line of thinking, natural rights are more robust and more important than legal or 'positive' rights: people retain their natural rights whatever the laws say, and laws that deprive them of such rights are illegitimate. If there is a natural right to welfare, then, governments have an obligation to fulfil it and are forbidden to obstruct it. Of course, it is hard to see how exactly these lofty claims should be translated into practice – especially as regards a right that requires positive action on the part of the government, like a right to welfare. That is the burden of much of this essay.

2 Griswold describes Smith as having made a 'decision to focus on commutative justice and for the most part to assimilate distributive justice to [the private virtue of] beneficence' (Griswold, 1999: 250). Compare also Istvan Hont and Michael Ignatieff, who say that Smith's views 'effectively excluded "distributive justice" from the appropriate functions of government in a market society', and that he 'insisted' that only commutative justice could be enforced (1983: 24). Donald Winch speaks of 'the restriction of the application [of the notion of justice] in [Smith's] *Theory of Moral Sentiments* to commutative as opposed to distributive justice' (Winch, 1996: 100).

3 'Natural law' or 'the law of nature' is based on the idea that there is an ethical standard of right conduct that governs every human being. Some classical natural law theorists – beginning with Aristotle, although the idea is most developed in the Stoics – used a moralised idea of human nature as an ideal or telos, towards which our actual natures are directed by laws of different kinds. In the medieval period, Thomas Aquinas merged these classical notions of an ideal human nature with Christian theology: natural law was now drawn from God's eternal law, by way of the reason that God has implanted in us. This allowed him to carve out a perfectionist view of ethics that was supposed to guide politics: rulers should enforce only those laws that all human beings can grasp by way of reason. However, the complexities and ambiguities of defining the natural law, let alone how to act on it, still remain in dispute. For example, what obligations arise from natural law norms and how are these to be effected? The question of what creates moral obligation weighed on most early modern theorists of natural law, such as Grotius, Suárez, Pufendorf and Hutcheson. For studies of the natural law tradition see for instance Haakonssen (1996), George (1993) and d'Entreves (1994) remains a superb introduction to the subject.

4 For a superb survey of the debates among historians over whether the old English Poor Law embodied a right to relief, see Steve Hindle (2004: 398–405). Many historians, including Stedman Jones, have argued otherwise (Stedman Jones, 2004: 75). Joanna Innes says that England was often described as having a system that recognised a 'right to relief' by the mid-eighteenth century (2002: 381ff.). She describes an Irish cleric named Richard Woodward, in the late 1760s, and a Welsh judge of the same time period, as making an argument that the poor had a right to support and using that argument to urge the passage of Poor Laws similar to the English ones in Ireland and Wales (p. 388). This certainly suggests that some thinkers *saw* the English Poor Laws as embodying a right to relief before the 1790s, but does it show that the English Poor Laws in fact embodied such a right? Woodward could have been overly optimistic in reading them that way, or he could have had an impoverished notion of what a 'right to relief' properly entails.

Lynn Lees says that '"social citizenship" with a right to maintenance arrived in England and Wales with the poor laws, not with the Labour government of 1945'. She admits, indeed stresses, that the Tudor Poor Laws were drawn up with the primary purpose of forcing the able-bodied to work rather than of helping poor people, able-bodied or otherwise, but she argues that in practice the poor were often able to use these laws to establish an entitlement to certain benefits. People with a parish settlement, she says, 'had a right to relief and they knew it' (Lees, 1998: 39). But the evidence she brings for this claim is problematic. Many of the cases she discusses demonstrate the opposite, that overseers could throw off the claims of the poor or ignore them (see pp. 31 and 34), and the ones that best support her claim come from the period between 1790 and 1834 (see pp. 36–39). I also think she misreads some of the evidence she brings for the belief in such a right before 1790. She cites, for instance, a 1765 riot in which poor people proclaimed their right to be relieved in their own parishes, against a law that would have put the poor of several parishes into one large workhouse (pp. 79–80). But what was at stake here was removal from one's home, not relief per se. Steve Hindle has noted that '[a]lthough the language of rights did not surface in ... polemics on the poor law until the early nineteenth century, some recent commentators have argued that seventeenth-century practice ... actually embod[ied] what was later meant by a right to relief', but he goes on to raise many of the conceptual difficulties over what might be meant by this claim that are my topic in this paper. '[T]he language of rights', says Hindle, was not part even of the 'polemics on the poor law until the early eighteenth century' (Hindle, 2004: 399, see also 416–417). We shall also see good reason, below, to say that in practice the Poor Law did not grant anyone a right to what they received until the mid- or late eighteenth century. Hindle nonetheless speaks of some seventeenth-century magistrates as employing 'the rhetoric of social justice' (p. 412). None of the quotations he brings to support this remark actually use the language of justice, however; they speak instead of 'uncivil' or 'unmerciful' behaviour, of 'offence[s] against God' and of 'cruel and barbarous act[s]', and I think he simply misses the anachronism that might be involved in speaking of 'social justice' in the seventeenth century, especially if one wants to deny that the notion of 'rights' was in play.

5 Thomas Ruggles praises 'the Godlike laws' of England, for granting a right of maintenance to the poor (Jones, 2004: 75), and Eden and Malthus, while criticising the idea of such a right, seem sometimes to suppose that it was enshrined in English law. As we saw above, Innes notes that some writers believed this as early as the 1760s.

6 William Pitt 'the Younger' (1759–1806) was a Tory prime minister serving two terms in this position from 1783 to 1801 and 1804 to 1806 and was most notably responsible for the Act of Union (1800) and the India Act (1784).

7 I argued in *Short History* that the fact that Paine defended his proposal in the *Rights of Man* for a retirement benefit on the peculiar grounds that the elderly deserve a rebate on past taxes suggests that even radicals did not feel they could make a convincing case for the idea that *all* people have a right to maintenance in 1792. The fact that Paine appeals to a more comprehensive right to maintenance in his 1797 *Agrarian Justice* – written after the abortive uprising of Babeuf and apparently somewhat under Babeuf's influence (see Fruchtman, 1994: 355–356) – reinforces this interpretation of the *Rights of Man.*

8 I am grateful to email exchanges with Jonathan Healey for the impetus to revise my views in this respect, and for alerting me to the works of Hindle, Slack and King mentioned in these notes.

9 Hindle also raises doubts about whether a right to relief can be seen in sixteenth- and seventeenth-century English practice, whatever may have been the case in the eighteenth century (pp. 401–403). See Botelho (2004: 22–23), on the obsequious process by which the poor claimed their relief: 'need alone', she says, 'was not enough' to make such a claim. Hindle also notes that lack of deference was often considered grounds to diminish or withdraw relief (Hindle, 2004: 387–390).

10 'In February 1682, the Middlesex justices agreed that "such poor people as shall go to any meeting house and not to their parish church shall have no benefit of the parish collections but be put out of the poor's book"' (Hindle, 2004: 382). The Devon bench issued a similar general order denying relief to those who did not conform to the Anglican rites from 1684.

11 'Over the longer run,' as Lees writes (1998: 19), 'some of the harsher elements of the poor laws lost their sting.' She also delineates ways in which the poor actively participated in the processes by which they were granted relief (pp. 30–32, 36–37) – processes that begin to resemble a way of claiming relief by law. See also Hindle (2004: 404–432).

12 As Lees says: 'the conviction of the wealthy's social duty to aid the poor *became* ... a conviction of the legitimacy of relief' (p. 163, my emphasis).

13 Stedman Jones points out that several writers in the 1790s themselves seem to have believed that the Tudor Poor Laws contained a right to relief (see note 5 above). But this does not settle whether the old Poor Law did contain such a right or not. Those who claimed that it did, in the 1790s, may have been reinterpreting the original English Poor Laws, rather than reporting on their content.

14 The case is *Cerro Gordo County vs Boone County* (1911).

15 Compare Marshall (1981: 84):

> But did the duty to care for the poor [in nineteenth century and early twentieth century law] ... imply a right of the poor to be cared for? In England, the answer was an ... unqualified 'no'. The pauper was a person deprived of rights, not invested with them. The duty to relieve him was admitted, but its source did not lie in any rights possessed by the person relieved.... The duty to relieve the poor, says Sir Ivor Jennings (writing about the Poor Law of 1930), was 'a duty owed to the public and not to the poor person himself'.

16 Jose Harris notes that a series of mid-Victorian lawsuits established the principle in English law that the poor could sue for relief if wrongly denied assistance, and that the public officers who denied it to them could be punished (Harris, 2002: 416–417, 426).

17 There was a short-lived experiment in the nineteenth century with establishing a legal right to relief in some of the Scandinavian countries (see Nelson, 1953: 448).

References

Abbott, Edith (1940), *Public Assistance, Vol. I, American Principles and Policies*, Chicago: Chicago University Press.

Botelho, L. A. (2004), *Old Age and the English Poor Law, 1500–1700*, Chippenham: Boydell Press.

D'Entrèves, A. P. (1994), *Natural Law*, Livingston, NJ: Transaction Publishers, 1994 (originally published in 1951).

Eden, Sir Frederic Morton (1966), *The State of the Poor*, London: Frank Cass (facsimile of 1797 edition).

Fichte, Johann Gottlieb (2000), *Foundations of Natural Right*, translated by M. Baur and edited by Frederick Neuhouser, Cambridge: Cambridge University Press.

Fleischacker, Samuel (2004), *A Short History of Distributive Justice*, Cambridge: Harvard University Press.

Fruchtman, Jack Jr (1994), *Thomas Paine: Apostle of Freedom*, New York: Four Walls Eight Windows.

George, Robert P. (ed.) (1993), *Natural Law Theory: Contemporary Essays*, Oxford: Clarendon.

Glendon, Mary Ann (1992), 'Rights in twentieth-century constitutions', *University of Chicago Law Review* 59: 519–538.

Griswold, Charles L. (1999), *Adam Smith and the Virtues of Enlightenment*, Cambridge: Cambridge University Press.

Haakonssen, Knud (1996), *Natural Law and Moral Philosophy*, Cambridge: Cambridge University Press.

Harris, J. (2002), 'From Poor Law to welfare state: a European perspective,' in D. Winch and P. K. O'Brien (eds), *The Political Economy of British Historical Experience*, Oxford: Oxford University Press, pp. 409–439.
Hindle, Steve (2004), *On the Parish? The Micro-Politics of Poor Relief in Rural England, c.1550–1750*, Oxford: Clarendon Press.
Hont, Istvam and Ignatieff, Michael (1983), 'Needs and justice in *The Wealth of Nations* – an introductory essay', in Istvam Hont and Michael Ignatieff (eds), *Wealth and Virtue – The Shaping of Political Economy in the Scottish Enlightenment*, Cambridge: Cambridge University Press, pp. 1–44.
Innes, Joanna (2002), 'The distinctiveness of the English Poor Laws 1750–1850', in D. Winch and P. K. O'Brien (eds), *The Political Economy of British Historical Experience, 1688–1914*, Oxford: Oxford University Press, pp. 381–407.
Jones, Gareth Stedman (2004), *An End to Poverty?* London: Profile Books.
King, Steven (2000), *Poverty and Welfare in England, 1700–1850: A Regional Perspective*, New York and Manchester: Palgrave and Manchester University Press.
Lees, Lynn Hollen (1998), *The Solidarities of Strangers: The English Poor Laws and the People, 1700–1948*, Cambridge: Cambridge University Press.
Locke, John (1988), *Second Treatise of Government*, in John Locke, *Two Treatises of Government*, edited by Peter Laslett, Cambridge: Cambridge University Press.
Marshall, T. H. (1981), *The Right to Welfare and Other Essays*, New York: The Free Press.
Nelson, George (1953), *Freedom and Welfare*, Westport, CT: Greenwood.
Peacock, A. J. (1965), *Bread or Blood: A Study of the Agrarian Riots in East Anglia in 1816*, London: Victor Gollancz.
Slack, P. (1998), *Poverty and Policy in Tudor and Stuart England*, London: Longman.
Smith, Adam (1976), 'Early lecture notes', in D. D. Raphael and A. L. Macfie (eds), *Theory of Moral Sentiments*, Oxford: Oxford University Press.
Thomson, David (1947), *The Babeuf Plot*, London: K. Paul, Trench, Trubner.
Young, Arthur (1804), *General View of the Agriculture of the County of Suffolk: Drawn Up for the Consideration of the Board of Agriculture and Internal Improvement*, London: Richard Phillips.
Winch, Donald (1996), *Riches and Poverty: An Intellectual History of Political Economy in Britain 1750–1834*, Cambridge: Cambridge University Press.

2 Luck Egalitarianism and the History of Political Thought

Carl Knight

Introduction

Luck egalitarianism is a family of egalitarian theories of distributive justice that give a special place to luck, choice and responsibility. These theories can be understood as responding to perceived weaknesses in influential earlier theories of both the left – in particular Rawls's liberal egalitarianism (1971) – and the right – Nozick's libertarianism (1974) stands out here. Rawls refused to give a fundamental or systematic role to individual choice or responsibility when it came to the distribution of goods, and is therefore subject to the traditional complaint that theories of the left fail to reward hard work and prudent decision-making. Nozick, by contrast, gave choice a central role, rewarding those who appropriate unowned goods or receive them through free exchange, but his refusal to acknowledge any duties of justice to support those who miss out on these processes (for instance, because they are born later when there are no unowned goods left) leaves him open to the usual complaint that theories of the right are unduly harsh on the poor and dispossessed. Like Rawls, luck egalitarianism calls for a significant redistribution of resources, especially to the benefit of the worst off. But it does so in a 'responsibility sensitive' way, so that those who are responsible for bringing about greater benefits receive greater rewards. In this way luck egalitarianism's proponents see it as drawing from the strengths of left-wing and right-wing thought alike.

Unlike Rawls and Nozick, luck egalitarianism's main proponents have shown virtually no interest in the historical antecedents of their view. Rawls put great emphasis on the continuity of his theory with the great social contract theories of modern political thought, particularly emphasising its Kantian character, while Nozick overtly develops his theory as an elaboration of John Locke's account of property. By contrast, how luck egalitarianism is related to the history of political thought or philosophy more generally has been left unexplored by its proponents. Perhaps this is because they see luck egalitarianism, with its focus on individual choice and association with such contemporary concerns as equality of opportunity, as without significant predecessors in the canon.

My purpose in this chapter is to make the tentative first steps towards identifying some historical antecedents of luck egalitarianism among the main works of Western political thought. I do not claim that any full-blown luck egalitarian theory can be found prior to the 1980s articles by Richard Arneson, G. A. Cohen and (though he subsequently denied that he is a luck egalitarian) Ronald Dworkin (Arneson, 1989; Cohen, 1989; Dworkin, 1981, 2003). Certainly, no historical theory as closely approximates the mainstream forms of luck egalitarianism as Locke approximates Nozickian right-libertarianism on the one hand and left-libertarianism on the other (see Steiner, 1994; Vallentyne and Steiner, 2000). Rather, I argue that there are *precursors of certain distinctive aspects of luck egalitarianism among the great texts of political thought.* This is really all that Rawls can claim of Locke, Rousseau, Hume or Kant. Since certain parallels between Rawls's ideas and those advanced by historical writers are considered of wide interest, so I believe there should be at least some interest in the similar parallels, so far neglected, concerning luck egalitarianism.

Before I begin in earnest, a brief note on method is in order. I broadly follow the approach to the history of ideas pioneered by Arthur O. Lovejoy. Lovejoy's

> initial procedure may be said – though the parallel has its dangers – to be somewhat analogous to that of analytical chemistry. In dealing with the history of philosophical doctrines, for example, it cuts into the hard and fast individual systems and, for its own purposes, breaks them into their component elements, into what may be called their unit-ideas.
>
> (Lovejoy, 1936: 3)

In this spirit, and notwithstanding the 'dangers', I aim to identify certain recognisably luck egalitarian unit-ideas – or perhaps more accurately, idea-complexes (see Knight, 2012) – in major historical works. In doing this, I do not of course claim that any thinker's overall system of thought, as opposed to specific ideas therein, has a proto-luck egalitarian character.

Definitions

In order to locate luck egalitarian ideas in texts, we must get clear what we mean by luck egalitarianism. In broad terms, we can define luck egalitarianism as a family of egalitarian theories of distributive justice that give a special place to luck, choice and responsibility. From that point, we can develop two more specific definitions of luck egalitarianism.

A common alternative name for luck egalitarianism is 'responsibility-sensitive egalitarianism'. This suggests something like the following:

> *Responsibility sensitivity* – each individual's advantage level should reflect the individual's exercises of responsibility.

For the view to be a responsibility-sensitive *egalitarian* view, something else is needed in addition to responsibility sensitivity. In the absence of responsible choices, responsibility sensitivity by itself says nothing about a distribution, so inequality might be permitted, which seems unfairly arbitrary from an egalitarian point of view. Hence a further condition is needed (Hurley, 2003):

> *Equality default view* – in the absence of responsibility, advantages should be distributed equally.

Responsibility sensitivity and the equality default view together provide a first, responsibility-based definition of luck egalitarianism.

A second definition focuses on luck. Specifically, it says that luck egalitarianism endorses the following proposition:

> *Luck neutralisation* – the distributive effects of some or all luck should be nullified.

The 'some or all' equivocation is explained as follows. The standard luck egalitarian position, 'brute-luck egalitarianism', only neutralises the distributive effects of brute luck – that is, the upshot of unanticipated and non-declinable risks (Dworkin, 1981; Arneson, 1989; Cohen, 1989). The less common 'all-luck egalitarian' view additionally neutralises the effects of option luck (the upshot of anticipated and declinable risks) (Knight, 2013; cf. Segall, 2010: ch. 3).

Most luck egalitarians treat the two definitions set out above as equivalent, and freely move between describing their view in terms of responsibility sensitivity and luck neutralisation. It is worth bearing in mind that this is only the case where we make further assumptions. For one thing, we have to assume that responsibility is the inverse of luck (Hurley, 2003; cf. Nussbaum, 1986: 4). Nevertheless, for most purposes in normative political philosophy the two definitions can safely be treated as equivalent. However, as we shall see, there is value in distinguishing them when it comes to the history of political thought.

Aristotle on Justice

An obvious starting point when discussing the roots of any theory of distributive justice is Aristotle's famous account. I will argue, however, that that account has rather more of a connection to luck egalitarian themes than it does to other contemporary egalitarian views.

Aristotle argues that justice

> does mean equality – but equality for those who are equal, and not for all. Again, inequality is considered to be just; and indeed it is – but only for those who are unequal, and not for all … a just distribution is

> one in which there is proportion between the things distributed and those to whom they are distributed.
>
> (Aristotle, 1995: 1280a)

So on Aristotle's account, neither equality nor inequality are intrinsically just; what matters is whether an individual's share is proportional to some relevant property or characteristic of that individual.

Even at this preliminary stage we can see a structural similarity between Aristotle's view and luck egalitarianism. Both views maintain that where individuals are identical in their relevant properties, their distributive shares should be equal, and where individuals are non-identical in relevant properties, their shares should be unequal. This may seem such a general view that it has nothing in particular to do with luck egalitarianism, but several of its egalitarian rivals would not endorse the view. Outcome egalitarianism would not accept it, as it would not allow that individuals are ever non-identical in a distributively important sense. Nor would democratic equality (Anderson, 1999) accept it. As this view says that the distributively important respect is community membership, it will, (1) like outcome egalitarianism, deny that members are ever non-identical in a distributively important sense, and (2) deny that members should be (un)equal with non-members – it offers minimum guarantees for members but makes no attempt to regulate distributions between members and non-members. Finally, Rawls's justice as fairness only achieves proportional justice in respect of one of its three principles (Rawls, 1971). The principle of equal basic liberties again denies that individuals can be non-identical in the relevant sense. The fair equality of opportunity principle does seem to achieve a kind of proportional justice, as it allows inequalities to arise in response to individual efforts to acquire offices and positions. The difference principle may also seem promising, as it too allows inequalities. However, these inequalities cannot be portrayed as necessary to achieving a proportion between the goods being distributed and the relevant personal properties of those receiving them, but are rather designed with the very different goal of maximising the position of the worst off. In short, whatever the merits of these non-luck egalitarian theories, they cannot satisfy even the loosest definition of proportional justice, as luck egalitarianism can with ease.

Are these findings reinforced when we consider which particular personal properties Aristotle considers to be relevant to distributive justice? Aristotle holds that this must be a matter of personal merit or desert (Aristotle, 2000: 1158b). This is in turn set by the end for which the city has been formed:

> For everyone agrees that justice in distribution must be according to merit, but not everyone means the same by merit; democrats think that it is being a free citizen, oligarchs that it is wealth or noble birth, and aristocrats that it is virtue.
>
> (Aristotle, 2000: 1131a; see also Aristotle, 1995: 1280a–1281a)

Here we can see two contrasts between luck egalitarians and Aristotle's account. In terms of justificatory strategy, luck egalitarians do not see the end for which the community was established as part of the argument about appropriate distributive shares. In terms of substantive principle, luck egalitarians do not give a role to the personal property of virtue or excellence.

Nevertheless, we can find similarities here too. First, some versions of luck egalitarianism are directly responsive to desert (see Arneson, 2001; Vallentyne, 2003). Second, even the standard version of luck egalitarianism, which does not respond to desert or virtue, nevertheless responds to responsibility. This is clearly a related notion; for Aristotle, virtue is in large part a matter of action.

These remarks do not, of course, show any tight fit between Aristotle's account of the personal properties relevant to distribution and luck egalitarian's account of these properties. It seems, however, that there is more of a fit than one would find when considering other modern egalitarian theories. Like luck egalitarianism, there is no role within outcome egalitarianism, democratic equality and justice as fairness for justifications based on the end of the community, nor is there any substantive distributive role for virtue or excellence. But these latter three theories are less potentially accommodating of desert than luck egalitarianism is, and they do not make use of the related concept of responsibility.

To make the main point clear, we can formulate Aristotle's view on distribution as follows:

> *Desert sensitivity:* each individual's advantage level should reflect the individual's desert.

This view is the same as the luck egalitarian principle of responsibility, except that 'exercises of responsibility' are replaced by the related notion of desert. There is no even vaguely similar principle in major recent non-luck egalitarian theories. Even Nozick, seemingly favourably disposed to desert claims (e.g. Nozick, 1974: 154–155), is hostile to 'patterned' principles such as this.

Furthermore, Aristotle also seems to be committed to an analogue of the equality default view, the second part of the first, responsibility-based definition of luck egalitarianism provided above. Just as luck egalitarianism holds that, in the absence of responsibility or choice, equality is required, so Aristotle would seem to hold that in the absence of desert or merit, equality is required. So Aristotle's account of proportional justice has a double structural similarity to luck egalitarianism. Both views are distributively sensitive to broadly similar personal properties, and in the absence of these properties insist on equality.

Machiavelli on Fortuna

We have seen that there is a structural resemblance between Aristotle's account of proportional justice and the first, responsibility-orientated definition of luck egalitarianism. Though we have noted some differences in the substance of these views, we have thus far neglected the greatest one. Aristotle clearly makes no attempt to neutralise luck. Indeed, of all the political thinkers in the canon, he may be the most overtly 'luck sensitive', as is especially clear in his account of natural slavery (Aristotle, 1995: 1254a–1254b). Though desert and responsibility are related, Aristotle evidently uses desert in such a way that distributive shares are set largely on the basis of brute luck. Even in considering personal conduct, Aristotle concludes that the good life has at its heart pursuits that are open to great misfortune (Nussbaum, 1986: chs 11–12).

Augustine queried the worship of the Roman goddess Fortune ('How, then, is the goddess Fortune good, when she comes to both good men and bad without any discrimination': Augustine, 1998: IV. 18), but it is with Machiavelli that we see a systematic but – crucially – prudential form of luck neutralisation. His recommendations in this respect are manifold. A wise prince does not use mercenaries or auxiliaries, which makes one 'completely subject to Fortune', but rather uses his own soldiers (Machiavelli, 1979a: XIII). He does not relax in times of peace, but prepares so that he might survive misfortune (Machiavelli, 1979a: XIV). Those that are armed with prudence and weapons can keep a state even when fortune turns against them (Machiavelli, 1979b: I, XIX). Just as one can prepare for floods with embankments and dikes, so too can Fortuna be resisted by 'organised strength' (Machiavelli, 1979a: XXV).

It may be doubted here whether Machiavelli is really proposing that luck be neutralised. The central support for this doubt is his view 'that men can assist Fortune but not oppose her; they can weave her schemes but they cannot break them' (Machiavelli, 1979b: II, XXIX). In reply, we should note that the textual support for the view that Machiavelli advises active resistance to, and even mastery of, Fortune is overwhelming. In addition to the material cited in the previous paragraph, we may note Machiavelli's suggestion that states will often change as Fortune does 'until someone arises so devoted to antiquity that he will rule Fortune in such a way that she will have no reason to demonstrate, with every revolution of the sun, how powerful she can be' (Machiavelli, 1979b: II, XXX). To this we must add his remarkable claim that 'Fortune is a woman, and it is necessary, in order to keep her down, to beat her and to struggle with her'. She can be 'taken over' by the young and impetuous, who 'command her with more audacity' (Machiavelli, 1979a: XXV). It is difficult to reconcile these with the 'assist but not oppose' quotation, but not impossible. Machiavelli pictures Fortune as a force of nature, to be harnessed for the benefit of the prince or the republic. Here, the earlier flood metaphor provides a helpful illustration. One cannot literally oppose a great deluge by returning it to the sky, but one can master it with earthworks to direct it away from where it does harm. Such an approach seems to amount to luck neutralisation. Luck egalitarians do not propose to stop all forms of luck from ever occurring. It is enough to neutralise its bad effects by, for instance, compensating people with congenital disabilities.

This comparison leads us back to the central contrast between the contemporary egalitarian notion of luck neutralisation and Machiavelli's account of Fortuna. The former is a thoroughly normative ideal, an attempt to achieve distributive justice, while the latter is an exercise in prudence, for either the prince personally or the republic more generally. The gulf between the two here may seem so great that it obliterates any similarity between doctrines. This would, however, be too hasty. It is not at all unusual to draw parallels between principles of morality and principles of prudence. Such parallels are at the heart of the utilitarianism of Bentham (1996) and Mill (1998) and the liberal egalitarianism of Rawls (1971) and Dworkin (1981) alike. Where one principle says that 'outcome X be achieved as a matter of justice' and another says that 'outcome X be achieved as a matter of prudence', it is clear that these are (at least) structurally related principles, whether the outcome in question is maximisation of the worst outcome, utility maximisation or luck neutralisation.

Machiavelli's prudential focus has an implication which bears on the structural parallel with normative luck neutralisation. Machiavelli is concerned only with neutralising *bad* luck; good luck serves one's interests, so obviously should not be resisted. For example, he has no quarrel with new princes' efforts 'to preserve what Fortune has put in their laps' (Machiavelli, 1979a: ch. VII). Luck egalitarianism does not at its heart treat good and bad luck differently, so there is a further contrast with Machiavelli here. However, this is mitigated in a couple of respects. First, it has been suggested that luck egalitarianism might treat good and bad luck asymmetrically, as Machiavelli suggests, while retaining its normative focus (de Shalit and Wolff, 2011). Second, luck egalitarians invariably endorse additional principles (for instance, prioritarian ones) that would recommend that good luck on a societal level be allowed to stand rather than be squandered (Arneson, 2000; Knight, 2009: ch. 6; Segall, 2010: ch. 8). Luck egalitarians do sometimes treat good and bad luck differently, but not in anything like the comprehensive way that Machiavelli does.

Machiavelli does, then, advocate a form of luck neutralisation, but only regarding bad luck, and most importantly, only as a prudential doctrine. While his account of distributive justice arguably has a meritocratic character (Benner, 2009: ch. 8; but cf. Barnes Smith, 2006), it makes no serious attempt to neutralise luck.

Locke on Property

With both Aristotle and Machiavelli we found significant structural similarity between the historical figure and luck egalitarianism, paired with major departures in terms of substance. To achieve some significant degree of convergence in substance we must move forward to the Enlightenment. Here we see a rejection of the hierarchies taken as given by earlier writers, and renewed emphasis on the equal moral standing of all persons. The connections between recent theories of justice and Enlightenment philosophers are myriad, and explored in great depth elsewhere. To keep things manageable, my exploration of luck egalitarian themes in this context will be limited to one such philosopher, John Locke. I think this is appropriate given that Locke has been claimed by both the left and right wings of contemporary political theory, and that friends and foes of luck egalitarianism seem to agree that it combines the traditionally left-wing idea of equality with the traditionally right-wing idea of individual choice (Cohen, 1989; Anderson, 1999). I will argue that this combination is already apparent, in nascent form, in Locke.

Locke's account of distributive justice is articulated as an account of property. To modern ears, to focus on property rights is already to suggest a conservative bias. However, Locke has a rather broader sense of 'property' than modern usage allows. He says that men join in society 'for the mutual Preservation of their Lives, Liberties and Estates, which I call by the general Name, Property' (Locke, 1988: §123). Locke's sense of property is, then, close to what modern egalitarians call primary goods, resources or (possibly) welfare. What we would now call property is only a subset of this, which Locke calls 'Estates'.

Locke assumes that all humans should be 'equal one amongst another, without Subordination or Subjection' (Locke, 1988: §4). (This equality, like much of Locke's political theory, has a theological basis, which I set aside in order to bring out the features of his view that are relevant for our purposes.) This seems to have distributive implications similar to (though, for reasons that will become clear, not as strong as) the luck egalitarian's equality default view. That is, prior to individual labour, Locke does not seem to believe that there are grounds for distributive inequality. Also like luck egalitarians, he believes that moral equality is compatible with unequal outcomes created by individual choices. The first part of his argument in this respect is as follows (Locke, 1988: §25–26):

1 Humans have the right to preserve themselves.
2 In order to preserve themselves, humans must be able to appropriate things.

Point (1) seems fairly straightforward but (2) requires explanation. Locke remarks that

> The Fruit, or Venison, which nourishes the wild Indian ... must be his, and so his, i.e. a part of him, that another can no longer have any right to it, before it can do him any good for the support of his Life.
>
> (Locke, 1988: §26)

Explained in this way it does seem that *some* appropriation is required for human survival. However, this would only seem to establish the appropriation of a limited class of things (like 'The Fruit, or Venison') as justified on the basis of preservation. As Locke does not limit his account of property to these survival-orientated goods, it seems that he cannot ultimately rely on preservation as a basis for this account. Nor does preservation have anything in particular to do with luck egalitarianism. We should, I think, set aside (1) and (2), and focus on a more direct argument for appropriation:

3 'every man has a Property in his own Person' (Locke, 1988: §27)
4 'The Labour of his Body, and the Work of his Hands, we may say, are properly his' (Locke, 1988: §27).
5 'Whatsoever then he removes out of the State that Nature hath provided, and left it in, he hath mixed his Labour with, and joined to it something that is his own, and thereby makes it his Property' (Locke: 1988, §27).

Point (3) seems a reasonable claim, though, aside from the left libertarian branch of the family, luck egalitarians are not committed to it (or to its denial). Point (4) seems a reasonable extension of (3), which again luck egalitarians may or may not accept. I would suggest that (5) is the pivotal claim, and here there is something of a luck egalitarian flavour. The act of mixing labour is plausibly an exercise of responsibility. Since Locke intends to base distributive shares in such acts, his view seems to be to some extent responsibility sensitive. For instance, if one individual picks up acorns from under a tree, which another individual ignored, Locke maintains that the former can legitimately become better off than the latter on account of their respective choices.

Locke does not think that just any appropriation is permissible (1988: §27, 31–38):

6 Appropriation is permissible only if it does not result in spoilage.
7 Appropriation is permissible only if enough and as good is left in common for others.

Shorn of Locke's theological assumptions, (6) may seem obscure. But there are similar ideas within contemporary thought. For instance, where fruit is allowed to rot, it is highly likely that the distribution is not Pareto optimal. (A distribution is Pareto optimal where no alternative distribution makes at least one individual better off without making at least one other individual worse off.) An alternative distribution may well be available in which the fruit is spread more widely, benefiting others at no cost to the original possessor. As most or all luck egalitarians accept Pareto optimality, it seems that they would have little quarrel with (6). In any case, Locke considers it to be bypassed where there has been tacit consent to money as a durable instrument of exchange (Locke, 1988: §36, 45–50), so it need not detain us.

In spite of Locke's emphasis on spoilage, it is his second limitation on appropriation, the Lockean proviso (point (7) above), that has received most attention. Nozick (1974: 176) argues that the proviso has stringent and weaker interpretations. On the weaker interpretation, appropriations are permissible only if others can still *use* what they could before. On the stringent interpretation, appropriations are permissible only if others can still *use and appropriate* what they could before. The stringent interpretation seems more plausible. It is hard to see how A can be said to have enough and as good as B, where B is able to appropriate and A is only able to use, as the weaker interpretation allows. Were an appropriation to have this result, it would seem very much to be 'to the Prejudice of others' (Locke, 1988: §37).

The stringent Lockean proviso might seem, at first glance, to reduce the responsibility sensitivity of the theory by limiting the available choices. In fact it strengthens it. Without the proviso, and after the invention of money, agents would have complete freedom to appropriate the commons. Individuals would be able to claim vast tracts of land. Others would have no opportunity to appropriate land for themselves, or even be able to use land freely, as there would be no commons left. They would be forced to work as hired hands for the lucky few, or face starvation. This is very far removed from luck egalitarian ideals. In the earlier example, an individual became disadvantaged as a result of choosing not to pick up acorns, as responsibility sensitivity and luck neutralisation allow. Here we see individuals become disadvantaged without having made relevant choices – they are simply locked out of valuable appropriation opportunities. With the proviso, by contrast, each appropriator must, in effect, only appropriate an equal share of the commons. For instance, if there are ten acres and ten individuals, each individual can only appropriate one acre. If they appropriate any more, they will fail to leave enough land that other individuals are able to appropriate as much as they could before. This means that each individual has a reasonable chance to appropriate, and luck will play less of a role in the generation of inequalities.

This is not to say, however, that the Lockean proviso makes Locke's theory strongly egalitarian. With her fairly appropriated land, an individual may be able to generate much more than an equal share. Some ways in which this comes about may be fair from a luck egalitarian perspective. For instance, if an individual works harder or makes better decisions (while having average initial effort- or decision-making abilities), luck egalitarians view resulting inequalities as justified. But there are three problems from a luck egalitarian perspective.

The first problem arises when we consider later generations. Locke makes no attempt to constrain the intergenerational transmission of wealth. Justly acquired property can be passed on to children and grandchildren. Considering these later generations, then, there will be dramatic differences in life chances grounded in parents' or grandparents' choices. For the current generation this is a matter of brute luck. Such inequality of life chances is clearly radically at odds with responsibility sensitivity and luck neutralisation. (This is why I said that Locke endorses a weaker view than the equality default view. Prior to *any* choice, equality is required, Locke and the equality default view agree. But after early generations' choices, Locke believes that equality is not required, even if the current generation have not made relevant choices. By contrast, the equality default view insists on equality in that case.)

A second problem is present in all generations. Though luck egalitarianism has no complaint with inequalities grounded in individuals working harder or making better decisions *while having average initial effort- or decision-making abilities*, these conditions might not be satisfied, yet Locke would still allow inequality. An individual might work harder and have above average effort-making abilities on account of brute luck. In that case it would seem that there were not, in Arneson's (1989) terms, 'effectively equivalent options', a precondition for egalitarian justice to be satisfied. Even if appropriation options were nominally equivalent because the Lockean proviso had been satisfied, they would not be effectively equivalent if some could navigate those options more effectively, owing to unchosen differences in temperament or ability.

The first two problems concern different ways in which brute luck interacts with choice. The final problem also concerns brute luck, but requires no involvement of choice. Every luck egalitarian seeks to neutralise the effects of brute luck. Though Locke partially achieves this objective through such measures as the proviso, he obviously does not target it as a general goal. He makes no attempt, then, to protect people from brute luck. Suppose a farmer's crop is devastated by storms. Suppose also that the farmer had no alternative means of subsistence, and that no insurance against such storms was available. In such a case, it seems clearly a matter of brute bad luck for the farmer that she has lost her crop. But Locke makes no suggestion that compensation for such bad luck should be made available, not even from a neighbouring farm which miraculously evaded the storms.

Of course, it is hardly surprising that someone writing hundreds of years prior to the welfare state did not take the alleviation of luck as a general social goal. The same point can be made of Aristotle, Machiavelli or any other such figure. But it does show that, while in certain respects Locke approximates luck egalitarian objectives, in others he departs from them significantly.

Conclusion

I have surveyed three historical political thinkers, picking out certain ideas as having something of a luck egalitarian quality, though always to a heavily mitigated degree.

Aristotle maintains that, where individuals are identical in their relevant properties, their distributive shares should be equal, and where individuals are non-identical in relevant properties, their shares should be unequal. While that may seem an obvious position to take, it is not actually common among current theorists of equality, but it is endorsed by luck egalitarians. Furthermore, Aristotle favours a merit- or desert-sensitive account of justice with broad similarities to the core luck egalitarian idea of responsibility sensitivity, as well as a counterpart to the luck egalitarian equality default view. Of course, in spite of these parallels, there is major substantive disagreement, most notably on the issue of luck neutralisation.

This latter topic was viewed through the perhaps surprising prism of Machiavelli's account of Fortuna. It was argued that this account has structural similarity to the luck neutralisation proposed by luck egalitarians. Nevertheless, there are major differences, most obviously that Machiavelli is proposing a prudential doctrine, not a normative one. This has the further effect that Machiavelli aims to neutralise only bad luck, whereas luck egalitarianism generally (though not unreservedly) aims to neutralise good luck as well.

Finally, Locke's account of property was found to show a significant degree of responsibility sensitivity, as to an extent it seems to assume equality as a default, and its account of appropriation allows responsible choices to give rise to inequalities. This is reinforced by the Lockean proviso, which prevents individuals from suffering the brute luck disadvantage of not having 'enough and as good' as earlier appropriators. However, brute luck can still arise through the intergenerational transmission of wealth, differential natural abilities and unfavourable natural events.

With all three writers, though there is no systematic attempt to make distributions insensitive to luck, as luck egalitarianism proposes, there are nevertheless parallels with luck egalitarian thought.

References

Anderson, Elizabeth S. (1999), 'What is the point of equality?' *Ethics*, 109: 287–337.

Aristotle (1995), *Politics*, translated by Earnest Barker and revised by Richard F. Stanley, Oxford: Oxford University Press.

Aristotle (2000), *Nicomachean Ethics*, translated and edited by Roger Crisp, Cambridge: Cambridge University Press.

Arneson, Richard J. (1989), 'Equality and equal opportunity for welfare', *Philosophical Studies*, 56: 77–93.

Arneson, Richard J. (2000) 'Luck egalitarianism and prioritarianism', *Ethics*, 110: 339–349.

Arneson, Richard J. (2001), 'Luck and equality', *Proceedings of the Aristotelian Society*, supplement, 75: 73–90.

Augustine, (1998) *The City of God Against the Pagans*, edited and translated by R. W. Dyson, Cambridge: Cambridge University Press.

Barnes Smith, Margaret Michelle (2006) 'The philosophy of liberty: Locke's Machiavellian teaching', in Paul A. Rahe (ed.), *Machiavelli's Liberal Republican Legacy*, Cambridge: Cambridge University Press.

Benner, Erica (2009), *Machiavelli's Ethics*, Princeton, NJ: Princeton University Press.

Bentham, Jeremy (1996), *An Introduction to the Principles of Morals and Legislation*, edited by J. H. Burns and H. L. A. Hart, Oxford: Oxford University Press.

Cohen, G. A. (1989), 'On the currency of egalitarian justice', *Ethics*, 99: 906–944.

de Shalit, Avner and Wolff, Jonathan (2011), 'The apparent asymmetry of responsibility', in Carl Knight and Zofia Stemplowska (eds), *Responsibility and Distributive Justice*, Oxford: Oxford University Press.

Dworkin, Ronald (1981), 'What is equality? Part one: Equality of welfare. Part two: Equality of resources', *Philosophy and Public Affairs*, 10: 185–246, 283–345.

Dworkin, Ronald (2003), 'Equality, luck and hierarchy', *Philosophy and Public Affairs*, 31: 190–198.

Hurley, S. L. (2003), *Justice, Luck, and Knowledge*, Cambridge, MA: Harvard University Press.

Knight, Carl (2009), *Luck Egalitarianism: Equality, Responsibility, and Justice*, Edinburgh: Edinburgh University Press.

Knight, Carl (2012), 'Unit ideas unleashed: a reinterpretation and reassessment of Lovejovian methodology in the history of ideas', *Journal of the Philosophy of History*, 6: 195–217.

Knight, Carl (2013), 'Egalitarian justice and expected value', *Ethical Theory and Moral Practice*, 16: 1061–1073.

Locke, John (1988), *Second Treatise of Government*, in John Locke, *Two Treatises of Government*, edited by Peter Laslett, Cambridge: Cambridge University Press.

Lovejoy, Arthur O. (1936), *The Great Chain of Being: A Study of the History of an Idea*, Cambridge, MA: Harvard University Press.

Machiavelli, Niccolò (1979a), 'The prince', in *The Portable Machiavelli*, edited and translated by Peter Bondanella and Mark Musa, New York: Penguin.

Machiavelli, Niccolò (1979b), 'The discourses', in *The Portable Machiavelli*, edited and translated by Peter Bondanella and Mark Musa, New York: Penguin.

Mill, John Stuart (1998), *Utilitarianism*, edited by Roger Crisp, Oxford: Oxford University Press.

Nozick, Robert (1974), *Anarchy, State and Utopia*, Oxford: Blackwell.

Nussbaum, Martha (1986), *The Fragility of Goodness: Luck and Ethics in Greek Tragedy and Philosophy*, Cambridge: Cambridge University Press.

Rawls, John (1971), *A Theory of Justice*, Cambridge, MA: Harvard University Press.

Segall, Shlomi (2010), *Health, Luck, and Justice*, Princeton, NJ: Princeton University Press.

Steiner, Hillel (1994), *An Essay on Rights*. Oxford: Blackwell.

Vallentyne, Peter (2003), 'Brute luck equality and desert', in Serena Olsaretti (ed.), *Desert and Justice*, Oxford: Oxford University Press.

Vallentyne, Peter and Steiner, Hillel (eds) (2000), *The Origins of Left-Libertarianism: An Anthology of Historical Writings*, London: Palgrave.

3 Radical Distributive Justice

Fichte's *The Closed Commercial State*

David James

Introduction

Johann Gottlieb Fichte's *The Closed Commercial State* (*Der geschlossene Handelsstaat*) published in 1800 has received little attention in the English-speaking world.[1] This neglect is exemplified by its omission from a history of distributive justice in which John Rawls is credited with being the first philosopher to define clearly the modern notion of distributive justice, thereby making explicit what this notion had previously been taken to mean (Fleischacker, 2004).[2] Yet in *The Closed Commercial State*, Fichte can already be seen to set out a clearly defined modern notion of distributive justice that 'calls on the state to guarantee that property is distributed throughout society so that everyone is supplied with a certain level of material means' (Fleischacker, 2004: 4). Indeed, as we shall see, it is hard to imagine a clearer and bolder statement of such a notion of distributive justice.

The Closed Commercial State also exhibits the following essential features of the modern notion of distributive justice of which Rawls is said to be the first real exponent. This work is based on the idea of a human good that ought to be respected and to which individuals have a right. It also constitutes an attempt to offer a rational, purely secular justification of the claim to this right at the same time as the required distribution of the relevant good is viewed as something that the state can actually achieve. Thus Fichte's *The Closed Commercial State* serves to highlight the perils of writing the history of a concept in the face of limited knowledge resulting from the neglect of a philosopher's work within a particular philosophical tradition with its own historically conditioned standpoint and corresponding blind spots. More importantly, *The Closed Commercial State* represents a serious attempt to define what distributive justice means both in theory and in practice.

The issue of distributive justice concerns the identification of principles according to which certain goods ought to be distributed, with the legitimacy of any given pattern of distribution being held to depend on whether or not the pattern in question accords with these principles. Yet there are other questions that a complete theory of distributive justice needs to address. To begin with, there is the question as to the nature of the primary object of distributive justice. This question in turn relates to the issue of the amount of the good or goods that ought to be distributed to individuals and to the issue of the mechanisms whereby this good or these goods are to be distributed according to the relevant principles. The second issue arises because no principle can apply itself. Then there is the question concerning the type of being to which this form of justice is owed and the question of how many beings of the relevant type are owed it: that is to say, the question of what, if any, are the limiting conditions of the scope of distributive justice. Fichte's *The Closed Commercial State* attempts to address all of these issues. I shall begin with the issue of the principles according to which goods ought to be distributed by the state and then turn to the issue of the fundamental good or goods to which individuals have a right before looking at the issue of the amount of this good or these goods that ought to be distributed and the issue of the scope of distributive justice.

Property as the Object of Distributive Justice

The Closed Commercial State rests on a theory of pure political right (*reine Staatsrecht*) which sets out how the rational state (*Vernunftstaat*) is to be generated in accordance with concepts of right (*Rechtsbegriffen*) (Fichte, 1962–2012, I/7: 51; Fichte, 2012: 87). No attention is paid at this level to existing constitutions or to the legal relations in which individuals stand with each other in any existing state. Rather, pure political right is concerned only with the principles that determine whether or not an actual existing state may count as a rightful one. Fichte provides a theory of this type in his *Foundations of Natural Right* (*Grundlage des Naturrechts*) from 1796/1797, in which he seeks to deduce the concept of right itself as a transcendental condition of the practical form of self-consciousness which consists in awareness of oneself as a rational agent capable of forming ends and acting with a view to their realisation in the world. In other words, he seeks to demonstrate that this form of self-consciousness is not possible at all unless the validity of the concept of right is presupposed. Fichte then attempts to show that state authority is a necessary condition of the application of the concept of right. Moreover, on the basis of the social contract through which any rightfully constituted form of political authority must be generated, the state is invested both with the responsibility and with the right to distribute property in such a way that each and every citizen is able to live from his or her own labour.[3]

The Closed Commercial State represents a further application of the concept of right and the concept of property developed and partially applied in the *Foundations of Natural Right*. It also represents an attempt to show how an existing state can be transformed into a truly rational state with particular regard to the economic relations existing (1) between its citizens, (2) between its citizens and the citizens of other states and (3) between the state itself and other politically independent states. Given this intention, *The Closed Commercial State* is a project consisting of three main stages: first, an account of what constitutes right within the rational state in general and with respect to commerce and trade in particular; second, an account of what is customary with regard to commercial relations, both internal and external ones, in existing states that are products of history and have so far been the result of a spontaneous, uncontrolled process, as opposed to being products of a rational form of organisation undertaken in accordance with the idea of what ought to be the case; third and finally, an account of how an existing state can be transformed into a truly just and rational one, a task which for Fichte is the concern of politics.

As regards the first stage of this project, even if a fuller understanding of the principles of distributive justice that are the concern of this part of the project requires taking a closer look at the *Foundations of Natural Right*, Fichte offers a condensed argument for the principles that he wishes to apply in *The Closed Commercial State* in the first chapter of the first book of this work. This argument begins with the idea of natural freedom. In a condition of natural freedom, individuals acting in pursuit of the means of subsistence and pleasure can claim equal entitlement to parts of a world which cannot be thought to be the rightful property of any one individual, and to which, therefore, everyone originally possesses a right to use as he or she sees fit. In the *Foundations of Natural Right*, Fichte describes the right in question as the right of a person 'to extend his freedom as far as he wills and can, and – if he so desires – the right to take possession of the entire sensible world' (Fichte, 1962–2012, I/3: 412; Fichte, 2000: 111).

These individuals do, however, have a non-moral, prudential reason for agreeing among themselves to limit their natural freedom in relation to each other. The reason in question concerns the fact that it is impossible to realise one's ends effectively in the world in a condition of unlimited natural freedom, for in such a condition stable conditions of agency that allow one to predict with reliability the actions of others and the effects of one's own actions in the world are lacking. It makes sense, then, to agree partially to limit one's freedom in relation to others, provided that they agree partially to limit their freedom in relation to oneself. This form of agreement amounts to the mutual renunciation of the natural right to everything that individuals originally enjoy through granting others the right to some things but not to others so long as they equally grant you the right to some things if not to others.[4] Yet such acts of freely limiting one's own original right to everything in the form of an agreement to recognise the rights of others to possess and to use determinate parts of the world and objects within it can only be of limited effectiveness, since anyone who is not party to this agreement will not be obliged to abide by its terms to which he or she has not consented.

Fichte claims that this problem can only be solved by means of the establishment of a state invested with the authority to decide to whom certain parts of the world and certain objects within it should belong and with the coercive power needed to enforce its decisions. In other words, only with the establishment of state authority can everyone be thought to have consented to subject themselves to the same conditions. No individual is therefore in the position to claim that he or she is not bound by the terms of an agreement into which others have entered provided that he or she wishes to remain a citizen of the state. For the conditions to which each individual subjects him- or herself to be genuinely the same for all, however, each and every individual must benefit from his or her membership of the state as well as bearing the burdens that citizenship imposes on him or her. Indeed, any individual who does not benefit by receiving something that is exclusively his or her own cannot be thought to have renounced his or her original right to everything and thereby 'retains the rightful claim that was originally his to do whatever he pleases wherever he wants' (Fichte, 1962–2012, I/7: 89; Fichte, 2012: 133). Thus it is not a matter of what individuals happen to agree to among themselves; rather, it is a matter of what it would be reasonable for them to agree to.

Given that state authority is a necessary condition of right, that is to say a condition in which each and every person is guaranteed a sphere of personal freedom and the conditions of free, effective rational agency, Fichte denies that there could be property rights outside a state. Consequently, although Fichte does not object in principle to the idea that the state does nothing more than preserve and protect each individual's personal rights and property, he is at pains to point out that this is true only if it is not assumed that property can exist independently of the state. It is instead the state that first gives to each person that which is rightfully his or hers and subsequently protects it (Fichte, 1962–2012, I/7: 53; Fichte, 2012: 91). Fichte's theory of property turns out in this way to be compatible with the idea of a set of rights that may be subject to constant revision because they cannot be held to be valid independently of a pattern of distribution which accords with principles of distributive justice. Yet we must continue to examine what exactly are these principles which ought to determine the state's distribution of property rights.

In relation to this question, it is to be noted that Fichte's theory of property is ultimately concerned with the conditions of effective rational agency. Thus property rights are viewed simply as conditions of a practical form of self-consciousness. In this respect, these rights must be thought to have only instrumental value in the sense of being the means to an end which is the source of their value and in the absence of which they would lack any real meaning and justification. The right to everything that individuals originally enjoy means, moreover, that any legitimate pattern of distribution must sufficiently compensate the loss of natural freedom which results from entering into a legal and political community in which individuals recognise the rights of others by limiting their own freedom in relation to them or, when necessary, are coerced into recognising these rights. In the *Foundations of Natural Right*, Fichte expresses this reciprocity in terms of the idea that if a person wants to coexist peaceably with others, and thereby possess a sphere free from external interference in which to exercise the capacity for self-determination under reliable, stable conditions of agency, he or she must will the rule of right. This rule expresses the principle that must govern a condition of right and it reads as follows: 'limit your freedom through the concept of the freedom of all other persons with whom you come in contact' (Fichte, 1962–2012, I/3: 320; Fichte, 2000: 10). The act of willing this rule in effect amounts to limiting one's activity in such a way that others can also be free, though only because logical consistency requires willing the necessary means to any end that one sets oneself, which in this case is the end of securing for oneself a sphere of personal freedom and the conditions of free, effective rational agency. Thus, although Fichte claims in the corollary to his deduction of the concept of right that 'we are both *bound* and *obligated* to each other by our very existence', the consistency in question relates only to the rules of thinking in general that he describes in the same paragraph as being 'scientifically presented in general *logic*' (Fichte, 1962–2012, I/3: 354–355; Fichte, 2000: 45). Consequently, the reciprocity in question does not entail any distinctively moral considerations such as recognition of the dignity of others, in the sense of holding their freedom to be something which ought to form one of our own ends, irrespective of what we desire to do.

For Fichte, the only pattern of distribution which could truly satisfy the conditions stated above would be one that enables all individuals to achieve awareness of themselves as effective rational agents. It is not, then, simply a matter of being granted and guaranteed some property rights. Rather, these rights must be sufficient in relation to the end in question. This focus on activity can be seen as justified since only a practical, as opposed to purely theoretical, relation to the world and to objects within it is liable to give rise to conflict between human beings and thereby generate the need for a theory of right, as Fichte himself points out (Fichte, 1962–2012, I/7: 86–87; Fichte, 2012: 131). This focus on activity leads Fichte to claim that in the first instance types of activity are to be divided among individuals. He accordingly describes the original and primary form of property as '*an exclusive right to a determinate free activity*', and claims that the right to property is to be understood first and foremost as the exclusive right to actions rather than a right to things (Fichte, 1962–2012, I/7: 85–86; Fichte, 2012: 130).

From what has been said above, the human goods which form the primary object of distributive justice can be identified as the fundamental conditions of effective rational agency in a condition in which there exists the potential for conflict between individuals pursuing their own ends. The division of these goods is to be explained in terms of a purpose that all human activity must be thought to share, namely the purpose of being able to live. This claim should not, however, be understood to mean that self-preservation is the sole purpose and ultimate end of human activity, making it the object of each and every human action. In the *Foundations of Natural Right*, Fichte makes clear that being able to live is the purpose of all human activity only in the sense of constituting the most basic condition of all world-directed human agency when he claims that it is not a matter of willing to continue to exist simply for the sake of existence as such, but a matter of willing to continue to exist for the sake of a determinate state of existence (Fichte, 1962–2012, I/3: 408; Fichte, 2000: 107). In other words, individuals will to continue to exist only for the sake of other ends, so that although existence is a condition of such ends, it is not itself the ultimate end of their willing. The other ends for the sake of which individuals will to exist vary. The realisation of such ends, whether they have to do with mere enjoyment or some higher end, nevertheless require the exercise of some degree of rational agency, even though some ends will require considerably more in the way of such agency than will others. The idea that self-preservation is a condition of all other purposes only in this sense is important, for if self-preservation were treated as an end in itself, the object of distributive justice could be reduced to a bare minimum in the form of the basic means of human subsistence. Fichte, by contrast, wants to claim that something more than this is required, as is signalled by the following claim:

> the division must be made in such a way that one and all can live as pleasantly as is possible when so many men as they are exist next to one another in the given sphere of efficacy. Each, in other words, must be able to live about as pleasantly as the other.
>
> (Fichte, 1962–2012, I/7: 55; Fichte, 2012: 93)

Although the idea that the basic human good which forms the primary object of distributive justice is rational, purposive agency in general in this way suggests that the goods that ought to be distributed equally must include more than the basic means of human subsistence, this idea does not by itself tell us what other conditions of such agency are to be included in the absence of a more precise account of what it means to live as pleasantly as possible. Some indications of what it means to do so are provided in *The Closed Commercial State*.

After identifying the first thing that will have to be distributed as the determinate activity by means of which one is able to live from one's labour, Fichte turns to explaining how the just distribution of such a good can take place. In the second chapter of the first book, he introduces a 'chief division of free activity' (Fichte, 1962–2012, I/7: 56; Fichte, 2012: 95). This division results in two main occupations: that of the producers (*Producenten*), whose activity is directed towards the materials that nature immediately provides, and that of the artists or artisans (*Künstler*), who work upon the raw materials obtained from nature by the producers. Presumably, the state will have to distribute not only the occupations which enable individuals to live from their labour, many of which will be subsets of these two general forms of activity, but also the means (e.g. land, tools and other equipment) needed to undertake effectively the tasks connected with these occupations. In this way, what is distributed turns out to be a function of the determinate type of productive activity that an individual performs. Fichte then introduces another occupation or, as he calls it, estate (*Stand*). This is the estate of merchants, whose members are responsible for the exchange and distribution of the goods provided by the two other estates.[5] The various estates enter into agreements with each other that the state must then supervise and when necessary enforce. Beyond the determinate activity through which one is able to live from one's labour and the means of performing this activity effectively, Fichte implies that other goods such as leisure will also form the object of distributive justice when he claims that right itself demands that humanity

> live on the earth as easily, as freely, with as much command over nature, in as truly *human* a way, as nature will permit. Man should labor, and yet not as a beast of burden who sinks into sleep under the weight of its load and, having just barely refreshed its exhausted forces, is roused to bear it anew. He should labor without fear, with pleasure and joy, and have time left over to raise his spirit and eye to the heavens, which he has been formed to behold.
>
> (Fichte, 1962–2012, I/7: 71; Fichte, 2012: 110)

Here we have the right to labour only under certain conditions and the right to be free from having to labour for a sufficient period of time, with both rights being ones that individuals possess in virtue of their humanity alone. Fichte accordingly wants to measure the wealth of a nation not merely in terms of what it produces but also, and more fundamentally, in terms of the ease with which the means of satisfying those needs whose satisfaction is demanded by right can be attained (Fichte, 1962–2012, I/7: 71–72; Fichte, 2012: 110). This could mean measuring national wealth in terms of the amount of time that each individual must work in order to achieve this end. A state would then be richer or poorer according to the extent to which each individual had more or less time free from work. This idea implies that the state must aim to create and to distribute equally as much time as possible free from work. Fichte draws this conclusion in his *Rechtslehre* from 1812, in which leisure has clearly become an object of distributive justice (cf. James, forthcoming b and James, 2013: 207–211). The same idea also allows the right to equal access to the resources needed to gain an awareness of oneself as a rational agent to be extended to include that which is needed to spend one's state-guaranteed leisure time as agreeably and effectively as possible. As with the question of what it means to live as agreeably as possible in a given state, the amount of leisure time that can be created and distributed equally will depend on such factors as the efficiency with which the labour process is organised and the technological means that can be utilised in the production process.

Fichte's view of distributive justice invites the following question which becomes central to debates about distributive justice once it is accepted that any principled distribution of goods must in some sense be an egalitarian one: how equal must the distribution of goods be? Fichte claims that what is available within a state must be divided equally among all (Fichte, 1962–2012, I/7: 56; Fichte, 2012: 94). Evidence of the literalness of this demand is provided by his claim that in the case of 100 people living together working the land, the law of right entails the division of the land into 100 equal parts, one part of which is given to each person as his or her own (Fichte, 1962–2012, I/7: 88; Fichte, 2012: 132).[6] This example creates a significant problem if this equal division of land is taken to concern the size of the individual pieces of land that are distributed, for one piece of land could be more fertile than another piece of land of equal size, so that in terms of quality the division would be an unequal one. Such a literal interpretation of the equal division of goods and resources demanded by distributive justice as Fichte understands this notion is not, however, entailed by his theory of property, which, as we have seen, provides the basis of his account of a just distribution of goods. For all that must be distributed equally according to this theory is an activity by means of which each and every individual with the capacity to do so is able to live from his or her own labour in a way that allows him or her to gain more than the basic means of subsistence if this is possible given the level of development enjoyed by the state of which he or she is a citizen. There is therefore no demand for absolute equality with respect to the benefits enjoyed as a result of having use rights to certain resources or goods.

When it comes to any actual distribution of goods, natural inequality will also surely have a role to play, even if Fichte does not explicitly acknowledge this point, for one individual may be more naturally suited to performing one particular activity rather than another one in virtue of such factors as physical strength or intelligence. The successful performance of one particular activity may require, moreover, a certain amount of material inequality, in that it demands the possession and use of more resources than those required by another activity. Fichte himself points out that the successful performance of certain activities may not require anything more in the way of property rights than the right to perform the determinate activity in question (Fichte, 1962–2012, I/7: 88; Fichte, 2012: 132). Thus the amount of property owned by any one individual will be determined by what is required for him or her to engage in the activity by means of which he or she is able to live from his or her labour. Fichte also views different occupations as reflecting and fostering different needs, so that once again the distribution of goods and resources may vary. He does not, however, provide a clear principle for determining what should be distributed to whom in such cases. Rather, he assumes that someone engaged in certain forms of art or science will generally require finer food, better clothing and more attractive surroundings than those required by someone engaged in manual labour (Fichte, 1962–2012, I/7: 67–68; Fichte, 2012: 106; see also James, 2011: 82–86).

Although Fichte is not, with one important exception, committed to a notion of absolute equality which rules out any unequal distribution of goods or resources whatsoever, he introduces such a high level of state control and regulation of economic life when explaining how the principles of distributive justice that he sets up can be applied that the question arises as to whether he ends up doing something that strong forms of egalitarianism are often claimed to do, namely to sacrifice freedom for the sake of equality. This state control and regulation extend beyond supervising and enforcing the agreements made between the members of the various estates to include such forms of oversight as ensuring that there are a sufficient number of people belonging to each estate at any given point in time. Another measure is that of arranging matters in such a way that the value of the sum of money in circulation at any given point in time simply represents the value of the sum of goods in circulation at the same point in time. The money supply must therefore be increased or decreased with the aim of ensuring that the relation between the value of the sum of goods in circulation and the value of the sum of money in circulation remains consistent.

The sacrifice of freedom for the sake of equality would represent a problem for Fichte given that he sets out a theory of distributive justice which seeks to explain how each and every individual, rather than only those people who happen to benefit from existing economic conditions, can be thought to have a compelling reason for renouncing their natural freedom and the right to everything which accompanies it. This is because this aim demands that freedom be in some sense preserved in the state if the benefits gained from citizenship are to outweigh the loss of natural freedom. A good example of this problem concerns the extent to which Fichte's talk of a division of 'free' activity is compatible with the state's function of determining the number of people belonging to each estate in accordance with the number of producers needed, since it is they who provide the raw materials upon which the so-called artists work, while the merchants distribute and exchange either these end products or the raw materials themselves. Even if it is logically possible for each and every person to be able to choose the occupation which enables him or her to live from his or her labour in accordance with this requirement – in which case all the state would effectively need to do is to endorse decisions that individuals have already freely made – the more likely scenario is one in which at least some people, and perhaps many of them, will be compelled to enter an occupation not of their own choosing so as to be able to live from their labour. In this scenario, the occupations into which some individuals enter will be determined more, and perhaps exclusively, by natural necessity (that is to say, the need to secure the means to live) than by free choice.

Although this subjection to natural necessity can be equally recognised as a feature of a free-market economy which is said to preserve natural freedom in the form of the freedom to sell and to buy goods including one's own labour, while putting many people in the position of being forced to work in order to survive, this subjection to natural necessity poses a particular problem for Fichte. This is because he wants to ensure that the freedom that is partially preserved in the state is not the freedom of a minority or even a majority of people, but is instead the freedom of all citizens. Thus the measures that Fichte introduces to guarantee this outcome threaten to suppress freedom not only through the introduction of a high level of state control and regulation, but also through his failure to explain how the activity that each individual performs so as to be able to live from his or her labour will always be freely chosen rather than being forced upon individuals by material need.

This difficulty can be related to the argument on which Fichte's theory of distributive justice is based. As we have seen, this argument appeals to the idea of a natural freedom which consists in everyone having the equal right, if not the power, to take possession of as much of the world as they desire for themselves. This natural right can be limited only by means of mutual agreement to limit one's natural freedom in such a way that everyone is left with a sphere of freedom in which it becomes possible to achieve full awareness of oneself as a free, rational agent capable of effecting changes in the world in accordance with ends that one has formed. Freedom and equality are therefore both essential aspects of the original right which must be partially preserved in the transition from a condition of natural freedom to membership of a legal and political community. It is not clear, then, why the demands of freedom should be subordinated to the demands of equality. Fichte could respond by claiming that although the type of freedom associated with choice of occupation may be lacking in some cases, the loss of this freedom together with the loss of freedom that comes from a high degree of state control and regulation are compensated for by an increase in freedom in other senses, such as the freedom associated with increased amount of leisure time that can be equally distributed among the citizens of a state. Freedom from work might therefore compensate lack of freedom with respect to one's choice of occupation. Another response would be to try to detach Fichte's commitment to the principles of distributive justice that he identifies from his proposals concerning how these principles might be applied, for it is possible that these principles could be effectively applied independently of the particular measures that Fichte himself identifies. They could, for example, conceivably be realised in a condition of full employment that is, if need be, created by means of state initiatives, and in which there exist various economic rights that the state dutifully enforces without, however, the same level of state control as that envisaged by Fichte proving necessary.

Fichte is arguably right to seek to show how the principles of distributive justice that he identifies can be applied as opposed to offering a merely formal account of distributive justice, even if in so doing he generates a problem faced by any egalitarian theory of distributive justice that is committed to the idea of freedom, namely the problem of how the demands of freedom and equality can be reconciled at a practical level as well as at a purely theoretical one. To claim that an imperfect application of these principles is justified simply because of the insurmountable practical difficulties faced by any attempt to apply them fully invites the question as to what may legitimately count as a reason for not seeking to apply them fully despite such difficulties. The danger here is that the answer given to this question will ultimately rest on the dogmatic acceptance of certain features of existing society (for instance, the existence of a largely unrestricted free market in labour and goods). Fichte can at least be credited with avoiding such a capitulation to existing conditions despite his commitment to the notion of distributive justice.

I shall now turn to a radical proposal made by Fichte that not only limits freedom of choice in the shape of the freedom to trade with others of one's own choosing, but also concerns the issue of the scope of distributive justice: that is to say, the question concerning what people and how many of them fall under the principles of distributive justice identified by Fichte. The proposal in question is that the state must become economically self-sufficient and commercially independent of other states, which it can only do if its citizens are forbidden from entering into commercial relations with the citizens of other states. This measure is necessary to ensure that the state is in the position to control and regulate the economic life of society in such a way that each and every person is able to live from his or her own labour and enjoy other benefits including as much time as possible spent free from work, whereas any commercial relations between its citizens and the citizens of other states would threaten to undermine the careful calculations that the state must make and the steps that it must take in order to guarantee these ends. While this particular measure appears to restrict the scope of distributive justice, I intend to show that the matter is perhaps less clear-cut than it at first seems to be.

The Scope of Distributive Justice

Fichte appears to provide a clear answer to the question of the scope of distributive justice when he defines the state viewed as a juridical entity as a closed multitude of human beings living under the same laws and the same supreme coercive power. Fichte then defines a closed commercial state as this same multitude of human beings viewed as standing in commercial relations with each other that they engage in for mutual benefit and subject to the same laws and the same supreme coercive power (Fichte, 1962–2012, I/7: 38; Fichte, 2012: 79). In short, the scope of distributive justice is restricted to the members of the same closed economic, legal and political community. As Fichte bluntly puts it, 'just as the rational state is a closed realm of laws and individuals, it is also an entirely *closed commercial state*. Every living human being is either a citizen of the state, or he is not' (Fichte, 1962–2012, I/7: 70; Fichte, 2012: 108).

This restriction appears to make distributive justice into something that is owed only to one's fellow citizens. It could, in fact, be interpreted even more narrowly given that the immediate object of distributive justice is the activity by means of which an individual is able to live from his or her labour, an object to which individuals have a right because it constitutes a condition of effective rational agency. In this way, Fichte appears to restrict the scope of distributive justice to citizens of the same individual state who are autonomous, rational beings able to work for the benefit of themselves, each other and the state as a whole. This narrowing of the scope of distributive justice could be avoided by treating both those citizens who cannot be regarded as autonomous and rational because of some form of mental incapacity and those citizens who cannot work as a result of physical incapacity as exceptions for whom the distribution of productive activities would be inappropriate. At the same time, the principle of equality demands that they enjoy the same basic level of economic well-being as that enjoyed by other citizens. This line of argument is compatible with the way in which Fichte himself does not explicitly tie the right to live as pleasantly as possible to the ability to work. Rather, since 'everyone demands this as a human being, and no one is more or less human than anyone else, everyone has an equal right in [making] this demand' (Fichte, 1962–2012, I/7: 55; Fichte, 2012: 93). Are there any grounds, though, for attributing to Fichte a more cosmopolitan position that allows that at least some non-citizens ought to fall within the scope of the distributive justice exercised by a state which has closed itself off commercially from other states with the aim of securing its economic independence and self-sufficiency?

There are at least two ways in which the scope of distributive justice might be extended to include non-citizens. First of all, it could be extended by the citizens of other states becoming citizens of a closed commercial state, making them subject to the same principles of distributive justice as all its other members. Second, it could be extended by granting the citizens of other states some kind of moral right to the economic goods that a closed commercial state which has achieved the necessary degree of economic independence and self-sufficiency is able to distribute. As regards the first possibility, Fichte does not oppose the idea of the citizens of other states becoming citizens of a closed commercial state in the case of foreign experts whose services this type of state may buy with the aim of developing science and industry in such a way as to guarantee its economic independence and self-sufficiency (Fichte, 1962–2012, I/7: 132; Fichte, 2012: 187). Here, however, it is a matter of people who bring certain clear benefits becoming citizens of a closed commercial state. This example does not show, therefore, that Fichte would also endorse the idea of people who do not bring obvious economic and scientific benefits becoming citizens. Could there nevertheless be some people with a moral right either to become citizens of a closed commercial state or to fall within its scope of distributive justice in some other way, irrespective of whether or not they benefit it in economic or scientific terms? Fichte cannot be said to address this issue explicitly. Yet some things that he has to say in *The Closed Commercial State* are relevant to it.

To begin with, Fichte accuses the European states of his own time of economically exploiting other nations by employing their stronger economic position in relation to them to dictate the terms of trade, and he claims that this form of exploitation would stop with the commercial closure of the state (Fichte, 1962–2012, I/7: 44; Fichte, 2012: 85). The reason for this is clear: in the absence of commercial relations between states, one state could not economically exploit another one except through sheer force, in which case there would be no question of right or justice. In the second book of *The Closed Commercial State*, Fichte offers an account of a process whereby the increasing economic power enjoyed by one state in relation to other states generates a form of economic dependence, leading to a weaker state's complete impoverishment, enslavement to an economically more powerful state and other evils such as depopulation caused by its citizens seeking work abroad (Fichte, 1962–2012, I/7: 101–104; Fichte, 2012: 148–151; see also James, 2011: 87–111). This critique of the economic imperialism of the European states of his own time suggests that *The Closed Commercial State* should partly be read as a blueprint of how the evils associated with this form of imperialism can be overcome. One particular measure that Fichte thinks must precede the effective commercial closure of the state is of particular relevance in this regard.

This is the measure of securing the state's natural borders. These borders are defined in terms of what a state needs to become economically independent and self-sufficient (Fichte, 1962–2012, I/7: 117; Fichte, 2012: 169). Needless to say, this measure could be used to sanction wars of conquest, and Fichte does not provide any clear principle by which it could be determined when a state has rightfully attained its natural borders beyond the demand for economic independence and self-sufficiency.[7] We are left to ask whether this aim would have been achieved, for example, once a state was able to satisfy its citizens' basic needs alone. If so, the citizens may well end up having to forego the satisfaction of other needs that they were used to having satisfied at the time when the state did enter into commercial relations with other states. Or would it only be achieved if other needs that are products of culture and civilisation, and whose satisfaction has come to appear necessary even if it is not actually so, could still be met?

Fichte's claim that the state should enable its citizens to live as agreeably as possible suggests that at least some of these needs would have to be met, for the expectation of having them satisfied would be a reasonable one in the circumstances.[8] Although Fichte may have had in mind only the drawing of borders between contiguous states, an affirmative answer to the second question could be seen to provide a pretext for acts of colonisation in cases when particular raw materials, such as certain minerals, are not to be found either within a state's existing borders or in any neighbouring territory. Some form of territorial expansion may then become a necessary condition of economic independence and self-sufficiency.

This brings me to Fichte's account of the genesis of the anarchic commercial relations that exist between the European states of his own time, despite the way in which these states have over time come to form distinct independent legal and political communities, provided in the second book of *The Closed Commercial State*. Part of Fichte's intention in providing a history of these relations is to show that the existing state of affairs is a contingent rather than necessary one and that it can therefore be transformed in accordance with the proposals that he makes. Fichte here recognises that the commercial closure of any state is something which must take place at a specific point in human history with all its attendant circumstances and relations. Given that his proposals were not implemented at the point in history occupied by him when he wrote *The Closed Commercial State* and had it published, the commercial closure of the state advocated in this work, or even just the aim of gaining economic independence, must be considered in the light of a different set of historical circumstances and relations.

Among these circumstances and relations, we may include the legacy of nineteenth- and twentieth-century European imperialism with its large-scale extraction and removal of raw materials found in the colonised lands. To this background we may add the fact that the relative economic independence enjoyed by many European states today – by which I mean the enjoyment of a degree of economic power that is sufficient for them to exercise a significant amount of control over economic policy at a national and transnational level and to meet a wide range of their citizens' needs – was arguably in some cases largely built upon the exploitation of their former colonies. On this basis, it might be said that if what Fichte proposes were to be implemented today, one would expect him to admit that the economic independence enjoyed by some states will have partly been made possible by certain historical injustices that they had committed. After all, although Fichte may not have been aware of the full extent of these injustices, he clearly had some inkling of them, and it appears fair to say, therefore, that the full extent of these injustices ought for him to form part of any revised account of the historical situation that precedes the commercial closure of the state.

If this is so, there is room for one or both of the following ideas: (1) that a transference of goods from one country to another ought to be made as a matter of justice: that is to say, so as to repair previous injustices with the aim of making the beneficiary state economically independent and self-sufficient; and (2) that there are some moral grounds for allowing the citizens of states which were the victims of such historical injustice, or which developed out of the process of colonisation if they did not exist beforehand, to enjoy the benefits and opportunities enjoyed by the citizens of states that engaged in acts of colonisation and as a result enjoy levels of economic independence that are not enjoyed by the states that were colonised or grew out of the process of colonisation. Admittedly, what I have said on this matter is highly speculative. Nevertheless, the fact that the issue of the moral right of certain non-citizens to be included within the scope of the distributive justice exercised by another state can be discussed in connection with Fichte's *The Closed Commercial State* demonstrates the extent to which Fichte deserves to be classed among the primary candidates for the honour of the first philosopher to have developed an explicit and fully worked-out theory of distributive justice. It is therefore certainly not the case that humanity had to wait until Rawls to encounter such a theory.

Notes

1 Two exceptions are James (2011) and Nakhimovsky (2011).
2 Fleischacker acknowledges this omission in a note (Fleischacker, 2004: 160–161). He also claims that the notion of distributive justice first found definite expression in Gracchus Babeuf's 'radical declaration that all human beings have an equal right to all wealth' (Fleischacker, 2004: 55). This claim is relevant because apart from the question of whether or not Babeuf directly influenced Fichte, the latter can be seen to share some of the former's ideas and to provide them with a philosophical basis (cf. James, 2011: 56–82).
3 For a fuller account of how the concept of right generates this right to property, see James, 2011: 21–55 and James, 2013: 102–119.
4 Fichte's position here appears to be close to the one adopted by Hobbes in so far as the latter speaks of individuals partially renouncing the right of nature, or that 'which Writers commonly call *Jus Naturale*', which he describes as follows:

> the Liberty each man hath, to use his own power, as he will himselfe, for the preservation of his own Nature; that is to say, of his own Life; and consequently, of doing any thing, which in his own Judgement, and Reason, hee shall conceive to be the aptest means thereunto.
>
> (Hobbes, 1996: 91)

While this characterisation of the right of nature brings to mind Fichte's 'infinite' right of the person to extend his freedom as far as he wills and can do so, as we shall see, Fichte does not identify this right simply with the right to do whatever one judges to be necessary to preserve one's life. Rather, he treats freedom as the individual's primary concern, so that preserving one's own nature for him ultimately means preserving the conditions of free, rational agency. This will ultimately require entering into a condition of right with others. This condition must, however, be one in which the full conditions of free, rational agency are met, so that in this respect personal security cannot be a sufficient condition of justified consent to the terms of any agreement to limit one's natural freedom so long as others limit theirs. For more on the connections and differences between Fichte's and Hobbes's standpoints see James, forthcoming a.
5 Fichte identifies various other estates, namely that of members of the government, that of teachers and that of the defence forces, but nevertheless treats the first three estates as the fundamental ones (Fichte, 1962–2012, I/7: 58; Fichte, 2012: 97).
6 This claim echoes a pattern of distribution and the reasons for it later described by Proudhon as follows:

> Man needs to labour in order to live; consequently, he needs tools and materials to work upon. His need to produce constitutes his right, and this right is guaranteed him by his fellows, with whom he makes a similar agreement. If one hundred thousand men settle in a large country like France with no inhabitants, then each man has a right to 1/100,000 of the land. If the number of possessors increases, each one's portion diminishes through this increase, so that, if the number of inhabitants rises to thirty-four millions, each one will have a right only to 1/34,000,000. Now, organise the police

system and the government, labour, exchange, inheritance, etc., so that the means of labour shall be shared by all equally, and that each individual shall be free, and then society will be perfect.

(Proudhon, 1994: 54)

7 Fichte optimistically views this measure as a necessary step towards global peace, even though he acknowledges that a state's act of attaining its natural borders may result in wars of conquest (Fichte, 1962–2012, I/7: 118–119; Fichte, 2012: 170).

8 Fichte identifies various measures whereby the state could satisfy such needs while aiming at absolute economic independence and self-sufficiency. In those cases in which the relevant raw materials are available within a state, there is no reason, he argues, that the means of manufacturing the goods needed to satisfy certain needs cannot be developed together with the necessary skills even when the goods in question have not traditionally been manufactured in this state, while in those cases in which the raw materials are lacking, they can either be cultivated or discovered in the state or substitutes for them can be developed. Should these measures not work, Fichte advocates the gradual withdrawal of the means of satisfying certain needs (Fichte, 1962–2012, I/7: 115–116; Fichte, 2012: 166). There must nevertheless be limits to the extent to which the citizens of a closed commercial state will be able to forgo the satisfaction of needs if they are to live as pleasantly as possible in line with their expectations regarding this matter based on previous experience. Another measure Fichte identifies concerns the fact that closed commercial states could engage in voluntary forms of exchange which involve the direct exchange of goods that can be found, cultivated or produced in one country but not in another one (Fichte, 1962–2012, I/7: 136; Fichte, 2012: 192). Such trade agreements will depend, however, on the wills of both parties and on each of them being able to provide something of benefit to the other party. This raises the question as to what is to happen when, for whatever reason, agreement cannot be reached or when a state which needs raw materials or other goods from another state has nothing to offer in return.

References

Fichte, J. G. (1962–2012), *J. G. Fichte – Gesamtausgabe der Bayerischen Akademie der Wissenschaften*, edited by R. Lauth, E. Fuchs and H. Gliwitzky, Stuttgart and Bad Canstatt: Frommann-Holzboog. Cited by series (Roman numeral) and volume (Arabic numeral).

Fichte, J. G. (2000), *Foundations of Natural Right*, edited by F. Neuhouser, translated by M. Baur, Cambridge: Cambridge University Press.

Fichte, J. G. (2012), *The Closed Commercial State*, translated by A. C. Adler, Albany: State University of New York Press.

Fleischacker, S. (2004), *A Short History of Distributive Justice*, Cambridge, MA: Harvard University Press.

Hobbes, T. (1996), *Leviathan*, edited by R. Tuck, Cambridge: Cambridge University Press.

James, D. (2011), *Fichte's Social and Political Philosophy: Property and Virtue*, Cambridge: Cambridge University Press.

James, D. (2013), *Rousseau and German Idealism: Freedom, Dependence and Necessity*, Cambridge: Cambridge University Press.

James, D. (forthcoming a), 'Fichte on personal freedom and the freedom of others', in G. Gottlieb (ed.), *Fichte's* Foundations of Natural Right: *A Critical Guide*, Cambridge: Cambridge University Press.

James, D. (forthcoming b), 'Conceptual innovation in Fichte's theory of property: the genesis of leisure as an object of distributive justice', *European Journal of Philosophy*.

Nakhimovsky, I. (2011), *The Closed Commercial State: Perpetual Peace and Commercial Society from Rousseau to Fichte*, Princeton, NJ: Princeton University Press.

Proudhon, P.-J. (1994), *What is Property?*, edited and translated by D. R. Kelley and B. G. Smith, Cambridge: Cambridge University Press.

4 Social Darwinism and Social Justice

Herbert Spencer and the Poor

Matt Zwolinski

Introduction

Libertarians are not well known for their concern for the poor. It is, after all, a common libertarian belief that the tax-funded welfare payments to the poor are the moral equivalent of theft, or even forced labour, and thus necessarily illegitimate (Nozick, 1974; Rothbard, 1973). And two of the twentieth century's most famous libertarian theorists, Robert Nozick and Friedrich Hayek, are famous (notorious?) for denying that the concept of distributive justice is even *coherent*, let alone morally defensible (Friedrich A. Hayek, 1976; Nozick, 1974). To those who believe that society owes aid to the poor as a matter of justice, and that state redistribution is an important mechanism for providing that aid, these beliefs might well appear to be sufficient evidence of libertarians' hard-heartedness. After all, if libertarians really cared about the poor, wouldn't they want the state to do more to help?

In recent years, a small group of libertarian theorists has begun to challenge this interpretation: to argue that libertarianism, properly understood, is *not* incompatible with the ideal of social justice (Tomasi, 2011), that it is not necessarily incompatible with the state provision of a social safety net (Zwolinski, forthcoming) and that it is certainly not incompatible with a serious moral concern for the welfare and dignity of the poor (Brennan, 2012).

In some ways, these ideas represent a departure from mainstream libertarian theory. They certainly look that way if we take the relatively hard-line, post-war American libertarianism of Murray Rothbard, Ayn Rand and Robert Nozick as paradigmatic representations of that tradition (Nozick, 1974; Rand, 1964a, 1964b; Rothbard, 1982). But if we take a somewhat longer historical view of libertarianism, matters become considerably more complex. The libertarian intellectual tradition, as I have argued elsewhere, is both far more diverse and far more *progressive* than has generally been understood (Zwolinski and Tomasi, 2016).

An interesting illustration of the diversity, complexity and progressivism of libertarian thought can be found in the writings of the late-nineteenth-century philosopher and social theorist Herbert Spencer. That I have chosen Spencer as the figure to represent the *progressive* nature of libertarianism will no doubt be surprising, even baffling, to many readers of this essay. Despite immense fame in his own time, little is remembered about the details of Spencer's social thought by academic philosophers today. But what *is* remembered is clear: Spencer was a social Darwinist, who was at best indifferent to, and perhaps positively *welcoming* of, the suffering and eventual extinction of the poor.

This belief reflects an interpretation of Spencer's thought that is common, and in many ways understandable. It is, nevertheless, also deeply mistaken. Spencer was not a social Darwinist; he was not opposed to charitable assistance to the poor; and he was not even necessarily opposed to what we would now describe as the idea of social justice. The social Darwinist interpretation of Spencer has dominated contemporary understandings of his thought not because of any historical merit, but simply because of the prominent articulation it was given by one influential critic, and the subsequent (and consequent) neglect that Spencer's work suffered by more serious scholars.

Getting Spencer's ideas right is thus an important exercise in intellectual history. We ought to understand the respects in which his ideas *were* deficient, but also to rediscover whatever insights those deficiencies may have previously blinded us to. We owe it to Spencer to understand his ideas correctly, and we owe it to ourselves to learn from those ideas what we can.

But a proper understanding of Spencer's social thought is not *merely* an exercise in intellectual history. In many ways, the twentieth-century criticism of and disdain for Spencer's thought mirrors the academic reaction to libertarian ideas more generally. Understanding where that criticism succeeds, and where it misses the mark, can thus potentially help us to understand the strengths and weaknesses of libertarianism as a contemporary social philosophy. And this is something that both critics and proponents of that doctrine ought to welcome.

Social Darwinism

The charge of 'social Darwinism' is not limited to the target of Herbert Spencer, or even of libertarians more generally. But it is typically reserved for the more libertarian *aspects* of the target at which it is directed. Even the mostly symbolic fiscal conservatism of the Republican Party in the United States, for instance, was enough to draw the charge from former labour secretary Robert Reich, who wrote in 2011 that 'If one of the current crop of Republican hopefuls becomes president, and if regressive Republicans take over the House or Senate, or both, Social Darwinism is back.' One year later, President Barrack Obama levelled a similar charge against Republicans who supported a deficit-reduction package that would cut various social welfare programmes while simultaneously extending certain Bush-era tax cuts. 'Disguised as a deficit reduction plan, it's really an attempt to impose a radical vision on our country. It is nothing but thinly-veiled Social Darwinism.'[1]

Phillips Thompson seems to have had a similar idea in mind over one hundred years earlier when he wrote the satirical poem, 'The Political Economist and the Tramp'.

> Walking along a country road,
> While yet the morning air was damp,
> As unreflecting, on I strode,
> I marked approach the frequent tramp.
> The haggard, ragged careworn man
> Accosted me with plaintive tone,
> 'I must have food—' he straight began;
> 'Vile miscreant,' I cried, 'begone!
> 'Tis contrary to every rule
> That I my fellows should assist;
> I'm of the scientific school,
> Political economist.
> Dost thou know, deluded one,
> What Adam Smith has clearly proved,
> That 'tis self-interest alone
> by which the wheels of life are moved?
> This competition is the law
> By which we either live or die;
> I've no demand thy labor for,
> Why, then, should I thy wants supply?
> And Herbert Spencer's active brain
> Shows how the social struggle ends;
> The weak die out the strong remain;
> 'Tis this that nature's plan intends.
> Now really 'tis absurd of you
> To think I'd interfere at all;
> Just grasp the scientific view,
> The weakest must go to the wall.'[2]

Thompson's poem captures the charge of social Darwinism in everything but name. The name itself would not be coined at all for another two years – in Italian – and would not find its way into the English language until 1895 (Bellomy, 1984; Hodgson, 2004). Certainly, Spencer never described *himself* as a 'social Darwinist'. Indeed, so far as we know, it is a term that no political thinker has *ever* used to describe their own position. From its beginning, 'social Darwinism' was a phrase people used almost exclusively to describe ideas with which they disagreed. In fact, the expression of disagreement often appears to be the *only* fixed element of the phrase's meaning. Different people at different times disliked and disagreed with different things, and 'social Darwinism' thus came at times to be a shorthand way of referring to ideas as various as racism, militarism, support of eugenics, indifference to the plight of the poor, an excessively biological view of humanity, or support of *laissez-faire* (Bellomy, 1984; Leonard, 2005b, 2009b).

The precise meaning of the term is barely more fixed today than it was over a century ago. But its transmission into popular political discourse, its association with the defence of *laissez-faire* and, most especially, its attachment to the thought of Herbert Spencer and the American sociologist William Graham Sumner can all be traced back to the work of a single intellectual historian: Richard Hofstadter. During the 1940s, first in the pages of the *New England Quarterly* and later in his influential book, *Social Darwinism in American Thought*, Hofstadter deployed the term in a forceful and eloquent critique of trends he found disturbing in American sociological and political thought. In so doing, Hofstadter popularised and defined the paradigmatic use of the term ever since (Hofstadter, 1941, 1992).[3]

For Hofstadter, as for others who had used the term before him, the primary function of the term 'social Darwinism' was the expression of contempt for ideas he disliked. And Hofstadter disliked the political idea of *laissez-faire* with a passion. A former member of Columbia University's Communist Party unit, Hofstadter wrote to friends that he 'hate[d] capitalism and everything that goes with it' (Hofstadter, 1992). In Spencer and Sumner, Hofstadter found two men who stood for everything he detested in social thought, and who fought bitterly against that which he himself prized – a progressive economy directed by enlightened expert rule. According to Hofstadter, these men found in the Darwinian idea of a struggle for existence 'a new sanction for economic competition' and in 'the survival of the fittest a new argument in opposition to state aid for the weak' (Hofstadter, 1941: 457).

On Hofstadter's reading, Spencer saw in the theory of evolution a ready-made justification for *laissez-faire* capitalism. After all, on Darwin's view the spontaneous, 'unplanned' evolution of the human species (and other well-adapted animals) was achieved through an unchecked process of competition. What better way to help along the evolution of the human species than to allow the competitive forces of capitalism to operate unchecked? The struggle for survival under capitalism is completely natural. Just as non-human animals compete within the natural environment, human animals must be allowed to compete in the economic environment. Let the free market separate the strong from the weak and, through the harsh discipline of competition, market forces will refine the species by weeding out the lazy and the less talented individuals. Within markets, as in the natural world, the effects of unchecked competition on the weak and less able may seem harsh. But any attempts to ameliorate the condition of the weak must necessarily come at the expense of the strong, and for that reason must retard the progress of the species as a whole. State assistance to the poor (and perhaps even charity of an entirely voluntary nature) are thus to be condemned. Such well-meaning initiatives are objectionable not only because they are inefficient. Worse, they threaten to impede, or even reverse, the evolutionary progress of the human race.

Thus, as one recent critic puts it, Spencer the 'social Darwinist' believes that the poor are 'unfit to survive and should be eliminated', and *this* was his grounds for arguing against state aid (Fleischacker, 2004: 87–88).

The Case Against Herbert Spencer

Hofstadter's charge had enough plausibility to make it stick. After all, it was Herbert Spencer, and not Charles Darwin, who originally coined the phrase 'the survival of the fittest', and it was this phrase more than anything else which the critics of 'social Darwinism' seem to have latched on to. Spencer first used the term in his 1864 *Principles of Biology*, writing that 'This survival of the fittest, which I have here sought to express in mechanical terms, is that which Mr Darwin has called "natural selection", or the preservation of favoured races in the struggle for life' (vol. 1: 444–445). Darwin, in turn, first used the phrase in his 1868 book on *The Variation of Animals and Plants Under Domestication*, where he wrote that 'This preservation, during the battle for life, of varieties which possess any advantage in structure, constitution, or instinct, I have called Natural Selection; and Mr Herbert Spencer has well expressed the same idea by the Survival of the Fittest.' Darwin would later incorporate the phrase into the fifth edition of *On the Origin of Species* in 1869.

Unfortunately for Spencer, his discussion of the survival of the fittest was not his only memorable passage. When it came to discussing the question of social obligations towards the poor and the weak, Spencer had a tendency to invoke broadly evolutionary ideas in a way that practically *invited* an uncharitable reading. This is especially true of his earliest treatise in social and political theory, *Social Statics* ([1851] 1995), from which almost all of the most objectionable passages cited by his critics have been drawn.

Take, for instance, the following lines, which were seized upon by Hofstadter and almost every critic of Spencer and social Darwinism since as damning evidence of Spencer's callous indifference to the fate of the weak (Hofstadter, 1992).

> Partly by weeding out those of lowest development, and partly by subjecting those who remain to the never-ceasing discipline of experience, nature secures the growth of a race who shall both understand the conditions of existence, and be able to act up to them.... Who, indeed, after pulling off the coloured glasses of prejudice, and thrusting out of sight his pet projects, can help seeing the folly of these endeavours to protect men against themselves? A sad population of imbeciles would our schemers fill the world with, could their plans last. A sorry kind of human constitution would they make for us – a constitution lacking the power to uphold itself, and requiring to be kept alive by superintendence from without – a constitution continually going wrong, and needing to be set right again – a constitution even tending to self-destruction. Why the whole effort of nature is to get rid of such – to

> clear the world of them, and make room for better. Nature demands that every being shall be self-sufficing. He on whom his own stupidity, or vice, or idleness, entails loss of life, must, in the generalizations of philosophy, be classed with the victims of weak viscera or malformed limbs. In his case, as in the others, there exists a fatal non-adaptation; and it matters not in the abstract whether it be a moral, an intellectual, or a corporeal one. Beings thus imperfect are nature's failures, and are recalled by her laws when found to be such. Along with the rest they are put upon trial. *If they are sufficiently complete to live, they* do *live, and it is well they should live. If they are not sufficiently complete to live, they die, and it is best they should die.*
>
> (Spencer, 1995: 337, 338–339, 339–340, emphasis added)

Elsewhere in the same book, Spencer writes that

> the poverty of the incapable, the distresses that come upon the imprudent, the starvation of the idle, and those shoulderings aside of the weak by the strong, which leave so many 'in shallows and miseries' are the decrees of a large, far-seeing benevolence.
>
> (Spencer, 1995: 289)

'Under the natural order of things', Spencer writes, 'society is constantly excreting its unhealthy, imbecile, slow, vacillating, faithless members.' The interferences of well-meaning men, he held, 'stops this purifying process [and] even increases the vitiation, absolutely encourag[ing] the multiplication of the reckless and incompetent' (Spencer, 1995: 289–290).

Thus, Spencer argued in *Social Statics*, laws which seek to relieve the suffering of the poor by funds raised through taxation are absolutely impermissible, imposing as they do an unjustifiable limitation on the liberty of the well-off in order to render succour to the weak (Spencer, 1995: 278). Poor Laws, just like restrictions on freedom of commerce (including restrictions intended to protect workers from exploitation) are forbidden by the fundamental principle of political morality – the law of equal freedom.

Whether or not these beliefs are indicative of an underlying 'social Darwinism' – and most serious scholars of Spencer have now concluded that they are not (Bannister, 1973; Bellomy, 1984; Leonard, 2009b; Weinstein, 2012) – they seem, at the very least, indicative of a callous indifference to the plight of the poor. And to the extent that such indifference played an important role, for Spencer, in the justification of libertarian political and economic institutions, whatever repugnance we attach to it might well seem to extend to those institutions as well. If Spencer's libertarianism was essentially hard-hearted, perhaps this is not because Spencer was exceptionally cruel, but rather because he was exceptionally *consistent*.

Spencer's Ethics in Context – Evolutionary Libertarianism

Before embracing this conclusion, however, it is important that we fully appreciate two important elements that pervade Spencer's social and political thought. The first is its deeply *evolutionary* character. The second is the nature of his thoroughgoing and principled commitment to libertarian freedom.

Understanding the evolutionary character of Spencer's thought can help us to better understand what he meant by such phrases as 'the survival of the fittest'. To many a modern ear, that phrase suggests a kind of moral endorsement of violent and cunning struggle, and a necessary approval of whatever happens to emerge out of that struggle. If the rich are succeeding while the poor have failed, it must be because the rich are 'fit' and the poor or not. And so it is *good* that the rich are flourishing, and it is *good* that the poor are dying out.

For Spencer, however, appeals to 'the survival of the fittest' were purely *descriptive* in nature. To label an organism as 'fit' is to make a largely formal statement about its adaptation to the conditions of survival in a particular environment. It does *not* imply any sort of normative judgement about the value of the organism, or the goodness of its survival. On this point, Spencer was explicit.

> The law is not the survival of the 'better' or the 'stronger'.... It is the survival of those which are constitutionally fittest to thrive under the conditions in which they are placed; and very often that which, humanly speaking, is inferiority, causes the survival.
>
> (Spencer, 1873a: 340)

Fitness was thus not only descriptive (rather than normative), but *relative* (rather than absolute). The biological and characterological traits that constitute fitness for one environment or stage of human development might well be wholly inappropriate for another. And, indeed, Spencer believed that human beings were in the process of a transition between two radically different stages of development, and that human morals, economic institutions and political systems were adjusting accordingly.

Human societies were evolving, Spencer thought, from *militancy* to *industrialism*. The former type of society was appropriate to those periods of human history marked by frequent violent conflict. Their organisation was centralised and hierarchical, and their mode of operation was highly coercive. This was necessary, Spencer argued, to effectively mobilise the persons and resources of society in order to carry out the primary purpose that this sort of society emerged to fulfil: defensive and offensive war. Industrial societies, on the other hand, emerge out of the peace and security that earlier militant forms of society made possible. Freed from the constant necessity of fighting and preparing to fight, industrial societies could afford to devote their attention to the protection of individual liberty, and the powers of government could be restrained by institutions of representative, decentralised government and economic *laissez-faire* (Mingardi, 2011: 56–63; Spencer, 1900: chapters XVII–XVIII).

Eventually, Spencer thought, both human beings and human societies would reach a stage of perfection. And as Spencer makes clear but as has often been misunderstood by casual readers, it is *only that stage of perfection* to which the doctrines of his *Social Statics* were meant to apply (Spencer, 1995: 51). The result, as W. L. Miller notes, has been a great deal of confusion regarding the nature of this work and its place in Spencer's thought more generally (Miller, 1982: 484). One cannot simply take moral principles that are appropriate for human beings in their highest stage of evolutionary development, and for societies untainted by injustice or imperfection of any sort, and apply them to *our* society, with all its immorality and imperfections. And one thus cannot assume that any of the practical precepts laid down in *Social Statics* were meant to be applied to the society of Spencer's time, or to ours.

Nevertheless, it is clear that the *ideal* morality towards which Spencer thought humanity was progressing was a libertarian one. For Spencer, the fundamental moral principle was a 'law of equal freedom' which holds that 'every man may claim the fullest liberty to exercise his faculties compatible with the possession of a like liberty by every other man' (Spencer, 1995: 69). This principle, the twentieth-century libertarian theorist Murray Rothbard would approvingly note, 'does not attempt to make every individual's total condition equal – an absolutely impossible task; instead, but advocates liberty – a condition of absence of coercion over person and property for every man' (Rothbard, 1970: 215).

Spencer's commitment to equal freedom is obviously incompatible with social Darwinism understood as a kind of 'might makes right', 'law of the jungle' philosophy.

> If every man has freedom to do all that he wills, provided he infringes not the equal freedom of any other man, it is manifest that he has a claim to his life: for without it he can do nothing that he has willed; and to his personal liberty: for the withdrawal of it partially, if not wholly, restrains him from the fulfilment of his will. It is just as clear, too, that each man is forbidden to deprive his fellow of life or liberty: inasmuch as he cannot do this without breaking the law, which, in asserting his freedom, declares that he shall not infringe 'the equal freedom of any other'. For he who is killed or enslaved is obviously no longer equally free with his killer or enslaver.
>
> (Spencer, 1995: 102)

A philosophical opposition to killing or enslaving others hardly strikes us as distinctive or worthy of note today. And yet, Spencer's firm libertarian commitment to non-aggression actually *did* set his system apart from many rival political ideologies of his day. Unlike many progressives of their era, for example, Spencer was strongly opposed to military imperialism, whether aimed at the glorification of the United States or at the civilisation of supposedly 'barbaric' peoples. Imperialism, Spencer argued, was really a kind of piracy writ large – a policy carried out largely for the benefit of 'rich owners of colonial property', involving unjustifiable 'deeds of blood and rapine' and the exploitation of 'the poor, starved, overburdened people' (Spencer, 1981b: 220–221; 1995, chapter 27). As for those ordinary citizens who volunteer to fight in imperialistic wars, Spencer had nothing but disdain: 'When men hire themselves out to shoot other men to order, asking nothing about the justice of their cause, I don't care if they are shot themselves' (Spencer, 1902: 126).

Moreover, whatever commitment he may have had to the biological advancement of the human race, Spencer was firmly opposed to the use of coercive central planning in order to achieve that advancement. And in this respect, too, he appears to have had a more genuinely progressive position than that held by the so-called progressives of their day. Oliver Wendell Holmes, in his dissenting opinion in *Lochner* v. *NY*, used Spencer, or the popular image of him, to attack the American constitutional doctrine of economic liberty: 'the 14th amendment does not enact Mr Herbert Spencer's *Social Statics*'. Yet it was Holmes who penned the infamous majority opinion in *Buck* v. *Bell*, in which the Supreme Court upheld a Virginia law allowing the state to forcibly sterilise persons deemed to be mentally or morally unfit. In his majority opinion, Holmes argued that mandatory sterilisation was justified 'for the health and protection of the state'. (In Holmes's chilling verdict regarding proposed forced sterilisation of Carey Buck: 'three generations of idiots is enough'.) Spencer, in contrast, trusted neither the wisdom nor the virtue of political elites to guide evolution along its proper path, nor would he tolerate the use of coercion to achieve that end, no matter how desirable or attainable it might actually be (Bernstein and Leonard, 2009; Leonard, 2005a, 2005b, 2009a, 2009b).

The connection between eugenicism and progressivism illuminates a more general point. It is not merely that Spencer was capable of advocating on behalf of socially and economically vulnerable groups *in spite of* his libertarianism. It is, rather, precisely *because* of his principled libertarian commitment to equal freedom that Spencer insisted on treating those groups with *more* respect and concern than was common among more mainstream ideological positions.

Perhaps nowhere is this point more clear than in Spencer's discussion of the moral questions pertaining to the treatment of women and children. The law of equal freedom, Spencer held, guarantees to each individual the right to exercise his or her faculties to the *fullest extent possible*, compatible with the like liberty of others. Thus, even if those who claim that women and children are mentally inferior to grown men turned out to be correct, this would in no way diminish their *moral* status.

> The fullest endowment of rights that any being can possess, is perfect freedom to exercise all his faculties. And if each of two beings possesses perfect freedom to exercise all his faculties . . . the rights of the two are equal; no matter whether their faculties are equal or not. For, to say that the rights of the one are less than those of the other, because his faculties are fewer, is to say that he has no right to exercise the faculties he has not got! – a curious compound of truism and absurdity.
>
> (Spencer, 1995: 156)

Perhaps surprisingly, Spencer did not stop at advocating merely *formal* equality of women before the law. Such formal equality was an important part of what morality required, and thus Spencer advocated extending to women the rights of property and franchise that were frequently withheld from them.[4] But Spencer's critique of inequality extended beyond *legal* inequality to encompass *domestic* inequality as well. Thus Spencer condemned not only 'despotism in the state' but 'despotism in the family', writing that:

> The arbitrary rule of one human being over another, no matter in what form it may appear, is fast getting recognised as essentially rude and brutal. . . . A further increase of this same refinement will show men that there is a fatal incongruity between the matrimonial servitude which our law recognises, and the relationship that ought to exist between husband and wife. Surely if he who possesses any generosity of nature dislikes speaking to a hired domestic in a tone of authority – if he cannot bear assuming towards his friend the behaviour of a superior – how utterly repugnant to him should it be, to make himself ruler over one on whose behalf all his kindly sentiments are specially enlisted; one to whom he is bound by the strongest attachment that his nature is capable of; and for whose rights and dignity he ought to have the most active sympathy!
>
> (Spencer, 1995: 146–147)

So Spencer had some surprisingly progressive views on a wide range of issues. Still, one might reasonably wonder whether all this is enough to overcome our initial concern about Spencer's indifference to problems of human need and suffering. At most, these examples show that Spencer's libertarian beliefs *sometimes* led him to advocate on behalf of the vulnerable. But perhaps those same beliefs *more often* interfered with such advocacy. After all, Spencer's commitment to equal freedom required him to reject measures that sought to aid the poor through taxation or other limitations on or infringements of the rights of private property. Libertarian rights, for Spencer, served as an absolute constraint on the pursuit even of desirable social goals. To many, then, it will still seem that Spencer's system, and libertarianism more generally, is ultimately incompatible with the fullest, most desirable form of concern for the poor and vulnerable.

Soft-Hearted Reasons for Hard-Headed Policy

Why, then, did Spencer oppose state aid? And why did he sometimes go even further than his libertarian principles required and caution against purely *voluntary* charity?

Part of the story concerns a distinction, common to the Victorian Age in which Spencer was writing, between the deserving and undeserving poor. In a free society, people sometimes become poor through no serious fault of their own. But sometimes poverty is the result of poor choices and irresponsible behaviour. In such cases, Spencer thought that using the power of the state to compel someone else to come to that person's aid is both ineffective and unjust. It is ineffective because giving more money to someone who is poor because of his own irresponsibility fails to address the person's problem in a long-term way. It is unjust because it penalises the prudent in order to reward the irresponsible. In expressing these points, Spencer's language could often be quite blunt, especially by the standards of contemporary academic discourse. But the idea that the poor have a claim of justice against others only insofar as their poverty is the result of bad luck, and not insofar as it is the result of bad choices, is one with which even many contemporary egalitarian philosophers would not disagree (Arneson, 1997). And no parent who has struggled to teach their children to become prudent and self-reliant, no one who has ever sought to aid a friend struggling with addiction, no teacher who has ever tried to help a student master difficult material, will argue with Spencer's general claims about the moral hazards of overprotectiveness, even if we might quarrel with the way he applies those lessons to particular cases (Spencer, 1995: 289, 338).

Thus, Spencer held that even well-intentioned efforts at state aid would be objectionable on grounds of both justice and expediency. But he frequently pushed his argument further, insisting that many, perhaps most, state policies were *not* well intentioned. Whatever rhetoric politicians might employ to justify a policy, and however they might describe its aims, the true guiding force of state policy, Spencer argued, is the self-interest of the legislators who create it. 'It is a tolerably well-ascertained fact that men are still selfish. And that beings answering to this epithet will employ the power placed in their hands for their own advantage is self-evident' (Spencer, 1995: 195). And the self-interest of legislators, Spencer recognised, is generally best served by aligning with the interests of the wealthy and powerful, not with those of the poor and weak. For those latter groups, then, legislation is more likely to be a source of continuing oppression than of salvation.

The specific examples that Spencer chooses to illustrate his point about state power and legislative self-interest are instructive. One who accepted the popular caricature of Spencer as social Darwinist might have expected him to illustrate his point with stories of the greedy but shiftless poor using political power to appropriate the wealth of the virtuous and industrious rich. Instead, almost all of Spencer's examples involve the use of state power to benefit the rich and powerful at the expense of the poor and marginalised. Thus Spencer describes how the English Enclosure Acts ran roughshod over 'the claims of the poor cottagers'; he decries the privileging of landed interests in electoral politics and tax law; he condemns the disparate legal treatment of 'gentleman sinecurists' and simple workmen, and so on (Spencer, 1995: 196). Thus Spencer held that it would be folly for the poor to look to the state for relief, or for society to entrust the state with power in the hopes that it would be used on behalf of the poor. State power is and always will be used for state interests, and state interests are rarely advanced by spending scarce resources on economically and socially marginalised groups.

But by far the most important aspect of Spencer's critique of poverty-relief programmes was derived from the twin ideas of complexity and unintended consequences – two ideas that would take an increasingly prominent role in libertarian thought during the twentieth century, especially in the work of Friedrich Hayek (Friedrich A. Hayek, 1971, 1976, 1994). For Spencer, society is best understood as constituted by a complex web of individuals, organisations and causal relationships. When we think about various social evils and what might be done to address them, our attention naturally focuses on certain particular elements of that web. But in focusing in this way, we easily forget that 'each phenomenon is a link in an infinite series – is the result of myriads of preceding phenomena, and will have a share in producing myriads of succeeding ones'. Because phenomena are complexly interrelated, it is always the case that 'in disturbing any natural chain of sequences, [legislators] are not only modifying the result next in succession, but all the future results into which this will enter as a part-cause' (Spencer, 1981a: 280).

Social systems thus exhibit a complexity that is 'utterly beyond human grasp' (Spencer, 1981a: 280). And thus, '[w]e need feel no surprise, then, that in their efforts to cure specific evils, legislators have continually caused collateral evils they never looked for' (Spencer, 1981a: 282). Legislation is a blunt tool, well designed, perhaps, to deal with average events, but extremely ill suited for adapting itself to the constant changes and surprises of a complex social world (Spencer, 1981a: 289). For Spencer, the attempt to stamp out evil by means of legislation was akin to an attempt to straighten out a wrought-iron plate with a hammer:

> [I]t sticks up a little here towards the left – 'cockles', as we say. How shall we flatten it? Obviously, you reply, by hitting down on the part that is prominent. Well, here is a hammer, and I give the plate a blow as you advise. Harder, you say. Still no effect. Another stroke? Well, there is one, and another, and another. The prominence remains, you see: the evil is as great as ever – greater, indeed. But this is not all. Look at the warp which the plate has got near the opposite edge. Where it was flat before it is now curved. A pretty bungle we have

> made of it. Instead of curing the original defect, we have produced a second.... The required process is less simple than you thought. Even a sheet of metal is not to be successfully dealt with after those common-sense methods in which you have so much confidence. What, then, shall we say about a society? 'Do you think I am easier to be played on than a pipe?' asks Hamlet. Is humanity more readily straightened than an iron plate?'
>
> (Spencer, 1873b: 270–271)

Thus, the attempt to prevent drunkenness among the working poor by placing restrictive licences on the sale of gin leads merely to black markets, new forms of crime and violence, and an actual *increase* in the production and consumption of liquor (Spencer, 1873b: 270–271). Thus, the attempt to ensure that the poor receive quality housing by mandating various requirements of structure and space leads the poor to be priced out of the rental market and crowded together in unregulated quarters 'unfit for human habitation' (Spencer, 1981a: 278–279). And, thus, the attempt to render banking secure by means of legislative restrictions and guarantees leads lenders and borrowers alike to act recklessly. After all, if the state is watching to ensure that lenders behave responsibly, and waiting to pick up the tab in the case that they don't, why should borrowers exert much effort in assessing and comparing the stability of potential lenders? And why should lenders expend much effort in *being* stable? And so, Spencer famously wrote, 'the ultimate result of shielding men from the effects of their folly, is to fill the world with fools' (Spencer, 1864: 320).

Even when legislation accomplishes its intended aims, it does so at a cost. Resources devoted to one social aim must necessarily be diverted from some other. And the complexity of social systems combined with the fact that legislators are spending *other* people's money means that the cost of those forgone opportunities will very rarely be recognised, let alone properly weighed against the expected benefits of the proposed legislative action (Spencer, 1981a: 287–289, 315). This is akin to the distinction emphasised by the French economist Fredric Bastiat between 'What is seen and what is not seen', in his 1848 essay of that name. The actions of legislators, in Bastiat's terms, are driven almost entirely by what they *see* – by 'proximate causes and immediate effects' – and almost not all by what is *unseen* – the spontaneous workings of social forces, indirect and remote effects of policies, and the lost opportunities of time, wealth and labour consumed by state action (Bastiat, 1995).

Spencer's objection was thus not to charity as such. Rather, his objection was to *coercive* 'charity' and to *injudicious* charity (Spencer, 1995: 285–286, 291). Aid to the poor that is extracted from persons against their will, or aid that actually *harms* the poor rather than helping them, is to be condemned by considerations of morality and expediency alike.

Libertarian Charity

But opposition to coercive and injudicious charity leaves plenty of conceptual room for the advocacy of charity that is voluntary and effective. And, indeed, Spencer was a consistent and sometimes impassioned proponent of precisely that.

Spencer's advocacy of voluntary, effective charity was present in his work from the very beginning. But his discussions of the issue in *Social Statics* were often lost to readers amid the harsher passages reviewed in 'The case against Herbert Spencer', above. In his later work, *The Principles of Ethics*, Spencer would express regret regarding the 'very erroneous impression' produced by his earlier work: 'In its full scope, the moral system to be set forth unites sternness with kindness; but thus far attention has been drawn almost wholly to the sternness. Extreme misapprehensions and gross misstatements have hence resulted' (Spencer, 1978: 30).

Throughout his career, Spencer expressed his approval of charity that was voluntary and that would help to relieve suffering without creating further suffering as an unintended byproduct. Because of his concern to avoid moral hazard, Spencer was most enthusiastic regarding charity to victims of brute bad luck. Since the suffering of such individuals is entirely (or mostly) outside of their control, we need not worry so much about our aid generating perverse incentives and therefore can, and should, give freely.

> To that charity which may be described as helping men to help themselves, [my argument] makes no objection – countenances it rather. And in helping men to help themselves, there remains abundant scope for the exercise of a people's sympathies. Accidents will still supply victims on whom generosity may be legitimately expended. Men thrown upon their backs by unforeseen events, men who have failed for want of knowledge inaccessible to them, men ruined by the dishonesty of others, and men in whom hope long delayed has made the heart sick, may, with advantage to all parties, be assisted. Even the prodigal, after severe hardship has branded his memory with the unbending conditions of social life to which he must submit, may properly have another trial afforded him. And, although by these ameliorations the process of adaptation must be remotely interfered with, yet in the majority of cases, it will not be so much retarded in one direction as it will be advanced in another.
>
> (Spencer, 1995: 291–292)

Success and failure in life, Spencer recognised, are not always a matter of virtue or vice, skill or ineptitude. Of course, those who are successful would like to *believe* that their success is due entirely to their own merit and that the failings of the poor are due entirely to their own deficiencies.

But Spencer had little patience with this sort of self-congratulatory rationalisation for stinginess.

> It is very easy for you, O respectable citizen, seated in your easy chair, with your feet on the fender, to hold forth on the misconduct of the people – very easy for you to censure their extravagant and vicious habits.... It is no honour to you that you do not spend your savings in sensual gratification; you have pleasures enough without. But what would you do if placed in the position of the labourer? How would these virtues of yours stand the wear and tear of poverty? Where would your prudence and self-denial be if you were deprived of all the hopes that now stimulate you ...? Let us see you tied to an irksome employment from dawn till dusk; fed on meagre food, and scarcely enough of that.... Suppose your savings had to be made, not, as now, out of surplus income, but out of wages already insufficient for necessaries; and then consider whether to be provident would be as easy as you at present find it. Conceive yourself one of a despised class contemptuously termed 'the great unwashed'; stigmatised as brutish, stolid, vicious ... and then say whether the desire to be respectable would be as practically operative on you as now.... How offensive it is to hear some pert, self-approving personage, who thanks God that he is not as other men are, passing harsh sentence on his poor, hard-worked, heavily burdened fellow countrymen ...
>
> (Spencer, 1995: 203–205)

In these passages, Spencer displays a real empathy with the plight of the poor. And he recognises, moreover, that aid to the poor can be and sometimes is a matter of moral *duty* – not merely a sort of supererogatory virtue. It is, to be sure, an *imperfect* duty of beneficence, rather than a perfect duty of justice, and it is for this reason that Spencer believes that it is not a duty that may properly be enforced by means of coercion. But this classification is simply a reflection of the fact that ascertaining the conditions in which aid is appropriate requires the exercise of flexible moral judgement, rather than fixed, absolute rules (Spencer, 1978: 375, 405–406). It certainly does not suggest that he thought these duties *unimportant*.[5]

Libertarian Social Justice?

Even critics of libertarianism may well concede that the doctrine is compatible with the advocacy of purely private, voluntary charity. But, even if this is so, libertarianism would certainly seem to be deeply incompatible with a more robust notion of *social justice*. It cannot admit that it makes sense to speak of the justice or injustice of social institutions as distinct from the justice or injustice of the particular actions of individuals. And it cannot hold that the needs or suffering of some give rise to a claim of justice against society as a whole, regardless of whether those needs or suffering were the product of wrongdoing by some assignable individual.

As applied to Spencer, this assessment is *largely* correct. The most well-developed contemporary libertarian theories of social justice are constructivist in nature. Tomasi's theory, for example, follows that of John Rawls in holding that the principles of justice that ought to govern the basic structure of society are those that would be chosen by rational individuals in an initial condition of freedom and equality (Tomasi, 2011).[6] Spencer's theory, in contrast, is probably best read as grounded in a kind of indirect utilitarianism (Gray, 1982; Weinstein, 1998). He is therefore committed to holding that people's legitimate moral claims on each other are a function of the aggregate consequences such claims would produce, and in a way that is largely independent of the *distribution* of such consequences.

Largely, but perhaps not entirely. In one fascinating passage from *Social Statics*, for instance, Spencer seems to suggest that even if justice is entirely a matter of individual rights, nevertheless there is a sense in which injustices against 'the humblest' cry out for a special sort of concern. Consider this excerpt from Spencer's discussion of allowing working-class citizens to vote, and notice how he responds to the objection that this would lead to policies hostile to the interests of the wealthy.

> Even were there no answer to this, the evidence would still preponderate in favour of popular enfranchisement. For what at the utmost does the argument amount to? Just this: – that the few must continue to trespass against the many, lest the many should trespass against the few. The well fed, the luxuriously housed and clothed, the placemen and pensioners, may perhaps think it better that the masses should suffer for their benefit (as they do) than that they should suffer for the benefit of the masses (as they might). But would a just arbitrator say this? Would he not say, on the contrary, that even if their respective members were blessed with equal advantages, the minority ought to be sacrificed rather than the majority; but that as the most numerous are at the same time the least favoured, their claim becomes still more imperative. Surely, if one of the two parties must submit to injustice, it ought to be the rich hundreds, and not the poor thousands.
>
> (Spencer, 1995: 198)

This is far from a full-fledged theory of social justice. But it is equally far from the crude social Darwinism that is usually associated with Herbert Spencer. And it does seem to be at least a step in the *direction* of a theory of social justice – something akin to the 'preferential option for the poor' endorsed by the United States Conference of Catholic Bishops in their *Economic Justice for All*.

Consider, also, Spencer's little-noticed treatment of the Poor Law in his later work, *The Principles of Ethics*. That treatment begins in a familiar way, reaffirming Spencer's long-held belief that 'relief of the poor from public funds raised by rates, is, if considered apart from certain antecedents to be presently named, inconsistent with that limitation of state functions which ethics insists upon' (Spencer, 1978: 394).

So far, this is just Libertarianism 101. Taxation violates individual freedom, and therefore tax-funded welfare is morally impermissible. But wait, what exactly is Spencer referring to as 'certain antecedents to be presently named'? In the next paragraph, he says that what he has in mind are the conditions that existed in feudal and pre-feudal times in which the serfs had certain established rights to the produce of the soil. The abolishment of serfdom freed the serf from his tie to his lord's land, but it also destroyed his claim upon the produce of the soil. This, Spencer argued, was a kind of injustice. 'Entire usurpation of the land by the landlord, and entire appropriation of the labourer, were unjust' (Spencer, 1978: 394). The Poor Law sought to compensate the labouring classes for this injustice and thus may, to that extent, 'be said to have an equitable basis', and the relief that it offers is thus 'something more than a charitable dole' (Spencer, 1978: 394). That 'something more', I think it is reasonable to infer, is a requirement of *justice*. And insofar as it is a requirement of justice based on class membership (the tax would be paid by the landowning class to the labouring class), rather than the specific behaviours of particular individuals, it seems not too implausible to construe it as a claim of *social justice*.

Almost a hundred years later, the libertarian philosopher Robert Nozick would suggest that perhaps something like a Rawlsian difference principle or other 'patterned principles of justice' could serve as 'rough rules of thumb meant to approximate the general results of applying the principle of rectification of injustice' (Nozick, 1974: 230–231). The convergence between Spencer and Nozick on this point suggests what might be a fruitful way forward in developing a libertarian account of social justice. Even if such a principle cannot be defended in terms of the kind of first-best ideal society described by Spencer in his *Social Statics*, it may well be defensible in our decidedly *non-ideal* reality, as a rough-and-ready mechanism for providing approximate compensation to those whose libertarian rights were violated in the generation of the present distribution of wealth and other resources.

Conclusion

Today, advocates of social justice focus their efforts almost entirely on thinking about what the state can *do* to help the poor more – enforcing laws against non-discrimination, providing greater educational opportunities and, of course, redistributing wealth. And understood in this way, it is hard to accept either Spencer's theory or libertarianism more generally as a plausible theory of social justice.

Historically, however, the greatest social injustices were not a matter of things that the state failed to do *for* the poor, but rather things that the state actively did *to* them. And in this respect, both Spencer's theory and libertarianism more generally look much more viable. Spencer's libertarianism is a theory devoted to ending oppression, not to equalising opportunity or well-being (Anderson, 1999). And its principled commitment to non-aggression, as Spencer's thought demonstrates, put libertarians in a strong position to condemn many of the most dangerous and destructive forms of oppression practised against the most vulnerable classes of persons.

To many modern advocates of social justice, this will not be enough. Of course, they hold, it is good to despise imperialism, to oppose eugenics and to advocate for the negative freedom of women and children. But it would be better if the state did *more* – if it did not merely refrain from oppressing, but took the further positive steps involved in *aiding* the poor, the vulnerable and the marginalised.

This is a formidable challenge for the libertarian. But it is one to which Spencer has articulated a powerful response. The belief that the state ought to be entrusted with the power to render positive aid to the poor presupposes both that the state is *capable* of rendering such aid and that it can be *trusted* to do so. And neither of these presuppositions, Spencer argued, are warranted. Considerations of complexity and moral hazard make it likely that genuine efforts by the state to improve the condition of the poor will be ineffective. And the fact that legislators are often motivated by self-interest means that power entrusted to the state will often be used on *behalf* of the state and the state's interests, which interests are very often antagonistic with those of the poor and vulnerable.

The charge that Spencer is indifferent to the suffering of the poor cannot stand up to a close scrutiny of his views. A full view of Spencer's writings gives every indication of an author who was capable of real empathy with the suffering of the vulnerable. And his system of thought sometimes reflects that sympathy in direct and obvious ways – as his consistent and well-developed endorsement of a positive duty of beneficence makes clear. Even when it does not, however, it is not because the sympathy was lacking. Rather, it was because Spencer thought our duty to aid must be matched by a duty to *know what we are doing* so that the aid we render might be effective rather than counterproductive (Spencer, 1978: 213). Reasonable people can disagree with Spencer about the correct application of this cautionary principle to particular cases. But Spencer's caution, his concern with moral desert, and his emphasis on the importance of non-aggression and the long-term sustainability of aid, must be *some* part of any reasonable modern conception of social justice.

Notes

1 'Remarks by the President at the Associated Press luncheon' (3 April 2012), www.whitehouse.gov/the-press-office/2012/04/03/remarks-president-associated-press-luncheon (accessed 10 August 2015); 'The rebirth of social Darwinism' (30 November 2011), http://robertreich.org/post/13567144944 (accessed 10 August 2015).

2 Phillips Thompson, 'The political economist and the tramp', *Labor Standard* (New York) (14 December 1878).

3 The influence of Hofstadter's work has been noted by virtually all historians of 'social Darwinism' such as Bellomy and Leonard. One of the most persuasive demonstrations, however, can be found in Geoffrey Hodgson's bibliometric analysis, which traces the use of the term before and after the 1940s, and uncovers an explosion in the term's popularity following Hofstadter's work. See Hodgson, 2004 (especially pp. 445–448).

4 Spencer advocated extending the right to vote to women in the original 1851 edition of *Social Statics*. However, he would later appear to change his mind on the issue, dropping the claim from the 1892 edition of *Social Statics*, and explicitly arguing against it in Chapter 20 of his 1897 *Principles of Ethics*. There, he argued that political rights come along with political responsibilities, and until women exercised the same responsibilities as men (specifically, military service), they could not legitimately claim the same rights. Much earlier, in 1867, Spencer expressed a different argument in a letter to John Stuart Mill, writing that voting rights are 'simply means to an end', that end being 'real liberty', which could only be secured by 'the limitations of the functions of the state'. Because women 'as a mass, are habitually on the side of authority', giving them the vote would likely 'stimulate all kinds of state administrations, the great mass of which are necessarily antagonistic to personal freedom'. Spencer still viewed the extension of the franchise to women as a moral ideal, to be pursued in the long term. But because of the dire threat to liberty he saw posed by socialism, he withheld support for it as 'an *immediate* measure, or even as a measure to be shortly taken'. See his letter to J. S. Mill, 9 August 1867 (in (Duncan and Spencer, 1908: 138–139) Unfortunately, Spencer was not the only libertarian thinker to stake out an (uncharacteristically) reactionary position on the issue of women's suffrage. The nineteenth-century American libertarian anarchist Lysander Spooner famously argued that since all legislation (as opposed to natural law) is necessarily unjust, *no one* should have the right to vote, and therefore denying the right to women was no injustice. See Spooner, 1877.

5 Spencer's *Social Statics* was explicitly designed as a work about what philosophers would now describe as perfect duties of justice under conditions of ideal theory. Accordingly, there is little discussion of beneficence within its pages. See, for a discussion, Spencer, 1995: Part I. In his later and more substantial work on ethics, however, Spencer devoted eight full chapters to the discussion of 'negative beneficence' and another ten to 'positive beneficence'. His discussion of the latter category of action includes pleas for children to devote greater care to parents in their old age, aid to the sick and injured, succour to the ill-used and endangered, and relief to the poor and destitute. See Spencer, 1978: Parts V and VI.

6 Interestingly, Tomasi suggests that Friedrich Hayek, despite his frequent assaults on the idea of 'social justice', might not have differed much from Rawls on this point. He notes that Hayek concedes that there is a 'genuine problem of justice in connection with the deliberate design of political institutions, the problem to which Professor John Rawls has recently devoted an important book', that the disagreement between his own account and Rawls's is 'more verbal than substantive' and that he and Rawls 'agree on what is to me the essential point'. He also notes that Hayek apparently developed on his own a principle very much like that expressed in Rawls's conception of the original position, namely that 'we should regard as the most desirable order of society one which we would choose if we knew that our initial position in it would be decided purely by chance'. (See Friedrich A. Hayek, 1976: xii, 100, 132, 188–189.)

References

Anderson, E. (1999), 'What is the point of equality?', *Ethics*, 109: 287–337.

Arneson, R. (1997), 'Egalitarianism and the undeserving poor', *Journal of Political Philosophy*, 5: 327–350.

Bannister, R. C. (1973), 'William Graham Sumner's social Darwinism: a reconsideration', *History of Political Economy*, 5: 89–109.

Bastiat, F. (1995), 'What is seen and what is not seen', in G. B. De Huszar (ed.), *Selected Essays on Political Economy*, Irvington-on-Hudson, NY: Foundation for Economic Education.

Bellomy, D. C. (1984), 'Social Darwinism Revisited', *Perspectives in American History*, N.S. 1: 1–129.

Bernstein, D. and Leonard, T. C. (2009), 'Excluding unfit workers: social control versus social justice in the age of economic reform', *Law and Contemporary Problems*, 72: 177–204.

Brennan, J. (2012), *Libertarianism: What Everyone Needs to Know*, Oxford: Oxford University Press.

Duncan, D. and Spencer, H. (1908), *The Life and Letters of Herbert Spencer*, London: Methuen.

Fleischacker, S. (2004), *A Short History of Distributive Justice*, Cambridge, MA: Harvard University Press.

Gray, J. N. (1982), 'Spencer on the ethics of liberty and the limits of state interference', *History of Political Thought*, 3 (3): 456–481.

Hayek, F. A. (1971), 'Principles or expediency?' in F. A. Hayek, H. Hazlitt, L. E. Read, G. Velasco and F. A. Harper (eds), *Toward Liberty: Essays in Honor of Ludwig von Mises*. Menlo Park, CA: Institute for Humane Studies.

Hayek, F. A. (1976), *Law, Legislation and Liberty, Vol. 2: The Mirage of Social Justice*, London, Routledge & Kegan Paul.

Hayek, F. A. (1994) 'The theory of complex phenomena', in M. Martin and L. C. Mcintyre (eds), *Readings in the Philosophy of Social Science*, Cambridge, MA: MIT Press.

Hodgson, G. M. (2004), 'Social Darwinism in Anglophone academic journals: a contribution to the history of the term', *Journal of Historical Sociology*, 17: 428–463.

Hofstadter, R. (1941), 'William Graham Sumner, social Darwinist', *The New England Quarterly*, 14: 457–477.

Hofstadter, R. (1992), *Social Darwinism in American Thought*, Boston: Beacon Press.

Leonard, T. C. (2005a), 'Eugenics and economics in the progressive era', *Journal of Economic Perspectives*, 19: 207–224.

Leonard, T. C. (2005b), 'Mistaking eugenics for social Darwinism: why eugenics is missing from the history of American economics', *History of Political Economy*, 37: 200–233.

Leonard, T. C. (2009a), 'American economic reform in the progressive era: its foundational beliefs and their relation to eugenics', *History of Political Economy*, 41: 109–141.

Leonard, T. C. (2009b), 'Origins of the myth of social Darwinism: the ambiguous legacy of Richard Hofstadter's social Darwinism in American thought', *Journal of Economic Behavior & Organization*, 71: 37–51.

Miller, W. L. (1982), 'Spencer's drift to conservatism', *History of Political Thought*, 3 (3): 483–497.

Mingardi, A. (2011), *Herbert Spencer*, New York: Continuum.
Nozick, R. (1974), *Anarchy, State, and Utopia*, New York: Basic Books.
Rand, A. (1964a), 'Man's rights', in A. Rand and N. Brandon, *The Virtue of Selfishness*, New York: Signet.
Rand, A. (1964b), 'The nature of government', in A. Rand and N. Brandon, *The Virtue of Selfishness*, New York: Signet.
Rothbard, M. N. (1970), *Power and Market*, Kansas: Sheed Andrews & McMeel.
Rothbard, M. N. (1973), *For a New Liberty*, New York: Collier.
Rothbard, M. N. (1982), *The Ethics of Liberty*, New Jersey: Humanities Press.
Spencer, H. (1864), 'State-tamperings with money and banks', in H. Spencer (ed.), *Essays: Scientific, Political, and Speculative, volume 2*. New York: D. Appleton.
Spencer, H. (1873a), 'Mr Martineau on evolution', in H. Spencer (ed.), *Recent Discussions in Science, Philosophy, and Morals*. New York: D. Appleton.
Spencer, H. (1873b), *The Study of Sociology*, London, Henry S. King.
Spencer, H. (1900), *The Principles of Sociology*, New York, D. Appleton.
Spencer, H. (1902), 'Patriotism', *Facts and Comments*. New York: D. Appleton.
Spencer, H. (1978), *The Principles of Ethics*, Indianapolis: Liberty Fund.
Spencer, H. (1981a), 'Over-legislation', in H. Spencer, *The Man Versus the State*, Indianapolis: Liberty Classics.
Spencer, H. (1981b), 'The proper sphere of government', in H. Spencer, *The Man Versus the State*, Indianapolis: Liberty Fund.
Spencer, H. (1995) *Social Statics*, New York: Robert Schalkenbach Foundation.
Spooner, L. (1877), 'Against woman's suffrage', *New Age* (24 February).
Tomasi, J. (2011), *Free Market Fairness*, Princeton: Princeton University Press.
Weinstein, D. (1998), *Equal Freedom and Utility: Herbert Spencer's Liberal Utilitarianism*, New York: Cambridge University Press.
Weinstein, D. (2012), 'Herbert Spencer', in Edward N. Zalta (ed.), *The Stanford Encyclopedia of Philosophy*, Fall 2012 edn, http://plato.stanford.edu/archives/fall2012/entries/spencer/ (accessed 8 August 2013).
Zwolinski, M. (forthcoming), 'Libertarianism and the welfare state', in J. Brennan, B. Van Der Vossen and D. Schmidtz (eds), *The Routledge Handbook of Libertarianism*, New York: Routledge.
Zwolinski, M. and Tomasi, J. (2016), *A Brief History of Libertarianism*, Princeton, NJ, Princeton University Press.

Part II

Distributive Justice Reconsidered

Forging New Debates

In the previous section, we were exposed to historical aspects of distributive justice. Commentators of these areas showed us how conceptual hurdles may be contingently distinct, but illuminating, as they inform our study of these issues and ways to approach them. As we move forward towards the observational, applicative and emerging issues of the contemporary world, theoretical perspectives and the African region as an exemplar of how a specified area of thought and policy has been marginalised, we must make a crucial step. This section takes that step by exploring how contemporary and emerging conceptual debates bridge the gap of the conceptual lineage of the past and observational shortcomings of our contemporary world to forge a new or more detailed horizon of the obstacles that face our concepts. These new horizons show us where our perceptions of what ought to be are being actively forged in relation to what has been and what exists, in order to direct and refine what will be.

In this section, the chapters will centre around critical approaches to current trends in political thought. This criticism will be informed distinctly and examine, critique and illuminate issues of distribution in ways reflective of specific approaches to and challenges of conceptualising justice. In our chapter, we illustrate this very point by showing how Nussbaum's search in the historical lineage under-represents a necessary step in building obligations towards her social approach to capabilities. Daniel Engster takes a seemingly compartmentalised aspect of justice, in care ethics, and shows how it can be a powerful tool in envisioning broad consideration of just distribution. Lawrence Hamilton questions the primary liberal focus on rights and asks us to consider needs as the appropriate and necessary starting point of justice. Chris Allsobrook discusses the potential scope of predominant socioeconomic ideological positions and their ability to consider progressive distributive and redistributive reforms. These chapters in their own way show what exists at the edge of the contemporary conceptual debates and the challenges, demands and promise of moving conceptual arguments forward.

As we move forward towards finding a fair share, this section serves as a link between the historical frameworks of thought and concept and the emerging ideas and observations that we seek to use to inform the development of our debates of justice. In order to understand the power of the past and the observations of what it has missed, ignored or under-represented, we must examine the space in which these two forces meet and confront each other. These chapters ask us to diverge from the paradigmatic path of how we have historically and philosophically approached an issue and instead argue for a change, broadening or refocusing of how we approach it. These chapters serve as examples of the exercise of engaging critically and precisely within debates of distribution. The key role these exercises serve is in forging our narratives in academic, social and political discourses about distribution. These chapters will help us understand an important part of how our narratives about distributive justice are created and refined.

5 Dignity, Sociability and Capability

Exploring Nussbaum's Interpretation of Grotius

Camilla Boisen and Matthew C. Murray

Introduction

Martha Nussbaum begins her work at the convergence of humanity's social nature to build an argument forward towards human equality, flourishing and entitlements through her specific development of the capabilities approach. The power of the argument comes from the social aspects of humanity, particularly in the settings of social justice, as the obvious point of intersection between most if not all meta and comprehensive accounts of the human condition. It is from this point of departure that she sees a path forward in cashing out this concept and what it implies of us as individuals, groups, societies and nations in facilitating the essential 'dignity' of human beings. This leads Nussbaum to a primary set of ten capabilities (Nussbaum, 2006, 2011) that are basic entitlements needed to ensure justice for historically under-represented groups in the Western rationalist traditions, namely the disabled, women, economic minorities (international and domestic), other minority groups and even non-human animals. Nussbaum's theoretical approach for all of its nuances, strengths and weaknesses makes a strong contribution to the literature on conceptualising the application of justice (including distribution) and takes the brave and increasingly rare task of making 'real' and palpable suggestions for policy approaches to and outcomes of human flourishing that come from the often abstract world of political theory. Whether Nussbaum's project succeeds or fails in this comprehensive task, or in equal measure to all of the groups and issues to which it is propounded to be applicable, is debated, but one cannot deny its impact or potential importance not simply as a philosophic exercise but as a legitimising benchmark for future leaders and policy makers.

Nussbaum pays interest to the often neglected historical discourse of political thought, taking seriously its contributions to issues, framing of rhetorical debates and the concepts and tools it lends the politically minded to grapple with contemporary problems. We share her concerns and admire and support her work in raising specific issues of inequality, developing approaches to these issues and utilising philosophy as an important and frequently under-represented aspect of changing our world for the better. She gives us powerful arguments in *Frontiers of Justice* and her many other works woven masterfully through the observable, emotive and conceptual narratives of our world to raise the discourse of justice. It is this power that we argue implies we must take the arguments and traditions that Nussbaum presents as preferable or outright support of her particular conceptual turns seriously, critically and comprehensively particularly in light of the critiques that have been raised about the justificatory claims she makes or fails to make in *Frontiers of Justice* and preceding and subsequent texts (see Nussbaum, 2001, 2004a, 2004b, 2006, 2011, 2015).

In this chapter, we will explore one of these aspects of her work presented primarily in *Frontiers of Justice*, that is, Nussbaum's sympathetic leaning towards the tradition of Hugo Grotius (1583–1645) and his exploration of natural sociability as a response to particular advantage-based social contract traditions and realist constructions of international relations. Nussbaum argues that these kinds of theories, in varying degrees, are overly focused on the autonomous individuality/agency, rationality and individual advantage seeking of individual moral agents. Instead Nussbaum seeks to use ideas of basic equal human dignity and natural sociability (humanity's proclivity for social arrangement) as starting points for a political theory much as she claims Grotius did.

> The general idea of Grotius' natural law theory is that these two features of the human being, and their ethical value, suggest a good deal about the treatment to which every human being is entitled. Thus political theory begins from an abstract idea of basic entitlements, grounded in the twin ideas of dignity (the human being as an end) and sociability. It is then argued that certain specific entitlements flow from those ideas, as necessary conditions of a life with human dignity.
>
> (Nussbaum, 2006: 36)

Nussbaum concedes that 'Grotius does not ask how one might use these insights to think about the just structure of an individual state' (Nussbaum, 2006: 36) but argues this can be made when we look at Grotius's use of the ideas in international relations to justify specific distributive and social justice norms. Nussbaum implies that arguments like hers, in the tradition of Grotius, use sociability and its collective nature to explain distributive, social and political implementations of 'core human entitlements'[1] (Nussbaum, 2006: 70) to provide capabilities and then subsequent political autonomy. As Nussbaum explains:

> Grotius does not distinguish between political and moral autonomy, as I (with Rawls) would like to do. So my version of the Grotian argument would say, instead, that by giving themselves laws, human beings assert a political autonomy that can be agreed to be important by citizens who differ about the value of a comprehensive moral autonomy.
>
> (Nussbaum, 2006: 441 fn. 30)[2]

Though Nussbaum seeks to develop core ideas and concepts, she does see herself in some way of making a Grotian argument. It is our contention that Nussbaum's 'version of' Grotius leads her to overstate Grotius's usefulness and symmetry as an allied argument to her capabilities approach. Nussbaum does not develop or expand on how deeply she seeks to develop the foundations or outcomes from Grotius's work in her own perspectives but does repeatedly allude to them as a valuable critique to individualistic contractarianism (especially against John Rawls as a contemporary hybrid representative of the tradition). She sees a Grotian argument as supportive if not formative in her position of building sociability as intertwined with human dignity and that a commitment to the latter, through her version of 'overlapping consensus' and supported by international and domestic norms and precedents,[3] dictates the former. As Nussbaum puts it in her extensive historical exposition in the opening of *Frontiers of Justice*:

> I begin with Hugo Grotius, since his natural law approach to basic principles of international relations is the one I shall attempt to revive; but Grotius's approach suggests a general template for thinking about domestic issues as well, although he does not so apply it.
>
> (Nussbaum, 2006: 36)

This shows how deeply Nussbaum believes that a Grotian approach is not only distinct and valuable but that its revival is ultimately a 'template' or pattern, to envision justice with a different individual vs social balance.

In this chapter, we explore what the Grotian template is if we view it with all of its complexity and problems. On a Grotian view of justice, individuals are social and ought to share in a protective and productive society which is very much in keeping with Nussbaum's general method of argument. However, we argue Grotius held that human sociability is the result of a thin universal account of their metaphysical nature based upon the assumption of natural law that characterises, specifies and most importantly obligates individual social members to moral claims of autonomy, advantage and social cohesion. In Grotius's political thought, a concept of the individual is needed for concepts of the social and the fulfilment of human dignity. Though Nussbaum shares and articulates the importance of human dignity, her willingness to adapt the economic capabilities approach of Amartya Sen[4] into an ethical and political approach leaves her to give the concept of dignity and our obligations to fulfil it for ourselves and others to the outcomes of overlapping consensus to avoid any specific meta or reasonably rejectable moral claims. Grotius, we argue, does not leave the concepts of inviolability or dignity undefined in some key ways. They are instead assumed or implied, if not stated outright, and provide the individual and social obligatory aspect of Grotius's project that is needed to sustain his later claims about sociability and political justice.

For all the value Nussbaum brings to the table of tackling issues of social justice, raising awareness of them and noting the limitations of particular policy approaches to address them, we argue in this chapter that seeing a supportive tradition of her particular prescriptions for the expansive provision of social capabilities in Grotius is overstated or implies extensive defence and development.[5]

This chapter proceeds to first investigate Nussbaum's account of the capabilities approach and her use of a thick conception of natural sociability as fulfilling a consensus-driven concept of human dignity that she implies is a similar point of convergence with Grotius against individualised or advantage-based contractarianism and illiberal theories of justice (Nussbaum, 2006: 20–21). Second, we interrogate Grotius's account of sociability and 'distributive justice'. We argue that Grotius's political philosophy cannot lend itself explicitly to this adaptation owing to his overt and implied exposition that sociability serves an inviolable and pre-political purpose in fulfilling a specific account of human dignity and the obligations we have to fulfil it for ourselves and others. Dignity and sociability are specific in what they do and mean for Grotius in a way that Nussbaum expressly rejects in seeking many domestic, international and even interspecies applications for her approach. This inspection will allow us to see some specific hurdles for Nussbaum's capabilities approach which may ultimately lead away from the Grotian tradition rather than towards it.

Nussbaum's Capabilities Approach, Equality and Sociability

> Since we live in a world in which it is simply not true that co-operating with others on fair terms will be advantageous to all, we must boldly insist that this account of social co-operation, even in its moralized Kantian form, is not the one we need to guide us. We have, and use, ideas of co-operation that are much richer than this. These richer ideas already inhabit the pre-contractarian natural law tradition, as my epigraph from Grotius makes clear. With Grotius, we ought to think of ourselves as people who want to live with others. A central part of our own good, each and every one of us, is to produce, and live in, a world that is morally decent, a world in which all human beings have what they need to live a life with human dignity.
>
> (Nussbaum, 2004b: 12)

In *Frontiers of Justice* Nussbaum later notes, 'My aim is to supply something both new and old, resurrecting the richer ideas of human fellowship across national boundaries that we find in Grotius and other exponents of the natural law tradition' (Nussbaum, 2006: 227).

As the above quotes indicate, it is vital to relate the concepts Grotius develops to Nussbaum's use of natural sociability and human fellowship to provide the basis for her development of the capabilities approach. Her conceptual argument has much symmetry to Grotius at first blush. Nussbaum sees the presence of conceptions of human dignity being present in societies all over the world and in international law. She however sees no need to describe what dignity is in a conceptual sense, conceding that people may have many comprehensive ideas about dignity and that our mere observation of overlapping consensus[6] on the idea and that this has applicability to everyone (including to some degree animals, which is a claim we will not address in this chapter) is all we need to move forward. It is at this point that we will see the start of Nussbaum's conflict with Grotius, but it is important now to unpack her approach and show how its elements and claims work as the conflict we see here will have ramifications throughout the unfolding of the argument.

Nussbaum argues that dignity has an essentially social element as humans are naturally given to social behaviour. The existence of rough/consensus-created human dignity, then, requires us to make each other capable of interacting in the kinds of social behaviours that facilitate our functioning and flourishing. These are our capabilities, and Nussbaum gives us a list of ten types of capabilities (described in detail in Nussbaum, 2006: 76–78, 393–400) that she argues are all equally required elements of social justice. These are, in the order of presentation, Life, Bodily Health, Bodily Integrity, Senses/Imagination and Thought, Emotions, Practical Reason, Affiliation, Other Species (the opportunity to interact with and value them), Play, Control of One's Environment.

Importantly, these have an explicitly distributive element not just in a non-tangible opportunity sense that a capability might mean, but in that we must work to facilitate through resources the capabilities of others, no matter the costs or economic demands of doing so. It is to be our priority of implementation when and where possible. The social element of dignity breeds a 'collective obligation' (Nussbaum, 2006: 275) to capabilities and the entitlements to facilitate them. As Nussbaum notes in her 2003 Olaf Palme Lecture,

> The focus on capabilities reminds us that we shall need to make special efforts to address the unequal needs of those who begin from a position of social disadvantage. Moreover, a focus on capabilities, although closely allied with the human rights approach, adds an important clarification to the idea of human rights: for it informs us that our goal is not merely 'negative liberty' or absence of interfering state action – one very common understanding of the notion of rights – but, instead, the full ability of people to be and to choose these very important things. Thus, all capabilities have an economic aspect: even the freedom of speech requires education, adequate nutrition, etc.
>
> (Nussbaum, 2004b: 13)

This positions her conception of the capabilities approach 'as an alternative to the economic–utilitarian approaches that dominated and to some degree still dominate decisions of quality of life in international development and policy circles' (Nussbaum, 2006: 71). Utility approaches and general GDP, or means-based measures of development that emulate its method, use the basic human experience of pain and pleasure to create obligations to the maximisation of pleasure and avoidance of pain. As a form of reflective and measurable human good, it creates an obligatory argument as to why particular courses of action are good and hence right-based from the idea of absolute human equality in the existence of these experiences, which when applied in policy approaches result in specific methodological and conceptual hurdles and shortcomings as Nussbaum notes (see Nussbaum, 2006: 72–80, 282, 338–346, 394, 447). Importantly for Nussbaum, and for Amartya Sen whose capabilities approach Nussbaum is ultimately developing, this powerful form of obligation in the public sphere places constraints of economic growth and resource efficiency as primary, and thus creates duties only to utility maximisation and not to any substantive and enduring principles of human flourishing and dignity; it assumes, worryingly, that wealth and means are the measure of pleasure, opportunity, development and welfare. The needs of people to participate in society are constrained by collective utility as measured by efficiency and the level of resources available, leading to troubling outcomes for minority or under-represented groups, peoples or nations.

Although it is not articulated in *Frontiers of Justice*, Nussbaum's assertion of respecting the plurality of concepts of social good expressed by peoples of the world will likely not exclude eventual decisions of utility in public expenditure or resource allocation, but will rather place such occasions in a different realm of decision-making that happens in social contexts well after the essential attributes of justice motivated by a shared duty to fulfil dignity (in her case capabilities) are provided to citizens.

The benefits here are potentially extremely large for incorporating under-represented groups into societies using existing norms and values to build a socially rooted account of political autonomy. The fraternity she sees broadly with human rights approaches is clear. Nussbaum states, 'the capabilities approach is, in my view, one species of a human rights approach, and human rights have often been linked in a similar way to the idea of human dignity' (Nussbaum, 2006: 78). Nussbaum continues by approaching the long and storied tradition of the social contract, contractarian approaches to justice more broadly and the more contemporary theories of this general kind utilising reciprocity or agreement, of various kinds, between individual agents in a collective arrangement. Nussbaum shares some common ground with many utilitarians both in respect to animal rights (see Nussbaum, 2006: III, 338) and in seeing that comprehensive accounts of inviolable, rational and advantage-based individual rights that subordinate social-rooting have led to dubious historical outcomes and contemporary inequalities. History has shown that, through intention or accident, accounts of individual rights, when created with particular understandings, predispositions or non-universal understandings of humanity, can serve equally to alienate, disenfranchise and stigmatise individuals and groups. This happens as these rights are formed in relation to a concept of humanity that obligates people into conducts or the expectations of conducts to ensure justice that does not reflect physical diversity, social diversity or social nature. As a result, these kinds of rights can legitimise and enforce unfair, undignified and even inhuman treatments of groups of people and the resources distributed through the collective association to or for them.

Nussbaum sees these failings as being acute particularly for citizens of developing countries, social minorities, women and the handicapped/disabled.[7] She notes, as many commentators have, that the atomised individual agent fixation of contractarian or reciprocal forms of social justice are, in spite of their best efforts, to blame, in part or in totality, for the inequalities we can see in the outcomes visible today for these groups. These kinds of approaches place humans in a form of atomised position that is not, in one sense, a total account of what it is to be a human being (socially encompassed). Nussbaum argues that obligations between people in these accounts comes down to mutual advantage and rationalisation which is not encompassing of all the people, beings and elements that ought to be the subject of and be served by actions of justice. Nussbaum articulately and persuasively notes the equal capacity of individuals to care, the human requirement for social interactions which may have little value to others and the validity of human flourishing in spite of ideal rational capabilities. Nussbaum is critical of Hobbes, Locke, Kant and later, in a qualified way Rawls, among others, on these grounds, as they all start with the primary foci of individual autonomy that is bias in troubling ways in light of the aspects she places back into the conversation about justice and the obligations that are subsequently placed on, from, of and by such individuals in a just collective arrangement. Of these, she is most sympathetic to Rawls and his hybrid contract position. Nussbaum's exhaustive critique of Rawls ultimately seeks to reconstitute several of his ideas and conceptual turns, but her concern about how he has allowed advantage to troublingly leak into his thought device remains throughout. Nussbaum has a greater affinity for the contractarian approaches of Thomas Scanlon and Brian Barry, whom she sees as more closely aligned with her own perspectives but ultimately lacking, in that both approaches require development or amendment to support her particular conception of capabilities (see Nussbaum, 2006: VI, 54). Nussbaum therefore urges that we need another way forward, and Grotius and pre-contractarian thought more broadly are key figures for Nussbaum in finding this new path. Nussbaum sees potential convergence on issues with contractarians of the Barry/Scanlon type but asserts that the capabilities approach she is positing is distinct in demanding a different articulation of social justice that does not need to retreat into hypotheticals to make real commitments and developments.

Though contractarian approaches are problematic in how, why and who they include and the value judgements they include or exclude in the reciprocity arguments they all uniquely apply, the idea of having a discrete conception of human beings, and facilitating their flourishing socially from this conception, does provide theories of justice with an important coercive tool: the ability or duty to act on these grounds that comes from an individual obligatory source. For our fellow humans, we must act to protect/secure or even facilitate their humanity depending on the contract/agreement. The development of these explanations of just societies and governments historically, particularly in the modern era, indicates these were not intended as a tool of oppression or disenfranchisement, but rather an attempt to emancipate and empower individuals and their collective groups from relativist, collective and nationalist concepts that were oppressive in their own ways. The human rights approaches of which Nussbaum finds her own theory a 'species' are a result of these ideas and their unfolding historically. They were arguably flawed but an important tool in asserting autonomy from social schemes that eroded or impinged this autonomy in troubling ways. It is worth noting that Nussbaum does not wish to avoid confrontation and debate with such theories and as such shows a level of academic respect we rarely witness in what are often charged debates about justice. At the same time, the clear implication of *Frontiers of Justice* in particular is that these theories are equally incomplete in what they do or claim, so her criticism is apparent, even if it is presented with deep admiration and respect.

Nussbaum does not wish us to throw out the importance of individual autonomy and acting based upon it. In fact, her capabilities approach requires individuals and states to act, and act frequently, to intervene in domestic and more vaguely/narratively/facilitatively in international affairs. She merely seeks to provide us with a distinct and non-atomised account of people that subsequently does not apply contractarian advantage leverage to the obligations we have to act in the ways she suggests. Nussbaum notes the need for this development in a Neo-Aristotelian sense (Nussbaum, 2006: III, 159–160, 216). This oversight in Western philosophy we can trace arguably to Aristotle himself, in observing the deeply social and interdependent nature of animals, including humans, in the collective sense but creating distinctness to human socialisation as a mechanism for ideal behaviour, reason, political power and advantageous arrangement, which has caused fault-lines dividing political scholars to this day. Nussbaum's acknowledged Neo-Aristotelianism, which somewhat lacks exhaustive defence aside from her aversion from potential Roussean, Marxist or illiberal interpretations (Nussbaum, 2006: 216) is clear about how sociability facilitates dignity and flourishing which ought to be the focus of applying justice. This task is a tall one and the argument has far more moving parts than we can assess here or, in fact, are given by Nussbaum expressly. It would involve coherently piecing together and subsequently rejecting aspects of liberalism, Aristotelianism, utilitarianism, care ethics, customary and normative human rights conventions, the natural law tradition and even parts of the contractarian traditions into a comprehensive argument. It is clear she sees them functioning as a coherent whole, but that coherency without exhaustive defence remains assumptive. Though this is expressly not Nussbaum's concern or project, she does allude to intuitions in ways that are assumed to work together in making claims about and from her starting point of consensus-driven dignity accounts and provisions for sociability, human flourishing and capabilities based on this shared value of dignity. Nevertheless, it is a task made conceptually easier if a historical approach provides some guide or template for how to ally these historically competing claims and ideas from a point of consensus like the one she posits.

It is here that we see how important a Grotian lineage is in her approach. Grotius is useful for Nussbaum in developing a kind of theory of political and social harmony and intervention on ends of collective interdependence. This move in drawing kinship cannot be oversold in its importance as Nussbaum treads a similar path to Grotius in observing sociability, arguing that it requires specific interventionalist actions domestically and internationally no matter why individuals may come to understand why dignity happens for humans, which in her specific case leads us to pursue the capabilities approach and/or her specific list of capabilities. Grotius shows this in his work as he takes the concept of natural sociability and works it into a non-conventional, arguably pluralistic and arguably minimal approach to social justice, distinct (as might be expected) from the capabilities approach but similar in its conceptual aims and ends. Grotius provides an exemplar for how this kind of conceptual argument would work.

Nussbaum treads a similar path in seeking a 'partial and minimal account of social justice' (Nussbaum, 2006: 71) that works only to speak to social arrangements. Nussbaum states, '[t]he capabilities approach is not remote and impractical, but urgently practical, when it urges us to rethink our ideas of social cooperation' (Nussbaum, 2006: 306). She stipulates this further in stating, 'the capabilities approach criticizes the approach to human rights that defines rights in terms of "negative liberty" alone' (Nussbaum, 2006: 372).

We can see these threads come together in discussing the capabilities approach to disability that uniquely deals with the frequently contentious relationship between natural individual distributions and their effect (rightly or wrongly) on external and social resources.[8] Nussbaum argues that in getting away from advantage and rationalisation in socialisation, we allow individuals with disabilities, particularly mental and cognitive disabilities, to participate in meaningful social activities they are capable and willing to undertake. We revisit the social arrangement and our commitments to it given the dignity the disabled have and the necessity of social opportunities (the capabilities list in Nussbaum's terms). And last, the considerations of A and B lead us to act facilitatively when we look at the policies of social equality, inclusion and development. It is in this light that we see the great appeal of what Nussbaum seeks to do and why it can have applicability to other groups of individuals who face social inequalities through seeking capability outcomes.

What is of primary concern to us is whether this account of consensus dignity and sociability Nussbaum wants is congruent to what Grotius uses to ground and obligate actions of sociability. We will move on now to show how Grotius builds up a priori obligations into his account of human dignity, practices of sociability and common human fellowship that Nussbaum has taken as primary and why these are such an important move for arguments of this type to make if they are to be obligatory to individuals. We will also show why Grotius's form of consensus (which is not well expressed by that term) expresses a form of obligation to dignity that is deontological in nature and creates the force and structure of his later arguments, which diverge from Nussbaum's in ways it is important to consider.

Grotius, Sociability and 'Distributive Justice'

The Self and Sociability

By taking a closer look at what can be ascribed as Grotius's account of sociability and 'distributive justice', we argue that owing to Grotius's *individual account* of why sociability is a common good to individuals, he does not give us a 'thick' account of what counts as a good social life, the capabilities required to fulfil it or the specific ways in which it fulfils human flourishing. In fact, he would have had good reasons to desist from any prescription as to what constitutes the good social life. What Grotius *does* give us is the reason why we are sociable and have sociability, which obligates us to actions of human fellowship and an account of human dignity, something which is a point of consensus but is not left to be defined by this consensus.

Although man is sociable by nature, according to Grotius,[9] the laws of nature do not imply any positive obligation on behalf of the owner to do more than respect the rights of others, to leave them alone or render what was theirs. In social terms, allowing someone to speak or express themselves is an inherently different act from facilitating their ability to say it. As Harvey demonstrates, in a similar vein to Knud Haakonsson, 'Grotius's conception of sociability is rather meagre at best: essentially it entails leaving others alone to the unmolested enjoyment of their "suum" as long as they likewise leave you to yours' (Harvey, 2006: 32). This would at first appear to mimic the distinction made by both prominent capabilities approaches to separate functioning from capability in society.

However, Grotius is using sociability as a non-interventionist account of individual liberty. As long as conduct does not violate the preservation of a virtuous society, individuals are obligated (by God) to be virtuous people (kind, charitable and empathetic) but government serves only to ensure people can live this kind of life, not compel them to conduct in keeping with these ideal virtues. The political and legal obligation stops at ensuring the ability to be virtuous, not at enforcing what these virtuous behaviours require for conduct of them or others in positive terms, as these are liberties that one must feel and interpret to act upon. It is non-interventionalist in a compatible way to Nussbaum, but it is also non-facilitative in a way contrary to Nussbaum as social space is left free for people to use in ways in keeping with their nature to fulfil their sociability and dignity. Though Nussbaum argues that she is non-specific in the actions people undertake and is providing us with 'a partial and minimal account of social justice' (Nussbaum, 2006: 71), a point we will return to later, her list of capabilities does tell us the types of activities and intellectual, bodily and emotional opportunities individuals need to flourish. These are instrumentally used by Nussbaum to make judgements on action and inaction in the public sphere, which are expressly facilitative (see, e.g., Nussbaum, 2006: XII, 199–212). Grotius, instead, created commentary on many matters of law and juridical decision-making, but none that were prescriptive about how society must facilitate avenues of specific types to be coherently just to its own commitments to dignity and society.

It is worth noting here that Grotius may actually be far more minimal and partial in some key ways and equally that there is potentially ample room for criticism of him for not seeing a facilitative aspect of social behaviour. It is important, when seeking a historic precedent or form of argument, to present it as it stood, the good and the bad. Grotius does give us extensive argument as to why he holds specific positions.

Grotius believed that fundamental to law was the necessity of maintaining social order. Humanity, Grotius contends, possesses 'an impelling desire for society' (cited in Simmonds, 2002: 212). This desire to lead a sociable life is derived from divine design, to satisfy our material needs within society; and we are constrained by our lack of things to be more inclined to cultivate the social life. This is most clearly asserted in Grotius's earlier works[10] and in the early edition of his famous *De Jure Belli ac Pacis* ('The Law of War [Rights] and Peace', 1625). Here he writes that morally necessary acts must be 'understood as necessarily commanded or forbidden by God' (I.1.10.2).

However, even if we wanted for nothing, our nature would still lead us into mutual relations of society. Our material needs are there to encourage us to a social life. In this way, we have divine intentions for being naturally sociable and wanting to lead a social life (Simmonds, 2002: 212). Our dignity is a bipartite concept. It is fulfilled through society and the recognition of it by others but also exists as a divine concept saturated with meaning and obligation. This is not where Nussbaum starts her project. Dignity is presumed to be a point of convergence between people and hence the capabilities approach can use 'a freestanding moral argument to support its claims about the connection between capabilities and a life with human dignity' (Nussbaum, 2006: 370).

For Grotius, dignity itself does not determine our need for sociability; instead, it is the components of the self, endowed by the author of that nature, that exist to affirm a necessary and inviolable part of our dignity. Sociability is instead the residue of the discrete nature of our human condition. For Grotius, our possession of this nature is the individual metaphysical reason for being obligated to the claims that follow. This nature, limits and empowers equally our social understandings, prescriptions and structures. However, Grotius's troubled and fluctuating explanations of this nature cause these dependant claims to be extremely vague.

This notion of natural sociability and divine obligation is different from Aquinas. Grotius desired to move away from the teleological perfectionism of Thomistic natural law and appealed to the fact of human desires rather than the Neo-Aristotelian claim that we can only realise our true nature in society. He does not seek to determine what the best form of life or of government is. As Simmonds notes, Grotius 'seeks only to find a possible basis for shared social order.' (Simmonds, 2002: 213). It is easier to see the way in which this position may appeal to Nussbaum and others, but the shared order and sociability seek to fulfil a precise assumption as to the nature of humanity that serves to obligate disparate parties to fulfilling those obligations.

To understand Grotius's defence of this position, it is important to understand his context. A seventeenth-century Dutch natural law jurist personally vested in the religiously fuelled political turmoil in the Lowland Countries of Europe, Grotius postulated a reconsideration of natural law and issues of 'distributive justice' in a clear attempt to bring an increasingly splintered and contentious political environment together. Grotius's project, then, interrogates whether we can find a source of principles of justice and right that may bind human beings in general irrespective of their religious and political allegiances (Frykholm and Rutherford, 2013: 418).

On this account, Grotius saw a need to utilise the naturally social aspects of individuals' behaviour to legitimise new conceptions of property rights (famously in his *Mare Liberum*), reinterpretations of natural law and perhaps most notably a distinct argument for religious, cultural and social toleration to build political consensus in spite of deep metaphysical discrepancies between parties, and doing so without the advantage and rationalism arguments we see in other theories. It is this last factor that lends much to how a capabilities approach, such as Nussbaum's seeks to be grounded in human 'fellowship'. Nussbaum's application would on these grounds seem appropriate, but this would be to dismiss the deeper assumed commonality in the metaphysical accounts of the parties at hand, which are distinct interpretations of a common core that neither Grotius nor they would have disputed. This shared core creates the obligation in Grotius's project and leaves approaches without it, or assuming overlapping consensus to create it, grasping for a new form of obligation to replace it that comes not from what follows dignity, but from what proceeds it.

Most recently Hans W. Blom argues that in conjecture with his 'rudimentary theory of sociability' Grotius never really arrives at an answer to 'what commits men to the pursuit of justice' (Blom, 2014: 1). This might very well prove to be the case, in that his works never tie themselves together to solve their dichotomies and make their commitments *coherent*, a claim we could lodge against pretty much any philosopher. We can equally say that although Grotius's solution to this conundrum of what obliges us is not definitive, in Grotius it is still implied that man has an obligation to his nature endowed in all and dictated by God in the same way as the natural law. As Blom notes, 'Grotius achieved this context for sociability in phases, through a series of writings' (ibid.). Though these writings may not speak to what *does* commit human beings to justice, it does in places clearly state what *ought* to commit humans to justice. Grotius's own lack of retractions and changing strategies can be traced in his work, as Blom shows, and this seems to indicate Grotius's deep commitment to understanding, and explaining, what motivates individuals to create a better world for ourselves. He is ultimately writing about justice and attempting to motivate disparate parties in moving towards it. For this reason, it could equally be that he felt no need to explain a presupposition he knew they held to the parties he was addressing. Grotius's sense of capabilities is not rich. If a capabilities approach is what Grotius provided, he addressed a single capability, that of self-preservation, the constituency of which is autonomy and property. This solitary capability, if properly called, that is our lone obligation. It does not, however, follow from social cohesion, but instead from human nature. In this light, we might also say that many contractarians and deontological accounts of justice equally provide some account of 'capabilities'.[11]

This undertone of an implied God dictating human nature and breeding metaphysical commonality that dictates sociability and its value is conveniently jettisoned by reconstituted utilisations of Grotius that ignore his context. It is this that seems to have challenged his commentators over the years, and Grotius has been the subject of scholarly scrutiny, some purporting that he 'secularised' the natural law tradition (e.g. Tuck, 1999). The contention in such a move is that with a secularised account of interhuman obligation due to a social and collective nature, it would provide a strong universal applicability. One can, of course, be sympathetic with such endeavours given the philosophic rewards, but as we move on to show, as others have done, pushing Grotius in such a direction is unhelpful in understanding his position in totality.

Grotius, Sociability and the Impious Hypothesis

David Boucher has noted that the secularisation of the natural law tradition emphasised the need for a natural law in a theory of morality based upon natural rights. The purpose of the law of nations and civil law, then, was to protect and facilitate the free use of these rights (Boucher, 1998: 209). Grotius, like some of his medieval predecessors, has a conception of a right, or *ius*, as something we possess: it is a moral quality. Grotius argues that 'in this sense a right becomes a moral quality of a person, making it possible to have or to do something lawfully' (Grotius, 1925: I, 1, §iv). For Haakonssen, this is a main indicator of Grotius's move to secularising the tradition. In his words, Grotius's natural law theory has a secularising effect – or what we might call thin moral law. Haakonssen notes that honouring rights, perfect and imperfect, is for Grotius a good in itself, and although it is prescribed by God it is obligatory in itself. This means that the natural law is obligatory without God. On this line of reasoning then, for Grotius the natural law is morally insufficient in the sense that it only prescribes negative justice and not positive virtues and obligations (and hence no capabilities). Haakonssen then deduces that without the moral intervention of God into human life there is no moral community between the two. This is to be understood in the idea that although Grotius accepts the authorship of God, his conception of human sociability is such that God says nothing about the form of this sociability (Haakonssen, 1996: 30–33; 1985: 247–248).

However, for Grotius the natural law is self-evident, the proof of which is found in human sociability. In this sense, natural law is so inextricably tied to human nature that even if it were the case that God did not have an interest in the welfare of humanity, the law prescribing this welfare would remain valid:

> What we have been saying would have a degree of validity even if we should concede that which cannot be conceded without the utmost wickedness, that there is no God, or that the affairs of men are of no concern to Him. The very opposite of this view has been implanted in us partly by reason, partly by unbroken tradition, and confirmed by many proofs as well as by miracles attested by all ages.
>
> (Grotius, 1925: *Prolegomena*, §11)[12]

Regardless of the inundated role God plays in Grotius's political theory, the commitment to Him and to a natural law instilled in man by God is very much still at work; it is simply unspoken to avoid potential interpretational/hermeneutic issues at the very basis of religious rupture at the time. The character of man, to be X, Y and Z is one that comes from God, including being social and providing a non-interventionist or prescriptive social and political framework of social capability in respect of each other's dignity. Because the conduct within the state is not dictated, the state is tolerant of many kinds of conduct and allows this conduct so that people may find their path to virtue. One can be seduced by this natural fraternity implied in saying everyone should have room on the social playground to interact, but for Grotius it is an environment that exists only because God has dictated it. For those living in virtue, a virtue that presumably must be adhered to in order to receive eternal reward, humans are obligated by this dictate of God revealed in our nature as human beings. As Grotius notes in *On the Truth of the Christian Religion* ([1627] 2013):

> That since God has a Regard to human Actions, who is himself just; and yet these Things come to pass in the mean Time; we ought to expect a Judgement after this Life, lest either remarkable Wickedness should continue unpunished, or eminent Virtue go unrewarded and fail of Happiness.
>
> (I, Section XXI, 78)

God had instilled reason in man to make His will intelligible so that men could live according to His commandments, bestowing on them dignity, worth and the responsibility to participate in their own salvation.[13] The virtuous conduct underlying the demands of your own salvation is not something that can be dictated by explicit conduct or mandatory distributive schemes. We will return to this below when discussing Grotius's distributive justice theory. The point is that, without God and the coercive punishment to be levied on the soul, individuals would have no obligation to undertake the conduct of ensuring duties to themselves and others, social harmony and, hence, room for socialisation.

The dichotomies in divine authorship and the role of knowledge in knowing where obligations to justice come from that lead Blom, as we saw above, to this conclusion about Grotius's coherency, are not as incongruent as it would first appear. The strategy in part could have been to accede more to knowledge (historic, contemporary, social) and, as such, acknowledge that natural law continues to be revealed rather than sits in some static, stated form. Therefore, Grotius could have been appealing to it as a basic argument of obligation as the authorship exists, even if humanity is still reading the pages for the details small and large. Given that Grotius was writing from a position of seeking an outcome he thought was in some sense just, the practice of what he was doing would be futile without some sense of his own obligation to it, even if he sought not to be specific about what it meant for himself, his fellow citizens or states of the world.

One might want to say yes, this is what Grotius thought, but does his theory need to be read exclusively in these terms? The reason why God cannot be separated from Grotius's conceptualisation of the law of nature is not that a different metaphysical reason could be put in its place or overlap to form it, but rather that the content of the qualities he sees in why people socialise are the cornerstone of his project.

For Grotius, a specific god creates the attributes of man. It is the nature and understanding of this metaphysical force that creates the theories and ideas to follow for Grotius. They must adhere to this metaphysical concept of human nature. Replacing or secularising the concept changes its attributes, most notably why humans are obligated to protect, secure and act upon these naturally endowed aspects of humanity. God is the necessary and specific force that propels the project for Grotius, no matter how thinly or vaguely it is stated. Simply arriving at this point and working forward is to explain a play from the second act. All arguments of this type, Nussbaum's included, need the force of what comes prior to the point of socialisation, which is the content and not the mere concept of dignity, to have the obligations to social intervention that are desired. The social nature of man is not enough for Grotius or arguments like his to explain why we are bound by our existence to undertake it. Something else must be at play, and it is necessary and critical to the fruition of the argument.

As we have seen, Grotius utilises distinct levels and qualifiers on obligations which mean that different actions have different priorities. Though accounts in the field differ on this point (see Tuck, 1987, 1999; Haakonssen, 1996; Tierney, 2002; Simmonds, 2002), something has to do the work here to say that what is natural is what is good. Natural law theories, broadly construed, do this by saying that the nature of man, revealed through inspection, is God's design (however that might be asserted). Furthermore, this inspection, allowed through man's unique capability to reason and reason 'rightly', is also placed in man by God and has a perfect form. Violating this design and, by extension, man's nature, makes an action wrong. So it is wrong to violate man's social nature because of common design created by God, not just the common design itself. Common design alone would imply obligations to animals that share our social proclivities or, if we may be so bold, clear capabilities to reason in a non-idealised form. Nussbaum is quite clear in extending her project to encompass the treatment of animals and people unable to engage or express ideal reason or advantageous conduct. Some may find this a positive outcome of working from natural sociability forward, but even if God is removed from the equation, what Grotius is saying specifically about how sociability serves the good of human beings, as primary and in some degree based on ideal reason, cannot be escaped. An argument here as to why or how these would be replaced beyond observing man's social nature is requisite in creating actionable obligations, be they negative or positive, to act coercively through government and to extend them to the groups and species Nussbaum seeks to cover. Nussbaum does not engage with the question of *why* people are obligated to dignity when they may not agree what constitutes it, only *that* people are sociable through agreeing to its existence (and further in themselves and in others equally, that are all potentially rich claims) which will serve as a point of consensus in order to implement her account of capabilities. Grotius, on the other hand, does give us obligatory individual symmetry.

If we take seriously Grotius's conception of natural sociability and the nature he gives to the individuals who undertake it, we get an account of 'distributive justice' that is conspicuously non-interventionalist and 'thin'. That is, for Grotius, the rights we have to lead a virtuous life do not dictate explicit type of conduct or privilege or entitlement, nor is it exact what that virtuous life social or private might be. Benjamin Straumann, for instance, has observed that Grotius is sparse, negative and minimal rather than prescriptive in what people owe to one another in terms of social capacity (Straumann, 2015: 4).

Grotius's Idea of Attributive and Expletive Justice

In Grotius's justification of natural law, he allows the individual and states the right to intervene and take action against violators of said law. Grotius explains these rights in greater detail in his discussion of attributive and expletive justice. His argument for a moral right to punish arises out of his criticism of Aristotle. It is well known that Grotius seeks to distinguish between questions of entitlement and questions of worthiness or rights and aptitudes. Grotius notes 'when the moral quality is perfect we call it *facultas* … when it is not perfect, *aptitudo*' (Grotius, 1925: I, 1, §iv). For Grotius, rights are a matter of expletive justice in that they follow from the *basic* requirements of the social order. Aristotle is concerned with aptitudes in his account of distributive justice – which is directed towards those virtues which have as their purpose the good of others and society by making the best of oneself. The central point underlying this distinction between rights and aptitudes is Grotius's denial that juridical rights and duties, which bear some key similarities to Nussbaum's entitlements, are derived directly from the requirement of the common good. For Grotius, rights were in the domain of liberty – where one might pursue one's preferences – but they could not be seen as being directly related to the requirements of the common good, even if one understands Grotius to have a 'thicker' understanding of natural sociability (ibid.: §iv–ix; see also Simmonds, 2002: 216–224). This provides non-infringement at best, which at first blush appears congruent with capability facilitation instead of functioning facilitation, but we will return to this point.

In relation to attributive justice, Grotius argues that it is not true to say that all punishment comes from the whole to the part – that is, the individuals comprise society. The essence of punishment is to take into account its notion of aptitude, which by way of definition 'does not contain in itself right strictly so called, but furnishes an opportunity for it' (Grotius, 1925: II, 20, §ii). Here, some clarification is needed to discern the philosophical devices Grotius uses in his conception of distributive justice from any modern account we might want to draw from it. Samuel Fleischacker rightly notes that it is a misconception on the part of Jerome Schneewind and Knud Haakonssen that Grotius introduced a distinction between 'perfect' and 'imperfect' rights. Grotius does not use the word 'right' for his notion of aptitudes. Instead, Grotius wants to distinguish between perfect rights and moral claims that do not have the status of a right. Thus, the phrase 'perfect right' is redundant. Rather, it was Pufendorf who first distinguished between 'perfect' and 'imperfect' rights, claiming some sort of quasi legal status for the latter (Fleischacker, 2004: 139–140, fn. 16). Attributive justice, then, unlike expletive justice for Grotius, governs whatever is required by human law and satisfies the criteria of 'legal rights', addresses all 'those virtues which have as their purpose to do good to others, as generosity, compassion, and foresight in matters of government' (Grotius, cited in ibid.: 22).

Grotius also talks about 'rules of love', conceived within a Christian ethics model. As examples of what the 'rules of law' demand of us as acts expressing attributive justice, Grotius includes not harming innocent civilians in wartime, showing mercy to debtors who are needy, being honest when going into business ventures, sacrificing your life for your country, and the granting of legacies. Grotius's attributive justice goes beyond merely showing generosity to the poor, and as such is equivalent to social virtue in general (ibid.). Grotius asserts

> But from hence all that can be gathered is, that no subject is, by any Right strictly so called, obliged to this, but not that Charity permits him to do otherwise. For there are many Duties, not of strict Justice but of Charity, which are … very commendable.
>
> (Grotius, 1925: II, xxv, ii, 3)

Drawing on Aristotle, and the stoics, Grotius wants to say that because we have a duty to live a life of virtue in working to be the best we can be and providing the same effectively for others, these rights to lead a virtuous life do not dictate types of conduct, but rather focus on the development of elements of our character and ideal as being pre-conduct.

The 'rules of love', then, are more broadly conceived than 'rules of laws' and there is a basis to suggest that the law of love is equivalent to the demands of attributive justice. In developing this very point, Fleischacker astutely points out that Grotius's attributive justice relates intimately to social virtue in general, going beyond mere generosity to the poor. What is of particular interest is the claim that, for Grotius, this law of love is equivalent to the *Christian* conception of social virtue. This necessarily entails that the law of love cannot be mandatory, else it would cease to be love at all. Such demands can never be enforced in legal obligations. Such endless obligation, Fleischacker notes, cannot belong to justice in the strict sense. An enforcement mechanism cannot be attached as it is unjust to punish people for something they cannot do, as an endless obligation implied by ideal virtue can never fully be satisfied. Thus, the law of love is something that transcends human virtues and something we set alongside institutions of law. To impose the realm of virtues in the legal domain would go against what Christ demanded of his followers. For Grotius, then, generosity to the needy is not something that should be undertaken in law; rather, being a core example of attributive justice, it is something that goes beyond law (Fleischacker, 2004: 22–23).

To sum up, we have an obligation to commit to the demands of attributive justice, being the requirements of virtuous living. For Grotius it can never be part of explicit justice as this implies conduct rather than virtue and we cease to have the opportunity for virtuous Christian life. This is not a small conclusion when we take on the intuitions about the primacy of dignity, the role of sociability and the applications of care, compassion and guardianship that come from Nussbaum's argument that societies ought to 'cultivate sentiments' of benevolence. (Nussbaum, 2006: 412). As Nussbaum writes,

> The capabilities approach demands a great deal from human beings. It demands a great deal more from them than classical theories of the social contract, and somewhat more than Rawls demands of citizens in the Well-Ordered Society, although Rawls's demands are already very substantial. The solution to our three unsolved problems requires

> people to have very great sympathy and benevolence, and to sustain these sentiments over time.
>
> (Nussbaum, 2006: 410)

To do this, Nussbaum advocates that societies engage in 'social teaching' (Nussbaum, 2006: 413). Our rejoinder here is not to undermine the potential need or desirability of this presumption, though we can fairly question if didactic, narrative or instructive approaches do any more than form a horizon for the engaged rather than foster the sentiments, or if such an approach can be squared with her other intuitions about justice. Instead, it is to highlight how in conflict with Grotius this particular suggestion could be or if not clarified, worked through.

When these attributes exist in a state, they are still not actionable or obligatory in a coercive sense by the state as that would undermine their nature which is expressly discussed by Grotius.[14] No list of capabilities or concern with outcomes *in law* is possible in the way Nussbaum has formulated them even if he is likely to agree, in keeping with his metaphysical beliefs, that they are the right thing for individuals to do.

Where does this leave Nussbaum? Grotius presumed homogeneity in the authorship of dignity and thus it having an obligatory nature to individuals and others is the cornerstone of his sociability project. He is willing to accept plurality, but we have argued that it is implied this plurality and consensus happens in a specific frame of reference. His theory, by design, coincidence, or accident, treats obligation and justification as distinct in some sense that actions may be justified to an individual through some process of authentication that is multifaceted, but the obligation to fulfil these aspects of oneself and the self in others are not. One can justify an action beyond its obligations to oneself and others even if Grotius remains unclear and even inconsistent on why this is so, leading to much philosophic debate and historical recovery. His balancing between claims of obligation to specific sets of laws and concepts of justice, being divine, rational and social all in some measure, is an enduring question of his work and certainly provides a unique position in that he clearly sees all having a role in the formulation of justice in a way that is quite distinct for his era. A reduction of the comprehensiveness of natural law theory, a thicker role for society and a complex relationship of the individual utilising natural attributes to live a life of moral coherency make this an alluring theory in many ways.

However, we cannot escape the obligatory aspect of the dignity being asserted here in how it precisely makes claims about why we must be aware of our own complexity, the complexity of others and the larger social structures we implement. The consequences are seen in the pointed forms of intervention and toleration[15] Grotius sees in international law and the non-interventionist and negative aspects of rights that he expressly argues for (see, e.g., Blane and Kingsbury, 2010; Piirimäe, 2010). Grotius wants humans to pursue their own interests and preferences without intervention to preserve this complicated and socially rooted authentication process. Our obligation to dignity in ourselves and others leads us to a very specific position about the rights we recognise and systems of justice we seek to justify that looks significantly different from the one presented by Nussbaum. This is not to support Grotius on these points or to insinuate that his theories are not fraught with hanging questions, debates and inconsistencies. Nor do we seek you, the reader, to escape the claims of Grotius and Nussbaum as important and useful. However, our discussion here does raise serious questions about their congruency without some significant development and defence of contentious positions that run deep into comprehensive claims about dignity, human flourishing and our duties, natural and political, to facilitating and securing both.

Conclusion: Grotius-Inspired or Neo-Grotian?

What often goes amiss in contemporary recoveries of early modern political thought is its reliance on God as the author and *enforcer* of moral obligations. As such, we have to look at what God *does* for Grotius to give his claims force and obligation rather than simply looking at what they say about people and their nature. The institution of God makes natural law not just natural but obligatory. Though our ability to deny the natural law or act against it or the interests of mankind in some ways is possible, it is clear for Grotius these are wrong. Grotius may be unclear on who is to levy this punishment, to what degree and how we justify those claims in domestic (and international law), but the claim stands and comes inexorably from the authorship of God in writing what it is to be human. Our ability to deny an obligation does not subsequently imply that it does not exist. It makes the claims right and wrong but also builds the obligatory force individuals have to these concepts into them. Any overlap in consensus in what dignity is or how it is socially fulfilled, then, is in any case reflective of this obligation we all have to fulfil it in ourselves and others that Grotius presumes, overtly or tacitly, into the consensus on the concept of dignity. You do what is in keeping with human nature, particularly sociability and fellowship, not simply because it is natural but because failing to do these things in precise and understood ways violates God's natural law. God, then, is a coercive force behind the character and content of Grotius's theory and the power it was intended to have over humans because it specified sociability, intervention and punishment for violations of this natural obligation in ways distinct from Nussbaum's account of these matters. Nussbaum thus has no coercive force from a foundational or meta-ethical standpoint, because the punishment for not living up to the obligation to allow equal socialisation is only a violation of an undefined, undescribed and expressly non-Grotian account of what a human being is and why we are motivated in terms of obligation, rather than convergences of intuition, to act to ensure these aspects of human flourishing and capabilities.

Furthermore, it is clear that any assertion that a Grotian foundational argument and conception of natural sociability will legitimise the comprehensive list of capabilities and obligate societies to provide them for individual human persons is incompatible with the character, colour and content of Grotius's actual argument, which urges non-intervention because of the nature of the obligations we have to each other as individuals with a precise account of dignity in a shared society. We are left to ask whether an argument of Grotius's type can defend the kind of extrapolation Nussbaum presents. This too presents certain challenges as Nussbaum has taken it that sociability is natural to human beings or ensures their flourishing through a consensus that any concept of dignity requires, rather than explaining why all accounts of dignity will involve sociability and also obligate individuals to her concept of this sociability, social flourishing and individual political autonomy. This is not to say one approach is preferable to the other, just that they build their argument from fundamentally different presuppositions.

The Grotian concepts of what individuals and their social-rooting are may be reconstituted in a Neo-Grotian way if, and only if, some alternative form of pre-political obligation is built into their account of individual dignity and then is subsequently unpacked, explained and defended. In the philosophic account of the capabilities approach we have had presented so far, this unpacking is not present. It may have been the re-packing of this touchy subject that led Grotius into his own issues, confusions and position in the canon as, for all their shortcomings, contractarian approaches lacked this obligatory problem when 'secularising' their accounts of justice and society. It is an impasse Nussbaum herself faces in trying to lodge a partial and minimal account of social justice. We may seek to speak to a compartmentalised part of justice, but why and how it can be treated this way is ultimately the measure of its viability. A further lesson from Grotius may be that compartmentalising and minimising an argument for easier digestion in a plural situation leads to its own problems. Either these arguments are there and require defence or their lack of articulation allows individuals to read unintended meanings or contrary prescriptions, or even to reject outright, as incomplete or inconsistent, what such a theory says about justice.

Furthermore, Grotius does not draw sociability to encompass the broad forms of flourishing that Nussbaum and other capability theories advocate, nor does he affirm an enforcement device implied by socialisation itself, actual or philosophic, to ensure human flourishing through specific capabilities. Grotius was himself deeply concerned with the nature of obligations to act, coerce and punish that we have to ourselves, other citizens and international actors. As we have shown, this concern ultimately is cautionary, erring on the side of non-intervention and negative liberty. The reason for this is that the aforementioned constituency of the dignity afforded to social agents directly informs the socialisation that is seen as natural by Grotius. His position is one that is neither 'thick' in what it wants for human flourishing or the duties and conducts individuals and states have to provide, enable or protect it, nor is it 'thin' enough to leave such decisions about what makes individuals obligated to honour and secure a particular form of dignity to overlapping consensus. Though we may fairly say this is a real shortcoming for Grotius in light of the way Nussbaum has argued that negative approaches cannot provide dignity to all who deserve it, it is certainly unfair to say that Grotius *did support* as opposed to *should have supported* a capabilities list of some type.

It is here that we wish to sympathise with Nussbaum and her project of bringing these issues into the scope of these discussions and hope she will take our critique as a constructive attempt to ask her for more rather than an attempt to tear down what could in some way be defended. The authors of this chapter can relay the troubling inability of liberalism and some of those who research within it to realise these limitations or feel they have any force or relevancy to their work. They do. The outcomes we see for the disabled, women, minority groups, international inequalities, animals and elements of the environment are unjust and not simply remedied by moving piles of money or empowering these groups in ways that only further entrench their absence from the societies that made the structures to which they have access. It is this importance, however, that begs us not to leave an argument like this one as incomplete or 'partial', and in doing so not to give it the force it ought to have in some sense in how we envision justice. Working to change outcomes and seeing philosophy's role in motivating those changes are important contributions. In working to address a conclusion, we must be aware of the limitation this places on what we say as much as starting from a specific moral or meta-ethical claim does. How we motivate our remedies of outcomes of present thought and policy are as important, even if they are hard or difficult to assess. We use them in building our projects and as such it is important to put them on display in some unified form if we are to build projects with the force they need to have. Avoiding these discussions, does not avoid the criticisms that can be levied against a political theory; instead, it allows the theory to be dismissed or ignored for implying or omitting an aspect of obligation that has not been addressed or displayed and is, or has to be, at work. Grotius himself faces this problem, which is an aspect of Neo-Grotian recovery that ought to concern us. We may fairly become Nussbaumians/Cravenites, if that were in fact a position we were given to digest why it obligates us to a specific form of dignity, sociability and capabilities. Simply because we pose a critique of how Grotian that position may ultimately be does not mean that it would be better or worse than that account if it were presented in totality. To draw a constellation of justice is a matter of explaining and defending all the parts of the practice, lest we leave our work unfinished to our fellow observer even if we see a single or set of lines and stars as the most important ones to connect.

Whether one ascribes to the intuitive power of the capabilities approach in the face of the shortcomings other approaches may have, it does not excuse the need for a foundational explanation of humanity that not only describes the nature of human dignity but equally obligates individuals and states to the actions we find intuitively appealing within the capabilities approach. This is the lesson from Grotius, no matter how well or poorly he accomplished it himself. Why people are social, what that concept means and why it obligates us are as, if not more, important than simply arriving at the point of consensus or convergence that social structures allow people to flourish, fulfil their dignity and occur naturally. It is the hard work of political theory, but it is necessary even if pragmatically the capabilities approach is replacing policy approaches that are, at best, impoverished. We can equally claim that is the lack of an obligatory aspect to individuals (or collectives given moral autonomy/recognition) that makes the legal standards in international and domestic law toothless. Their violation is lamentably rampant, repeated and undeniable. Treaties, further cited by Nussbaum as an example of normative consensus building, are by their very nature advantage-based, which presumably makes them subject to her already stated critique of such approaches (Nussbaum, 2006: 243; 260–261; 316).

It is in this light that the convergence Nussbaum sees with forms of contractarianism is far more concerning to accepting her approach that would first appear. Contractarians express claims about human beings, and what fulfils their autonomy, that may be troubled but that give the reader, the advocate and even the policy maker a stated non-dogmatic meta or existential account of individual autonomy and obligations to it to reflect upon, which will motivate political and social structures that encompass distinct individuals and their conceptions of the good. This is not to say that Nussbaum's scepticism in the atomised account of flourishing is without merit. These kinds of accounts, as Nussbaum herself notes, have great issues in their scope, prescriptiveness and depth which have caused issues not just philosophically but in how governments and international entities approach the needs and rights of human beings and the natural world when they present divergent needs and perspectives. If we look at what is actually lost when perspectives are absent from society (both for the individuals or beings or objects who hold or present them and for the society and individuals who subsequently lack them to engage with)[16] we could look at Nussbaum's theory in a different light, as a way of illuminating the values of arrangement in the contract/agreement device rather than a refutation of the device itself to do something important in creating the obligations we have to these values.

If Nussbaum truly believes the device to be deficient in deriving political obligations, then how her various positions can be placed together to accomplish individual obligations is requisite regarding the collective obligations that consensus or something else will always provide in the liberal/ autonomy-valuing, socially rooted and care-driven way she advocates. Exploring the Grotian claims of the debate makes this need clear in certain ways that are helpful in understanding how historical recapturing is difficult and may conceptually undermine an argument rather than support it, if significant and pointed defence of its specific interpretation is not presented.

Sociability may be natural to human beings, but societies are structured in the image of the individuals they serve. The balancing of how these elements feed into each other has challenged philosophers for millennia, Grotius and Nussbaum being only two examples. Societies observably change and morph, which is the residue of individuals willing their perceptions into social realities. Allowing people to access these structures and institutions of society is only part of a question of how they are justly constructed, and likely not the primary one. Foundational arguments are requisite to creating the motivation for undertaking the political ideas, structures, principles and subsequent institutions that are built upon them. In Grotius, we find that necessity – that is, that you can have a principle of 'moral intervention' in violations of the natural law (even though no enforcement mechanism is necessarily attached) – is clearly what appeals to Nussbaum. However, this notion of 'moral intervention' in Grotius does not end up being mere moral intuitions about what is right and wrong, because ultimately God provides its obligatory force for Grotius by exercising a punishment or reward on the metaphysical aspect of people who uphold or violate the natural law: free to be evil but never free of the punishment of that choice. This is not how we would, of course, suggest grounding such a project but something must provide this force as it did for Grotius, inclusive of secularised accounts of this type for Nussbaum. We would not only welcome this kind of contribution by Nussbaum to strengthen her position, the intuitive power of her argument and her proscriptions for policy makers, but we would argue that it is needed to ensure that her theory of justice, no matter how 'partial and minimal', is not eroded and left on the sidelines of a debate in which it firmly and absolutely deserves marque status.

Notes

1 'Entitlements' have a long historical tradition and baggage which it is important to note here are not expressly intended to be conveyed as part of the term when Nussbaum uses it. She does address in various places the historical use and its troubling background. They are in the capabilities sense better understood as things people owe to each other (physically, conceptually and protectively) as dignified social actors.

2 Here, Nussbaum also writes that she intends to develop Grotius in her political thought.

3 Nussbaum mentioned many aspects of legal precedents in domestic (state-specific) applications, such as the Americans with Disabilities Act (Nussbaum, 2006: 199), and rights treaties/agreements at the international level such as the Universal Declaration of Human Rights by the United Nations (Nussbaum, 2006: 248). We will return to some of these discussions later in the chapter.

4 Amartya Sen is a Nobel Laureate, Thomas W. Lamont University Professor and Professor of Economics and Philosophy at Harvard University and perhaps the best known advocate of the capabilities approach within international political development. The authors would like to extend Professor Sen and his faculty assistants present (Chie) and past for their assistance in attaining lists of and handicap-accessible versions of Professor Sen's work, particularly his 2009 work *Ideas of Justice*.

5 There have been attempts to square Nussbaum's project with a Grotian foundation. An example of this is Jeffrey Spring (2010). It is our contention that this particular attempt to extract a Grotian rights theory from the rest of his discourse is unconvincing as it utilises the argument without fully taking into account the obligatory aspect of Grotius's thought in giving content and character to his theory of rights and larger arguments about justice.

6 In May 2015 (after the proof deadline for this chapter) Nussbaum is scheduled to release an introduction on Rawls in *Rawls's Political Liberalism*, edited by Thom Brooks and Martha C. Nussbaum, that appears (from the pre-release notes) to have added elaboration on the ideas of Rawls and overlapping consensus which we are unable to appraise or for which we are unable to retrieve an ADA compliant copy at this time. As this is an element of Rawls that Nussbaum expressly uses, this exposition is likely to be important and enlightening, particularly in how she sees the concept and its viability in her project. However, for our purposes here, the consensus on dignity is not going to be enough as we argue in looking specifically at Grotius that he will seek specific individual obligatory aspects to the concept that consensus alone is not guaranteed and potentially unlikely to supply adequately. Furthermore, in our initial searching of the text, Grotius was not extensively addressed in this work.

7 Nussbaum's primary point of contact with disability tends to be related to mental and cognitive impairment in *Frontiers of Justice*, but even more starkly in her previous work. She shares dialogues that are deeply personal in one case and the expressions of other authors in others, that collectively and exquisitely capture the depth and value of social interaction for both the disabled and 'normal'/typically embodied individuals. Though she does make contact with the potential difficulties of expanding the observations of one form of disability into others, it is a complex issue in need of exhaustive examination particularly when other critical genres of thought are used to assess and empower a group the critique was not designed explicitly to approach (see Matthew C. Murray, forthcoming).

8 The medical vs social approach to defining disability and the subsequent effect on means or resources and the justness of these outcomes is an area of great and needed debate in legal, philosophic and political circles.

9 Grotius's claim that human nature contains both the urges associated with self-interest and sociability has not achieved a consensus on whether one inclination has a primacy over another in Grotian scholarship (see Tuck, 1999; Tierney, 2002).

10 The source of our obligations, how they are prescribed by the law of nature and why we are obliged to act on them is a long-standing debate between voluntarism and intellectualism, which medieval philosophers such as William of Ockham and St Thomas Aquinas attempt to reconcile in their thought. The early modern thinkers of the seventeenth century equally attempt to avoid the implication that the content of natural law is arbitrary, and Grotius is no exception here. Giving a full account of this debate is no easy task. No one thinker adopted either of the positions in their simple or pure forms. Painting with a broad brush, it can be said that voluntarism is the position from which moral standards are derived from the divine will, whereas intellectualists believed that divine will was determined or guided by independent standards. For the voluntarist, God is the absolute power, and His actions should not be explained or rationalised. The good is good because God has willed it. By an act of will God created morality. For the intellectualist, the good is willed by God in recognition of its intrinsic goodness (see Simmonds, 2002).

11 In discussions of an early draft of this chapter, Hans W. Blom adroitly helped us refine our perspective and expression of this important aspect of Grotius's thought. We would like to thank him for his generous attention and

response. As it was already in proofing stage, we were unable to incorporate more responses into the chapter but we felt the point noted here is a point of common ground we share with Hans Blom who expressed it so clearly, we felt it benefited the reader immensely to include it into the dialogue.

12 This is the contested passage which scholars use to place Grotius as the scholar who spearheaded a secular natural law. The origin of the contested passage, as Brian Tierney explains, is to be found in the 'common topos of late scholastic discourse and that Grotius could have picked it up from Suárez or from any one of half a dozen sixteenth-century authors' (Tierney, 1997: 319–320). Instead, Grotius's impious hypothesis, rather than giving credence to a new foundation for the natural law, locates him instead in the long-running debate within Christian theocentric natural law writing, which highlighted the two positions of voluntarism and intellectualism (see note 10). Here, Grotius takes the middle position of the two. Those who seek to defend Grotius's originality – that the Grotian natural law has a new and somewhat secular character – will not find the impious hypothesis a fruitful avenue to pursue. Rather, the impious hypothesis instead begs the question of whether Grotius was an intellectualist. Pufendorf certainly interpreted Grotius as one (see also Simmonds, 2002: 219–220).

13 As an Arminian Calvinist Grotius affirmed the freedom of the human will, and thereby rejected the religious predestination determinism which ruled orthodox Calvinism of his time. For a good discussion on this see Bryner and Vetterli, 1993). In the theological dispute between Remonstrants (followers of Jacobus Arminius) Calvinists, Grotius found himself on the losing side and was arrested in 1618 and subsequently sentenced to life imprisonment in Loevestein Castle (from which he would later escape).

14 This is analogous to Grotius's notion of what duties and rights states have. In fact, the object of Grotius's exercise of natural law was to find international rules basic or useful, though not clearly consented to by states, as we identify with modern general principles of law (Janis, 2003: 60–61). For Grotius's international justice system, we see that the moral requirements that arise from human natural sociability cannot furnish states with absolute obligations to intervene when the natural law is grossly violated, precisely because such obligations are not 'thick' enough. This is why he talks of states' or sovereigns' *rights* to punish and not obligations as such. For this reason, obligations to punish crimes for breaches of the natural law on humanitarian grounds stand on much weaker foundations. What we can derive from the idea of aptitudes is the issue of appropriation and proportionality. Nature cannot determine to whom punishment is directly appropriated, which remains at the core of Grotius's idea of enforcement: 'For Reason declares that the criminal may be punished. It does not, however, declare who ought to inflict the punishment' (Grotius, 1925: II, 20 §iii; see also Boisen, 2013: 77).

15 The issue of 'Toleration' within Grotius, and the natural law tradition is debated. Our emphasis here is that precise treatments of toleration can cast its value in a specific light. These interpretations may be at odds with a specific reading of Grotius or natural law theories more broadly on the subject, but equally, if congruent with them, may still not be motivated by a concern for diversity and toleration as a social good, but that deviant behaviour can act socially to reinforce or buttress conceptions of the good, making toleration an instrumental aspect of justice by revealing imbalances in social order, rather than holding a deeper social or normative value. On the idea of toleration and the natural law see, for instance, Parkin and Stanton, 2013. More specifically on the emerging idea of toleration in the Dutch republic and in Grotius's writing, see Israel, 1997.

16 Disability poses a distinct challenge to political philosophy as it is identified as a group with a social and physical make-up but lacks the experiential symmetry

of many if not all other social minorities. The claim expressed and not exhaustively defended here is likely to be the crux of the position stating the thin identity of disability and the challenges it poses when considering social inclusion (see Matthew C. Murray, forthcoming).

References

Blane, A. and Kingsbury, B. (2010), 'Punishment and the *ius post bellum*', in B. Kingsbury and B. Straumann (eds), *The Roman Foundations of the Law of Nations: Alberico Gentili and the Justice of Empire*, Oxford: Oxford University Press, pp. 241–265.

Blom, Hans W. (2015), 'Sociability and Hugo Grotius', *History of European Ideas*, 41 (5): 589–604.

Boisen, C. (2013), 'Subjecting international relations to the law of nature: a neglected aspect of the early modern jurists and Edmund Burke', *Theoria*, 60 (134): 69–90.

Boucher, D. (1998), *Political Theories of International Relations: From Thucydides to the Present*, Oxford: Oxford University Press.

Boucher, D. (2009), *The Limits of Ethics in International Relations: Natural Law, Natural Rights and Human Rights in Transition*, Oxford: Oxford University Press.

Bryner, Gary C. and Vetterli, Richard (1993), 'Hugo Grotius and natural law: a reinterpretation', *The Political Science Reviewer*, 22 (1): 370–402.

Comim, Flavio, Qizilbash, Mozaffar and Alkire, Sabina (eds) (2010), *The Capability Approach: Concepts, Measures and Applications*, Cambridge: Cambridge University Press.

Finnis, J. (1980), *Natural Law and Natural Rights*, Oxford: Clarendon Press.

Fleischacker, S. (2004), *A Short History of Distributive Justice*, Cambridge, MA: Harvard University Press.

Frykholm, Erin and Rutherford, Donald (2013), 'Hedonism and virtue', in Peter R. Anstey (ed.), *The Oxford Handbook of British Philosophy in the Seventeenth Century*, Oxford: Oxford University Press, pp. 416–441.

Grotius, H. ([1627] 2013), *On the Truth of the Christian Religion: In Six Books*, corrected and illustrated with notes by Mr Le Clerc, London: H. Balwin & Son.

Grotius, H. (1925), *On the Law of War and Peace, Three Books* [*De Jure Belli ac Pacis*, 1625], introduced by James Brown Scott, translated by Francis W. Kelsey, Oxford: Clarendon Press.

Grotius, H. (2005), *On the Law of War and Peace* [*De Jure Belli ac Pacis*], Jean Barbeyrac 1738 edition], Indianapolis: Liberty Fund.

Haakonssen, K. (1985), 'Hugo Grotius and the history of political thought', *Political Theory*, 13 (2) (May): 239–265.

Haakonssen, K. (1996), *Natural Law and Moral Philosophy: From Grotius to the Scottish Enlightenment*, Cambridge: Cambridge University Press.

Harvey, M. (2006), 'Grotius and Hobbes', *British Journal for the History of Philosophy* 14 (1): 27–50.

Israel, Jonathan (1997), 'The intellectual debate about toleration in the Dutch republic', in C. Berkvens-Stevelinck, J. Israel and G. H. M. Posthumus Meyjes (eds), *The Emergence of Tolerance in the Dutch Republic*, Leiden: Brill, pp. 3–36.

Janis, M. W. (2003), *An Introduction to International Law*, fourth edn, New York: Aspen Publishers.

Murray, Matthew C. (forthcoming), 'Subaltern? Disability as a critical theory of justice' (working title).

Nussbaum, M. (1990), *Love's Knowledge: Essays on Philosophy and Literature*, Oxford: Oxford University Press.

Nussbaum, Martha C. (2001), *Upheavals of Thought: The Intelligence of Emotions*, Cambridge: Cambridge University Press.

Nussbaum, Martha C. (2004a), *Hiding from Humanity: Disgust, Shame, and the Law*, Princeton: Princeton University Press.

Nussbaum, Martha C. (2004b). 'Beyond the social contract: capabilities and global justice' (an Olaf Palme Lecture, delivered in Oxford on 19 June 2003), *Oxford Development Studies*, 32 (1) (March).

Nussbaum, Martha C. (2006), *Frontiers of Justice: Disability, Nationality, Species Membership*, Cambridge, MA: The Belknap Press of Harvard University Press.

Nussbaum, Martha C. (2011), *Creating Capabilities: The Human Development Approach*, Cambridge, MA: Harvard University Press.

Nussbaum, Martha C. (2015), 'Flawed foundations: the philosophical critique of (a particular type of) economics', in Aristides N. Hatzis and Nicholas Mercuro (eds), *Law and Economics: Philosophical Issues and Fundamental Questions*, New York: Routledge, pp. 16–31.

Parkin, Jon and Stanton, Timothy (eds) (2013), *Natural Law and Toleration in the Early Enlightenment*, Oxford: Oxford University Press/British Academy.

Piirimäe, P. (2010), 'Alberico Gentili's doctrine of defensive war and its impact on seventeenth-century normative views', in B. Kingsbury and B. Straumann (eds), *The Roman Foundations of the Law of Nations: Alberico Gentili and the Justice of Empire*, Oxford: Oxford University Press, pp. 187–209.

Pogge, T. (2002), *World Poverty and Human Rights: Cosmopolitan Responsibilities and Reforms*, Cambridge: Polity Press.

Rawls, John (1999), *A Theory of Justice – Revised Edition*, Cambridge, MA: Harvard University Press.

Rawls, John (2001a), *The Law of Peoples and the Idea of Public Reason Revisited*, Cambridge, MA: Harvard University Press.

Rawls, John (2001b), *Justice as Fairness – A Restatement*, edited by Erin Kelly, Cambridge, MA: The Belknap Press of Harvard University Press.

Sen, Amartya (1992), *Inequality Re-examined*, Cambridge, MA: Harvard University Press.

Sen, Amartya (1999), *Development as Freedom*, New York: Alfred A. Knopf.

Sen, Amartya (2009), *The Idea of Justice*, Cambridge, MA: The Belknap Press of Harvard University Press.

Simmonds, N. E. (2002), 'Grotius and Pufendorf', in Steven Nadler (ed.), *A Companion to Early Modern Philosophy*, Oxford: Blackwell, pp. 216–224.

Straumann, B. (2015), *Roman Law in the State of Nature – The Classical Foundations of Hugo Grotius' Natural Law*, Cambridge: Cambridge University Press.

Spring, J. (2010), 'The Grotian rights tradition and the capabilities approach', *Science et Esprit*, 62 (2–3): 275–291.

Tierney, B. (2002), *The Idea of Natural Rights: Studies on Natural Rights, Natural Law and Church Law 1150–1625*, Cambridge: William. B. Eerdmans Publishing.

Tuck, R. (1987), 'The "modern" theory of natural law', in Anthony Pagden (ed.), *The Languages of Political Theory in Early-Modern Europe*, Cambridge: Cambridge University Press, pp. 99–119.

Tuck, R. (1999), *The Rights of War and Peace: Political Thought and the International Order from Grotius to Kant*, Oxford: Oxford University Press.

6 Care Ethics and Distributive Justice

Daniel Engster

Introduction

What should a distributive justice theory aim to distribute? In 'Equality of what?' (1980), Amartya Sen took up this question in a particularly fruitful way. Starting out from the assumption that any meaningful account of distributive justice must invoke some notion of equality, he divided distributive justice theories into three main categories: those that aim to equalise individual utility or welfare, those that aim to equalise resources, and those that aim to equalise capabilities. Highlighting the limitations of welfare- and resource-based approaches, he suggested that the capabilities approach more fully captures widely held intuitions about what a distributive justice theory should distribute than these other theories. In arguing this way, Sen launched the capabilities approach as an important new perspective in philosophical debates about distributive justice.

Sen's essay spawned an important new literature about the nature of distributive justice and the adequacy of resource-, welfare- and capabilities-based theories. Meanwhile, in the years these distributive justice debates were taking shape, a new moral and political theory was emerging: care ethics. Care ethics was originally formulated as an alternative to rule-bound and abstract ethical theories. Early care theorists such as Carol Gilligan (1982) and Nel Noddings (1984) defined it as personal ethic concerned primarily with meeting the needs of others in particular and contextual ways. A second generation of care theorists nevertheless extended care ethics beyond personal relations to political theory, and today there exists a rich literature on care ethics and justice (Engster, 2007; Engster and Hamington, 2015; Held, 2006; Kittay, 1999; Tronto, 1993, 2013). Yet care ethics remains on the margins of debates about the proper aims of distributive justice. Very few care theorists have directly engaged with mainstream distributive justice debates (see, however, Gheaus, 2005, 2009a, 2009b), and recent surveys of major distributive justice theories (Brighouse and Robeyns, 2010) hardly mention care ethics at all.

This chapter situates care ethics in relation to mainstream distributive justice debates. It offers answers the following questions: Can care ethics plausibly be framed as a distributive justice theory? If so, what exactly does it suggest we should distribute? How does it differ from other distributive justice frameworks? What, if any, are its unique merits?

The value of my argument is twofold. First, by bringing care ethics into more direct conversation with mainstream political philosophy, I hope to increase awareness and appreciation of this theory. One reason care ethics has been overlooked in distributive justice debates is because so few care theorists have been willing to frame their arguments in distributive justice terms. Some theorists have even suggested that care ethics cannot plausibly be understood as a distributive justice theory (Gheaus, 2005, 2009a, 2009b; Noddings, 1984; White, 2000: 72–73, 88–93). As I hope to show in this chapter, this is not the case. Care ethics can be faithfully translated into the language of distributive justice and set alongside resource-based theories, welfare-based theories and capabilities theories as a unique approach to distributive justice. Second, my argument also aims to demonstrate the merits of care ethics as a distributive justice theory. My intention is to show that care ethics offers a more intuitively plausible and satisfying answer to the question 'What should a distributive justice theory aim to distribute?' than other distributive justice theories. The implication of my argument is that distributive justice should be re-oriented around care or, at the very least, that care should become much more of a focal point of distributive justice theories than it is at present.

I begin by briefly describing the three major approaches to distributive justice and some of the standard criticisms of them.[1] I do not pretend to provide here a comprehensive review of all the possible criticisms and defences of all the various distributive justice theories but merely to summarise the general contours of the debate so that care ethics can be situated within it. I next turn to characterise care ethics and compare it with other distributive justice theories. Care ethics is unique in comparison with other distributive justice theories because it aims to distribute care which is a complex entity encompassing resources, welfare, capabilities and relational values. In the third section, I argue for the importance of care as a distributive good and refute the contention that care cannot be the proper subject of distributive justice. In the final section, I highlight some of the theoretical and practical advantages that care ethics enjoys over other distributive frameworks.

This chapter is suggestive more than anything else. Just as Sen introduced the capabilities approach into distributive justice debates by highlighting certain advantages it enjoys over other distributive justice frameworks, I hope to do the same for care ethics here. Much work nonetheless remains to be done on the subject of care ethics and distributive justice.

Three Theories of Distributive Justice

Theories of distributive justice necessarily rest on some claim about the proper subject of distribution. Before there can be any meaningful discussion about standards of distribution (desert, choice, effort, need), the subject of distribution needs first to be decided. In contemporary political debates, most distributive justice theories define the subject of distributive justice in terms of one of three goods: resources, welfare or capabilities. The most obvious subjects for distribution are resources or primary goods. In fact, all theories of distributive justice distribute some resources or primary goods. The distinguishing feature of resource-based justice theories is that they treat resources or primary goods as the main subject of distribution and, at least when measuring the justice of a distributive arrangement, as ends in themselves.

John Rawls (1999) and Ronald Dworkin (2000) are the two most famous proponents of resource-based approaches to distributive justice. Rawls argued that a just society should aim for a fair distribution of primary goods, consisting of rights, liberties, opportunities, income, wealth and self-respect (1999: 54). Dworkin claimed that the main subject of distributive justice should be external resources, including material resources, occupations and liberties. Neither Rawls nor Dworkin favoured a completely equal distribution of resources. Rawls claimed that primary goods should be distributed in a manner supportive of his two principles of justice, which allow for some inequality as long as it does not interfere with liberty or equal opportunity and benefits the least advantaged. Dworkin argued that a just distribution of resources should be sensitive to inequalities in natural endowments and individual choices (2000: 81). Individuals with unequal natural abilities should be compensated for their 'fewer resources' through an insurance scheme, by his account, but individuals who experienced resource inequalities as a result of their preferences and ambitions should be held responsible for them. He ultimately suggested that an ideal distribution of resources would be one that could pass the envy test, meaning no one would prefer someone else's bundle of resource to their own. Like Rawls, Dworkin nonetheless defended resources, broadly understood, as the proper subject of distributive justice.

There are some clear advantages to orienting a justice theory around resources: above all, they are easy to distribute and measure. Sen and others have nevertheless highlighted a number of shortcomings of resource-based distributive justice theories. The main complaint is that resource distribution does not get at what we really care about in matters of justice. If people were basically the same, Sen notes, an index of primary goods might be a good way of judging justice. 'But, in fact, people seem to have very different needs varying with health, longevity, climatic conditions, location, work conditions, temperament, and even body size (affecting food and clothing requirements)' (1980: 215–216). Simply to distribute resources and be done with it fails to account adequately for the diversity of persons, their circumstances and their varying abilities to convert resources into other valuable goods. It fetishises resources rather than focusing on their effects on persons or what people can do with them. At an extreme, a resource-based theory of justice might conceivably regard some distribution of resources as just even if some individuals remained exposed to harm due to their inability to effectively convert resources into utilities. This is true even of Dworkin's theory, which compensates individuals for any 'handicaps' they may have with cash payments based on the average insurance policies that prudent individuals would purchase to protect themselves against various disadvantages. His insurance market solution does nothing to ensure that these average benefits are adequate to meet the needs of all individuals and fails to consider the possibility that disabled individuals might want something other than financial compensation (e.g. social accommodations) to make up for living in a social environment that devalues their particular endowments.

Defenders of resource-based approaches have retorted that it is possible to calibrate resources to many of the differences among people (Pogge, 2010). But this response misses the point. The critique here is not so much that resource-based theories are not precise and flexible enough. It is that one needs to look beyond resources when measuring justice. Even supposing a resource-based theory did distribute resources in a finely tuned way, we would still want to look to welfare, capabilities or some other outcome to see if resource distribution was finely tuned enough. Resource distribution by itself is a rather cold and impersonal way of thinking about justice; it does not pay sufficient attention to whether resource distributions actually benefit individuals in the ways they are implicitly intended to do.

Welfare-based theories of distributive justice avoid the fetishism of resource-based theories by measuring justice in terms of human well-being – most usually defined by contemporary philosophers as individual preference satisfaction. Resources are valuable from this perspective only instrumentally for the contribution they make to individual welfare. Because welfare-based theories focus on what people actually do with the resources available to them, they account better for the diversity of persons and circumstances than resource-based theories. They also measure justice directly in terms of people's well-being rather than the resources available to them, which seems intuitively more important (Sen, 1980: 216). In these respects, welfarist theories enjoy important advantages over resource-based theories.

There are, however, a number of drawbacks to welfarist theories (Cohen, 1990: 360–361; Dworkin, 2000; Sen, 1980). Inasmuch as welfarist theories are committed to equally satisfying the subjective preferences of different individuals, it follows that individuals with expensive tastes (e.g. drinking champagne and taking helicopter rides) should be entitled to a larger share of resources than those with cheap preferences (e.g. drinking tap water and taking walks). Alternatively, individuals with easy-going and naturally jolly dispositions might receive very little under welfarist schemes – even if living in hovels and lacking adequate food – because of their innate happiness and naturally high level of welfare. The happy and content Tiny Tim might receive less under a welfarist scheme than the perpetually discontent and greedy Scrooge (Dworkin, 2000: 60). Because of these problems, welfarist theories are often said to be an inadequate guide to just distribution. Some non-subjective standard seems necessary to guide our thinking about which preferences deserve or do not deserve support.[2]

Sen summarises his criticisms of resourcist and welfarist justice theories in the following way:

> Primary goods suffers from the fetishist handicap in being concerned with goods … rather than with what these good things *do* to human beings. Utility, on the other hand, *is* concerned with what these things do to human beings, but uses a metric that focuses not on the person's capabilities but on his mental reaction. There is something still missing in the combined list of primary goods and utilities.
>
> (1980: 218)

What is missing from resourcist and welfarist theories, according to Sen, is 'basic capabilities'. We should be concerned, Sen argues, not so much with the resources a person has or how fully his or her preferences are satisfied as with his or her ability (or capabilities) to do certain important things (218). The capabilities approach moves beyond both resourcist and welfarist theories by shifting attention from resources in themselves and individuals' subjective preferences to how resources can help individuals to achieve some objectively specified goods. 'A person's "capability",' Sen writes (1999: 75), 'refers to the alternative combinations of functionings that are feasible for her to achieve.'

Relevant capabilities have to be specified, of course, before the capabilities approach has any traction. There are otherwise simply too many capabilities that human beings might exercise, most of which do not matter from a moral perspective (Arneson, 2010). Sen (1999) notes the importance of some basic capabilities such as being nourished, sheltered, educated and healthy, but generally maintains that people should define for themselves the capabilities that matter to them through participatory public discussions. Martha Nussbaum (2000, 2006), by contrast, has produced a list of ten capabilities that she claims has universal applicability, including life, health, protection, sensation and imagination, emotion, practical reason, artistic expression, religious freedom and affiliation, living with concern for plants, animals and nature, and having political and economic control over one's environment.

The capabilities approach is unique because, as G. A. Cohen (1990: 368) observes, it captures something 'which had, amazingly, been largely neglected in previous literature': it focuses on what goods can do for persons apart from their personal evaluations of them. Yet it, too, runs up against some problems. Some critics have questioned whether capability should really be the ultimate aim of justice. Richard Arneson (2006: 32) asks us to imagine a case where providing some capability to some individual is expensive and the capability, if provided, would certainly yield nothing valuable for the person because it would be ignored, wasted or mishandled. If it is known that a capability will never be used, Arneson asks, why should we trouble ourselves to provide it, particularly when the available resources might be used to promote some other capabilities. If resource-based theories fetishise resources, the capabilities approach can similarly be said to fetishise capabilities. It prioritises capabilities over persons.

The capabilities approach likewise tends to stigmatise individuals who fail to achieve the objectively designated capabilities (for a related argument, see Pogge, 2010: 46–48). Nussbaum writes, for example, that if any person is for any reason incapable of achieving at least a threshold level of any of the ten capabilities – say, because of severe cognitive or physical disabilities – their life must be deemed 'a tragedy' or at least 'extremely unfortunate' and 'unhappy' (2000: 83; 2006: 192–193). She even notes at one point (2000: 73, emphasis added) that

> at one extreme, we may judge that the absence of capability for a central function is so acute that the person is *not really a human being at all*, or any longer – as in the case of certain very severe forms of mental disability, or senile dementia.

In order to avoid allowing anyone to exist in a sub-human state, Nussbaum argues that we must 'work tirelessly' to bring all people 'up to the same threshold of capability that we set for other citizens', since any life that fails to achieve a threshold of capability in any area is 'not a fully human life, a life worthy of human dignity' (2006: 181, 190). We should, for example, operate on individuals with subnormal capabilities or otherwise do whatever we must to assure that everyone achieves a threshold level of the species norm (2006: 193). Otherwise we cannot really regard them as human at all.

A final critique of the capabilities approach relates to the specification of capabilities. As noted above, Sen resists outlining any list of capabilities, arguing instead that people should develop their own lists through democratic deliberation. In the absence of any list of capabilities, however, his capabilities approach seems to collapse back into something closely resembling a welfarist theory of distributive justice. 'We may doubt,' Richard Arneson writes, 'whether there are any objectively decidable grounds by which the value of a person's capabilities can be judged apart from the person's (ideally considered) preferences regarding those capabilities' (1989: 91–92, see also 2006: 19–22, 2010). Nussbaum, by contrast, has outlined a well-known list of capabilities based on an ethical conception of a 'truly human' life (2000: 71–72; 2006: 74–75, 182). Her list, however, makes some controversial claims about what does and does not constitute a dignified human life. Many have questioned whether Nussbaum's list is truly universal or instead reflects only her own personal, cultural and political biases (Clark, 2006; Engster, 2007, 167–168; Okin, 2003).[3]

Care Ethics

Care ethics offers a unique answer to the question: what should a distributive justice theory aim to distribute? Before discussing how it answers this question, however, it is first necessary to say a few words about the theory itself.

Care ethics is usually characterised as a needs-based philosophy. 'What is definitive about care ethics,' Joan Tronto (1993: 105) writes, is 'taking the other's needs as the starting point for what must be done' (see also Engster, 2007; Gheaus, 2005; Held, 2006; Kittay, 1999; Noddings, 2002: chapter 3). Although some care theorists define needs very broadly (e.g. Tronto, 1993, 2013), I consider a narrower definition to be more useful for developing a moral and political theory (Engster, 2007: 24–25). By my account, care involves everything we do directly to help individuals: (1) to meet their vital needs for food, water, shelter and other goods necessary to survive, develop and function; (2) to develop and sustain their basic physical, mental and emotional capabilities (for sensation, movement, communication, feeling, imagination, reason and sociability) and other important skills and knowledge necessary for successful functioning; and (3) to avoid or alleviate unnecessary and unwanted pain and suffering (Engster, 2007: 28–29). The ultimate goal of care ethics is to enable individuals to survive, develop as fully as possible given their innate capacities, and live and function in the world as well as possible, including being able to care for themselves and others, form meaningful relationships, engage in productive work, participate in social activities and pursue some conception of a good life.

Although care ethics identifies some objective needs as definitive of what it means to care for others, it also highlights the importance of relational values or virtues in meeting these needs. Simply shipping off food or blankets to earthquake survivors is at best only minimally and contingently caring. Care involves engaging with others and addressing their needs in particular ways: attending to the specific nature of their needs; responding to their preferences; seeking their input about our care; adjusting our care to their suggestions; and acting towards them in a manner that is respectful, acknowledges their agency and does not belittle them or assume their complete incapacity simply because they are dependent in some way.

In matters of distributive justice, care ethics (or what is often referred to as a public ethics of care) aims to ensure that everyone can satisfy their needs at least at levels sufficient to survive, develop and function. In setting standards of sufficiency, a public ethics of care further favours relatively high thresholds. While physiological requirements are clearly important in thinking about threshold levels of social support, social norms are also relevant. Even if disadvantaged individuals might technically be able to survive on nutritionally enriched gruel, it would be uncaring to provide them solely with this food source when most people in society have access to more diverse and exciting food options. Care-like behaviour that falls below social norms will in many cases fail to support decent social participation (an old paint-stained shirt may keep a person warm but not support his or her ability to find a job or attend social events) or may be perceived as disrespectful and rejected by the very individuals whom it is intended to help (nutritionally enriched gruel might be stigmatised to the point where even hungry individuals lose their taste for it). For an action to be caring, it must at least meet standards of social decency. Since in some societies norms of decent care may themselves be degraded (Nussbaum, 2000: 114–115, 136–142), cross-society comparisons of similarly positioned societies can be valuable in determining norms of social decency.

Although a public ethics of care is for the most part a sufficientarian theory, aiming to ensure that individuals have access to enough resources and personal attention to survive, develop and function at decent social levels, there is one area where it departs from this sufficientarian standard – or, perhaps more accurately, foregoes sufficiency in one area to achieve it in another. Because a public ethics of care is ultimately concerned with supporting decent functioning, it suggests that society should aim to develop and maintain the basic capabilities of all children and adults as much as reasonably possible and not just up to decent threshold levels. 'As much as reasonably possible' here means as much as society can support given reasonable resource constraints (e.g. limits on justifiable taxation), other social commitments (e.g. health care, elder care, national defence, etc.) and individuals' own innate capacities. The innate or basic capabilities in question here include sensation, movement, emotion, imagination, reason, communication and sociability. The development and maintenance of one's basic capabilities is so important for decent functioning that sufficientarian standards are misguided in this area. We generally need the fullest development and maintenance of our innate capabilities in order to be able to meet whatever challenges we may confront in life and maintain our survival and decent functioning. Indeed, while it is possible to identify some standards of sufficiency for food, clothing, shelter and the like, it is very difficult to say what should count as a sufficient level of reason, imagination, sociability or emotional intelligence. Given the fact that some individuals may have below-average capacities in some areas (e.g. sociability), it is particularly important that their other capabilities (emotion, imagination, reason) are developed as much as possible in order to provide them the best chance possible of decent social functioning. Overall, our basic or innate capabilities stand in a different relation to the ultimate aims of care than do the instrumental goods of life like food and shelter (Feinberg, 1980: 125). Where the goal is to ensure that individuals have a real opportunity to care for themselves and others, form meaningful relationships, engage in productive work, participate in social events and pursue some conception of a good life, the most prudent course is to help all individuals to develop and maintain their basic capabilities as much as possible.

Care Ethics and Other Distributive Justice Theories

Inasmuch as a public ethics of care may be considered a distributive justice theory, the good it distributes – the subject of distributive justice – is care. Care consists most fundamentally of all the personal and interpersonal practices that serve to translate resources into human utilities (feeding, sheltering, protecting), help to develop or maintain basic capabilities and skills (e.g. teaching) and mitigate pain and suffering (e.g. health care). Care ethics posits the equal entitlement of all human beings to the care they need to survive, develop and live and function as well as possible free from pain, suffering or other significant blights.

Our equal right to care follows from the fact that we have all depended on care for our survival, development and functioning (Engster, 2007; Kittay, 1999). Because we have all depended on the care of others to survive, develop and function, we can all be assumed to have made claims on others for care at some time in our lives (at the very least during infancy). We should therefore as a matter of moral consistency recognise the validity of the claims that others make on us for care when they need it and provide them with the care they need to survive, develop and function just as others have done for us.

As the subject of distribution, care includes elements of resourcist, welfarist and capabilities theories. As such, care ethics overlaps in part with other distributive justice theories. Yet, it also departs from these other distributive justice theories in significant ways. Although resources (income, liberties, opportunities) are necessary to care for oneself and others, for example, care ethics is not a resource-based theory. Resources are valuable in care ethics only to the extent that they support care. We may be said to successfully care for someone in care ethics only when his or her welfare has been enhanced (Kittay, 2015; Noddings, 2002; Tronto, 1993). Simply distributing resources is not enough. Eva Kittay (1999: 102–103) argues that care might be appended to Rawls's theory of justice as one more primary good. Care is, however, quite unlike the other primary goods on his list. It is an interpersonal good concerned with outcomes – specifically the particular welfare and capabilities of the cared-for. If appended to Rawls's list of primary goods, it would change the nature of his justice theory away from its resource-based focus.

Care ethics is also not a traditional welfare-based theory. Care ethics picks out some needs as objectively important (those that contribute to survival, development, functioning and the avoidance or alleviation of pain and suffering) while treating other subjective preferences as a personal responsibility. Preference satisfaction is important from the perspective of care ethics in some close personal relationships (the relationship between spouses or other committed adults), but remains an imperfect duty and one that is subject to interpersonal negotiation. Since care ethics does identify some needs as objectively important, one might classify it as an objective welfare theory. Even as an objective welfare theory, however, care ethics remains unique because of its emphasis on relational values, meeting needs in context and taking account of the preferences of others.

The relationship between care ethics and the capabilities approach is perhaps the most complicated. Care ethics has been characterised as a minimal capabilities theory (Engster, 2007: 12). Nussbaum likewise acknowledges that her capabilities theory (2006: 168–169) depends heavily on care:

> Good care for dependents, whether children, elderly, ill, or disabled, focuses on support for capabilities of life, health, and bodily integrity. It also provides stimulation for senses, imagination, and thoughts. It supports emotional attachments and removes 'overwhelming fear and anxiety'.... Good care also supports the capacity of the cared-for for practical reason and choice ...

Despite significant overlap between care ethics and the capabilities approach, the two theories diverge on a number of important issues. First, care ethics aims to distribute care rather than capabilities. Rather than attempting to distribute outcomes themselves, care ethics aims to ensure a fair allocation of the resources and interpersonal care necessary to ensure that everyone can achieve outcomes as much as possible given their innate abilities and preferences. While care ethics ultimately judges whether the distribution of care is just based on whether individuals have the capability to care for themselves and others, engage in productive work and so forth, the subject of distribution under care ethics remains care rather than capabilities. As will become clear below, this difference in emphasis has important ramifications for how one thinks about justice in distribution.

Second, and relatedly, care ethics also endorses a more interpersonal approach to capability development. In contrast to Nussbaum's capabilities approach, care ethics does not posit any normative conception of a truly human life that we should tirelessly work to achieve for all individuals. It aims instead to help all individuals to develop as much as possible their innate capabilities for sensation, movement, emotion, imagination, reason, sociability and the like, as well as important skills and knowledge. If a person plainly has no aptitude for developing some capability or no interest in exercising it, care ethics suggests that energies might be legitimately redirected towards developing other capabilities. Tirelessly working to bring someone up to a threshold level of capability can at some point become uncaring, particularly if it involves making the person work tirelessly to develop a capability that he or she has no aptitude for or interest in. There are, of course, some dangers associated with this more relational approach to development. In the hands of poor caregivers, it can mean giving up too quickly on a person's developmental potential or acquiescing to shortsighted preferences. As long as caregivers remain focused on the long-term goal of developing all a person's basic capabilities as much as possible, however, and every effort is made to ensure that care is attuned to the characteristics of individual persons and not based on group stereotypes, this danger can be avoided. The main point here is that care ethics focuses on persons rather than fetishising capabilities.

Third, care ethics also supports a more minimal list of capabilities than Nussbaum endorses. Care means helping individuals to survive, develop their basic capabilities and cultivate the skills and knowledge necessary for successful functioning (reading, writing, mathematics, science, etc.). It does not necessarily require, however, fostering artistic expression, a love of nature and animals, political participation or the other higher capabilities on Nussbaum's list. Parents who do not cultivate their children's artistic talents or political interests may be less than ideal by Western liberal standards, but they are not necessarily uncaring. Care has more minimal and general aims than those encompassed by Nussbaum's capabilities list.

Care Ethics and Distributive Justice

Care ethics aims to ensure that all individuals have access to the care (encompassing resources and interpersonal attention) that they need to survive, develop and avoid pain and suffering so that they can function at least at decent social levels (or as much as possible if decent social functioning is not possible). Although most political philosophers have overlooked care as a distributive good, there are some very good reasons for including it in a theory of distributive justice (Gheaus, 2005, 2009a, 2009b; Robeyns, 2011).

Care is a fundamental need that everyone requires. Without an adequate provision of care during childhood, no human being would survive or develop. All adults further depend on care (of self and others) throughout their lives to survive and function. If one believes that human beings have a prima facie right to survive, develop and function at decent social levels, it therefore follows that care should be subject at least in part to public distribution.

Care is also closely tied up with equal opportunity. The quality of care one receives when young is the single most important determinant (perhaps even more so than one's own innate capacities) of one's opportunities in life. How well one is cared for by one's parents or parent-like caregivers and the quality of the education one receives virtually dictate one's opportunities for finding productive work, supporting oneself, forming relationships and pursuing happiness later in life. A person's access to health care, long-term care, disability care and the like can further have profound effects on what he or she can do in society. If society is to support equal opportunity in any meaningful way, it should therefore promote the fair distribution of care.

Care is further essential for the existence and reproduction of society. If no one cared for anyone else, society would collapse. The well-being of nearly all persons would then be dramatically diminished. Ensuring an adequate provision of care is thus a social good that all individuals have a personal interest in.

A final significant reason for treating care as an important distributive good is its cost for caregivers. Because of the extensive time commitments and high interpersonal expenditures usually required to care for others, caregiving carries high opportunity costs. Individuals who care for others usually miss out on significant earning, career and social opportunities. Since women have traditionally taken on most caregiving responsibilities, they have borne most of these opportunity costs. The distribution of care thus raises important questions about gender justice. Unless care is treated as a public distributive good, women and others who take on significant caregiving responsibilities are likely to pay high personal costs for performing an essential form of social labour. Rules of fairness suggest that caregivers should be at least partially compensated and supported for their efforts so that they do not have to bear all the costs of caring by themselves. The public distribution of care is also important for freeing women from the unsubstantiated, inefficient and exploitative belief that they, but not men, are naturally inclined to care for others.

If, then, care is a good that we all need, has a profound influence on our life opportunities, represents a fundamental social good and carries significant costs for those who provide it, a good case would seem to exist for treating it as a (or even the) central subject of justice. States should do what they can to distribute the costs and benefits of care fairly. Some theorists have nevertheless argued that, because of its relational components, care cannot be distributed.

Onora O'Neill and Barbara Arneil have developed one version of this argument with regard to children's rights. They argue that rights frameworks are inappropriate when thinking about justice for children because rights do not very well capture what children need (Arneil, 2002; O'Neill, 1992). Children need the love and engagement of their parents and other caregivers in order to enjoy a happy life and healthy development, but these relational goods are inexpressible in the language of distributive justice or rights (Arneil, 2002: 87). Even if one might proclaim something like a right to be loved, it would be impossible, or at least very difficult, to enforce it.

Anca Gheaus has developed this line of argument more fully with regard to care ethics (2005, 2009a, 2009b). Relationships are morally important in care ethics, according to Gheaus, for two reasons. Care ethics values them instrumentally for the role they play in meeting needs; and it values them intrinsically as important goods in themselves. We all have a need for close emotional relationships – or more simply, for love – Gheaus claims (2005: 17–18, 186–189; 2009a), and care ethics is unique among moral theories in recognising this need for close personal relationships and love. But this creates a problem for care ethics. Caring relationships cannot be fully distributed because institutions cannot distribute love. Mandating love is, in fact, counterproductive. We value love precisely because it is voluntarily given. If the state were to declare that everyone had a right to be loved, many individuals, including those who were truly loved, might wonder whether their partner's love was authentic or merely an expression of duty. This does not mean, Gheaus emphasises, that care stands entirely beyond distribution. Some forms of care (e.g. access to medical care) can be distributed, but the most important part of care – love – cannot.

Is, then, care ethics best understood as something other than a distributive theory? I do not think so. Although O'Neill and Arneil rightly suggest that there are limits to the ability of states and other institutions to distribute care, these limits should not be overstated. States and other institutions can support and meet most needs that most people have for care through financial support, childcare, education, health care, long-term care and other services. They can further support a variety of policies that can greatly enhance parenting quality and even provide the conditions for love to flourish within families. Arguing for a state-based duty to ensure that all children are loved, Luara Ferracioli (2014: 16) writes,

> The duty in question is not so much to facilitate the development of an emotion, but for the state to do what it legitimately and feasibly can to ensure that children are raised by those who are likely to love them.

If states were to support family planning policies, parent-training classes and general family welfare policies (paid parenting leaves, child cash and tax benefits), most parents would show appropriate love for their children. In most cases, if love is absent from or poorly expressed in a parent–child relationship, it is not because of any lack of feeling on the part of parents but rather a lack of time and money and relational support. States do not need to mandate love in most parent–child relationships but merely to facilitate its expression.[4]

As for Gheaus's claim about the centrality of love to care, this, too, seems overstated. While care does involve a high degree of empathy and emotional engagement, it does not necessarily entail love. One certainly wants attentiveness, responsiveness and respect from one's doctor, but not usually his or her love. Even teachers of small children are generally not expected to love their students as their parents do. In most cases, a teacher who loved his or her students (or more likely, loved some of them) like a parent would probably be a less competent educator than one who cared for them in a competent, professional manner. A loving teacher would be much more likely to show favouritism for some students over others, to devote more time to some students than others, and to blur personal beliefs and goals with his or her professional responsibilities.

If love is important to care, then, it is only in some particular personal relationships. Parent–child relationships would seem to be the main example. Children certainly do need to form attachments with a few personal caregivers during infancy. They further seem to need to feel loved throughout childhood in order to be happy and develop in full and healthy ways. Thus, insofar as we are speaking of care and children, Gheaus's argument appears correct. Yet, as was pointed out above, even though states cannot mandate or distribute love to children, they can do a lot to ensure that all children have competent parents or parent-like figures to care for them and that all parental caregivers have adequate resources to care well for and love their children.

Gheaus's broader claim about the intrinsic value of love relationships for care ethics is more dubious. While most people may seek love and emotional intimacy with another human being, not everyone does. Monks and nuns appear more interested in a close relationship with a higher power than in forming loving human relationships, and some people similarly seem to be more interested in art, science or philosophy than close personal relationships. It therefore seems highly questionable that love is a fundamental need of all adults on a par with eating and drinking or developing one's ability to communicate or think rationally. Rather, love seems an important good that many people pursue as part of their vision of a good life. As such, it is not something with which a public ethics of care need directly concern itself. States should help individuals to meet their vital needs and develop their basic capabilities and otherwise promote the social and environmental conditions that enable individuals to function and pursue some vision of a good life. Having a meaningful adult love relationship is, however, rightfully a personal responsibility that individuals must attempt to achieve on their own.

The argument for treating care ethics as something other than a distributive justice theory thus comes down to this: care contains relational components that cannot be distributed, and good parental care for children, in particular, entails love. These limits on the distributive scope of care ethics nonetheless need not render it something other than a distributive theory, but may be understood as checks on its ability ever to achieve perfect justice. We can distribute resources to persons in need of care or their caregivers, assign caregivers to those who need them, create a public ethos that encourages only those individuals who want to become parents to have and raise children, and ensure that nearly all caregivers have some training and are subject to some oversight. We cannot, however, guarantee that all caregivers will care well. Of course, this problem is inherent to any justice theory that contains service components, including resource-based theories. Inasmuch as we consider safety to be an important distributive good, we ultimately must rely on police officers and military personnel to behave in honest, fair and responsible ways, but there is only so much we can do to assure their good conduct. No one, however, would suggest that safety is a good that defies distribution; it is simply taken for granted that there is only so much states can reasonably do to provide it. So it is with good care.

The argument can perhaps be clarified by considering a distinction that Nel Noddings makes between 'caring-for' and 'caring-about'. Caring-for occurs in the 'face-to-face occasions in which one person, as carer, cares directly for another, the cared-for'. Caring-about, by contrast, 'moves us from the face-to-face world into the wider public realm' where institutions and policies establish and promote 'the conditions under which caring-for can flourish' (2002: 22–23). By Noddings's account, institutions cannot directly care-for others but they can support good care relations. The responsibility of states from this perspective is to distribute resources to those in need so that they can care for themselves or their dependents directly. By empowering care agents at the personal level, states can largely avoid dominating individuals and encourage the flexible and particular delivery of care. Justice is achieved (or at least approximated) when all individuals receive the care they need (including both material resources and interpersonal attention) in order to survive, develop and function without pain, suffering or other significant blights, and caregivers are supported at levels that enable them to care decently for themselves and others without grave personal sacrifice.

The Comparative Merits of Care Ethics as a Distributive Justice Theory

Care ethics has a number of advantages over other distributive theories. Most generally, care ethics brings the concept of care to the fore of discussions of distributive justice. As highlighted above, care is an important good necessary for individual survival, development and functioning. It is also essential for the reproduction of society. Yet, aside from Nussbaum and a few other political philosophers, care has been generally overlooked as a significant distributive good. Care ethics highlights the need to include care in any satisfactory distributive framework. If one considers individual survival, development and functioning to be important outcomes that states should try to promote, then it follows that one should also view care as an important component of distributive justice. States should, from the perspective of care ethics, ensure that all individuals have access to sufficient levels of resources (income, personal liberties, etc.) and interpersonal care (good parental care, health care, long-term care, disability care and so forth) so that they can survive, develop and function decently (including having real opportunities to work, care for themselves and others, form relationships, participate in social activities and pursue some conception of the good life).

In comparison with resource-based theories, care ethics enjoys two particular advantages. First, it focuses on the particular needs of different individuals (children, the sick, disabled persons and so on) and distributes resources accordingly, thus avoiding the usual criticism of resource-based theories that they are insensitive to human heterogeneity. Perhaps more importantly, care ethics gets more directly at what most people seem to really care about in thinking about justice: not what they have but what they can do and how they are doing.

Care ethics' primary advantage over welfare-based theories stems from its identification of certain objective outcomes that it aims to promote for all people: survival, development and functioning in certain core areas. By focusing on objective outcomes, care ethics avoids the problems of expensive tastes and adaptive preferences. A person who refuses to drink anything but champagne can be informed that society has an obligation under care ethics only to meet her needs at decent social levels (e.g. through a small allocation of funds for clean water and other common beverages). A person who says he is happy enough living in a cardboard box can be encouraged to see whether he might not prefer living in a permanent apartment building with heating and air conditioning and other amenities.

Care ethics further enjoys a number of advantages over capability theories. It avoids fetishising capabilities by emphasising the importance of developing people's capabilities in relationship with them rather than setting objective thresholds as goals for their development. In this way, it also avoids the potentially stigmatising character of the capabilities approach. From the perspective of care ethics, we should help individuals to develop as much as possible and live as well as possible given their innate capacities and (within limits) their preferences. There is no imperative, however, to bring everyone up to a threshold of capability in all areas and no suggestion that anyone who fails to achieve a threshold level of some capability – say, sociability or reasoning – should be regarded as subhuman.

There are also two advantages to care ethics' more limited or basic capability set. First, by positing a thinner set of goods, care ethics outlines a distributional justice theory that reasonable individuals from diverse cultures and religions are more likely to endorse. Second, care ethics also provides a more focused approach to development. Whether we are talking about the post-industrial countries of Western Europe and North America or the developing countries of Africa, Asia or South America, the primary focus of justice, from the perspective of care ethics, should be making sure that everyone has enough to eat, sufficient shelter, the interpersonal care necessary to develop their basic capabilities and a real opportunity to care for themselves and others, form meaningful relationships, engage in productive work, participate in society and pursue some vision of a good life without pain, suffering or other significant blights. Fostering artistic appreciation, a love of nature and other goals are arguably not as pressing.

Aside from its comparative theoretical advantages, the value of care ethics as a distributive justice framework can also be demonstrated by looking at practical applications. A test case of sorts in recent debates about distributive justice theories, for example, is how well a given theory can address justice for disabled persons. It has been argued that the capabilities approach is preferable to resource-based theories in addressing disability justice for a couple of reasons: it is more sensitive to differences among persons; and it goes beyond mere resource distribution in order to measure actual capability to function (Nussbaum, 2006; Terzi, 2010). For reasons listed above, care ethics is further preferable to the capabilities approach – or at least Nussbaum's version of it. While aiming to ensure that all disabled persons are able to meet their vital needs, develop their basic capabilities and function as much as possible without any blights, care ethics avoids the stigmatising aspects of Nussbaum's capabilities list. It suggests that we should aim for the full development and integration of disabled people into society on their own terms by subsidising the care they need and reforming the social environment so that they can live their lives as they want. We should not, however, force upon them a thick conception of truly human functioning and work tirelessly to ensure they achieve it.[5]

Children's justice provides another area where care ethics appears superior to other distributive frameworks. Traditional resource-based theories are not particularly appropriate for thinking about justice for children since they generally rely on human agency to translate resources into welfare or functioning (Macleod, 2010). Providing a six-month-old infant with money, opportunities, liberties and the like is hardly sufficient for achieving justice. Infants need care to translate resources into benefits. Welfare-oriented theories are also poorly suited for addressing justice for children because children's preferences are not always a good guide to what they need. Similar criticisms apply to the capabilities approach. Narrowly conceived, the capabilities approach is inappropriate for children because many children lack the agency to make capability choices (Macleod, 2010). Nussbaum (2006: 172) partially acknowledges this point by suggesting that for children 'functioning may be made the goal in many areas'. Yet even this acknowledgement misses the point. Children do not so much need functioning in many capability areas as they need competent caregivers who can make capability choices for them. Care ethics orients a theory of children's justice directly around the care they need to survive, develop and eventually function in the adult world.

Another area where care ethics has notable advantages over other justice frameworks is gender justice. As feminists have long noted, the gendered distribution and devaluation of care work is a central contributing factor to the inequalities that exist between men and women (Gheaus, 2009b: 112). One reason that women have less income and power and fewer opportunities than men is because women traditionally have taken on more care responsibilities – particularly unpaid and informal responsibilities in the family. Most distributive frameworks say very little about care, and thus fail to address this important source of disadvantage for women. Care ethics, by contrast, directly addresses this source of injustice and inequality. Society should from the perspective of care ethics aim to educate all individuals about the value of care, emphasise the universal responsibility of both men and women to care for others, support and subsidise individuals who are doing necessary care work, and ensure that all those who need care receive it in sufficient amounts. Women and men under a caring welfare state would have equal opportunities to work, care, participate in society and pursue their own visions of a good life.

There are other areas, too, where care ethics arguably supports a superior distributive justice theory than existing frameworks, including health care, education and old age justice (see Engster, 2015). I will pass over these subjects here, however, in order to address a possible criticism of the account of care ethics outlined in this chapter. My account of a public ethics of care is in large part a sufficientarian theory. It aims to ensure that everyone has enough care to meet their needs and live decently. As with other distributive frameworks, there exist a number of criticisms of sufficiency-based distributive justice theories (Arneson, 2006; Brighouse and Swift, 2009; Casal, 2007). Above all, sufficientarian theories are often said to invoke ambiguous standards of sufficiency and pay inadequate attention to distribution above the threshold. The account of care ethics that I have outlined here largely avoids these criticisms. It defines the threshold of sufficiency for most goods in terms of physiological needs and social norms. A threshold income thus might be defined in terms of the amount a person or family requires to meet their basic needs and participate in society at decent levels – often associated with the international poverty line (50 per cent of median income adjusted for household size). Virtues such as empathy nonetheless remain important in care ethics in defining sufficientarian standards. In developmental matters, care ethics suggests that states should aim to enable all individuals the highest achievement possible consistent with resource constraints and other public commitments. In this important area, care ethics is therefore concerned with distribution above the threshold. Although there may be some shortcomings to care ethics as a distributive justice theory, standard criticisms of sufficientarian theories have limited force against it.

Conclusion

What should a distributive justice theory aim to distribute? This chapter has argued that care represents one very plausible answer to this question. My central claims have been (1) that care ethics can be plausibly framed as a distributive justice theory; and (2) that it compares favourably with other distributive justice theories. Because of the heterogeneous character of the concept of care, care ethics avoids many of the standard criticisms of resource-based, welfare-based and capabilities-based distributive justice theories. Care ethics also seems better suited than other distributive justice frameworks for guiding our thinking about what justice means for children, disabled people, women and a number of other groups. It further has much to offer in thinking about development in poor and disadvantaged countries.

This chapter obviously does not settle the case. Debates about the proper standards of distributive justice are complex. My purpose here has been simply to survey contemporary debates about distributive justice, situate care ethics in relation to them, and offer some arguments for why political philosophers and others should take care ethics more seriously as a distributive justice theory.

Notes

1 A fourth approach, articulated most clearly by Elizabeth Anderson (2012), focuses on equalising social relations. The approach I outline in this chapter shares a number of commonalities with this relational conception of distributive justice. It particularly provides a clear vision of how some very fundamental aspects of social relations can be equalised. A full comparison between care ethics and this relational approach to distributive justice nonetheless could not be undertaken within the bounds of this chapter.

2 'Opportunities for welfare' theories (Arneson, 1989; Cohen, 1989, 1990) avoid some of these problems by compensating individuals 'only for those welfare deficits which are not appropriately traceable to the individual's choices' (Cohen, 1990: 362). This perspective nonetheless still seems to suggest that individuals raised in wealthy homes should be subsidised throughout their lives in order to help them fulfil their taste for the finer things in life, since the development of expensive tastes in them was unchosen.

3 Nussbaum sometimes presents her capabilities as 'the source of political principles for a liberal pluralistic society' (2006: 70). Framed narrowly in this way, her list avoids in part – but not completely – the above criticism. More generally, Nussbaum treats her capabilities list as the basis for a theory of global justice and universal human rights.

4 Ferracioli (2014: 16) argues that 'the state must develop and implement parenting and procreation policies geared toward a public ethos in which those who are not subjectively attracted to parenting are much less likely to have children'. Elsewhere (Engster, 2015) I suggest that states should also require or at least strongly encourage parents to take parenting classes prior to the birth of their first child. Other measures are likewise necessary to protect children against abuse and neglect. I do not mean to suggest here that all family problems would disappear if parents had more time and money.

5 This point is further argued in Chapter 5 of my book *Justice, Care, and the Welfare State* (Engster, 2015).

References

Anderson, Elizabeth (2012), 'Equality', in David Estlund (ed.), *The Oxford Handbook of Political Philosophy*, Oxford: Oxford University Press, pp. 40–57.

Arneil, Barbara (2002), 'Becoming versus being: a critical analysis of the child in liberal theory', in David Archard and Colin Macleod (eds), *The Moral and Political Status of Children*, Oxford: Oxford University Press, pp. 70–94.

Arneson, Richard (1989), 'Equality and equal opportunity for welfare', *Philosophical Studies*, 56 (1): 77–93.

Arneson, Richard (2006), 'Distributive justice and basic capability equality: "good enough" is not good enough', in Alexander Kaufman (ed.) *Capabilities Equality: Basic Issues and Problems*, New York: Routledge, pp. 17–43.

Arneson, Richard (2010), 'Two cheers for capabilities', in Harry Brighouse and Ingrid Robeyns (eds), *Measuring Justice: Primary Goods and Capabilities*, Cambridge: Cambridge University Press, pp. 101–127.

Brighouse, Harry (2002), 'What rights (if any) do children have?' in David Archard and Colin MacLeod (eds), *The Moral and Political Status of Children*, Oxford: Oxford University Press, pp. 31–52.

Brighouse, Harry and Robeyns, Ingrid (eds) (2010), *Measuring Justice: Primary Goods and Capabilities*, Cambridge: Cambridge University Press.

Brighouse, Harry and Swift, Adam (2009), 'Educational equality versus educational adequacy: a critique of Anderson and Satz', *Journal of Applied Philosophy*, 26 (2): 117–128.

Casal, Paula (2007), 'Why sufficiency is not enough', *Ethics*, 117 (2): 296–326.

Clark, David (2006), 'Capability approach', in D. Clark (ed.), *The Elgar Companion to Development Studies*, Cheltenham: Edward Elgar, pp. 32–44.

Cohen, G. A. (1989), 'On the currency of egalitarian justice', Ethics, 99 (4): 906–944.

Cohen, G. A. (1990), 'Equality of what? On welfare, goods and capabilities', *Economiques de Louvain/Louvain Economic Review*, 56 (3–4): 357–382.

Dworkin, Ronald (2000), *Sovereign Virtue: The Theory and Practice of Equality*, Cambridge, MA: Harvard University Press.

Engster, Daniel (2007), *The Heart of Justice: Care Ethics and Political Theory*, Oxford: Oxford University Press.

Engster, Daniel (2015), *Justice, Care, and the Welfare State*, Oxford: Oxford University Press.

Engster, Daniel and Hamington, Maurice (2015), *Care Ethics and Political Theory*, Oxford: Oxford University Press.

Feinberg, Joel (1980), 'The child's right to an open future', in W. Aiken and H. Lafollette (eds), *Whose Child? Parental Rights, Parental Authority and State Power*, Totowa, NJ: Littlefield, Adams, pp. 124–153.

Ferracioli, Luara (2014), 'The state's duty to ensure children are loved', *Journal of Ethics and Social Philosophy*, 8 (2): 1–19.

Gheaus, Anca (2005), 'Care and justice: why they cannot go together all the way', unpublished dissertation, Philosophy Department, Central European University, Budapest.

Gheaus Anca (2009a), 'How much of what matters can we redistribute? love, justice, and luck', *Hypatia*, 24 (4): 63–83.

Gheaus, Anca (2009b), 'The challenge of care to idealizing theories of distributive justice', in L. Tessman (ed.), *Feminist Ethics and Social and Political Philosophy: Theorizing the Non-ideal*, New York: Springer, pp. 105–119.

Gilligan, Carol (1982), *In a Different Voice: Psychological Theory and Women's Development*, Cambridge, MA: Harvard University Press.

Held, Virginia (2006), *The Ethics of Care: Personal, Political, and Global*, Oxford: Oxford University Press.

Kittay, Eva (1999), *Love's Labor: Essays on Women, Equality, and Dependency*, New York: Routledge.

Kittay, Eva (2015), 'A theory of justice as fair terms of social life given our inevitable dependency and our inextricable interdependency', in Daniel Engster and Maurice Hamington (eds), *Care Ethics and Political Theory*, Oxford: Oxford University Press.

Macleod, Colin (2010), 'Primary goods, capabilities, and children', in Harry Brighouse and Ingrid Robeyns (eds), *Measuring Justice: Primary Goods and Capabilities*, Cambridge: Cambridge University Press, pp. 174–192.

Noddings, Nel (1984), *Caring: A Feminine Approach to Ethics and Moral Education*, Berkeley: University of California Press.

Noddings, Nel (2002), *Staring at Home: Caring and Social Policy*, Berkeley: University of California Press.

Nussbaum, Martha (2000), *Women and Human Development: The Capabilities Approach*, Cambridge: Cambridge University Press.

Nussbaum, Martha (2006), *Frontiers of Justice: Disability, Nationality, Species Membership*, Cambridge, MA: Harvard University Press.

Okin, Susan (2003), 'Poverty, well-being, and gender: what counts, who's heard?' *Philosophy and Public Affairs*, 31 (3): 280–316.

O'Neill, Onora (1992), 'Children's rights and children's lives', *International Journal of Law and the Family*, 6 (1): 24–42.

Pogge, Thomas (2010), 'A critique of the capability approach', in Harry Brighouse and Ingrid Robeyns (eds), *Measuring Justice: Primary Goods and Capabilities*, Cambridge: Cambridge University Press, pp. 17–60.

Rawls, John (1999), *A Theory of Justice*, revised edn, Cambridge, MA: Harvard University Press.

Robeyns, Ingrid (2010), 'Gender and the metric of justice', in Harry Brighouse and Ingrid Robeyns (eds), *Measuring Justice: Primary Goods and Capabilities*, Cambridge: Cambridge University Press, pp. 215–235.

Robeyns, Ingrid (2011), 'A university duty to care', in Axel Gosseries and Yannick Vanderborght (eds), *Arguing About Justice: Essays for Philippe Van Parijs*, Louvain: Presses Universitaires de Louvain, pp. 283–290.

Sen, Amartya (1980), 'Equality of what?' in S. McMurrin (ed.), *The Tanner Lectures on Human Values, Vol. 1*, Cambridge: Cambridge University Press, pp. 197–220.

Sen, Amartya (1999), *Development as Freedom*, New York: Anchor Books.

Terzi, Lorella (2010), 'What metric of justice for disabled people?', in Harry Brighouse and Ingrid Robeyns (eds), *Measuring Justice: Primary Goods and Capabilities*, Cambridge: Cambridge University Press, pp. 150–173.

Tronto, Joan (1993), *Moral Boundaries: A Political Argument for an Ethic of Care*, New York: Routledge.

Tronto, Joan (2013), *Caring Democracy: Markets, Equality, and Justice*, New York: New York University Press.

White, Julie (2000) *Democracy, Justice, and the Welfare State*, University Park, Pennsylvania: Penn State University Press.

Wilkinson, Richard, and Pickett, Kate (2009), *The Spirit Level: Why Greater Equality Makes Societies Stronger*, New York: Bloomsbury Press.

7 Justice and Real Politics

Freedom, Needs and Representation

Lawrence Hamilton[1]

Introduction

Today most political theorists and philosophers view justice as the central concept or concern in politics. More exactly, political thinkers have come to assume that a particular form of justice – distributive justice – is the central question; and that just *institutions* are those that can be stipulated based upon *transcendental* principles of justice antecedent to the messy business of real politics. It is not too much of an exaggeration to say that the work of John Rawls, while important in resuscitating political philosophy is the main source of this state of affairs (Sen, 2009). The industry that has grown up around his work has generated half a century of misguided approaches to the central problems we face in local, national and global politics.

In this chapter I am going to question the view of politics as ultimately a matter of justice. I submit, rather, that justice is just one among many goals and points of difference and discord that characterise politics; and, moreover, that justice itself should be characterised more realistically. That is, as I argue here, justice is not exempt from the disagreement that pervades politics – 'there are many of us, and we disagree about justice' (Waldron, 1999: 36) – and thus that the basic structure, or legal and political framework, of modern democracies as well as the fair distribution of goods therein depend not on pre-political and universally applicable legal structures, but on representative and participative institutions that enable the articulation, identification and evaluation of actually existing needs directed towards overcoming domination.

In order to make this argument, I use some of Amartya Sen's main contributions to various debates as a helpful foil, arguing that his 'realisation' or 'accomplishment-based' approach to justice does not go far enough (Sen, 2009: 18). Even if articulated in pluralist, social choice outcomes of individual preferences and judgements, what we are left with is a strong and unrealistic role for what he calls 'public reason' based on rational deliberation as central to politics: that it can produce just outcomes agreeable to all from near and far. Contrary to what Sen suggests, the reference to Adam Smith's idea of an impartial spectator is not that far from the various pre-political ideals of agreement common in the political theoretical literature: that the fair distribution of goods depends upon agreement – via the heuristic device of a 'veil of ignorance' (Rawls, 1971, 1993) or by means of deliberation that generates consensus (Habermas, 1984, 1987, 1996) or through pre-political, constitutional determinations that safeguard the common interests of 'the people' (Rousseau, 1997; Pettit, 2006). In place of this faith in 'public reason', I meet head-on the reality of the irrevocability of conflict in justice and politics and propose, therefore, a series of *partisan* institutions that would both enable citizens to participate more actively in the determination of their needs and give their representatives greater autonomy in the process of identifying and evaluating existing needs and interests, and provide citizens with the means meaningfully to control, critique and veto the decisions of their political representatives.

Justice

As an aside in an essay on another topic, Raymond Geuss provides a telling critique of the common current tendency to take justice as central in politics (Geuss, 2014: 156–161). He suggests that there are at least four distinct notions of justice to hand. First, 'just' designates that which accords with existing legal codes. Second, 'just' accords with what we – which 'we'? – think *ought* to be the enforced legal code. Third, 'justice' is used to refer to 'all the human excellences together', as Aristotle (1980: 1129b–1130) argued – what he called 'universal justice'. 'Just' here refers in a rather indeterminate way to that which is 'socially excellent, desirable, and so on' (Geuss, 2014: 157). It is important not to confuse this third sense with the second sense as there might well be things we think are *socially desirable* that we also think cannot be formulated in a legal code. Take, for example, gratitude: it is precisely an important part of the value of gratitude that it is exhibited and linked to those from whom I might receive benefits *without* it being legally required or associated with sanction (Geuss, 2014: 157). Fourth, a conception of justice that focuses on questions of distribution. Although there has been theoretical disagreement about what should be distributed – goods, welfare, opportunity, possibilities of agency, rights, and so on – *and* about whether the principles of distribution should be some version of equality (goods distributed equally to each) or proportionality (goods distributed according to a person's perceived merit or contribution), over the last half-century there has been considerable consensus around the idea that the theoretical study of politics is (or at least ought to be) about the realisation of the ideal of distributive justice.

John Rawls's *A Theory of Justice*, coupled with his later corpus and the work of most of his acolytes, exemplifies these problems. Rawls argues that the health and stability of a modern democracy depends on the justice of its 'basic structure' and thus that the 'basic structure' of society is the primary subject of a theory of justice (Rawls, 1971: 7; Rawls, 1993:

257–289). The foundations for this institutionally ideal approach are a set of 'principles of justice' that will emerge with *unanimous agreement* in the 'original position', where all, it is supposed, do not know their status, power or wealth in the society about which they are deliberating. The two principles include lexical priority for all having a right to 'scheme of equal basic liberties' compatible with a 'similar scheme' for all *and* fair equality of opportunity vis-à-vis offices and positions, and social and economic inequalities must 'be to the greatest benefit of the least advantaged members of society' (Rawls, 1993: 291).

There are three broad problems with this approach to justice. First, it is hard to see how the lexical priority of liberty and the inequalities Rawls seems keen to retain will allow for the greatest benefit of the least advantaged. (Given that this has generated libraries of published debate, I will leave it to one side here.) Second, as argued by Sen, this is a 'transcendental' account of justice, which is concerned with institutions alone; that is, it is concerned primarily with providing an institutional answer to the idea of an ideally just polity as opposed to tackling the various injustices that bedevil modern life by means of a focus on outcomes or realisations – a form of consequentialism that does not eschew liberty but focuses on which decisions, judgements and forms of public reason enable better outcomes in terms of Sen's capability approach (Sen, 2009). Third, it is devoted to one particular social ideal, the ideal of justice.

Rawls's approach eviscerates both the concept of justice and our understanding of politics. If 'justice' is used in the third sense stipulated by Geuss (Aristotle's sense) then of course it comes as no surprise that all politics is about justice. It is no surprise because it is a tautology. The problem arises – as is clearly the case in Rawls – when a theorist moves, as it is easy to do, from the tautology that 'justice' is about what is socially desirable to something that is by no means a tautology, 'namely to the claim that all politics is appropriately construed as the equitable or proportional distribution of pre-existing goods and benefits' (Geuss, 2014: 158).

There are four problems with this now very prevalent slippage. First, as many have argued in the history of political thought and expressed during real struggles for liberation from domination under colonialism, imperialism, apartheid and patriarchy (among others), not all politics is about justice. Politics is also *at least* about freedom, security, the coordination of action, the exercise of influence, the regulation of power relations, the control of the use of force and so on (Geuss, 2014; Hamilton, 2003, 2014, 2015). Second, this unique focus on distributive justice presumes that justice will have something to do with rules (and principles) and conformity to such existing rules or conformity to a better set of ideal rules. In other words, there is also conceptual slippage back to the first two senses of 'just' described by Geuss. Third, the distributive view of justice always associates justice with the distribution of goods that are considered to exist antecedently. In other words, as Karl Marx pointed out regarding justice-centred theories of this kind propagated in his time, the goods in question are taken at face value, as objects that come into existence in ways that are irrelevant to discuss (Marx, [1867] 1976–1978). As is well known, Marx thought it more important for political theory to scrutinise the activities through which such goods were produced and the social relations that structured these productive processes. For Marx, these were the most important features of any society, and justice in the sense of rules of distribution, in the sense of conformity to a legal code or some more desirable scheme of distribution, was secondary (Marx, [1939–1941] 1973). Fourth, the predominant claims about justice refer to equal (or proportional) distribution of goods fundamental to our social order or to an ideally 'good' social order: but, 'what is so special about "*our*" notions of social order … [and why assume that] societal order is good in itself?' (Geuss, 2014: 160).

Conceiving of justice as central to politics may be the result of a number of understandable phenomena. Two are worth mentioning here. First, justice has historically been linked with the concepts of rationality and reasonableness, which in its extreme form (Plato, Kant, Rawls) leaves no room for actual political judgement and the conflict that might arise out of it (Hampshire, 2000: 15–22); but, even in its most subtle form (Sen), where consequentialism, real plurality of views and outcomes-oriented deliberation is made central it is difficult to see how real judgement and dispute is admissible. This is the case because it falls back on a conception of public reason that requires all claims to pass before the reasoned assessment of the public via the notion of an impartial spectator who would assess them from near and far (to avoid parochialism and to include all the necessary, global information in the assessment). How? As Smith and Sen both admit, this idea of an impartial spectator is another form of heuristic, as this 'position' is not that of the actual views of these near and far, but in fact the capacity for individuals to stand back and judge their own and others' values, judgements and claims based on the 'as if' assumption of adopting the position of the impartial spectator (Sen, 2009: 121–125; Smith, [1790] 1976: III, I, 2). This is to ask too much of the capacity for impartiality among citizens as they struggle to have their needs and interests heard and met. Also, why assume that all needs and interests could only be admissible were they to pass the full test of public reason? As I'll suggest below, there may be partisan, legitimate needs that 'the public' in general would not view as reasonable or rational.

Judgement is crucial too to the second phenomenon: given our horror at the uncertainty and indeterminacy of human life, and our anxiety at having to exercise judgement to decide in each case regarding how to act in the world, 'justice' provides us with a two-pronged exit out of this state of horror. It enables us to cling to theories we have once committed ourselves to, even if they have revealed themselves as flawed; and it upholds the objectivity and determinacy we seek – to start from 'justice' gives us the illusion that all the indeterminacies of our forms of valuation can be reduced to one objective, rational ideal. We therefore do not need to exercise judgement, or so the illusion is created (Geuss, 2014).

Even if these are understandable motivations for us to cling to justice as central to politics, they are seriously flawed for an attempt to get anywhere in understanding politics and judging how best to act in the world of politics. What is needed is the courage to jettison some of the main underpinnings of the received views on justice: (1) that a fully rational and objective account of justice, existing a priori or following deliberation, is necessary for humans to act in the world; that is, justice might always involve irreducible conflict (Hampshire, 2000); (2) that evaluation of the effects of social choice, individual behaviour (Sen, 2009) *and* the formative role of existing institutions lies at the heart of justice (Hamilton, 2003); and (3) that an assessment of existing power relations in terms of whether they generate states of domination cannot be avoided in assessments of justice and injustice. In order to right this ship of justice theorists need to take more seriously two related and under-emphasised components of justice. First, judgement, power relations and overcoming domination are central to achieving practical justice – justice on the ground, not aimed at castles in the air. Second, combine an account of freedom with the identification, satisfaction and evaluation of needs and show how a politics of needs is not first and foremost aimed at resolving conflict, but justifying *partisan* institutions of representation that may help institutionalise and control (class and other) conflicts.

Freedom, Needs and Power

Like Rawls and Sen, I take freedom to lie at the heart of justice. However, I get there via first proposing a distinct account of freedom, by making the argument that power is integral to freedom, particularly power through political representation. This is against the grain of the three main Western accounts of freedom, which *reduce* it to: (1) absence of external (physical or legal) impediments ('negative' freedom); (2) the ability to decide for oneself what to do ('self-determination' or 'positive' freedom); or (3) citizenship within a free state (republican freedom) (Berlin, [1958] 1969; Skinner, 2002; Pettit, 2006). These supposedly *universal* theories are unpersuasive as all three lead to the patently incorrect conclusion that, for example, South Africans are now free, despite the evident lack of power to act freely that characterises the lives of most – particularly the unemployed and working class – who live in this highly unequal, racially scarred and unsafe society.

So, we need to look elsewhere: to an account of freedom understood in terms of the power to act and the requirements for that power. And there is nothing crazy about this idea. When I say 'I am free' normally I am not saying, 'I am externally unimpeded' or 'I am self-determining.' What I usually mean is 'I am free to do X' which concretely means 'I have the power or ability to do X.' It follows that it is more helpful to conceive of freedom as a *combination of my ability to determine what I will do and my power to do it or bring it about.*

Moreover, freedom as power in this sense chimes with most of the struggles for freedom across the ages, including the sharp distinction between freedom and slavery in Antiquity, subsequent slave revolts like the Haitian Revolution and later liberation struggles, *and* the everyday attempts to gain more independence and freedom from, say, the state, the churches, the community, poverty and so on. As Livy puts it in his history of Rome, 'freedom is to be in one's own power' (Livy, 2005: book 35, ch. 32, 11).[2] Similarly, Frantz Fanon argues that the human condition is to be free and that freedom resides in the *capacity* to choose and to act (Fanon, 2008: 180). Moreover, perhaps surprisingly, in different ways, Thomas Hobbes (1996: 62, 91, 146), Jean-Jacques Rousseau (1997: 82), Edmund Burke (2004: 91) and John Stuart Mill (2008: 7, 16–17, 116, 121–122) – supposed standard-bearers of Berlin's 'negative' conception of freedom – are ultimately concerned with whether or not an individual is able to exercise his or her power to act, to do something. However, at least in the Western tradition, it is Marx who first unequivocally identifies freedom with power. Marx distinguishes three concepts of liberty, arguing that the third, 'materialist' conception is the full, sophisticated notion, in which freedom comprises the conjunction of the ability to determine what one will do and the power to do what one decides to do, and anything less than this is a mere shadow of the concept of freedom (Marx and Engels, 1976: 193–195, 304–306). This means that for Marx the other two concepts he discusses, and a fortiori the main three concepts analysed in the modern literature, are poor approximations of this real form of freedom.

Freedom as power also captures the fact that people are interested in freedom as a human ideal because it is connected with the actual attainment of 'something': that is, some good or set of goods. The liberation struggle in South Africa, for example, did not have as its goal the abstract idea of being 'free from impediment' or 'living in a free state'. Rather, it had more concrete political, economic and social goals: having the power to determine who rules and how they rule; to produce, exchange and consume; to love, procreate and seek entertainment; to bring up one's children, and so on; all in conditions free of poverty and racial and gender discrimination and domination, as both the 1955 Freedom Charter and the 1996 South African Constitution enunciate. So, to paraphrase Julius Nyerere (2002: 40), Frantz Fanon (1963: 43) and Nelson Mandela (1995: 617), the attainment of political freedom alone does not secure freedom; it is a necessary but not sufficient condition for the broader concrete goals that constitute freedom. The same is true for less stark struggles for freedom under less tyrannical conditions. The constant clamour for freedom of speech is ultimately about the power to hold political representatives accountable – or, as Simon Schama puts it, 'to keep the powerful awake at night' (cited in Armitage, 2014).

Freedom as power thus emphasises the effective exercise of our powers as individuals and groups. As John Dewey puts it: 'Liberty is power, effective power to do specific things.... The demand of liberty is the demand for power' (Dewey, 1968: 11). And Sen argues that '[t]he question whether a person can bring about the objects of her reasoned choice is crucial to the idea of freedom [by means of] *direct control* ... or 'indirect power' ... the issue of *effective power*' (Sen, 2009: 301–302).

As regards power, if we begin by combining Foucault's and Lukes's accounts, it is possible to identify power as: (1) connected to general concepts like *ability* or *capacity* to do (Lukes, 2005: 63, 109); (2) a relation between rather than a resource or a property of persons; (3) the socially determined abilities of agents to bring about significant effects, by furthering their own interests or affecting the interests of others, either positively or negatively (Foucault, 1991; Lukes, 2005: 65). In my first book I argued that these abilities depend upon the extent to which individuals are able to determine and satisfy their vital and agency needs, which in turn depends upon the extent to which they can evaluate and critique the prevailing political and economic institutions (Hamilton, 2003). In subsequent work I have focused this articulation in terms of domination: that is, freedom depends on whether or not citizens find themselves in situations of domination, especially vis-à-vis the determination of their needs and interests (Hamilton, 2014). A situation of domination can take various forms. Existing power relations may: (1) mislead me in my attempts to *identify* my needs, either through direct coercion, intentional manipulations or as a result of fixed, traditional norms and practices that have yet to be transformed, e.g. patriarchal institutions and norms; (2) ensure that I do not have the means or voice to *express* my needs, e.g. life under a regime that has taken away or never granted me the power to do so, such as apartheid South Africa; (3) disable meaningful *evaluation* of needs, e.g. unregulated liberal capitalism, even if the regime in question provides me with the *formal* means and freedoms (or rights) to make claims (Hamilton, 2014: 88; cf. Pettit, 2006; Lovett, 2010).

Freedom as power therefore depends upon avoiding or overcoming situations of domination by ensuring power, control and self-control over four dimensions: (1) the power to act or be as I would choose in the absence of either internal or external obstacles; (2) the power to determine the government of my political association or community; (3) the ability to exercise my powers and capacities self-reflectively against existing norms and power relations; and (4) the power to determine my social and economic environment via meaningful control over my economic and political representatives.

Given the complexity and division of labour of modern states and the global economy, this last dimension is the most important: our lives within and between these states are characterised by membership of a whole variety of overlapping and interdependent groups and various forms of associated representation. Our freedom is therefore determined to a significant degree by a number of different variables to do with the nature and power of these groups and their representatives (Mamdani, 1996; Hamilton, 2014).

Group Representation and Group Freedom

Western political thought tends to focus on two distinct groups of people – the rulers and the ruled – all being citizens with equal formal power. The rulers are the *representatives*; and the ruled are the *represented*. But this picture is too stark: both 'the rulers' and 'the ruled' are comprised of various different groups, many of which overlap. This is particularly important in Africa given the stubborn legacy of divide and rule, tribal invention, 'Native Administration' and racial repression, that not only treated the indigenous population as non-citizens, but generated racial, tribal, class and gender divisions that have proved very difficult to overcome following independence (Fanon, 1963; Mamdani, 1996; Freund, 2000).

This stark picture is mirrored in Western political theory's dependence on 'mandate' or 'independence' to understand political representation: that is, political representatives respond directly to the expressed opinions and interests of the citizens they represent (Dahl, 1989; Przeworski et al., 1999: 2); or they act independently of these interests and judge for themselves what is in the best interests of the citizenry and state (Hobbes, 1996: 121, 128, 184; Burke, 1999; Siéyès, 2003).

This rests upon one or both of two erroneous assumptions: (1) that the interests of group members cohere in such a way as to make them a plausible principle; and (2) that there exist a set of shared interests or identities *antecedent* to and necessary for political representation. In fact, citizens' and states' needs and interests are not pre-existing and fixed, waiting to be tracked through representation. Rather, they require identification, articulation, expression, evaluation and even construction. Like needs, interests have a dualistic nature – they are attached and unattached, subjective and objective – and, moreover, individual and group interests often only become *present* as a result of representation (Pitkin, 1967; Hamilton, 2003).

Thus, representative institutions will not be freedom-enhancing if they simply 'track' interests; rather, they must encourage the formation of new political interests. This is most obvious in a place like South Africa today where many existing felt needs and interests have been formed under conditions of racist policies, the 'bifurcated' apartheid state, poverty, inequality and unemployment. Under these conditions representatives have actively to generate new interests that enable groups to escape these situations of domination.

A more fruitful account of political representation, an 'aesthetic' theory, brings this out well. First, as we know from the world of art and literature, representation is never simply the copy of some pre-existing external reality. Representation always creates something new: Tolstoy's account of the Napoleonic War does not simply replicate the historical events, it creates a new version of them in the act of representing it. There is therefore always a 'gap' between an object and the representation of that object and this holds in politics too: political representation opens up a gap between the government and the people (Ankersmit, 1997: 47. Ankersmit, 2002).

Second, the aesthetic approach maintains that representatives often create a new version of the people and their interests, and this creative process gives representation its dynamism. Some people interpret this negatively in the sense that they suppose that it follows from this that political representation and freedom are antithetical (e.g. Rousseau, 1997). Others embrace this creative characteristic of political representation as it provides a unique means of understanding that political representation is not designed as a means either to 'track' pre-existing interests or provide an *exact* reflection of the people; rather, it is designed to give the people an image of themselves and their interests upon which to reflect (Ankersmit, 2002: 112ff).

Third, it follows therefore that in any system of representative democracy there will be more than one version of 'the people' at work. There is 'the people' conjured up by formal political representatives in the act of speaking for them; there are conflicting views of 'the people' generated by group membership and representation; and there are 'the people' who pass judgement on these conjuring acts. Indeed, the functioning of representative democracy depends upon politicians being able to offer *competing versions of the people to the people*, in order for the voters to be able to choose the one they prefer (Vieira and Runciman, 2008: 141). Given this, the aesthetic theory of representation allows us to view representative democracy as a form of politics that *accommodates* two further oft-forgotten central components of politics: political judgement among both representative and represented; and that this judgement is usually regarding partisan not general or common interests (cf. Rousseau, 1997; Rawls, 1971, 1993; Habermas, 1984, 1987, 1996; Pettit, 2006).

Finally, none of the versions of the 'the people' on offer to 'the people' ought ever to succeed in *closing the gap* between the represented and their representatives. Even the attempt to close the gap between the people and their representatives is futile and dangerous: it is not the realisation of democracy but an invitation to tyranny because it thwarts any opportunity for the people to reflect on and judge the decisions and actions of their representatives (Machiavelli, 2003; Madison, 2003; Ankersmit, 2002). This is the case because the effect of *closing the gap* – and at the extreme the complete identification of the rulers and the ruled – is (paradoxically) to *exclude* the people from politics in their active or judgemental, role. If the gap is closed there is no longer any room for the various groups and associated partisan interests that constitute 'the people' to evaluate the images of themselves on offer; and the effect of closing the gap will be to remove the possibility for the portrayal of other competing images, visions and interests of the polity.

The Nature of Needs and the Need for Partisan Political Institutions

Despite needs having been out of vogue for some time,[3] I submit here that the determination of needs, properly conceived, brings to the fore all four of the points highlighted by the aesthetic approach to representation. In particular, they highlight that values, judgements and claims are irreducibly partisan and thus that reversion to ideas of an institutionally ideal basic structure, communicative rationality or the general interests of 'the people' are all wide of the mark as regards how best to think about justice. The legacy of utilitarian and Kantian approaches to questions of justice crowd out a concept that calls for greater evaluative input, greater independence for representatives and yet increased citizen participation: that is, subjective and objective judgement about how best to proceed (cf. Nozick, 1975; Rawls, 1971, 1993).

What are needs and how might they help highlight freedom, power relations, domination and representation in the quest to understand and overcome injustices? First, it is important to see that they hinge on the conditions for power and agency in a way that is not true of other conceptual competitors. Human needs are the necessary conditions and aspirations for the individual and political agency that is characteristic of full human functioning. They are of three kinds: (1) vital needs, (2) agency needs and (3) particular social needs.

Vital needs are the necessary conditions for minimal human functioning. These include the need for water, shelter, adequate nutrition, mobility, social entertainment and so on. Calling them 'vital needs' captures the fact that their satisfaction is a necessary condition for *vita*, or life (Hamilton, 2003; Braybrooke, 1987; Doyal and Gough, 1991).

Agency needs are the necessary conditions and aspirations for individual and political agency, which include freedom, recognition and active and creative expression. Calling them 'agency needs' captures the fact that they are ongoing aspirations whose development increases an agent's causal power – and associated feelings of safety, self-esteem and confidence – to carry out intended actions, and satisfy and evaluate needs (Hamilton, 2003; cf. Doyal and Gough, 1991).

Needs, however, are normally felt not as abstract vital and agency needs, but as particular drives or goals, or 'particular social needs': for example, the desire to drink some apple juice or the felt need to work. These needs are brought to light in three different ways: by bald need-claims, for example the need for an efficient train service; by the content of public provision, for example the need for basic income support; and by patterns of production and consumption, for example the need for a car (see below). These are the needs that inspire modern analytical philosophy to treat 'need' solely as a verb and confine it to the logical or analytical form of '*A* needs *X* in order to *Y*'. The need-claim is then evaluated in the light of this, thus making *Y* the crucial normative variable (Connolly,

1983: 62; Thomson, 1987). For example, my claim that 'I need a house' cannot be evaluated until we know why I need a house. 'I need a house in order to shelter myself' is a distinct kind of claim to 'I need a house in the country for weekend trips.'

However, the clear analytical distinction between needs and wants that rests on this over-reliance on the supposed logical form of need generates an over-simplification in our understanding of the nature of needs. There exists a more complicated causal reality. First, particular wants over time can become interpreted as needs, as with the satisfiers of luxury wants for refrigerators and televisions becoming conceived as legitimate needs for these commodities.[4] Second, new satisfiers and commodities generate new wants that affect our ability to satisfy our needs. For example, the car produces both the desire for a car and a need for more motorways. Subsequent economic and political decisions that shift investment, for example from the upkeep of an efficient public transport system to the construction of more motorways, ensure that, in order for me to be able to satisfy my need for mobility, I need a car.

In other words, needs are not only normative; they are also ethical, historical and political. In other words, past and existing institutions and practices determine to an important degree the way we perceive our needs. We therefore need objective and subjective input by all citizens into the *political* determination of the contemporary state of need development and satisfaction in any particular economic and political context. And this input must include ethical reflection and judgement. Moreover, most issues under evaluation are not reducible to any single individual's needs or actions,[5] but larger political questions such as how we should live, who should govern us and how goods and resources and services should be distributed. All of these issues involve value judgements; the necessity to assess political and economic priorities in the past and present; and historical analysis of how existing institutions and past decisions have or have not generated the needs in question. It is therefore important for politics and how our needs develop (or our 'need trajectories') to get some grip on what our current needs are, what they ought to be, and what we, as a community, as a society, as a state, as a world, would like our needs to be. In sum, full participation in the determination of needs is vital because any ethical and material decisions that follow from it must be made with as much information as possible (Dunn, 2005: 94–97). Sen makes the same point with regard to the evaluation of 'capabilities' and the 'quality of life' (Sen, 1985a, 1987a, 1993a, 1993b). Moreover, this form of evaluation depends upon citizens being able to satisfy and develop their vital and agency needs.[6]

Given the complexity of our lives within and between large modern states and the persistence of domination, representation is not only unavoidable but a central cog in this evaluative process. The best way to control for these processes is to determine which power relations generate situations of domination; and then to identify the ways in which economic and political representatives act to underpin these situations of domination or overcome them (Hamilton, 2014). The legitimacy of representatives lies here; and the role of the citizen is, ultimately, in the assessment and veto of representatives in light of their evaluative and creative functions and capacities regarding the formation and regulation of needs and institutions that reduce the incidence of situations of domination.

Given this account of justice as the evaluation of freedoms, needs and representatives under conditions of moral and material disagreement, a state (or other kind of coercive authority) would be legitimate if it produced and maintained conditions in which citizens could effectively evaluate their needs, institutions and representatives and, simultaneously, provided representatives with sufficient power and capacity not only to act on these evaluative outcomes but also to forge new ways of conceiving of our needs and institutions. For this to obtain, theorists must remain realistic and sanguine about the need for partisan institutions, conflicting groups and interests and the kinds of antagonistic politics that follow. I now propose a few institutions in this realistic spirit. These are not intended to be comprehensive, but simply another contribution to those who view politics in agonistic terms and question the ideas of 'impartiality', 'common good' or 'public interest', especially given that these ideas are all too often hijacked to serve only the interests of economic and political elites.

The following political institutions would give citizens both the positive power to legislate and the negative power to repeal legislation, while also providing their representatives with more freedom to legislate. This seemingly paradoxical requirement is achievable if we take the need for both representation and participation seriously and thus institutionalise changes at local, legislative and constitutional levels that would empower citizens to participate periodically in the determination of their needs and their constitution and give them a power of veto or repeal over legislation and existing representatives. These proposals are an amalgamation of my own ideas regarding district assemblies, a revitalised consiliar system and so on (bolstered by some of Condorcet's ideas) and Machiavelli's arguments in support of the Roman tribunes of the plebs. I can but list them here without much explanation, but before I do, let me be clear that they are intended as *additions*, not replacements, to existing institutions of representative democracy; and they originate in the insight that all polities are characterised by moral and political conflict and disagreement and power relations that underpin more or less domination.

Four Main Institutional Arrangements Are Likely to Keep States of Domination to a Minimum

District Assemblies

These would be local physical sites with five main functions: (1) to enable the articulation and evaluation of needs and interests, the substantive outcome of which would then be transferred by the district's 'counselor' to the national assembly for further debate and, ultimately, legislation[7]; (2) to make available to citizens full accounts of all the legislative activity and results emanating from the national assembly; (3) to provide a forum for the presentation of amendments to existing legislation; (4) to vote on proposals coming from other assemblies; and (5) to select counselors for the revitalised consiliar system. The determination of the exact geography (and thus borders) of these sites would be a matter for context and practice, but at least one guiding principle must be kept to the fore: each district should always incorporate as diverse a group of the national population as possible, especially as regards social and economic power relations – the full spectrum of conditions, needs and interests must be incorporated.

A Revitalised Consiliar System

Such a system: (1) would rest on the network of district assemblies; (2) would involve each district assembly selecting one counselor for a two-year period, who would be responsible for providing information to the representatives in the national assembly regarding the *local* needs and interests of the citizenry and existing institutional configurations and their links to states of domination – that is, what changes may be required to better satisfy needs and interests and diminish the possibility for states of domination in the local area in question; (3) would mean that the main role of the counselors was therefore biased towards the defence of the interests of the various groups of citizenry within the district in question, whose needs and interests would surface within district assemblies; and thus not only that the powers and responsibilities of district counselors would be much greater than those of councillors within existing forms of local government, but also that, in order for them to carry out these functions, their independence from national representatives, political parties and social and economic elites would have to be procedurally safeguarded within the constitution. I say 'select' and not 'elect' counselors as, given the formal and merely procedural function of counselors in this proposal, their selection could be undertaken by election or sortition (lottery). I favour the latter as local, district assemblies are prone to fall prey to local factions and interests that may work against the point of this form of local participation; in other words, each counselor must literally advise – give counsel to – the national assembly on the conditions, needs and interests of these she or he represents. Were the counselors to be too easily captured by social and economic elites or always come from these elites – as is the case in most national assemblies within existing representative democracies – they would not help in the necessary process of countering domination as it would be in their interest to advance the interests of these elite groups. Checks and balances and forms of accountability and transparency could be included to ensure that they do carry forward the needs and interests as articulated and determined in the district assemblies; but, given that the district assemblies will be made up of normal citizens leading busy personal and commercial lives, even these kinds of institutional checks and balances may not ensure that counselors conform to their station, as citizens are likely not to have the time properly to monitor counselors 'all the way up the political chain of command'.

Updated Tribune of the Plebs

This would be: (1) a partisan, separate and independent institution of legislation for the exclusive membership of representatives of otherwise dominated groups and classes in society, whose membership could be made exclusively for representatives from this class either by a net household worth ceiling or associated measures, enabling those with the least economic power in any polity both to propose and repeal (or veto) legislation and impeach national representatives, but with strict and low per annum limits on the number of times this could be carried out – here too the selection of representatives could be by means of election or sortition, again favouring the latter, for similar reasons to those stated above (cf. McCormick, 2011: 178–188 and *passim*); and (2) a partisan, separate and independent electoral procedure by means of which the least powerful groups or classes in society would have exclusive rights to elect at least one quarter of national representatives for the national assembly, alongside the normal, open party-dominated processes of electing representatives within most existing representative democracies. This second component of the updated tribune of the plebs is intended to offset the potentially merely reactive character of the first and to withstand the real possibility that the national assembly or assemblies would hamstring a plebeian chamber of this kind by various means, such as using up its power of veto of one piece of legislation per annum by first proposing mock legislation that it knows will be vetoed and then, once the per annum quota of veto has been used up, going ahead with anti-plebeian legislation about which the tribune could then do nothing.

Constitutional Revision and Safeguard

This would entail: (1) a decennial plebiscite, following a month-long carnival of citizenship – a public holiday – in which all citizens would have equal formal freedom and power to assess existing social, economic and political institutional matrices and their effects on the determination and satisfaction of vital and agency needs (Hamilton, 2009); (2) a right of constitutional revision that would have to be procedurally safeguarded: that is, a right of any citizen at any point to propose the assessment and possible revision of a component of the constitution, which in Condorcet, as in Jefferson and Paine, is based on two important arguments, namely *anti-tyranny* (shielding present and future generations from the unchecked power of past generations) and *fallibility* (that reason is prone to error and subject to change over time and thus it is important to presume the need for permanent revision to the constitution) (Urbinati, 2008: 184–187); and (3) *procedural* safeguards giving priority to the satisfaction of *vital* needs, safeguarding counselors from manipulation, coercion and corruption, ensuring the administration of district assemblies and the partisan institutions, and enabling constitutional revision.

Conclusion

In the same way that a bicycle needs a chain to function, humans need certain things to function: we need water, sufficient nutrition, shelter and so on. But there is also another important way to look at this: we also need certain further requirements for both political and individual agency. Some have gone about clarifying this by removing all of the evaluative, historical and political mess that always surrounds these matters and focused in on immutable, fixed, even transcendental accounts of justice. I've suggested here that we should do the opposite, for what is really in question when we talk about needs is the evaluation of how we ought to live, how best it is to function as a human being, how we should proceed: central questions for justice and real politics. Much of what politics is about is about making these kinds of decisions regarding competing, substantive and institutionally determined needs and forms of domination that by their very nature normally do not admit of consensus. To help understand how these matters do and could occur, theorists of justice need to take three things more seriously: that needs are plural, historical and political; that conflict over needs, interests and judgements is irrevocable in politics; that these needs, conflicts and judgements normally take place via institutions of representation. So, in order to remain true to these characteristics of politics, partisan institutions are necessary, which not only act as checks on one another's power but also bring to the fore claims and judgements that might not otherwise find voice in existing accounts of justice. The four main institutional changes I propose would provide sufficient power, class antagonism and institutional checks and balances to generate these outcomes, or at least ensure against one powerful group usurping the freedom as power (and thus political agency) of all the citizens and groups that constitute the polity in question and thus undermining the possibility of dealing equitably with the practical matters of injustice that face us every day. In these terms, then, a citizen's fair share is their fair share of freedom as power to overcome situations of domination via the determination of who and how they are represented in the political institutions of their polity (and, by representative extension, global institutions).

Notes

1 My thanks to Mairéad McAuley, Moshibudi Motimele, Camilla Boisen, Matt Murray, Raymond Geuss, Laurence Piper, Ayesha Omar and many others in

various fora who have commented on parts of the argument submitted here. I am indebted to the University of the Witwatersrand and the South African National Research Foundation for institutional support.

2 *'Libertas suis stat viribus'*. I am indebted to the expert help of Mairéad McAuley in very slightly modifying the English rendition of this phrase found in the translation cited here.

3 This is the case for two main reasons. First, needs have become associated with thinking that falsely assumes the existence of a universal, unchanging list of basic human needs whose determination does not depend on or require the input or opinion of citizens: for example, (1) the 'dictatorship of needs' within the Soviet Union (Fehér et al., 1983) and (2) the prevalent idea that the development of the 'Global South' depends first and foremost upon the satisfaction of *basic* needs. Both undermine an important component of most forms of politics: political agency. Second, the concept of needs is rare because of the still hallowed position of utilitarianism within economic and political thought. Ever since the influential work of Jeremy Bentham, the legacy of utilitarianism has provided justification for purely preference-based economics and politics (Bentham, [1781] 1970; Becker and Stigler, 1977; cf. Menger, [1871] 1981; Arrow, [1952] 1963; Sen, 1970, 1973, 1976–1977; Sen and Williams, 1982). Utilitarianism's subject-relative approach to morality, which treats pleasure or desire-satisfaction as the sole element in the evaluation of human goods and actions, underpins the common tendency to reduce economics and politics to the aggregation of individual preferences (or expressed wants). This involves reducing all claims of need and interest to claims of individual preference. In economic thought, the conspicuous absence of the concept of need is exemplified well by the omission of an entry for 'need' or 'needs' in the four-volume *New Palgrave Dictionary of Economics* (Eatwell et al., 1998). There are some major exceptions to this rule: in economic thought, Smith ([1776] 1975, [1790] 1976), Marx ([1932] 1992, [1847] 1976, [1939–1941] 1973, [1867] 1976–1978, [1890–1891] 1996), Sen (1985a, 1985b, 1987a, 1987b, 1993a, 1993b); and, in political thought, Braybrooke (1987), Doyal and Gough (1991), Wiggins (1998), Brock (1998), Hamilton (2003).

4 For an excellent analysis from over a century ago of the way in which luxury items are transformed from indicators of 'taste' to the basic necessities of modern life, especially within the norm-creating 'luxury' or 'leisure' classes, see Veblen, [1899] 1973.

5 The identification of the question of need as an inherently evaluative, political question related to the fact that human nature and (thus human needs) is not historically invariable is made best by Hegel (1991) and Marx ([1932] 1992, [1847] 1976, [1939–1941] 1973, [1867] 1976–1978, [1890–1891] 1996). Moreover, in doing so, they depart from most of their predecessors in political philosophy, such as Plato, Aristotle, St Augustine, Kant and Smith, who all develop accounts of fixed, unchanging human needs.

6 This is not to suggest, of course, that all needs are subjective (and thus problematic as a basis of an account of justice). Quite the opposite: legitimate post-evaluation agency and vital needs are objective – in the case of some vital needs there will be little or no evaluation required (air, water and so on), while some vital and agency needs will attain their objectivity on the back of the processes of moral and political evaluation proposed in this account of the politics of needs, even if some emerge from partisan political institutions. As Sen (1993b) has argued convincingly, a difference of perspective does not have to leave us with an evaluation outcome that is subjective or relative to particular conditions or circumstances. Objectivity regarding needs and interests must be reached to enable justified judgement in politics.

7 For an explanation of my adoption of the term and institution of 'counselor' from Ancient Rome (as opposed to the more normal modern English term and

institution of 'councillor'), see below and Hamilton, 2008; and for how parts of my account of 'district assemblies' mirror aspects of Condorcet's notion of 'primary assemblies', see Urbinati, 2008: 207–213.

References

Ankersmit, F. (1997), *Aesthetic Politics: Political Philosophy Beyond Fact and Value*, Stanford, CA: Stanford University Press.

Ankersmit, F. (2002), *Political Representation*, Stanford, CA: Stanford University Press.

Aristotle (1980), *The Nicomachean Ethics*, translated by D. Ross, Oxford: Oxford University Press.

Armitage, D. (2014), 'Why politicians need historians', *Guardian* (7 October).

Arrow, K. J. ([1952] 1963), *Social Choice and Individual Values*, second edn, New Haven: Yale University Press.

Becker, G. S. and Stigler, G. J. (1977), 'De gustibus non est disputandum', *American Economic Review*, 67 (2): 76–90.

Bentham, J. ([1781] 1970), *Introduction to the Principles of Morals and Legislation*, London: Athlone.

Berlin, I. ([1958] 1969), 'Two concepts of liberty', in I. Berlin, *Four Essays on Liberty*, Oxford: Oxford University Press.

Braybrooke, D. (1987), *Meeting Needs*, Princeton: Princeton University Press.

Brock, G. (ed.) (1998), *Necessary Goods: Our Responsibilities to Meet Others' Needs*, Oxford: Rowman and Littlefield.

Burke, E. (1999), 'Speech to the electors of Bristol', in E. Burke, *Select Works of Edmund Burke, 4 vols*, Indianapolis: Liberty Fund.

Burke, E. (2004), *Reflections on the Revolution in France*, edited by C. C. O'Brien, London: Penguin.

Connolly, W. E. (1983), *The Terms of Political Discourse*, Oxford: Martin Robertson.

Dahl, R. (1989), *Democracy and its Critics*, New Haven: Yale University Press.

Dewey, J. (1968), *Problems of Men*, Westport, CT: Greenwood Press.

Doyal, L. and Gough, I. (1991), *A Theory of Human Need*, London: Macmillan.

Dunn, J. (2005), *Setting the People Free: The Story of Democracy*, London: Atlantic Books.

Eatwell, J., Milgate, M. and Newman, P. (1998), *New Palgrave Dictionary of Economics*, Basingstoke: Palgrave.

Fanon, F. (1963), *The Wretched of the Earth*, Paris: Présence Africaine.

Fanon, F. (2008), *Black Skin, White Masks*, edited by H. K. Bhabha and Z. Sardar, London: Pluto Press.

Fehér, F., Heller, A. and Markus, G. (1983), *The Dictatorship Over Needs*, Oxford: Basil Blackwell.

Foucault, M. (1991), *Discipline and Punish*, New York: Penguin.

Freund, B. (2000), 'Democracy and colonial heritage in Africa: revisiting Mamdani's *Citizen and Subject*', *Left History*, 7 (1): 101–108.

Geuss, R. (2014), 'Politics and architecture', in R. Geuss, *A World Without Why*, Princeton: Princeton University Press.

Habermas, J. (1984), *The Theory of Communicative Action, Volume 1: Reason and the Rationalization of Society*, translated by T. McCarthy, Boston: Beacon Press.

Habermas, J. (1987), *The Theory of Communicative Action, The Theory of Communicative Action, Volume 2: Lifeworld and System: A Critique of Functionalist Reason*, translated by T. McCarthy, Boston: Beacon Press.

Habermas, J. (1996), *Between Facts and Norms: Contributions to a Discourse Theory of Law and Democracy*, translated by W. Rehg, Cambridge: Polity.

Hamilton, L. (1999), 'A theory of true interests in the work of Amartya Sen', *Government and Opposition*, 34 (4): 516–546.

Hamilton, L. (2003), *The Political Philosophy of Needs*, Cambridge: Cambridge University Press.

Hamilton, L. (2008), 'Human needs and political judgment', in B. de Bruin and C. Zurn (eds), *New Waves in Political Philosophy*, London: Palgrave, pp. 40–62.

Hamilton, L. (2009), ' "(I've never met) a nice South African": popular sovereignty and virtuous citizenship', *Theoria*, 119 (June): 57–80.

Hamilton, L. (2014), *Freedom is Power: Liberty Through Political Representation*, Cambridge: Cambridge University Press.

Hamilton, L. (2015), 'Democratic theory: the South African crucible', *Democratic Theory*, 2 (3).

Hampshire, S. (2000), *Justice is Conflict*, Princeton: Princeton University Press.

Hegel, G. W. F (1991), *Elements of The Philosophy of Right*, edited by A. W. Wood, translated by H. B. Nisbet, Cambridge: Cambridge University Press.

Hobbes, T. (1996), *Leviathan*, edited by R. Tuck, Cambridge: Cambridge University Press.

Livy, T. (2005), *Ab Urbe Condita [History of Rome from its Foundation: Rome and the Mediterranean]*, translated by H. Bettenson, London: Penguin.

Locke, J. (1988), *Two Treatises of Government*, edited by P. Laslett, Cambridge: Cambridge University Press.

Lovett, A. (2010), *General Theory of Domination and Justice*, Cambridge: Cambridge University Press.

Lukes, S. (2005), *Power: A Radical View*, second edn, New York: Palgrave Macmillan.

McCormick, J. P. (2011), *Machiavellian Democracy*, Cambridge: Cambridge University Press.

Machiavelli, N. (2003), *The Discourses*, edited by B. Crick and translated by L. J. Walker with revisions by B. Richardson, London: Penguin.

Madison, J. (2003), 'Federalist No. 10', in A. Hamilton, J. Madison and J. Jay, *The Federalist*, edited by T. Ball, Cambridge: Cambridge University Press.

Mamdani, M. (1996), *Citizen and Subject: Contemporary Africa and the Legacy of Late Colonialism*, Princeton: Princeton University Press.

Mandela, N. (1995), *Long Walk to Freedom: The Autobiography of Nelson Mandela*, Johannesburg: Macdonald Purnell.

Marx, K. ([1847] 1976), *The Poverty of Philosophy*, in Karl Marx and Frederick Engels, *Marx/Engels Collected Works, Volume 6*, London: Lawrence & Wishart.

Marx, K. ([1867] 1976–1978), *Capital*, three volumes, introduced by E. Mandel, translated by D. Fernbach, Harmondsworth: Penguin.

Marx, K. ([1890–1891] 1996), *Critique of the Gotha Programme*, in T. Carver (ed.), *Marx: Later Political Writings*, Cambridge: Cambridge University Press.

Marx, K. ([1932] 1992), *Economic and Philosophic Manuscripts*, in *Karl Marx Early Writings*, edited by L. Colletti, London: Penguin.

Marx, K. ([1939–1941] 1973), *Grundrisse*, translated by M. Nicolaus, Harmondsworth: Penguin.

Marx, K. and Engels, F. (1976), *The German Ideology*, in Karl Marx and Frederick Engels, *Marx/Engels Collected Works, Volume 5*, London: Lawrence and Wishart.
Menger, C. ([1871] 1981), *Principles of Economics*, translated by J. Dingwall and B. F. Hoselitz, introduction by F. A. Hayek, New York: New York University Press.
Mill, J. S. (2008), 'On liberty', in J. S. Mill, *On Liberty and Other Essays*, edited by John Gray, Oxford: Oxford University Press.
Nozick, R. (1975), *Anarchy, State and Utopia*, Oxford: Basil Blackwell.
Nyerere, J. (2002), 'The process of liberation', cited in W. J. Foltz, 'African states and the search for freedom', in R. H. Taylor (ed.), *The Idea of Freedom in Asia and Africa*, Stanford: Stanford University Press.
Pettit, P. (2006), *Republicanism: A Theory of Freedom and Government*, Oxford: Oxford University Press.
Pitkin, H. (1967), *The Concept of Representation*, Berkeley: University of California Press.
Przeworski, A, Stokes, S. and Manin, B. (1999), *Democracy, Accountability and Representation*, Cambridge: Cambridge University Press.
Rawls, J. (1971), *A Theory of Justice*, Oxford: Oxford University Press.
Rawls, J. (1993), *Political Liberalism*, New York: Columbia University Press.
Rousseau, J. J. (1997), 'The social contract', in J. J. Rousseau, *Rousseau, The Social Contract and Other Later Political Writings*, edited by V. Gourevitch, Cambridge: Cambridge University Press.
Sen, A. K. (1970), *Collective Choice and Social Welfare*, San Francisco: Holden-Day.
Sen, A. K. (1973), 'Behaviour and the concept of preference', *Economica*, 40 (159): 241–259.
Sen, A. K. (1976–1977), 'Rational fools: a critique of the behavioral foundations of economic theory', *Philosophy and Public Affairs*, 6: 317–344.
Sen, A. K. (1985a), 'Well-being, agency and freedom: the Dewey Lectures 1984', *The Journal of Philosophy*, 82 (4): 169–221.
Sen, A. K. (1985b), *Commodities and Capabilities*, Amsterdam and Oxford: North-Holland.
Sen, A. K. (1987a), 'The equality of what', in S. M. McMurrin (ed.), *Liberty, Equality and Law*, Cambridge: Cambridge University Press.
Sen, A. K. (1987b), *On Ethics and Economics*, Oxford: Basil Blackwell.
Sen, A. K. (1993a), 'Capability and well-being', in M. C. Nussbaum and A. K. Sen, *The Quality of Life*, Oxford: Clarendon Press.
Sen, A. K. (1993b), 'Positional objectivity', *Philosophy and Public Affairs*, 22 (2): 126–145.
Sen, A. K. (2009), *The Idea of Justice*, London: Allen Lane.
Sen, A. K. and Williams, B. (1982), *Utilitarianism and Beyond*, Cambridge: Cambridge University Press.
Siéyès, E. (2003), *Political Writings*, edited by M. Sonenscher, London: Hackett.
Skinner, Q. (2002), 'The idea of negative liberty', in Q. Skinner, *Visions of Politics Vol. II*, Cambridge: Cambridge University Press.
Smith, A. ([1776] 1975), *An Inquiry into the Nature and Causes of the Wealth of Nations*, 2 vols, edited by R. H. Campbell, A. S. Skinner and W. B. Todd, Oxford: Clarendon Press.
Smith, A. ([1790] 1976) *The Theory of Moral Sentiments*, edited by D. D. Raphael and A. A. Mackie, Oxford: Clarendon Press.

Thomson, G. (1987), *Needs*, London and New York: Routledge.
Urbinati, N. (2008), *Representative Democracy: Principles and Genealogy*, Chicago: Chicago University Press.
Veblen, T. ([1899] 1973), *The Theory of the Leisure Class*, Boston: Houghton Mifflin.
Vieira, M. B. and Runciman, D. (2008), *Representation*, Cambridge: Polity Press.
Waldron, J. (1999), *The Dignity of Legislation*, Cambridge: Cambridge University Press.
Wiggins, D. (1998), *Needs, Values, Truth*, Oxford: Clarendon.

8 A Conservative Response to Piketty's 'Unthinkable' Top Rate Income Tax

Christopher Allsobrook

Introduction

On the occasion of the visit to King's College, London, of Thomas Piketty on 30 April 2014, the editor of the *New Statesman*, commenting on contemporary reception of *Capitalism in the Twenty First Century*, writes,

> That a 690-page treatise on inequality has become an international bestseller is surely symptom of our anxieties and of a yearning for something better. Most of us sense that something is seriously wrong in our politics and economics, at a deep structural level.
>
> (*New Statesman*, 7 May 2014)

Looking out, in this heated reception of Piketty, for 'a counter-hegemonic project comparable to Thatcherism', he continues: 'From as early as the mid-Seventies Thatcher and those who followed her had a philosophy and a message' (ibid.). Thatcher was profoundly influenced by the libertarian economists, Friedrich Hayek and Milton Friedman for instance, writing in her memoirs that 'the most powerful critique of socialist planning and the socialist state' she had read and to which she 'so often returned was F. A. Hayek's *The Road to Serfdom* (Thatcher, 1995: 50). The editorial continues: 'She wanted to privatise, liberalise and roll back the state. She had a distinct world-view ... the Thatcherites were prepared to "think the unthinkable"' (*New Statesman*, 7 May 2014).

Piketty, arguing for an 80 per cent top rate tax for the highest earners, makes a related comment on Thatcher, noting, with irony, that public tolerance of inequality rose during the same period in which inequality widened, in part, due to Thatcher's agenda:

> Up until the 1970s, policymakers and public opinion probably considered – rightly or wrongly – that at the very top of the income ladder, pay increases reflected mostly greed or other socially wasteful activities rather than productive work effort. This is why they were able to set marginal tax rates as high as 80 per cent in the US and the

> UK. The Reagan/Thatcher revolution has succeeded in making such top tax rate levels unthinkable since then.
>
> (Piketty et al., 2011)

Debates in distributive justice have tended to focus on challenges of relative inequality in society. But on the question Rawls asks, of how much inequality we ought to desire at the very bottom, one may ask: how long is a piece of string? The issue of relative inequality represents various social ills which its broad, abstract terms of opposition often override. The aim of this chapter, then, is not to argue for 80 per cent top rate tax, but, modestly, to question why it cannot be thought and to help render it thinkable, by refocusing the terms of the debate in distributive justice from the merits of the relative *equality* and *inequality* of winners and losers in capitalism to the common ground of *civil order* and *social rights*, which conservatives traditionally sought to preserve with cautious adaptation and gradual reform.

Unthinkable Conservatism

We are left to ask, in liberal democratic states which once valued extensive redistribution through means-based taxation, why is this now an 'unthinkable' course of action to revisit or re-implement? Opponents argue such a policy discourages wealth-creators and encourages tax avoidance. John Stossel, author of *No They Can't: Why Government Fails – But Individuals Succeed*, puts the point nicely: 'Rich people wouldn't work if government takes all their earnings' (*Forbes*, 4 March 2012). It is argued that a high wealth tax would be impractical and counter-effective, since (1) the rich will find ways to avoid it, increasing tax avoidance, and (2) where they cannot avoid it, they will not earn the income. Work effort and business creation among the most talented will thus be discouraged, hurting everyone (Piketty et al., 2011).

Thatcher and Reagan's conservative leap forward revolutionised public attitudes by raising the prominence of capitalist market economics not just as a tool of distributive justice but as the primary procedural device to provide it. To stimulate economic growth, civil bureaucracies and labour unions were dismantled, finance and commerce deregulated and public services privatised. We now accept extreme inequalities of wealth since we think this consequence of market forces favours private initiative that benefits the common good. An 80 per cent top rate tax on income is thought to slow economic growth and deter choices the talented and industrious make, which harms the poor. Thus, we accept the dictum that a rising tide lifts all boats, even if some are yachts and liners, with the rest on the *Raft of the Medusa*.

'In the end,' Piketty recognises, 'the future of top tax rates depends on the public's beliefs of whether top pay fairly reflects productivity or whether top pay, rather unfairly, arises from rent-seeking' (ibid.). The unthinkable status of 80 per cent top rate tax must, on this analysis, reflect public belief that top pay reflects productivity. But Piketty's comment on 'unthinkability' reveals more, about inequality and its remedy. I would suggest public opinion is not deceived by the libertarian abstractions of right-wing economic interest groups, but, more generally, we are resigned to the inevitability of the trend. There is, first, a practical problem: even though income inequality is obviously rising, progressive tax measures to reduce such uneven distribution have been defeated by the opinion that such a disincentive to productivity harms everyone. This, in turn, reflects a deeper ideological problem: there can be no debate over higher taxes on higher incomes. It is 'unthinkable' that such policy could be raised as a serious political initiative today. Why is this?

In the late 1970s and early 1980s, radical conservative politicians established the proposal that liberalisation of the economy was needed to revive flagging Western economies. Suddenly the trend from 1949 to 1979 to a declining share of wages accruing to the top 1 per cent of earners was decisively reversed. The subsequent thirty-year period, though accompanied by deeper cyclical fluctuations, has seen no greater average growth rate, nor more efficient output per person employed, than the previous period (Chakravarty et al., 2014: 1). Chakravarty et al. argue that growing public acceptance of inequality that accompanied economic liberalisation 'has been possible due to a change in social attitudes tolerating earnings that are not related to any productive contribution' (2014: 16). But this explanation does not accord with their earlier claim that market-determined wages 'enjoy legitimacy only if distribution of income is not contaminated by rent' (ibid.: 8). Outside of coercion, inequality is tolerated only if income is thought to reflect a relative degree of contribution (if top pay reflects productivity).

It is generally accepted that, in a free-market economy, you get what the market pays for what you do. Wealth is earned and deserved, since individual and social interests are thought to be aligned by prices that obtain for goods and services on the market. On the 'unthinkable' status of high top rate tax, the problem is not just that public opinion is heavily decided against such a tax, despite widening inequality, but, more dangerously, that debate is off limits. The libertarian monetarist political economic revolution of the 1980s forced left-leaning welfare state liberals and social democrats to endure the preponderance of private over public ownership, of corporate over state enterprise, and of low tax on high wealth and private enterprise, to keep the economy going. By 1998, the Labour secretary for trade and industry in the UK, Peter Mandelson, was prepared to state publicly that the New Labour government was 'intensely relaxed about people getting filthy rich'. It is blindly accepted that high tax on entrepreneurial activity acts as a barrier to economic growth, perversely impoverishing the intended beneficiaries of redistribution, the poor. Reagan and Thatcher drastically cut top marginal tax rates by 40 per cent within a decade. Yet, although they increased inequality, those that made large cuts in top tax rates like the United Kingdom or the United States did not grow significantly faster than countries that did not, such as Germany or Denmark (Piketty et al., 2014: 27).

Stiglitz (2013: 83) notes that before the mid-1970s there was a broad social consensus that executives were well paid but not fabulously so. Since then, executives have seen their share soar in relation to workers with no corresponding rise in productivity. The top 1 per cent of earners saw their share of national output steadily increase as lavish executive pay rises became the norm in financial services even though average growth remained the same. All this is generally accepted, yet, I would argue, *non-productive* executive wage inflation has not become *legitimate* during this period – reflecting rising public tolerance of rent-seeking oligarchy. Rather, the economic dogma, that such wage inequalities benefit the common good (at first, buoyed by cheap credit and rising asset prices) obscured the contrary economic fact that it benefits only the few. Over time, especially since the 2008 financial crisis, the trend grew impossible to ignore. Now it is accepted, not as a set of radical ideas, but as an inevitable economic condition. This chapter questions the conservative merits of such *ideological blind spots*. The 'unthinkable' status of high tax on high wealth is due not to practical economic considerations but to dogmatic, abstract, revolutionary ideology that does not befit traditionally pragmatic, flexible conservatism.

Ethics First

To help explain the blind spot which has made high top rate tax unthinkable, I draw on the insights into ideology of the critical theorist Raymond Geuss. Geuss describes the ideological mechanism at the basis of the problem discussed, to explain how the rise of theoretical debate in the abstract ethics of distributive justice, focused specifically on the problem of inequality, has tended to overlook the actual rise in inequality that it accompanied. John Rawls's social democratic treatise on justice as fairness gives a nice account of legitimate inequality with his formulation of the 'difference principle'. By this rationale, unequal distribution is considered just *if this improves the position of the least advantaged.*

Tax strategies to narrow the inequality gap have been rendered unthinkable by widespread acceptance of the doctrine that economic growth depends on these unequal income distributions, such that the least well-off benefit more from present inequality than they would from its reduction. 'The structure and ethos of this theory,' remarks Geuss, is 'complacent and smug' – 'as if developed and fortunate nations like the US have got it basically right' (1999: 38). The problem is not that Rawls's theory failed to reverse widening inequality in the West, as he imagined, but, worse, that actually increasing inequality was overlooked by a theory designed to ignore historical, social and economic institutions. 'After all, a major danger in using highly abstractive methods in political philosophy,' explains Geuss, 'is that one will succeed merely in generalising one's own local prejudices and repackaging them as demands of reason. The study of history can help to counteract this natural human bias' (ibid.: 38–39).

Rawls's 'veil of ignorance' is 'designed to occlude any empirical information that might prejudice the normative force of the outcome' (ibid.: 22). Considering what free and rational beings would ultimately agree under ideal conditions, Rawls imagines a constitutional structure that happens to coincide with that of the United States. The coincidence, comments Geuss, 'stretches credulity' (ibid.: 34). Rawls's 'purported egalitarian theory became more entrenched and influential in the US at the same time as social inequalities in the world increased drastically in almost all industrialized states.' (ibid.: 34). 'Toward the end of his life,' he recalls,

> Rawls had a vague awareness of the gross discrepancy between the aspirations and self-conception of his theory and the way the world was going, and was disturbed by it … He did not, however, seem to have the conceptual tools to make any real sense of it.

The problem for Rawls is that he 'was up against the basic limitations of his approach to the world and of the kind of theory he was trying to develop' (ibid.: 38).

In effect, Rawls shifts the terms of a debate about acceptable inequality from the straightforward empirical question, 'Does A have more than B?' to an unanswerable, complex counterfactual judgement without concrete variables: 'Would B have even less if A had less?' The burden of the answer is shifted from the rich to the poor, who have to come up with an alternative to the latter unfeasibly difficult counterfactual. This reflects a common problem in contemporary political philosophy, which, Geuss claims, moralises political discourse and politics as matters of applied ethics, putting ethics outside and before politics, as a separate discipline, which prescribes how humans should behave, in order to analyse politics with objective terms and natural principles of basic, rational, interested human behaviour (2008: 5).

The problem, he argues, is that ethics cannot reasonably be understood in a pre-socialised sense: that is, without reference to factors of history, sociology, economics, psychology, etc. (ibid.: 6). Political philosophy, he maintains, 'must be realist'; it 'must start with how social, economic and political institutions actually operate' (ibid.: 9). The meaning of our ideals is historically qualified and principles are only relevant if they have an effect (ibid.: 10–13). Ideology makes contingent features of power appear natural or inevitable (ibid.: 52). The idealised framework of ethics-first political philosophy functions ideologically by presuming effective rational ethical distance from existing motivations, social and political institutions, and historical sociological contexts (ibid.: 59).

The biggest problem with Rawls's approach to political philosophy, in his account of distributive justice, is that it avoids the topic of power. By drawing attention away from the issue of power, his theory begins to function as ideology. Geuss argues,

> to understand the political world by appealing to 'our' intuitions of what is just is to divert attention from where those intuitions come from, how they're maintained, what interest they serve and the possibility that these intuitions themselves may be ideological.
>
> (Ibid.: 90)

An overview of social and political systems should pay attention to relations of power and their influence on thought, feeling and valuation. Without some account of relative powers, he maintains, with reference to Friedrich Nietzsche's *Genealogy of Morals*, 'Imposing one law for the vulture and the lamb can easily mean death for all the lambs' (ibid.: 92). He argues that, in 'real politics', theories like that of Rawls are only useful as 'potential ideological interventions' – they are 'actively pernicious, because mystifying' (ibid.: 94).

In Geuss's critique of Rawlsian distributive justice, we find an ideological explanation for the puzzle discussed at the outset of this section, of how rising inquiry into theory and ethics of distributive justice (focusing specifically on the problem of inequality) overlooked the rise in actual inequality it accompanied. Such an approach fails to consider the relationship between ethical principles and actual relations of power. Moreover, conceptually fixated political philosophies, of which Rawls's is just one, can function ideologically, to condone troubling power relations, when the concepts fail to use observable contextual inequalities as a relevant tool in understanding the conceptual nature of the philosophic objects that theoretical accounts of justice wish to move, equate and distribute. 'The 1 per cent' – who are the agents responsible – vs 'the rest of us' – the passive victims – is a conceptual dichotomy that is symptomatic of the failing of conceptual arguments that focus on the relative distributions people have or lack, instead of the real consequences these inequalities have on our contextual equity.

Ethical theories of distributive justice seeking to account for optimal levels of inequality have reinforced the inequality they ostensibly seek to redress, by wilfully abstracting norms and principles of political legitimacy from the context of historical, political conditions. We may, then, apply this ideological explanation to the puzzle of how a high top rate tax became unthinkable at the same time as inequality, indeed, widened, the doctrine that individual and social interests are aligned by market forces in a free economy has failed to explain *how* the mysterious beneficence of such freedom is historically and politically determined and constrained. In Rawlsian approaches to distributive justice, a priori norms are imposed on the evidence, without engagement with the operative norms, practices and moral reasoning of existing institutions, customs and relations of power.

Economic laws are similarly repeated as deontological facts, devoid of any 'interfering' political agenda. A major argument for liberalisation has been that *political* concerns of state should not meddle with the *economic* functioning of the market, whose direction is best left to the private interest of those with relevant financial expertise. Ironically, by renouncing *political* considerations in reasoning about the *economy*, neo-liberal doctrine functions ideologically, effectively asserting political conditions it neglects to deliberate. Piketty's work, by contrast, disarms such uncritical thinking by presenting empirical data on the actual effects of economic laws, about highly unequal rewards needed to incentivise private initiative for adequate economic growth. The majority of professional economists in the UK and the US were blinded to the problem of widening inequality by their belief that income distribution is patterned by benefits to others in a free capitalist society. But, as Geuss notes, a 'free market' depends on *specific* interventions, even if they may be so successful that they appear natural and inevitable (ibid.: 52).

It would seem from this critique that the political economic analysis and evidence which Piketty's *Capital* presents is precisely what we need to counter the ideological 'ethics-first' approach which has obscured widening inequality and its causes, the conservative ideology which renders a remedy like his 80 per cent top rate tax unthinkable. Unlike Rawls, Piketty draws on historically and statistically accurate empirical data to make an explicit judgement on optimal tax rates and levels of inequality for acceptable economic growth. *Capital in the Twenty-First Century* is a work of vast historical scope, grounded in exhaustive fact-based research, which is normative, political and, above all, empirical. In sympathy with this critique of Rawls's 'ethics-first' approach to distributive justice, Piketty rejects theories ungrounded in data and admits an explicitly political stance, insisting social scientists 'must make choices and take stands in regard to specific institutions and policies' (Wolf, 2014).

The central argument of *Capital* is built on more than a decade of research detailing changes in concentration of wealth and income, allowing Piketty to recount the evolution of inequality since the industrial revolution. He finds, unsurprisingly, that, until the two world wars and the Depression, Western European society was traditionally highly unequal, with private wealth concentrated in the hands of wealthy families. In the twentieth century, high taxes, inflation, bankruptcies and the growth of the welfare state disrupted this pattern, ushering in a period in which wealth and income were distributed in a more egalitarian fashion. This period did not last long. Once again inequality is approaching levels last seen since before the First World War (Avent, 2014). Piketty explains the cause of this trend to greater inequality according to a general rule of capital: $r>g$ (where r is the rate of return to wealth and g is the economic growth rate). When the rate of growth is slow, wealth tends to accumulate more from r than from labour, going mostly to wealthy investors, which inevitably increases inequality, in the absence of state intervention. Free-market capitalism does not spread the wealth around but, in the absence of any major redistributive interventions on the part of the state, it produces anti-democratic oligarchies. Piketty advocates progressive taxation and a global wealth tax as the only way to counter the trend (Harvey, 2014).

Despite the merits of this empirically grounded approach, compared with Rawls's ahistorical approach to distributive justice and the difficulty it has in making specific policy statements due to its conceptual focus, Piketty's deployment of masses of historical data to back his argument nevertheless still succumbs to the problem Geuss identifies, of imposing a priori ethical norms on the evidence, instead of working with the operative norms, practices and moral reasoning which are evident in existing institutions, customs and relations of power.

Criticism of the work has picked up on aspects of this underlying weakness. John Gray, for instance, points to 'the hole at the heart of Piketty's book *Capital in the 21st Century*: no agency is identified that could counteract the built-in tendency to inequality that the book diagnoses' (Gray, 2015). We are left to question who will establish and manage a global wealth tax and how they will apportion the spoils. Martin Wolf notes that Piketty's analysis, 'does not deal with why soaring inequality – while more than adequately demonstrated – matters. Essentially, Piketty simply assumes it does' (Wolf, 2014). This reflects the broader failure to contextualise the ethical principles of analysis applied to the evidence. Harvey complains, likewise, that, although Piketty helpfully shows statistically that capital tends to produce ever-greater levels of inequality, he merely states the 'central contradiction' of capital, which drives inequality, as a law of statistical regularity: the return on capital always exceeds the growth of income. Marx would have attributed the forces that sustain this contradiction to the imbalance of power between labour and capital, but for Piketty, 'the law is the law and that is that' (ibid.).

These weaknesses reflect a problem for the inequality debate, regarding the contextual significance of inequality. One may criticise current income inequality because of a specific drawback, problem or widening social gap, but it does not help to criticise inequality per se. Much legally created inequality (giving special powers to surgeons, the judiciary, etc.) has positive social value (Geuss, 2008: 79). As Marx argued, it is open to question where and when equality is desirable. Since no net gain in abstract equality is possible, inequality is always moved from one place to another. Any attempt to make people more equal on one dimension makes them more unequal on another (ibid.: 7). The significance of equality and inequality depends on relative historical circumstances that make sense of these contrasting terms. What agent or institution should reduce income inequality, by what practice, by how much and with what end in mind? How does the goal of inequality stand relative to other political goals? Who will institute a global wealth tax and how, when 80 per cent top rate tax is considered unthinkable?

Realistic Resignation

Geuss thinks it accommodates the status quo to treat abstract concepts of 'equality', 'liberty' and 'human rights' as absolute moral goods in political discussion without historical qualification, since this distracts from the socio-economic and cultural context of these norms, including the ideological agendas and relations of power that determine their significance. This explanation helps to show why solutions to actually widening inequality have been rendered *unthinkable* despite rising debates and data on inequality and distributive justice.

However, the critique of ideology presented so far fails to account for a further ideological feature of Piketty's approach which also features as a weakness in the 'realist' approach to political theory Geuss advocates. It is this further ideological feature I will now explain, drawing on the work of Theodor Adorno. The critique I have given so far of the ideological function of the concept of equality follows a typical Marxian form of *ideologiekritik*: abstract idealists are said to perpetuate the contradictions they criticise without historical qualification (e.g. *The German Ideology*: Adorno, 1970: 5). But the problem Adorno identifies with Marx's method of *ideologiekritik* is that this fails to address a form of late capitalist ideology: positivism.

For Adorno, such liberal egalitarian ideals as 'freedom' and 'equality' are never fully instantiated by the limited experience of actual freedom or equality of real historical individuals. The concept of freedom, or equality, does not exhaust individuals' particularity and no one has yet fulfilled the potential intimated in the concept (Cook, 2001: 7). Unqualified norms of egalitarian liberal ideology can shore up the status quo, conveniently turning attention away from historical socio-economic conditions, but these terms nevertheless also function as an index of truth for the ideology critic, to draw attention to inconsistencies. Despite its shortcomings, egalitarian liberal ideology can serve a basis for criticism, since it 'contains a historically conditioned moment of truth against which the pathic rationality of existing conditions can be judged.' (ibid.: 9).

A problem for the immanent method of *ideologiekritik* arises with a general shift in late capitalist ideology from aspirant idealism to resigned positivism. As Adorno observes:

> Critics confronted bourgeois society not only economically, but morally, with its own norms. This left the ruling stratum, in so far as it was unwilling simply to lapse into apologetic and impotent lying ... with no other defence than to reject the very principle by which society was judged, its own morality.
>
> (Adorno, 1974: §58)

By contrast with the utopian moralism of egalitarian liberalism, positivist ideology affirms existing social preferences in simple terms of inevitability.

It 'legitimates existing conditions by identifying its concepts with them', seeking to establish objectively what the world is already like (Cook, 2001: 10). While false legitimation of existing states of affairs can be confronted with inconsistency, positivism falls back on the argument that this is how things are (Adorno, 1974: §134). Whereas *ideologiekritik* used to reveal the gap between ideal universal liberty and actual unfreedom, it now confronts a different form of consciousness that has dispensed with all thought which does not conform to experience (Adorno, 1967: 29). The rapid rise of extreme inequalities in wealth and income is now treated as a regrettable fact, like climate change, which we know we constructed but we must accommodate, to secure growth and investment. With hard-hearted realism we resign ourselves to prevailing conditions, while the culture industry provides compensatory illusions of freedom.

Although Piketty goes to great lengths to give historical evidence for his claims about rising inequalities of income and wealth, I have argued that the value and significance of his notion of equality remains contextually unqualified. This followed Geuss's criticism of the ideological function of imposed ethical abstractions. Now, following Adorno's concern about positivism, a further problem with Piketty's analysis may be identified, concerning not the ideal of equality deployed but the impression of inevitability given by the data presented as evidence of widening inequality. Like a hopeless scientist monitoring ecological collapse Piketty notes that this trend appears inevitable without unthinkable public intervention.

Aside from the problem of idealism in abstract equality, a further explanation may be given for public tolerance of inequality and the unthinkable status of measures proposed to curb it, despite awareness of widening wealth and income gaps. Masses of historical data from expert economists, along with relentless realism in political theory, disempowers citizens. Dense empirical statistical evidence and sophisticated critique is presented as a radical challenge to the status quo but their effect is to beat the baffled bystander into desperate retreat. As James Alexander notes about socialism, 'the more abstract its criterion becomes, the more liberal; the more historical, the more conservative' (2014: 9). Realism about politics and history can function ideologically, by shoring up the status quo with disempowering radical criticism. This problem is discussed in Lorna Finlayson's critique of realism, 'With radicals like these, who needs conservatives? Doom, gloom and realism in political theory' (2015).

Realism is associated with criticism of ideal theory in liberal political philosophy and a corresponding drive to take the 'real world' and its contemporary politics seriously. Realists such as Bernard Williams, Richard Bellamy, John Gray, Judith Shklar and Stuart Hampshire call for reform of liberal theory. They insist politics is an autonomous domain, irreducible to ethics, and that order is the sine qua non of politics, criticising classical liberal emphasis on reason and equality. But this approach grows conservative, as Finlayson describes it, in three typical moves. First: the move from paying cautious attention to phenomena such as conflict, irrationality and passions, as features of human history, to treatment of these as historically constant features of human nature, failing to question the social conditions that shape such attributes. Second: a related move, to focus on constraints on what is politically possible without paying attention to what makes political organisation possible, such as communication, imagination, empathy, etc. The third move: to emphasise order and stability over ideals such as justice or equality (Finlayson, 2015).

In sum, Finlayson argues, realists' emphasis on *constraints* has a *conservative* effect in liberal theory. 'Realists generally ... preserve the areas where mainstream liberal theory affirms the status quo (e.g. the basic framework of liberal democracy) whilst eliminating points where liberal demands most visibly exceed what is realised' (ibid.). Despite these worries, however, in the remainder of this chapter I argue in favour of conservatism, partly for strategic reasons, related to *real politics*. I argue that conservative politics has been distorted by a neo-liberal agenda, launched by Thatcher and Reagan, that is overwhelmingly responsible for the social ills that drive concerns about inequality in liberal political theories of distributive justice. Deregulation and privatisation has torn apart communities, undermined civil liberties and failed to improve economic growth in the long run. Thatcherism as an ideology has led to blindness towards empirical economic conditions. Aside from a need for more imaginative, inspiring challenges from the left, explicit, consistent conservatism in real politics is overdue. Traditional conservatism has been missing from conservative party politics for forty years. Traditional anti-ideological conservatism sought not to impose revolutionary doctrine and radical initiatives on society but to conserve the wisdom and conciliation of existing institutions with the prevailing spirit of custom and tradition. The current crisis does not demand a revolutionary agenda. Revolutionary thinking, I argue, is part of the problem. That conservatism has been hijacked by ideological revolutionaries outstrips the danger, which Finlayson identifies, of conservative liberalism in realist political theory.

Aside from this strategic political objective, the argument I present stems from the aim to situate, historically, the concern with equality that stimulates engagement with distributive justice, even as tolerance of inequality has risen. Although I endorse Geuss's criticism of mystifying conceptions of equality, his realist approach tends to resignation, without recourse to secure normative grounds traditional conservatism would deem necessary for reform. To stay alive, Geuss's sceptical realism and Socratic interrogations parasitically depend on inadequate, but living, normative preconceptions. His criticism of egalitarian liberal idealism deflates reified terms of 'ethics-first' distributive justice, frustrating their ideological effect. But such realism can also function ideologically, in another way. Without a fat protagonist the relentless negativity of revolutionary critical theory holds no stakes and offers fewer returns. Misleading abstractions in distributive justice should not be dismissed for their idealist orientation. The contemporary significance of illusory ideals demands explanation. What social conditions determine the form the inequality debate has taken? The debate about inequality speaks to traditionally conservative concerns about social rights and civil order.

Conservative Ideology

Thatcher's revolutionary crusade, which continues to drive conservative policy today, was inspired by an ideological agenda, to privatise the state and to shrink the public realm, following the conviction of libertarian economists, such as Milton Friedman and Friedrich von Hayek, that free-market forces, unimpeded by interfering government enforcement, solve all social ills. A minister in Thatcher's cabinet in the early 1980s, Kenneth Baker, remarked that Thatcherism, at first, just stood for some basic 'instincts' that the state should do less, spend less and own less, so that 'the individual' could do more, spend more and own more (*Tory! Tory! Tory!* 2006). But, as British Conservative politician, David Willets admits, in 'Modern Conservatism', not long before New Labour took over the project, 'There is no disguising the political difficulty of getting across both the message of free-market radicalism and also the message of Conservative belief in the community' (Willetts, 1992: 420).

Acknowledging a credibility gap, Willetts maintains that conservatives understand the 'mutual dependence of markets and the community', recognising ties of 'community, affinity and shared culture' which have traditionally 'tempered' the market in Britain and which sustain capitalism (ibid.: 418). 'Without shared loyalties to institutions,' he continues, 'we lose any basis of legitimacy for the state.' Moreover, he acknowledges, 'if we are perpetually fighting to take resources from others ... we will indeed experience national disintegration', closing with a careful quote from Edmund Burke (in Willets, 1992: 421):

> The state ought to confine itself to what regards the state, or the creatures of the state, namely exterior establishment of its religion, its magistracy, its revenue, its military, the corporations that owe their existence to its fiat; in a word, to everything that is *truly and properly* public, to the public peace, to the public safety, to the public order, to the public prosperity ... the leading vice of the French ... was ... a restless desire of governing too much.

While Willets admits basic credibility problems for New Right Conservatism, he speaks up for New Right commitment to the minimal state by locating it in Burke's conservative political philosophy.

How close does 'modern conservatism' compare to Burke's traditionalist interpretation? For starters, traditional conservatism avoids ideology. It finds its bearing in precedent: that is, in evolving historical concessions established gradually, over time. It only allows for reform in continuity with the empirical past, and not out of speculative political convictions.

'Conservatism accepts that change is necessary', observes James Alexander, but it 'only concedes change; it does not try to force it' (2014: 10). Willetts, by contrast, writing on the direction of modern conservatism after Thatcher, claims conservatism is fundamentally based on commitment to the free market. He writes, 'A crucial task for the Conservative Party is therefore to ensure that the free-market agenda remains as substantial and vigorous in the 1990s as it was during the 1980s.' He enthuses,

> In the heroic early Thatcherite period there were enormous virgin lands, areas of government policy untouched by free-market thinking.... Now there is hardly an area of government policy which has not been reviewed.... People now simply want a quiet life. They think that after the turbulence and change of those years we can now put our feet up.
>
> (1992: 414)

This is no reluctant concession to changes in customs and civic order. By the poll tax riots at the end of the 1980s, Thatcherism was associated with policies which had torn apart settled communities.

Traditional conservatism, associated with One-Nation Conservatism in Britain, explains Dorey Garnett, fell out of favour in the mid-1970s for various reasons, mostly to do with demographic and economic shifts in the constitution of the leadership and the electorate. Crucially, Garnett claims, the Conservative Party was taken over by 'self-made lower middle-class politicians and City financiers' in 'a switch of power from estate owners to estate agents'. Unlike the aristocratic gentry in Britain, these 'provincial middle-class grammar school Conservatives felt less responsibility toward those who had not "earned" such success' (2015: 76). Thus,

> integral to Thatcherism is the view that State intervention is itself a major cause of economic and social problems; in the economy, it impedes enterprise, innovation and wealth-creation, while socially, the welfare state saps individual effort and self-reliance, and thus fosters dependency.
>
> (2015: 77)

Massive labour unrest and the economic crisis sparked by OPEC in the early 1970s finished off Heath's One-Nation Conservatives, who sympathised with the post-war welfare state consensus. Heath promoted rational agreement between labour and employers and failed. He asked the nation in a snap election to vote for an inclusive party but lost the gamble, leading Conservatives to 'ditch the half-baked One-Nation doctrine'. Garnett describes how Conservatives moved to a strategy of finding a leader who thrived on confrontation, rather than trying and failing like Heath to meet the socialists halfway (2015: 81).

Thatcher emerged in 1975 as the leader of a new Conservative Party, backed by academics and think-tanks, such as the Institute for Economic Affairs and the Freedom Association, with a powerful critique of the economic turmoil of the early 1970s. For Thatcher and these 'blue revolutionaries', it was essential to 'go over to the offensive in the supreme battle of ideas'. From her Conservative philosophy group, Thatcher demanded, 'We must have an ideology. The other side have got an ideology … we must have one too' (Garnett, 2015: 84). Her populist belief that people knew better than governments about what to do with their money led to a rise of 'conviction politics'. Conviction replaced consensus, competition overrode cooperation, individualism triumphed over collectivism, and public policy was geared towards profit, competition, shareholder value and 'consumer choice' (2015: 87). To save Britain from the unions, Thatcher set up a 'revolutionary free market government' (Hoskyns and Strauss, 1977). Her radical clique took advantage of the 'Winter of Discontent' to take on the unions and drive a radical privatisation initiative. This emerged from Thatcher's Treasury, under John Redwood and Nigel Lawson, as a revolutionary strand of policy which had never been attempted on such a scale. 'Popular capitalism', as Thatcher called the sale of national assets her government 'pioneered' to pay off current expenditure, was so popular it was 'catching on in country after country'. Her dream of a 'property-owning democracy' was, as she called it, 'nothing less than a crusade to enfranchise the many in the economic life of the nation … to return power to the people' (Thatcher, 1986). The state was to be managed by the market. 'That is the way to "one nation, one people",' she declared, seeing victory over traditionalists in the party (ibid.). There has since been no return to traditional conservatism, which has grown more Thatcherite than Thatcher over time.

Traditional conservatism is anti-ideological and avoids imposing such radical initiatives. It represents not so much a body of ideas but more of a positive disposition or orientation towards historical traditions, customs and prejudices (Vincent, 1994: 204). An explicit political ideology which offered to change the world in line with transcendent ideas would be anathema to traditional conservatism (ibid.: 210). Traditional conservatism has its roots in self-conscious criticism of the French Revolution. Burke's typical critique, interestingly, runs parallel to Napoleon's criticism of French *ideologues*, such as Destutt de Tracy, which had turned the term 'ideology' – originally, the objective study of ideas – into a term of abuse on the continent. Napoleon ridiculed *ideology* as a naive and abstract science, divorced from political reality, so focused on metaphysical speculation about ideal politics that it loses touch with the practical realities of political behaviour (Thompson, 1990: 32). Marx borrowed the term 'ideology' to mock Young Hegelian idealists, who neglected to account for the material conditions of the social 'illusions' they criticised – opposing ideas with ideas which leave the real world unchanged (Marx, 1970: 37).

Burke's critique of the French Revolution follows a similar line of reasoning to classical Marxist ideology criticism. His conservative disposition was to rely on experience and to distrust abstract theoretical speculation. He appealed only to principles rooted in long-standing custom and tradition. He opposed the dry, aberrant abstractions of metaphysical reason (Vincent, 1994: 213). Politics, for Burke, was not to be determined by abstract theories about 'natural rights' but by the accumulated wisdom of experience:

> The change is to be confined to the peccant part only; to the part which produced the necessary deviation; and even then it is to be effected without a decomposition of the whole civil and political mass, for the purpose of originating a new civil order out of the first elements of society.
>
> (Burke, 1909: 169)

This conservative reasoning traces back to early defenders of the common law who, from the seventeenth century on, had developed in Britain the vocabulary of 'artificial reason' famously articulated by Burke's critique of the French Revolution (Boisen, 2013: 83).

Burke's anti-ideological conservative disposition typifies eighteenth-century English approaches to common law. On his conservative understanding of 'artificial reason', years of practical experience and usage testifies to the ancient wisdom of the ancient law. Like Suarez before him, Burke took customs to be expressive of the will of the people (Boucher, 2011: 754). He is concerned less with the truth of the immemorial constitution than with the procedure by which the English tended to claim their social rights: that is, by appealing to antiquity and not justifications of metaphysical natural rights, grounded in speculative reason. Burke defended social rights 'not on abstract principles "as the rights of men" but as the actual social rights of Englishmen and as the patrimony derived from their forefathers' (in Vincent, 1994: 213). Rights, for Burke,

> are recognised and acknowledged as fundamental to the social, moral and political fabric of a society, which to some extent already structure and define, or are at least immanent in, that society in the form of customary, but not always fully articulated, rules.
>
> (Boucher, 2011: 761)

As Vincent puts it, 'the circumstances of an institution's or custom's existence, over time, was evidence of an intrinsic rationality or principle which might not be always immediately obvious to the superficial metaphysical observer' (1994: 214). Burke thought it an error to wipe out institutions and start with abstract rational premises.

He praised the American Revolution, unlike the French, for defending existing rights. Political or moral knowledge was not to be found in the speculative ideas of 'intellectuals' but in the concrete accumulated historical experience of actual communities (ibid.: 220). Burke's anti-absolutist inclination explains his conservative reluctance to impose norms where they are not already evident in the moral reasoning of existing customs. His conservatism is balanced with respect for the social rights which citizens secure in their subordination. Like Marx, Burke judges individual human beings for the most part to be incapable of adequately understanding the full meanings and modes of operation of social and political institutions and processes. The accumulated stock of institutional reason is inscrutable for individuals:

> We are afraid to put men to live and trade each on his own private stock of reason; because we suspect that this stock in each man is small, and that the individuals would be better to avail themselves of the general bank and capital of nations, and of ages.
>
> (Burke, 1839: 38)

In this, Burke shares Geuss's thought that theory is to be derived from practice, not imposed on it.

Like later Marxian critical theorists, Burke avoided constructing ideal metaphysical frameworks. He preferred to draw on the moral reasoning evident in actual institutions and social practices, to reform social ills while conserving the good, through continuity in change. Unlike Marxist revolutionaries, Burke thought the authority of international human rights to be derived, not from dictates of right reason, nor from logical deductions of universal natural attributes of man, but from the collective wisdom of ancient custom codified into a coherent body of ideas by learned legislators and judges (Boucher, 2011: 761). Burke criticises the French Revolution for 'sweeping away' the accumulated wisdom of generations, to install untested, abstract principles. Of the Revolution he writes,

> I cannot forward and give praise or blame to anything which relates to human actions, and human concerns, on a simple view of the object, as it stands stripped of every relation, in all the nakedness and solitude of metaphysical abstraction.
>
> (1909: 156)

By contrast with communist idealists and Thatcherite ideologues, Burke was practical: 'Circumstances,' he wrote, 'give in reality to every political principle its distinguishing colour and discriminating effect. The circumstances are what render every political and civil scheme beneficial or noxious to mankind' (1909: 152). On public or private enterprise, Burke left it open: 'Abstractly speaking, government as well as liberty is good', depending in reality on the government or liberty in question (1909: 156).

Reagan and Thatcher both promised to implement free-market, incentive-based, monetarist economic policy. By contrast with these modern conservatives, Burke 'drew a sharp distinction between gradualist reform or resistance to oppression and any ideologically driven, totalising, revolutionary transformation' (Hampsher-Monk, 2012a: 196). He recognised that 'liberty must be combined with government, with public force ... with peace and order, with civil and social manners', since 'all these things (in their way) are good things too, and without them liberty is not a benefit while it lasts, and is not likely to continue long' (in Boyd, 1999: 466). Against imposed rights of man, he warned, 'only if power is broken up, diverted, or checked and balanced by tradition, habit, and institutions with prescriptive roots in civil society will liberty be preserved.' (Boyd, 1999: 487) For Burke, the French Revolution 'destroyed the stable ground of inherited institutions and prejudices against which a political of judgment could conduct the pragmatic appraisal of benefit and possibilities of compromise' (Hampsher-Monk, 2012b: 211). He criticised 'natural rights' of liberty, without limit or qualification, which grounds libertarian conservative free-market doctrine today. 'For rights to be exercised morally, or even practically,' he wrote, 'they must be conventionally limited and institutionally incorporated.' For Burke, the assertion of natural rights presupposes the absence of all aspects of political society (ibid.: 212). 'When people appeal beyond agreed positive conventions to natural rights, they are dissolving their social bonds' (Burke, 1839: 82).

Wendy Brown describes the effects of the unholy convergence in the USA of two distinct political rationalities – 'neo-liberalism' and 'neo-conservatism' – during the Bush regime in the early 2000s, which reflects the problem discussed here, of revolutionary libertarian ideology in New Right conservatism. In this convergence, neo-liberal privatisation undermines public citizenship, political leadership, civil law and traditional community affiliations, while state power is used to reinforce market functions and boost military spending (Brown, 2006: 690). The libertarian chairman of the Federal Reserve, Alan Greenspan, for instance, refused to raise interest rates to correct a rising stock and housing asset bubble, but he socialised risk, releasing money and lowering interest rates against corrections to the long bull market, bailing out traders when bets failed (Einhorn, 2008).

The neo-liberal state has not stopped intervening, but, it intervenes on behalf of investors. Radical free-market policies have dismantled and privatised the welfare state in the North and wrecked representative sovereignty and economic self-direction in the South, as global income disparities reflect. This is more than *ideology*, which masks economic rationality, but a 'political rationality': a normative political form of reason about politics, that is the imposition of market rationality on governance and society, which governs what is sayable, true and intelligible ('thinkable') (Brown, 2006: 694). Not just trade but also governance and citizenship are construed in market terms of productivity and profit, not moral reasoning about norms of precedence. Government by law is replaced by government by business. Citizenship is reduced to rational economic self-care, with no concern for a common good or for the rule of law (ibid.: 695). Thus, neo-liberalism paves the way for neo-conservatism, which 'tries to preserve the moral fabric that corporate domination shreds' (ibid.: 700). Older forms of procedural juridical governance are undermined by openly partial, market-oriented policies, which erode civil liberties and the rule of law. This devalues political autonomy and transforms political problems into personal problems with market solutions, undermining public life for heavily governed consumer–citizens ruled by absolutist states (ibid.: 703).

Conclusion

The debate about equality in theories of distributive justice reflects deeper anxieties about the erosion of communal affinities, civil liberties, social ties, economic security and civic order, while rent-seeking, asset-stripping global private investors take control over all aspects of public national life. Concerns about inequality, xenophobic scapegoating and rising religious fundamentalism follow the insecurity of social rights and civil order. The supposedly conservative agenda, which sustains these processes that undermine traditional civil liberties, is explicitly ideological, grounded in convictions that obscure empirical economic conditions.

These dogmatic features of Thatcherite conservatism do not align with traditional conservatism. The revolutionary libertarian agenda of the New Right has proved to be as dangerously deluded about political economy as the utopian communism it opposes, refusing to countenance evidence against its position and rushing out policies based on speculative, ahistorical, abstractions and an ontology of personhood based on conflict and competition. Rising inequalities of wealth, income and access to resources accompanied these radical initiatives, concentrating economic power in fewer and fewer hands and undermining the independence of elected representatives and legislature. Private global investors threaten an absolutism Burke could not have imagined. His dismissal of abstract, revolutionary ideology, his defence of social rights and his critique of absolutism are ignored by the radical agenda of Thatcherite conservatives. For these reasons, I advocate consistent, coherent conservatism, against such imposture, to shift the focus of the debate about inequality in distributive justice to one of social rights and civil order, so that remedies, such as Piketty's high top rate of income tax, may at least be considered thinkable.

References

Adorno, T. (1967), 'Cultural criticism and society', in T. Adorno, *Prisms*, translated by S. and S. Weber, London: Spearman.

Adorno, T. (1974), *Minima Moralia: Reflections of a Damaged Life*, London: Verso.

Alexander, J. (2014), 'The major ideologies of liberalism, socialism and conservatism', *Political Studies* (June), DOI: 10.1111/1467-9248.12136.

Avent, R. (2014), 'The economist explains Thomas Piketty's "capital"', *The Economist* (4 May), www.economist.com/blogs/economist-explains/2014/05/economist-explains (accessed 11 March 2015).

Boisen, C. (2013), 'Subjecting international relations to the law of nature: a neglected aspect of the early modern jurists and Edmund Burke', *Theoria*, 60 (134): 69–90.

Boucher, D. (2011), 'The recognition theory of rights, customary international law and human rights', *Political Studies*, 59: 753–771.

Boyd, R. (1999), '"The unsteady and precarious contribution of individuals": Edmund Burke's defense of civil society', *Review of Politics*, 61 (3): 465–491.

Brown, W. (2006), 'American nightmare: neoliberalism, neoconservatism and de-democratization', *Political Theory*, 34 (6): 690–714.

Burke, E. (1839), *The Collected Works of Edmund Burke Vol. III*, Boston: Charles C. Little and James Brown.

Burke, E. (1909), *Reflections on the French Revolution*, New York: Collier & Son.

Chakravarty, S. P., Nikolopoulos, K. and Thomakos, D. D. (2014), 'Growth, deregulation and rent-seeking in post-war British economy', *Rimini Centre for Economic Analysis Working Paper Series*, 64 (13).

Cook, D. (2001), 'Adorno, ideology and ideology critique', *Philosophy and Social Criticism*, 27, (1): 1–20.

Einhorn, D. (2008), 'Private profits and socialized risk', *Global Association of Risk Professionals Review* (June/July), 42: 10–18.

Finlayson, L. (2015), 'With radicals like these who needs conservatives? Doom, gloom and political realism', *European Journal of Philosophy* (forthcoming).

Garnett, D. (2015), '"The weaker-willed, the craven-hearted" – the decline of one-nation conservatism', *Global Discourse*, 5 (1): 69–91.

Geuss, R. (1999), *Morality, Culture and History: Essays on German Philosophy*, Cambridge: Cambridge University Press.

Geuss, R. (2004), *Outside of Ethics*, Princeton, Princeton: Princeton University Press.

Geuss, R. (2008), *Philosophy and Real Politics*, Princeton: Princeton University Press.

Gray, J. (2015) 'Misunderstanding the present: Ed Miliband wants to govern a country that doesn't exist', *New Statesman* (19 February), www.newstatesman.com/politics/2015/02/misunderstanding-present-ed-miliband-wants-govern-country-doesn-t-exist (accessed 11 March 2015).

Hampsher-Monk, I. (2012a), 'Reflections on the revolution in France', in D. Dwan and C. Insole (eds), *The Cambridge Online Companion to Edmund Burke*, Cambridge: Cambridge University Press.

Hampsher-Monk, I. (2012b), 'Burke's counter-revolutionary writings', in D. Dwan and C. Insole (eds), *The Cambridge Online Companion to Edmund Burke*, Cambridge: Cambridge University Press.

Harvey, D. (2014), 'Afterthoughts on Piketty's *Capital*', *Davidharvey.org* (17 May), http://davidharvey.org/2014/05/afterthoughts-pikettys-capital/ (accessed 11 March 2015).

Hoskyns, J. and Strauss, N. (1977), '"Stepping Stones" report', Centre for Policy Studies (14 November).

Marx, K. (1970), *The German Ideology*, translated by C. Arthur, London: Lawrence& Wishart.

Piketty, T., Saez, E. and Stantcheva, S. (2011), 'Taxing the 1 per cent: why the top tax rate could be over 80 per cent', VoxEU, www.voxeu.org/article/taxing-1-why-top-tax-rate-could-be-over-80 (accessed 11 March 2015).

Piketty, T., Saez, E. and Stantcheva, S. (2014), 'Optimal taxation of top labor incomes: a tale of three elasticities', *American Economic Journal: Economic Policy*, 6 (1): 230–271.

Stiglitz, J. (2013), *The Price of Inequality*, New York: W. W. Norton.

Stossel, J. (2012), 'Tax the rich? the rich don't have enough. Really', *Forbes* (3 April), www.forbes.com/sites/danbigman/2012/04/03/john-stossel-tax-the-rich-the-rich-dont-have-enough-really/ (accessed 11 March 2015).

Thatcher, M.. (1986), Speech to the Conservative Party, 10 October.

Thatcher, M. (1995), *The Path to Power*, New York: HarperCollins.

Thompson, J. (1990), *Ideology and Modern Culture: Critical Social Theory in the Era of Mass Communication*, Oxford: Polity Press.

Tory! Tory! Tory! (2006), TV programme, BBC Television, London (8–22 March).

Vincent, A. (1994), 'British Conservatism and the problem of ideology', *Political Studies*, XLII: 204–227.

Willetts, D. (1992), 'Modern Conservatism', *The Political Quarterly*, 63 (4): 413–421.

Wolf, M. (2014), 'Review of *Capital in the Twenty-First Century*, by Thomas Piketty', *Financial Times* (15 April 2014), www.ft.com/intl/cms/s/2/0c6e9302-c3e2-11e3-a8e0-00144feabdc0.html#axzz3XGws1x00 (11 March 2015).

Part III

New Horizons Beyond the West

African and Global Issues in Distributive Justice

In the previous two sections, we have explored historical debates and their importance in expanding the approaches we take to distributive justice. We moved on to emerging arguments and critiques of justice through chapters that exposed important issues specifically and serve, more broadly, to show the importance of these kinds of pursuits in making distributive decisions in policy, practice and philosophy. This section moves our debate to another level of discussion, exposing the issues and perspectives outside of the typical framework of distributive justice. These will show us perspectives from outside of the typical Western framework through a specific focus on issues of global distribution and theoretical and applicative traditions and approaches from the, woefully under-represented and historically subverted African background of distributive justice.

This section will represent these issues first through Thad Metz and his chapter, which presents the distinct nature of an African concept of justice and the distributive implications it has. Marianne S. Ulriksen, Sophie Plagerson and Tessa Hochfeld show how the applicative hurdles of understanding African social protection derive in part from the lack of engagement with the philosophic concepts that motivate these policy approaches. Kim Angell exposes an emerging complication in global governance by revealing the limitations of reconstituting legitimising arguments for the territorial distributions. Peri Roberts and Peter Sutch ask us to reconsider the common heritage of humankind in relation to resources and global distributive claims. These chapters in their own way highlight distinct challenges, issues and perspectives which implore the broadening of our thought about distribution in relation to their subjects, foci and observations. They serve to inform us of the broad scope in which distributive debates form and are informed.

However, they also represent a larger concern about the practice and framework of how we explore distributive claims conceptually, motivationally and applicatively. They serve to show us the many ways in which our debates emerge and gain their constituency. They show us that no matter how complex, detailed and specified our pursuit of distributive justice is in our perception, it is ultimately constrained as much as it can be empowered by the aspects we see as relevant to understanding it. Our practice of study must be vigilant of these new, missed and under-represented tools, as we work to sculpt the face of distributive justice revealing it slowly, rather than assuming we can cast its visage in whole or in part with a single-stroke approach or consideration.

9 An African Theory of Social Justice

Relationship as the Ground of Rights, Resources and Recognition

Thaddeus Metz

Africa as a Neglected Intellectual Resource

Most people know that Africa is a continent rich in minerals and, indeed, has been exploited for them for centuries. However, few people, including theorists in the Anglo-American and Continental traditions, are aware of what this part of the world has to contribute intellectually. Upon having moved to South Africa more than a decade ago, I have been working to mine the worldviews of black peoples indigenous to the sub-Saharan region for ideas that can contribute to contemporary debates in moral and political philosophy. This chapter presents some of my key findings with regard to the latter.

The theoretical gem that I have encountered upon having become acquainted with sub-Saharan normative perspectives is the idea that a certain kind of communal relationship is morally worth pursuing for its own sake. The kind of communitarianism below the Sahara, which I sometimes label 'Afro-communitarianism', differs from the kinds salient in the contemporary Western tradition, mainly in that it focuses more on a certain kind of relationship as the normative ground of political choice and less on a group. It also provides an interesting, relational contrast to the Hobbesian, Millian, Lockean and Kantian traditions, which are all individualist in an important way, as I explain below.

In my work, I have studied Afro-communitarian approaches to politics under a philosophical loupe, and have also sought to refine and polish them in various ways. The theory of justice that I advance in this chapter is therefore not meant to *reflect* the views of any particular African people. Instead, I have drawn on values and norms that have been salient in sub-Saharan worldviews in order to *construct* an attractive basic moral principle[1] on which I here ground a novel, comprehensive conception of social justice. My aim is not merely to indicate how this theory of justice with an African pedigree differs from influential Western views, but also to contend that it is worth taking seriously as a rival to them.

In this chapter I address solely social or 'ideal' justice, as opposed to criminal, compensatory or more broadly 'non-ideal' justice. The latter concerns second-order duties about how to respond to the violation of other duties. My focus on the former means that I am instead concerned to specify some of the key first-order duties, binding principally on the state, that should not be violated in the first place when it comes to the protection of civil liberty, the distribution of property and the recognition of identity. Notice that I set aside issues of political power, for the sake of focus.[2]

I begin by distinguishing theories of social justice according to whether they are individualist, corporatist or relational, so as to make it clear how the latter category is under-developed in the English-speaking literature. Then, I advance a relational principle grounded on sub-Saharan ideas of community that is a strong candidate for a basic moral theory. In the rest of this chapter I apply this principle to three major issues in social justice, namely which civil liberties the state should protect, which resources the state should distribute and in what manner, and how people's identity should figure into state decision-making. Along the way I will have contrasted the Afro-communitarian approach with standard Western theories of justice, and conclude that, in light of its promise relative to them, it should not be neglected.

Individuals, Groups, Relationships

At a highly abstract level, theories of social justice are usefully characterised according to where moral status is located. By 'moral status' I mean what is entitled to moral treatment for its own sake, or what can be wronged. Most theories can be classified as (largely) either individualist, corporatist or relational.

An individualist theory of distributive justice (or of ethics more broadly) is one that implies that properties intrinsic to an individual are what ground moral status. It is the view that features of an individual that make no essential reference to anything outside it are what ground morality.

The most salient theories of distributive justice in the modern Western tradition are individualist in this way. Consider, first, Thomas Hobbes's (1651) egoist view that each agent, including the ruler of a state, ought to act in ways that are expected to satisfy his own long-term self-interest. Although interacting with others in various ways would of course be likely to improve an individual's self-interest, such interaction is of mere instrumental value; what matters morally for its own sake, and not merely as a means, is the satisfaction of a person's desires.

Similar remarks apply to John Stuart Mill's utilitarianism (1863). According to this theory, the state, among other agents, ought to do what will maximise expected interest satisfaction and minimise interest dissatisfaction over the long run, taking everyone's interests into account. Even though the interests of all are to be advanced as an aggregate, what has ultimate moral value from this perspective is, like egoism, an individual's capacity for pleasure/pain or for the desires she would have if informed to be satisfied/frustrated.

Turning to John Locke (1690), many political philosophers elect to read him as maintaining that individuals have basic natural rights of self-ownership. From this perspective, the sole job of the state is to protect people from interference with their bodies and minds and to protect the property they have acquired upon having either laboured on something unowned or been freely given something by another rightful owner (or having otherwise obtained something in a manner that has not harmed other persons). Again, the individualism is palpable.

For a last example, consider Immanuel Kant (1793), whose account of justice is largely grounded on the formula of humanity, according to which wrong acts are those that degrade a person's capacity for autonomy, roughly the ability of an individual to govern herself according to her reason, as opposed to be determined by natural instinct or conditioning. So stated, there is no essential reference to anyone but the individual when it comes what has moral status.[3]

From this sketch, one readily sees that individualism cuts across many of the usual ways of classifying theories of political and economic justice, e.g. egoist versus altruist, consequentialist versus deontological, rights-based versus duty-based, autocratic versus democratic, libertarian versus egalitarian, and so on. There is a real kernel of truth in the claim that the Western tradition, at least over the past few hundred years, largely ascribes basic moral value to the individual, and to the person in particular.

The starkest contrast with individualism is corporatism, according to which moral status inheres not in properties internal to an individual, but rather those of a group. From this standpoint, wholes are what ultimately matter and merit moral treatment for their own sake, and not their parts as distinct from them.

In the European canon G. W. F. Hegel (1837) is sometimes read this way, where he is taken to ascribe moral significance to spirit, a supra-individual agency that realises its freedom across society. In addition, there have been anthropologists who deem cultures to have basic moral value (e.g. Benedict, 1934), as well as other theorists who have deemed peoples or nations to have it, where this might include one of the founders of contemporary thought about crimes against humanity (cf. Kukathas, 2006). And then the Western 'communitarian' view that individuals can have unassumed obligations to support their community's way of life (e.g. Walzer, 1983; Sandel, 1984) might implicitly ascribe basic moral value to the latter.

The African tradition also has strains of corporatism, probably most clearly voiced in the work of Claude Ake when he remarks that

> in most of Africa ... people are still locked into natural economies and have a sense of belonging to an organic whole, be it a family, a clan, a lineage or an ethnic group.... All this means that abstract legal rights attributed to individuals will not make much sense for most of our people; neither will they be relevant to their consciousness and living

> conditions. It is necessary to extend the idea of human rights to include collective human rights for corporate social groups such as the family, the lineage, the ethnic group.
>
> (1987: 9; see also Kigongo, 2002)

Ake believes that individual rights might be appropriate for 'atomised' Western societies, in which people have a sense of their identity as persons separate from groups to which they belong, but that they are inappropriate in a context where characteristically African conceptions of the self and of the good predominate.

I implicitly argue below that Ake's interpretation of the African tradition is inaccurate, or at least incomplete; although he is correct that the notion of collective rights is part of it, it also includes individual rights, so that I believe it is no accident that the Organisation of African Unity's ('Banjul') Charter speaks of both 'human' rights and those of 'peoples' (OAU, 1981). My point at this stage, however, is merely to illustrate the differences between individualism, corporatism and relationalism.

Turning to the latter, it is the view that moral status is constituted by some kind of interactive property between one entity and another. It therefore stands 'in between' individualism and corporatism. Similar to individualism, a relational account implies that moral status can inhere in things as they exist apart from their membership in groups. A relational theory implies that something can warrant moral consideration even if it is not a member of a group or, more carefully (if every individual is necessarily part of a group), for a reason other than the fact that it is a member. Similar to corporatism, though, a relational account accords no moral status to a being on the basis of its intrinsic properties. A relational theory implies that something warrants moral consideration only if (and because) it can or does exhibit certain attitudes towards, or have a causal effect on, another being. It is an individual's extrinsic properties that count.

It is difficult to give clear examples from the Western tradition of justice; in fact, the closest cases come from theorists who are well known for rejecting distributive justice (construed in terms of giving people what they deserve, observing their rights or treating them impartially) as an ideal. Karl Marx, for instance, who in the *Critique of the Gotha Programme* (1875) is famously scathing of 'equal right' and 'fair distribution', at bottom prizes the realisation of a person's species-being, where that includes the capacity to relate to others in certain, communal ways (most clearly articulated in the early manuscripts, 1844a, 1844b). And more recently there is the ethic of care, normally contrasted with an ethic of justice, where the former maintains that the point of moral behaviour should be to develop, sustain and enrich caring relationships (e.g. Gilligan, 1982; Noddings, 1984).

Although there have been strains of relationalism in Western political philosophy, it has not been the dominant approach, particularly when it comes to justice. That is quite unlike the African tradition, by which I mean worldviews and cultures salient among indigenous sub-Saharan peoples.[4] They are routinely called 'communitarian', and, while that is not inaccurate, in the following section I demonstrate how African communitarianism is characteristically relational and not corporatist. Or at least I show that the relational interpretation is under-developed and merits much more attention than it has received as a potential ground of justice.

An Afro-Communitarian Moral Theory

In this section, I spell out a principled interpretation of relational themes that are prominent in the moral thought of sub-Saharan peoples and, especially, of contemporary, literate intellectuals whose ideas are grounded on theirs. I begin by indicating broadly how much of the African moral tradition is relational, after which I present a specific theory that I advance as a philosophically attractive reading of it.

To begin to see some of the respects in which African political thought has been relational, consider these remarks about sub-Saharan values and norms from theorists who are from places as diverse as South Africa, Zimbabwe, Uganda, Kenya and Nigeria:

> (I)n African societies, immorality is the word or deed which undermines fellowship.
>
> (Kasenene, 1998: 21; see also p. 67)

> The conclusion that Africans are persistently in search of harmony in all spheres of life is pertinently true of African thought. The concrete expression of African thought is the continual quest for consensus aimed to establish harmony.
>
> (Ramose, 1999: 59)

> Social harmony is for us [Africans – ed.] the *summum bonum* – the greatest good. Anything that subverts or undermines this sought-after good is to be avoided like the plague.
>
> (Tutu, 1999: 35)

> (O)ne should always live and behave in a way that maximises harmonious existence at present as well as in the future.
>
> (Murove, 2007: 181)

> A life of cohesion, or positive integration with others, becomes a goal, one that people design modalities for achieving. Let us call this goal communalism, or, as other people have called it, communitarianism. In light of this goal, the virtues … also become desirable.
>
> (Masolo, 2010: 240)

> The vast majority of norms, taboos and prohibitions [in the African tradition – ed.] is directed towards protecting the community and promoting peace and harmony.
>
> (Ejizu, 2011)

Talk of 'fellowship', 'harmony' and 'cohesion' is recurrent in the above quotations and in many other remarks from scholars of African thought.[5]

Corporatism is admittedly one way to interpret these remarks; one might think that ethics for much of indigenous Africa is more or less a matter of maintaining a certain kind of group, which, after all, must have its parts arranged in a certain way for it to exist. However, I believe that is not the best interpretation, at least for the purpose of developing a plausible theory of social justice. Instead of maintaining that community, understood as a group, is to be sustained, I focus on the idea of living communally or relating to others in a harmonious way.

I again quote representative African theorists about what it means to live in communion or harmony with others, after which I draw on their comments to advance a precise moral principle to guide thought about social justice.

> Every member is expected to consider him/herself an integral part of the whole and to play an appropriate role towards achieving the good of all.
>
> (Gbadegesin, 1991: 65)

> Harmony is achieved through close and sympathetic social relations within the group.
>
> (Mokgoro, 1998: 17)

> The fundamental meaning of community is the sharing of an overall way of life, inspired by the notion of the common good.
>
> (Gyekye, 2004: 16)

> (T)he purpose of our life is community-service and community-belongingness.
>
> (Iroegbu, 2005: 442)

> If you asked *ubuntu* advocates and philosophers: What principles inform and organise your life? What do you live for … the answers would express commitment to the good of the community in which their identities were formed, and a need to experience their lives as bound up in that of their community.
>
> (Nkondo, 2007: 91)

I do not deny that some of the above are using the word 'community' to refer to a group, most clearly Nkondo when he speaks of '*ubuntu*', the southern African Nguni term often used to capture traditional African approaches to morality and theories grounded on them. But what I submit all of them are at bottom prescribing is a certain way of relating to other persons.

In fact, notice that two distinct relational themes are recurrently mentioned. On the one hand, there is considering oneself a part of the whole, enjoying close ties, sharing a way of life, community-belonging and experiencing oneself as bound up with others. I most often call this way of relating a matter of 'identifying with others'. On the other hand, there is what I call 'exhibiting solidarity with others', namely achieving the good of all, being sympathetic, acting for the common good, serving others in the community, and being committed to the good of one's society (or rather its members).

Although several thinkers have obviously conceived of the key relationship in the African tradition as the combination of two major elements, I aim to be fairly precise and systematic about it, as I construct a moral principle that promises to make sense of social justice. More carefully, then, it is revealing to understand identifying with another (or being close, belonging, etc.) to be the combination of exhibiting certain psychological attitudes of 'we-ness' and cooperative behaviour. The psychological attitudes include a tendency to think of oneself as part of a relationship with the other and to refer to oneself as a 'we' (rather than an 'I'), as well as a disposition to feel pride or shame in what the other does. The cooperative behaviours include being transparent about the terms of interaction, allowing others to make voluntary choices, acting on the basis of trust, adopting common goals and, at the extreme end, choosing for the reason that 'this is who we are'.

Exhibiting solidarity with another (or acting for others' good, etc.) is similarly aptly construed as the combination of exhibiting certain psychological attitudes and engaging in helpful behaviour. Here, the attitudes are ones positively oriented towards the other's good and include an empathetic awareness of the other's condition and a sympathetic emotional reaction to this awareness. And the actions are not merely those likely to be beneficial – that is, to improve the other's state – but also are ones done consequent to certain motives, say, for the sake of making the other better off or even a better person.

Altogether, then, think of communal or harmonious relationship roughly as in Figure 9.1.

And keep in mind that it is possible to be in a communal or harmonious relationship in two ways. One way to be party to a communal relationship would be to exhibit identity and solidarity with others, as a subject. However, one could also be party to such a relationship by being identified with or exhibited solidarity towards, as an object. Similar remarks apply to the opposite of a communal (harmonious) relationship. One could either relate in a discordant manner as a subject or be subjected to discordance, as in Figure 9.2.

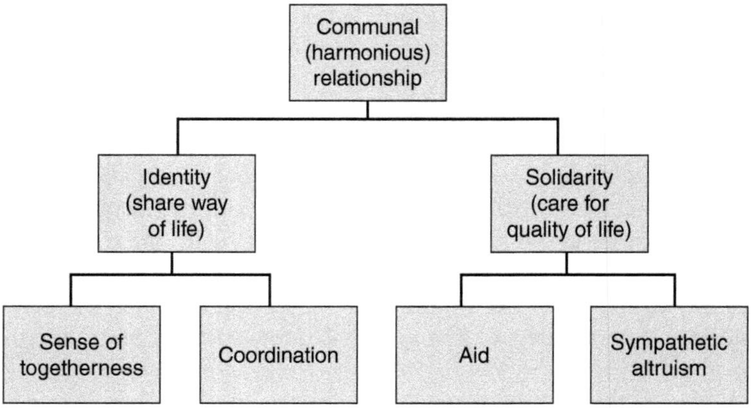

Figure 9.1 Communal or Harmonious Relationship.

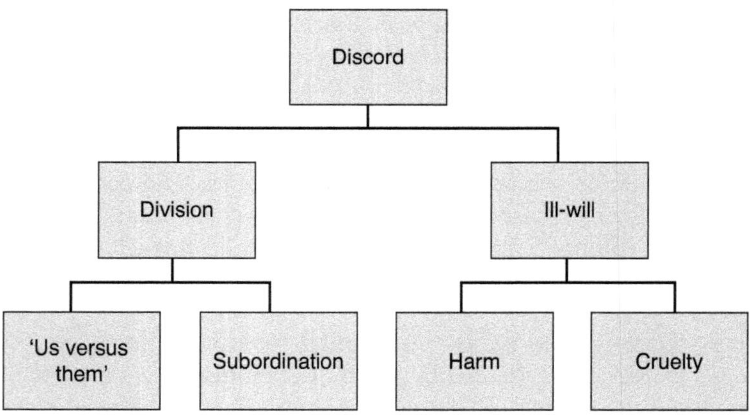

Figure 9.2 The Opposite of a Communal or Harmonious Relationship.

With this reconstruction of salient normative themes in the African tradition, I now advance the preferred statement of my moral principle[6]:

> An act is right if it prizes other persons in virtue of their natural capacity to relate harmoniously; otherwise, an act is wrong, and especially insofar as it prizes discordance.
>
> An agent must honour those who can by nature be party to relationships of identity and solidarity, and she ought above all to avoid honouring relationships of division and ill-will.

Notice that these statements, intended to be equivalent, imply that since people have a moral status in virtue of their capacity to relate communally, one generally ought to relate to people in that way for its own sake, a reconstruction of the African tradition that differs from the ways others have interpreted it. For example, some sub-Saharan theorists have maintained that relating communally is not to be done as a way to express respect for other human beings, but rather done merely as a means to the promotion of a common good in the long run (e.g. Gyekye, 2004, 2010). Others have held that communal relationships are a mere means to the ultimate end of promoting an invisible, vital energy in people's lives, a force that is widely thought in the African tradition to have come from God and to constitute the essential nature of everything in the world (e.g. Bujo, 1997; Magesa, 1997). Still others have contended that communal relationships are to be promoted as ends, with the most important relationships being with ancestors, progenitors of a clan who are normally understood not only to have lived to a ripe old age, achieved moral wisdom and survived the death of their bodies, but also to continue to interact with human beings on earth (e.g. Murove, 2007).

I lack the space here to show that my interpretation is no less African and is more philosophically plausible than these rivals. However, I can point out that, by making a certain way of relating to other human persons the focus and more than merely a means to an end, my principle best promises to ground individual rights. It does not instruct an agent to *promote* anything, not even communal relationship. In a word, the principle is not consequentialist, instead prescribing *respect* and specifically of another person's *ability* to relate harmoniously. It is only such a deontological interpretation of the African tradition, I submit, that can make reasonable sense of the judgements that all human persons matter morally and may not be treated as mere means to a greater good.[7]

To see more of the nature and promise of this principle, consider what it entails for intuitively wrongful actions. When dealing with an innocent party (the natural focus of an ideal theory of social justice), respecting her capacity to enter into communal relationship will typically mean relating to her communally: that is, enjoying a sense of togetherness with her, participating with her on a cooperative basis, doing what one can to help her, and doing so consequent to sympathy and for her sake. Conversely, wrongful treatment of an innocent would normally consist of discordant behaviour, in which one acts out of a sense of 'me versus you', subordinates another, seeks to harm another, and does so consequent to indifference or even cruelty. On the face of it, this is a compelling account of why it is typically wrong to steal, exploit, kidnap, assault, insult, lie, break promises and the like.

Notice that the Afro-communitarian account of right and wrong actions differs from the individualist views canvassed above. A prescription to honour people in virtue of their ability to relate harmoniously is distinct from the ideas that one should, at bottom, maximise long-term self-interest, maximise the general welfare in the long run, uphold natural rights of ownership and treat the capacity for autonomy with respect.[8] And it is on the face of it no worse an account than these, or at least so I now contend by applying it to three major dimensions of justice, concerning the protection of civil liberty, the distribution of property and the recognition of identity.

Rights[9]

Here, I appeal to the Afro-communitarian moral principle articulated in the previous section in order to show how it provides a novel and promising account of human rights to civil liberties. I address duties of the state to provide economic resources and to recognise people's identity in the following sections.

As is well known among Western political theorists, the most common way that human rights have been philosophically grounded has been on a principle of respect for human dignity. The standard thought has been that human beings characteristically exhibit a superlative, non-instrumental value that must not be degraded, where human rights violations are severe degradations of our worth. Quite often, a Kantian account of our dignity in terms of our capacity for autonomy or reason has been advanced to fill out this approach.

I continue to employ this overall view of how rights are a function of dignity, but do not conceive of dignity in an individualist manner; instead of rationality as its ground, I suggest relationality. The Afro-communitarian moral theory is well understood to entail that an individual has a dignity insofar as he is by nature capable of being both a subject and an object of a communal relationship.

Suppose, then, that what is special about human beings is their capacity to be in communal relationship with others. In that case, one should neither stunt that capacity for the sake of something worth less than it, nor treat (innocent) others in a discordant way. Respecting another's dignified capacity both to exhibit harmony and to be harmonised with means treating it as the most important value, and hence entails (in the case of innocents) not impairing their ability to be harmonious as well as not failing to be harmonious with them.

Now, characteristic negative human rights violations are behaviours that *do* impair others' ability to harmonise as well as constitute grave forms of discordance. What genocide, torture, slavery, human trafficking and apartheid have in common is more or less that those who engage in these practices treat people, who are special by virtue of their capacity for harmonious relationship, in an extraordinarily discordant way. Raping someone to feel a sense of power and torturing an innocent person for fun are actions that stunt another's capacity for identity and solidarity for a trivial end and evince enormous division and ill-will, the opposites of communal relationship, towards him. Instead of expressing togetherness, one creates distance; instead of engaging in coordinated behaviour, one subordinates; instead of helping another, one harms; and instead of being altruistic and sympathetic, one exhibits emotions such as *Schadenfreude* as well as motives such as self-interest.

Compare this account of (negative) human rights with the Kantian approach, well known for being more promising than utilitarianism as a ground of them. The Kantian standardly thinks of negative rights violations as restrictions on the ability to make an autonomous choice (e.g. Rawls, 2001), but that account does not fully capture why, say, rape is a human rights violation. Rape is wrong not merely because there is a lack of consent involved, for otherwise stealing someone's television would be equally wrong, but it is not; rape is much worse.

The Kantian will try to say that rape is worse than stealing a TV because the degree of infringement of the other's ability to choose is more severe. Perhaps. However, additional, and promising, explanations include the following ideas.

For one, rape is a form of ill-will beyond any restriction of autonomy (or, in my terms, division). It inflicts pain out of, at best, indifference to the other's good. It foreseeably, if not intentionally, hurts, both physically and psychologically, where it is implausible to think that pain is immoral to inflict merely because it prevents another from choosing a wide variety of ends (as per Rawls, 1988).

For another, rape foreseeably damages the other's ability to be romantically intimate, one of the most intense forms of how to commune. That is, the sexual dimension of rape is relevant to its moral dreadfulness, but that is difficult for a Kantian to acknowledge.

My aim is not to show that the Afro-communitarian account of rights to be free from interference and harm is better than the Kantian one, let alone the best full stop. It is rather to indicate an under-appreciated, relational strategy by which to ground negative human rights philosophically, one that gives the dominant approach an apparent run for its money.

Resources[10]

It is well known that over the past couple of decades there has been a marked shift in theorisation of poverty and socio-economic justice more generally away from subjective considerations. Instead of focusing on autonomous choice or preference satisfaction, many theorists and policy makers now contend that economic development is better conceived in terms of ensuring that people have the capabilities to live in a variety of ways that are objectively good for their own sake (Sen, 1999; UNDP, 2010; Nussbaum, 2011; OECD, 2013). As I explain below, the African tradition, at least as interpreted here, is in line with this trend, while adding in a robust relational approach to ideas about not only what should be distributed, but also how.

Treating people as special in virtue of (in part) their capacity to be party to a relationship of solidarity means helping them (when they are innocent). Help, though, can be interpreted in a variety of ways. A Kantian would think of it as enabling another person to achieve whatever (permissible) goals she might have adopted, and a utilitarian would tend to conceive of it as satisfying a person's desires or making her pleased. In contrast, the Afro-communitarian theory, as per most of the sub-Saharan tradition, instead focuses on particular ways of life that people *should* aim for, desire or find pleasing. These objectively good ways of life are usefully distinguished in terms of welfare and excellence.

People's welfarist good in characteristic African thought is largely conceived in terms of met needs, both physical and mental, as well as both biological and social. For example, Kwame Gyekye, the influential Ghanaian political philosopher, maintains that moral behaviour is a matter of working to satisfy 'needs that are *basic* to the enjoyment and fulfilment of the life of each individual' (2010: sec. 7), whereas Nhlanhla Mkhize, an academic psychologist in South Africa, remarks, 'A sense of community exists if people are mutually responsive to one another's needs' (2008: 39). My favoured theoretical rendition of sub-Saharan moral theory likewise is meant to imply that the core of improving others' well-being is a matter of meeting their needs, not merely basic ones but also those relevant to higher levels of flourishing, e.g. being creative, athletic, theoretical.

People's non-welfarist good, in contrast, is a matter of their ethical development. The focus here is not on a person's doing well, but on being a good person. Indeed, an important way to help others in the African tradition is to foster their moral virtue or human excellence (their *ubuntu* in the most literal sense of the word). And since morality is a function of honouring people's capacity to commune, relational factors take centre-stage when thinking of how to aid others. Consider an elderly African woman who during a community discussion about poverty remarked, 'For me, the problem with being poor is that I have nothing to give to others' (cited in Metz, 2011b). She objects to poverty primarily on the ground that it stunts her ability to care for others.

Concretely, by the Afro-communitarian theory, a central way for the state to exhibit solidarity with its residents would be to ensure they have access to things and services particularly useful for communing with others. So, in addition to food, water, shelter, clothing, health care and other goods essential for meeting needs, the state should distribute those resources particularly enabling people to share a way of life and to care for one another's quality of life, e.g. couples counselling, women's shelters, parenting classes, quality daycare, rehabilitation programmes, neighbourhood parks, densification in spacious (i.e. rich) neighbourhoods, job training, non-exploitive labour relations and grassroots organisations.

This relational approach to the kinds of resources that a state should ensure people can access marks a fairly novel contribution to thinking about economic justice. Kantian and utilitarian economic theories are both individualist for their focus on goods/services that will enable a given person to obtain her goals or satisfy her preferences. And note that the influential capabilities approach is also characteristically individualist. Aside from affiliation and political control, the rest of Martha Nussbaum's list of ten central capabilities makes no essential reference to any person but the individual with the capacity, e.g. life, bodily health/integrity, play, imagination, thought, practical reason, material control, other species (2011: 31–35, 46–62). And then Amartya Sen leaves the content of capabilities open, to be determined by democratic deliberation (2004). In contrast, the Afro-communitarian theory entails that some key socio-economic resources are those that enable people to engage in harmonious relationships with each other, an alternative approach that is worth consideration.

In addition to providing a novel account of what to distribute, the relational theory grounds a fresh view of how to distribute the relevant resources. The dominant views in the literature are currently: utilitarianism (or consequentialism more generally), distribution so as to maximise some state of affairs; prioritarianism (or the Rawlsian difference principle), distribution so as to make the lot of the worst-off the best it can be; sufficientarianism (basic income grant), distribution so as to ensure that everyone has a decent minimum; and egalitarianism, distribution so as to provide (roughly) equal opportunities and goods. In contrast to these views, my reading of the African tradition is that it prescribes what I call a 'balanced' distribution.

To begin to see what I mean, consider that the quintessential instance of communal relationship is the family; it is where sharing a way of life and caring for others' quality of life are expected to be found and to a fairly intense degree. As Augustine Shutte has noted in one of the first philosophical books devoted to the southern African ethic of *ubuntu*,

> The extended family is probably the most common, and also the most fundamental, expression of the African idea of community.... There is a sense in which 'the people', even humanity itself, constitutes a kind of family. The importance of this idea for ethics is that the family is something that is valued for its own sake.
>
> (2001: 29)

It is common to find the suggestion among sub-Saharan theorists that society ought to be modelled on a family. For instance, Julius Nyerere, the first post-independence political leader of Tanzania, says, 'Modern African Socialism can draw from its traditional heritage the recognition of "society" as an extension of the basic family unit' (1968: 12; see also Oruka, 1997: 148–150). The questions, therefore, are how an appealing sort of family distributes wealth, and whether this model would 'work' at a national level.

I submit that, intuitively, a family should distribute resources to its members so as to ensure that everyone receives some substantial and comparable meeting of needs, but with special consideration going to both the least flourishing and the most promising. When allocating time, attention, money and whatever else is likely to improve others' lives, a head of household should distribute them so that everyone gets a similar share, but with the particularly talented and the particularly untalented each getting something greater than a strictly equal share.

Consider that if only one child were gifted, say at piano, the *bulk* of resources should not go to her. However, she should get more than an average child; a head of household would be wrong to parcel out resources in a strictly equal manner, because the piano player should reasonably get more than that, to develop an unusually creative ability.

Another reason to avoid strict equality would be that a particularly untalented child should reasonably get more. And yet, again, a head of household would be wrong to devote the *bulk* of resources to the worst-off child, particularly if he were handicapped, so that there would be little or nothing left for those able to flourish at a higher level.

These reflections suggest a kind of *balancing*, in which there is no great inequality between family members and all receive some substantial consideration, but those who need more resources either to reach a decent minimum of good or to approximate a maximum should receive a larger share. If that is indeed the proper distribution for a family, and if a society ought to be modelled on an ideal family, then resources ought also to be distributed in a balanced way within a state's territory.

Such an approach would ensure that everyone receives a comparable share, but those who are particularly badly off would receive more, so as to reach a decent minimum, and those who are particularly talented would also get more, so as to be able to max out their development. This sort of scheme is neither utilitarian, as it in principle focuses to some degree on the worst-off, nor prioritarian, as it also implies that the best-off have a principled claim to flourish, nor sufficientarian, as people should generally receive a comparable share, nor egalitarian, as the least flourishing and the most talented should get more than others. If indeed this approach is characteristic of a family, the exemplar of communal relationship, then it should be given consideration as the way that a society should commune when it comes to the distribution of property. In addition, I submit that the respects in which balancing differs from other, more familiar principles in the Western tradition on the face of it count as advantages.

Recognition[11]

One reason I have avoided talk of 'distributive' justice, and have instead spoken of 'social' justice, is that there appear to be central facets of justice that do not concern the allocation of civil liberties or socio-economic resources (or political power). In particular, those who have reflected on identity politics contend that there is an important kind of justice that has to do with recognition, something that is not normally spoken of as 'distributed' (see, e.g., Honneth and Fraser, 2003). In this section, I consider what my Afro-communitarian moral theory entails for how the state and other agents ought to respond to people in light of their particular self-understandings, cultures and histories.

I first address issues of disrespect such as denigration and marginalisation of people deemed to be members of particular groups and then issues of whether and how the state should support them. My basic claim with regard to these matters is that, for a state to treat people as special in virtue of their capacity for communal relationship when it comes to their group membership, it must not degrade their psychological and social abilities to commune and their particular actualisations of this capacity, namely in the form of extant *communities*, by which I mean instances of identity and solidarity.

To begin, consider cases in which government agents publicly express negative attitudes towards, or judgements of, people because of their religion, race, gender or sexual orientation, at least for the purposes for which such judgements are typically made. Think of a judge who expresses abhorrence of gay sex when making a ruling, or a welfare official who makes derogatory comments to black people seeking social assistance, or a prime minister making a sexist remark about female Parliamentarians in a speech. Such behaviour is degrading, and is so in virtue of symbolic or expressive considerations.

By the Afro-communitarian theory, everyone has a moral status, even a dignity, by virtue of their natural ability to relate communally, and hence everyone merits equal respect. To verbally denigrate people on the basis of their group membership is to fail to treat them as special in virtue of their capacity for harmonious relationships. Of course, a given individual might have failed to exercise this capacity appropriately, or might not have taken care to develop it. However, to act as though members of an ethnicity or sex all (or even characteristically) have an impaired capacity to commune, or are otherwise inferior, is to fail to treat them as having a dignity.

Similar remarks apply to behaviour that is not insulting by virtue of something said or otherwise actively expressed, but that still conveys the view that others are lower by virtue of their group membership. Serving white people before black people who are in a queue would be an example.

In addition to being symbolically degrading, such behaviour can be expected causally to impair, and hence dishonour, people's capacity to be objects of caring and sharing relationships. Slurs and related forms of insulting behaviour do not cultivate a sense of togetherness, but rather divide people according to 'us and them'. They foreseeably reduce people's self-esteem, and hence make them less able to undertake cooperative projects. They often hurt people's feelings, and so are harmful. Finally, they are often done consequent to cruelty or indifference to others' well-being. In a word, they are instances of discordance (objectionably directed towards innocents).

Of course, all these points apply to more than just public agents. And, so, the state would be reasonable to forbid slurs and related insulting behaviour of people's identity not merely by those employed by the state, but also by other institutions that citizens cannot easily avoid. These include privately owned workplaces and stores, and perhaps even schools and churches (at least when there is not an array from which to choose).

So far, I have discussed negative responses towards people in virtue of their identities, and contended that the state has good reason to forbid ones that are difficult for people to avoid, given their other, legitimate interests. Here are some additional ways that people's identities can ground duties on the part of the state to support them.

Although a community, specifically understood here as the combined relationships of identity and solidarity, is of course not one and the same thing as the mere ability for it, it is people's exercise of that ability. And it is plausible to suggest that respecting the individual's capacity for communion requires recognition of the way he has actualised it or, equivalently, that degrading harmonious relationships is to degrade those individuals who have been party to them. When an agent such as the state foreseeably and avoidably disrupts such relationships, or even fails to support them when it could easily do so, it is *thereby* expressing disrespect of individuals who are special because of their ability to relate harmoniously.

It follows by the Afro-communitarian theory that if a group has established genuinely communal relationships, then the government should do what it reasonably can to avoid impairing them, and can also have some reason to go out of its way to protect them. These supportive activities could be a matter of making exceptions to rules, permitting some collective self-determination over, say, civil matters. Or they could be a matter of providing resources to support a group's intellectual or aesthetic culture. Or they could even involve imposing mild restrictions on others, so as to protect the group's identity, with an example being Israel's policy of requiring 50 per cent of all radio broadcasts to be in Hebrew, a language at the heart of many people's self-conceptions there.

Of course, not every widespread and long-standing tradition merits support from the state. A necessary condition for support would be that a group is not seriously degrading anyone's ability to commune, neither insiders nor outsiders. This natural qualification makes good sense of why only certain groups, which do not egregiously discriminate on grounds of race, gender or the like, can merit state protection.

Utilitarianism is well known for having difficulty giving appropriate weight to the interests of minorities; sometimes discriminating against them can be what produces the greatest good on balance. In addition, though, the present rationale for group rights or identity politics is on the face of it more compelling than, say, a typically Kantian one. The natural approach for a Kantian is to consider the bearing of culture and membership on the ability of the individual to make informed or intelligible, and hence autonomous, choices (e.g. Kymlicka, 1989; Rawls, 2001: 93–94; cf. Kukathas, 2006). However, when a practice has been willingly adopted by a large number of people for a long span of time and is central to their self-conception as members of a group, it plausibly has a moral significance that can be worth respecting, apart from the *effects* of membership in the group on the capacity for autonomy, and instead as an *instantiation* of the special capacity to relate communally.

Conclusion: Sub-Saharan, Not Sub-Standard

In this chapter I have sought to mine under-explored sub-Saharan approaches to moral and political philosophy with the aim of advancing a prima facie attractive theory of social justice. I noted that African normative ideas are characteristically relational, thereby contrasting with not only individualism but also corporatism. Specifically, I advanced a moral principle according to which people have a moral status in virtue of their capacity for communal relationships, ones of sharing a way of life and caring for others' quality of life. Then, I applied this principle to three major facets of social justice, namely how the state ought to protect civil liberties, allocate socio-economic resources and recognise people's identities. My suggestion has been that these three elements of justice are unified in virtue of being forms of honouring people's capacity for communal relationship. In each case, I submit that the Afro-communitarian ethic has grounded a reasonable approach, particularly in relation to Kantian and utilitarian theories of justice that have dominated Western political thought of late.

I have sought to argue neither that the African theory of social justice advanced here is the most defensible specification of sub-Saharan ideals, nor that it is more defensible than Western ones. My aim has been the more moderate goal of showing that there are perspectives salient in the African tradition that it would be unjust to neglect, with my views being one, prima facie attractive specification. I naturally think that my favoured theory has much going for it, but I will have succeeded in this chapter if the reader simply takes away the idea that a communal relational ethic of some kind or other is a promising ground for a theory of social justice and that the views of nearly a billion people below the Sahara should not be ignored when thinking about justice.

Notes

1 For some of this groundwork, see Metz, 2007, 2009, 2010, 2011a; Metz and Gaie, 2010.
2 For an Afro-communitarian approach to how political decisions ought to be made, as opposed to which decisions should be, see Metz 2009, especially pp. 344–348, and Metz 2012a.
3 Things are admittedly more complicated when it comes to Kant. According to him, the reasons one finds upon reflection are moral ones, and so one might think they include essential reference to others. However, they do not. Although one must treat the humanity of others with respect if they exist, one would still have duties to oneself if no one else existed.
4 For more on what I mean by 'African', 'sub-Saharan' and other geographical labels such as 'Western', see Metz, 2015.
5 In addition to these authors, one could appeal to Western writers such as Silberbauer, 1991: 20; Paris, 1995: 43, 56; Verhoef and Michel, 1997: 397.
6 In the following formulations, I focus on persons, since the topic of this chapter is justice. In other work, however, I broaden them to include certain non-persons such as sentient animals (see Metz, 2012b).

7 On which see Oyowe, 2013, and my reply to him in Metz, 2014a.
8 Some might argue that acting in accordance with the sub-Saharan principle would be equivalent to, or a reliable means to, one of the Western principles. Equivalence is not on the cards, at the very least, for the reason that the ultimate explanation the former provides of *why* an act or policy is wrong will necessarily differ from the latter (see also Metz, 2009: 339–344; 2011b, 2012b).
9 Many of the ideas and phrasings in this section are pieced together from Metz, 2010, 2011a, 2012a, 2014a, 2014b.
10 Many of the ideas and phrasings in this section are borrowed from Metz, 2011b, 2014c, 2016.
11 Some of the ideas and phrasings in this section are lifted from Metz, 2013, 2014b.

References

Ake, C. (1987), 'The African context of human rights', *Africa Today*, 34: 5–12.

Benedict, R. (1934), 'Anthropology and the abnormal', *Journal of General Psychology*, 10: 59–82.

Bujo, B. (1997), *The Ethical Dimension of Community: The African Model and the Dialogue between North and South*, translated by C. N. Nganda, Nairobi: Paulines Publications.

Ejizu, C. (2011), 'African traditional religions and the promotion of community-living in Africa', www.afrikaworld.net/afrel/community.htm (accessed 10 August 2015).

Gbadegesin, S. (1991), *African Philosophy: Traditional Yoruba Philosophy and Contemporary African Realities*, New York: Peter Lang.

Gilligan, C. (1982), *In a Different Voice*, Cambridge, MA: Harvard University Press.

Gyekye, K. (2004), *Beyond Cultures; Ghanaian Philosophical Studies, Volume III*, Washington, DC: Council for Research in Values and Philosophy.

Gyekye, K. (2010), 'African ethics', in E. Zalta (ed.), *Stanford Encyclopedia of Philosophy*, http://plato.stanford.edu/archives/fall2010/entries/african-ethics/ (accessed 10 August 2015).

Hegel, G. W. F. (1837), *The Philosophy of History*, www.marxists.org/reference/archive/hegel/hisindex.htm (accessed 10 August 2015).

Hobbes, T. (1651), *Leviathan*, https://archive.org/details/hobbessleviathan00hobbuoft (accessed 10 August 2015).

Honneth, A. and Fraser, N. (2003), *Redistribution or Recognition?* London: Verso.

Iroegbu, P. (2005), 'Beginning, purpose and end of life', in P. Iroegbu and A. Echekwube (eds), *Kpim of Morality Ethics*, Ibadan: Heinemann Educational Books, pp. 440–445.

Kant, I. (1793), *On the Common Saying: This May Be True in Theory but It Does Not Apply in Practice*, translated by H. B. Nisbet, www.sussex.ac.uk/Users/sefd0/tx/tp2.htm (accessed 10 August 2015).

Kasenene, P. (1998), *Religious Ethics in Africa*, Kampala: Fountain Publishers.

Kigongo, J. (2002), 'The relevance of African ethics to contemporary African society', in A. T. Dalfovo (ed.), *Ethics, Human Rights and Development in Africa*, Washington, DC: Council for Research in Values and Philosophy, pp. 51–65.

Kukathas, C. (2006), 'Genocide and group rights', unpublished lecture given at the Conference on Ethics in Africa held at the University of Cape Town.

Kymlicka, W. (1989), *Liberalism, Community, and Culture*, New York: Oxford University Press.

Locke, J. (1690), *Two Treatises of Government*, http://socserv2.socsci.mcmaster.ca/econ/ugcm/3ll3/locke/government.pdf (accessed 10 August 2015).
Magesa, L. (1997), *African Religion: The Moral Traditions of Abundant Life*, Maryknoll, NY: Orbis Books.
Marx, K. (1844a), 'Comments on James Mill', translated by C. Dutt, www.marxists.org/archive/marx/works/1844/james-mill/ (accessed 10 August 2015).
Marx, K. (1844b), 'Economic and philosophical manuscripts', translated by M. Mulligan, www.marxists.org/archive/marx/works/1844/manuscripts/preface.htm (accessed 10 August 2015).
Marx, K. (1875), *Critique of the Gotha Programme*, translated by F. Engels, www.marxists.org/archive/marx/works/1875/gotha/ (accessed 10 August 2015).
Masolo, D. A. (2010), *Self and Community in a Changing World*, Bloomington: University of Indiana Press.
Metz, T. (2007), 'Toward an African moral theory', *Journal of Political Philosophy*, 15: 321–341.
Metz, T. (2009), 'African moral theory and public governance', in M. F. Murove (ed.), *African Ethics: An Anthology for Comparative and Applied Ethics*, Pietermaritzburg: University of KwaZulu-Natal Press, pp. 335–356.
Metz, T. (2010), 'Human dignity, capital punishment, and an African moral theory: toward a new philosophy of human rights', *Journal of Human Rights*, 9: 81–99.
Metz, T. (2011a), '*Ubuntu* as a moral theory and human rights in South Africa', *African Human Rights Law Journal*, 11: 532–559.
Metz, T. (2011b), 'An African theory of dignity and a relational conception of poverty', in J. de Gruchy (ed.), *The Humanist Imperative in South Africa*, Stellenbosch: African Sun Media, pp. 233–241.
Metz, T. (2012a), 'Developing African political philosophy: moral-theoretic strategies', *Philosophia Africana*, 14: 61–83.
Metz, T. (2012b), 'An African theory of moral status: a relational alternative to individualism and holism', *Ethical Theory and Moral Practice*, 15: 387–402.
Metz, T. (2013), 'The Western ethic of care or an Afro-communitarian ethic? Finding the right relational morality', *Journal of Global Ethics*, 9: 77–92.
Metz, T. (2014a), 'African values and human rights as two sides of the same coin: reply to Oyowe', *African Human Rights Law Journal*, 14: 306–321.
Metz, T. (2014b), 'African values, human rights and group rights: a philosophical foundation for the Banjul Charter', in O. Onazi (ed.), *African Legal Theory and Contemporary Problems*, Dordrecht: Springer, pp. 131–151.
Metz, T. (2014c), 'In search of *Ubuntu*: a political philosopher's view of democratic South Africa', in B. Ngcaweni (ed.), *Liberation Diaries: Reflections on 20 Years of Democracy*, Johannesburg: Jacana Media, pp. 205–214.
Metz, T. (2015), 'How the West was one: the Western as individualist, the African as communitarian', *Educational Philosophy and Theory*, vol. 47, pp. forthcoming.
Metz, T. (2016), 'An African egalitarianism: bringing community to bear on equality', in G. Hull (ed.), *The Equal Society*, Lanham, MD: Rowman & Littlefield, pp. forthcoming.
Metz, T. and Gaie, J. (2010), 'The African ethic of *Ubuntu/Botho*: implications for research on morality', *Journal of Moral Education*, 39: 273–290.
Mill, J. S. (1863), *Utilitarianism*, www.earlymoderntexts.com/pdfs/mill1863_1.pdf and www.earlymoderntexts.com/pdfs/mill1863_2.pdf (accessed 10 August 2015).

Mkhize, N. (2008), '*Ubuntu* and harmony: an African approach to morality and ethics', in R. Nicolson (ed.), *Persons in Community: African Ethics in a Global Culture*, Pietermaritzburg: University of KwaZulu-Natal Press, pp. 35–44.

Mokgoro, Y. (1998), '*Ubuntu* and the law in South Africa', *Potchefstroom Electronic Law Journal*, 1: 15–26.

Murove, M. F. (2007), 'The Shona ethic of *Ukama* with reference to the immortality of values', *Mankind Quarterly*, 48: 179–189.

Nkondo, G. M. (2007), '*Ubuntu* as a public policy in South Africa: a conceptual framework', *International Journal of African Renaissance Studies*, 2: 88–100.

Noddings, N. (1984), *Caring: A Feminine Approach to Ethics and Moral Education*, Berkeley, CA: University of California Press.

Nussbaum, M. (2011), *Creating Capabilities: The Human Development Approach*, Cambridge, MA: Harvard University Press.

Nyerere, J. (1968), *Ujamaa: Essays on Socialism*, Dar es Salaam: Oxford University Press.

OAU (Organisation of African Unity) (1981), *African Charter on Human and Peoples' Rights*, www.achpr.org/files/instruments/achpr/banjul_charter.pdf (accessed 10 August 2015).

OECD (Organisation for Economic Co-operation and Development) (2013), *Better Life Index 2013: Definitions and Metadata*, www.oecd.org/statistics/OECD-Better-Life-Index-2013-definitions.pdf (accessed 10 August 2015).

Oruka, H. O. (1997), *Practical Philosophy*, Nairobi: East African Educational Publishers.

Oyowe, A. (2013), 'Strange bedfellows: rethinking *Ubuntu* and human rights in South Africa', *African Human Rights Law Journal*, 13: 103–124.

Paris, P. (1995), *The Spirituality of African Peoples: The Search for a Common Moral Discourse*, Minneapolis: Fortress Press.

Ramose, M. (1999), *African Philosophy through Ubuntu*, Harare: Mond Books.

Rawls, J. (1988), 'The priority of right and ideas of the good', *Philosophy and Public Affairs*, 17: 251–276.

Rawls, J. (2001), *Justice as Fairness: A Restatement*, Cambridge, MA: Harvard University Press.

Sandel, M. (1984), 'The procedural republic and the unencumbered self', *Political Theory*, 12: 81–96.

Sen, A. (1999), *Development as Freedom*, New York: Knopf.

Sen, A. (2004), 'Capabilities, lists, and public reason', *Feminist Economics*, 10: 77–80.

Shutte, A. (2001), *Ubuntu: An Ethic for the New South Africa*, Cape Town: Cluster Publications.

Silberbauer, G. (1991), 'Ethics in small-scale societies', in P. Singer (ed.), *A Companion to Ethics*, Oxford: Basil Blackwell, pp. 14–28.

Tutu, D. (1999), *No Future without Forgiveness*, New York: Random House.

UNDP (United Nations Development Programme) (2010), *Human Development Report 2010; The Real Wealth of Nations: Pathways to Human Development*, New York: Palgrave Macmillan.

Verhoef, H. and Michel, C. (1997), 'Studying morality within the African context', *Journal of Moral Education*, 26: 389–407.

Walzer, M. (1983), *Spheres of Justice*, New York: Basic Books.

10 Social Protection and Justice

Poverty, Redistribution, Dignity

Marianne S. Ulriksen, Sophie Plagerson and Tessa Hochfeld

Introduction

Debates and opinions on how public goods and opportunities in society are, and should be, distributed are invariably linked to understandings of the causes of poverty. Those believing that poverty is largely due to people's own (in)action and poor choice would tend to argue that the state has a limited obligation in distributing public goods and should only assist those who are 'deserving', those who are in absolute peril, and as a last resort. At the other end, those who regard poverty as primarily the cause of unjust and unequal structures in society would advocate a stronger role of the state in distributing goods to redress such unfairness.

Social protection policies, such as the provision of cash and in-kind transfers,[1] are particularly controversial in debates on what constitutes a fair distribution across society. This is because the provision of non-contributory benefits most clearly *gives* to identified, often poor, beneficiaries and *takes* from the better-off taxpayers. In this chapter, we discuss how social protection, a relatively new concept, has roots in two traditional, but different, types of social provisions, namely safety nets (the provision of small cash or in-kind transfers to the extreme poor) and social security (the combination of social assistance, social insurance and labour-market policies to ensure income and social security). The World Bank has favoured safety nets, whereas the ILO (International Labour Organisation) has promoted social security. More recently, however, there is consensus across these and many other international development agencies that social protection, cash transfers in particular, is a powerful tool for poverty eradication across developing countries, especially if transfers are targeted at the poorest and most vulnerable.

In recent years, social protection has gained prominence as an approach to distribution in the Global South (De Haan, 2014). However, social protection is hardly ever justified as an instrument by which the poor can get their 'fair share'. In fact, as we discuss, while the field of social protection is primarily focused on *how* best to implement social protection, there is only a small but growing academic literature that discusses *why* social protection should be promoted. We will analyse how this literature views social protection from a justice perspective. The term 'justice' is used to denote a *normative* rather than a pragmatic approach to the analysis and promotion of social protection. In this chapter, we attempt to clarify how different approaches to justice have different political and philosophical meanings, and expose some of the consequences of these for social protection. We understand social justice as a specific and substantive application of a justice lens of enquiry, which broadly encompasses notions of social and economic rights, and specifies their nature and fair distribution within society.

We argue that the full realisation of social justice draws on both relational perspectives on justice (rooted in an interpersonal understanding of the structural causes of injustice) and non-relational perspectives (in which injustice occurs when a person is deprived of the chance to live the life they *could* lead if circumstances were different). We suggest that prevailing social justice justifications for social protection largely take a non-relational view, arguing that a fair provision of social protection should focus on the poor, those below a certain standard of living. This perspective weakens the linkages between social protection and distributive justice as it downplays the significant relational dimensions of poverty. Being poor relates not only to 'material needs for food, water and shelter', but also to 'our relational needs for security, exchange and affection' as well as 'our cognitive needs for dignity, autonomy and sense of self-worth' (Devereux and McGregor, 2014: 300).[2]

Consequently, we suggest that a distributive justice framework is needed to capture these relational dimensions. Viewing social protection from a distributive justice perspective, and thereby recognising the relationship between individuals and communities, we see that social protection can promote redistribution, but also recognition and dignity. Some proponents of social protection appreciate its distributive role, but few acknowledge why dignity is also an important justification for social protection. We end the chapter by critically reflecting on the current approach to social protection and showing how a simple poverty focus can undermine dignity among social protection beneficiaries. Thus, without a proper justice framework, the current social protection bonanza fails to acknowledge some important trade-offs in the course of helping the poor.

Social Protection as a Key Developmental Objective

Increasingly acknowledged for its ability to address poverty, social protection has become a popular developmental mechanism among international development agencies operating in developing countries. Although this drive largely builds on the positive impacts revealed by nationally initiated and funded social protection programmes in middle-income countries such as Brazil, Mexico and South Africa (Barrientos, 2013), we focus here on international agencies as they have become the main promoters of social protection expansion in many low-income countries in the Global South, especially in Africa.

Social Protection as a Tool for Poverty Reduction: Consensus and Differences

Since the World Bank published its annual World Development Report in 1990 titled *Poverty* (World Bank, 1990), the main development goal of international aid organisations has been to address poverty in developing countries. This is evident first in the widespread promotion of Poverty Reduction Strategy Papers (PRSPs) in the 1990s and with the Millennium Development Goals campaign of the 2000s, where the first goal is to halve the proportion of people with an income less than US$1 a day by 2015. With the new Sustainable Development Goals the eradication of extreme poverty remains the first goal. In this fight against poverty, social protection has increasingly become embraced by international agencies as an essential tool (Cook, 2013), as is exemplified by the Social Protection Floor Initiative adopted in 2009 by all the main international organisations, including the International ILO and the World Bank.[3]

It is particularly interesting to compare the development of the social protection discourse between the World Bank and the ILO. Initially, both organisations operated with the more traditional term: social security. Social security is generally understood to include contributory (social insurance) and non-contributory (social assistance) income protection provisions. Both elements of social security are included in the broader, and newer, concept of social protection, although social insurance often receives much less attention. The World Bank, together with the International Monetary Fund (IMF), is often regarded as the most conservative international agency with respect to social security. The organisation has traditionally discarded social security as irrelevant to developing countries and instead argued to limit social provisions to safety nets for those unable to provide for themselves through economic activity (Mkandawire, 2004). The ILO, on the other hand, is the key international organisation mandated to extend social security worldwide.[4] In the following, we describe how these two extreme positions meet with the promotion of social protection and how, although there are still noticeable differences in their views, they agree that the primary goal of social protection in developing countries is to target the poorest and most vulnerable groups.

Starting with the World Bank: in the World Development Report of 1990, the World Bank promoted a two-part strategy to achieve 'sustainable improvements in the quality of life of the poor' (World Bank, 1990: iii). The two parts of the strategy were 'the pursuit of a pattern of growth that ensures productive use of the poor's most abundant asset: labour' and 'widespread provision to the poor of basic social services, especially primary education, primary health care and family planning'. Complementing the strategy would be 'well-targeted transfers, to help those not able to benefit from these policies, and … safety nets, to protect those who are exposed to shocks' (ibid.). Thus, cash or in-kind transfers and safety nets were viewed as a mechanism to reach the most vulnerable and help poor people through short-term stress and calamities.

It is widely agreed that the World Bank regards safety nets as the main relevant social protection programme for developing countries. Safety nets are generally defined as non-contributory transfer programmes (such as cash transfers and public works) targeted to the poor or vulnerable unable to benefit from mainstream economic growth (Monchuk, 2014: 2; World Bank, 2013). In the last two decades, following the tremendous growth of national social protection programmes in developing countries and volumes of research pointing to their positive impacts for the poor, social protection in the form of cash transfers in particular has become an increasingly popular policy instrument at the World Bank. Today, the Bank is a major player in promoting and funding social protection across developing countries (Hall, 2007; Babajanian and Hagen-Zanker, 2012; Barrientos, 2013).

However, although the Bank increasingly promotes social protection, their affection for safety nets (income transfers) and their hesitation to embrace comprehensive social security systems is still evident in the most recent World Development Report:

> Social protection can be criticized for not encouraging personal self-reliance and being an unsustainable burden to the state. The evidence, however, demonstrates that these problems can be avoided by a design that takes people's incentives directly into account. Well-designed safety nets – such as conditional cash transfers or workfare programmes, as implemented in Bangladesh, Brazil, India, and Mexico, to name a few – have promoted better household practices in the areas of education, health, and even entrepreneurship, while remaining fiscally sustainable.
>
> (World Bank, 2013: 40–41)

In one way, the World Bank has shifted somewhat, from regarding social protection as a safety net to manage risks, to recognising that income transfers can build human capabilities and increase livelihood capacity in the long term (Babajanian and Hagen-Zanker, 2012). However, social protection is still an instrument to target the poorest and most vulnerable and particularly conditional cash transfers[5] (CCTs) have become popular with the Bank. As Hall (2007: 159) explains: 'CCTs allow the poor to be targeted quite effectively and comparatively quickly, with benefits being directly channelled to vulnerable groups such as women and children, while generating additional benefits through education and health conditionalities'.

The World Bank has thus embraced social protection as an important policy instrument and today argues that 'inclusive social protection systems need to be in place to protect the vulnerable' (World Bank, 2013: 174). Particularly, conditional cash transfers targeted at the poorest fit well with the Bank's philosophy that views comprehensive social security with some disdain and that favours policies providing incentives for productive behaviour and limited interference in the market economy.

In contrast, comprehensive social security systems are the end goal for the ILO. The ILO regards social security as a human right and an integral part of the ILO Constitution, which aims to promote the extension of social security worldwide. Building originally on developed countries' social security systems that embrace both social insurance and social assistance programmes, for a long time the ILO implicitly assumed that developing countries would follow similar economic and social development patterns as the developed countries. However, as is evident in the 2001 ILO report on social security, the organisation has increasingly recognised that social security in developing countries has failed to reach the majority of people and that social insurance schemes have been inadequate due to large informal sectors (ILO, 2001).

In recognition of the different context of social insecurity in developing countries, the ILO – although still advocating the universality of social security – is now the lead organisation, together with the World Health Organisation (WHO), promoting the Social Protection Floor Initiative, which has led to the adoption of the ILO's Social Protection Floors Recommendation, 2012 (No. 202). The Social Protection Floor suggests a two-pronged strategy in which countries first ensure a minimum level of income security and access to essential health care, followed by a progressive expansion with wider coverage and higher levels of protection in the medium to long term (ILO, 2014). Although the Social Protection Floor has an ambitious end goal, there is an initial focus on the poor and vulnerable as exemplified in the call by tripartite delegates of the 183 ILO member states in 2011 for

> the rapid implementation of social protection floors, containing basic social security guarantees that ensure that over the life cycle all *in need* can afford and have access to essential health care and have income security at least at a nationally defined minimum level.[6]

Thus, arguably, the ILO has accepted that social protection targeting the poor is the feasible starting point for developing countries. In practice, then, both these international agencies and other development partners promote social protection in the form of targeted cash or in-kind transfers. There are, however, differences in approach. The World Bank tends to insist on the term 'safety nets' as appropriate programmes for developing countries and prefers the implementation of targeted conditional transfers (World Bank, 2013; Monchuk, 2014). The ILO, on the other hand, advocates that social protection should be given as a right, be based on social solidarity, redress not only poverty but also inequality and social exclusion, and therefore (in the ideal, long-term situation) should be universal (ILO, 2012, 2014).

Justice Perspectives on Social Protection

Social policy is inevitably informed and directed by political philosophies. Yet there has been a remarkable silence regarding philosophical antecedents to social protection in key discourses within international development (Barrientos, 2013; Sabates-Wheeler and Koehler, 2011). International organisations have tended to focus more on the *how* than the *why* of social protection. Justice frameworks for social protection have been introduced almost retrospectively, both to describe how concepts of social justice have inadvertently shaped different expressions of social protection, and to prescribe how ideas of justice *should* guide social protection in its wider policy context.

In this section, we discuss the different justice paradigms that do exist within the social protection literature. We argue that the dominant perspectives justify social protection from a non-relational argument, which is in stark contrast to distributive justice ideas where an essential factor is exactly the relation between individuals.[7] Although there are new and radical moves that take justice theories beyond the non-relational perspective, we end this section by discussing the implications of the weak justice foundations within the literature, and particularly in practice, leading to what we coin a 'philosophy of pragmatism'.

From Needs, to Rights, to Transformation

As discussed, the social protection movement has developed under the overarching aim of reducing global poverty. Therefore, the foundations of social protection policy have closely tracked the shifts in justifications for tackling global poverty. Poverty research has long focused on defining basic human needs – both as a mechanism to measure poverty levels and to define programme inputs to address poverty. Basic human needs were initially measured quite narrowly with reference to essential nutrition, food and shelter, but in recent years – particularly with the UNDP-led Human Development Index – basic human needs are understood more broadly to include aspects such as education and health. The UNDP, like many other international agencies, has been strongly influenced by Amartya Sen's work on capabilities (see for example, Sen, 1999, 2009). Sen's work marks a shift in development theory and practice from just outcomes to just opportunities, and the need to ensure that individuals can enjoy the freedom to live the life they value. Interestingly, this change in emphasis was motivated by a move away from universal and normative conceptions of justice towards the idea of justice as a dialectic tool for comparative reasoning, rooted in empirical observation (Sen, 2009).

According to Lauchlan Munro (2008: 35), proponents of the basic needs approach have seldom been explicit about the role of social protection, and even the justice theory underlying the school has not been very sophisticated – relying mostly on 'an intuitive approach to morality based on a sense of human solidarity and compassion in the face of unnecessary suffering'. The needs school has tended to be residualist, where the state should only step in when the market, individual and community fail to cover basic needs. From this perspective, the needs school is similar to the traditional World Bank view on the role of public interventions, such as social protection, which have been regarded as safety nets covering short-term risks and shocks (Munro, 2008).

Similarly, the historical progression of social protection policy and practice in many low- and middle-income countries started out as the provision of social safety nets and humanitarian assistance. In such contexts, often of emergency, relief was offered on a discretionary basis, typically for a limited time period (Devereux et al., 2011). Over time, social protection has been absorbed into development policy, to the point of becoming a central strategy for poverty alleviation. For example, in a World Bank report it is stated that the broader objectives of social protection have moved beyond mitigating risks and offering safety nets, to help the poor 'invest in productive and capital-forming activities' (Monchuk, 2014: 9). In this context, a justice perspective on social protection involves an evaluation of what a person's life could and should be. Barrientos (2013) refers to this as the *priority* validation for assisting the poor, justified on the basis that they are worse off than they could be. Parfit (1991: 22, cited in Barrientos, 2013: 35) states clearly that intervening in poverty has absolute merit, regardless of its comparative nature:

> On the priority view, we do not believe in equality.... We do of course think it is bad that some people are worse off. But what is bad is not that these people are worse off than others. It is rather that they are worse off than they might have been.

Thus, the priority view has an intra-personal (non-relational) rather than interpersonal (relational) emphasis, which puts it in contrast to distributive justice.

Though coming from a different perspective, a gradual re-emphasis on human rights as a foundation for poverty reduction and for social protection is in some ways similar to the priority perspective on justice. Human rights have been introduced as a framework for mandating and evaluating social protection. There has been a dramatic and rapid shift over the past two decades, from a discretionary approach, often dependent on donor aid and the prevailing global attitudes towards social protection, towards one of statutory rights, rooted in national sovereignty and international legislation (Tessitore, 2011). The benefits of this contemporary conception of rights is that fulfilling them should no longer depend exclusively on the benevolence of the individual donor, but should be a legally and morally protected claim, independent of local or donor politics and whims.

The rights discourse has gained momentum across the development sector. Cornwall and Nyamu-Musembi highlight the 2005 Paris Declaration as a significant marker in re-directing international donor funding towards supporting citizens to claim rights and hold institutions accountable (Cornwall and Nyamu-Musembi, 2005). This movement towards rights-based approaches has been paralleled by a broadening scope for social protection, from the provision of emergency relief to the sustainable protection of basic livelihoods in low-income households, to a view of social assistance as a tool for social and economic transformation (as discussed later in this section). Even changes in terminology have borne witness to the transition which is underway: social protection 'beneficiaries' have given way to 'participants', claimants' or 'citizens' (Devereux et al., 2011). A number of social protection programmes in emerging economies are designed to be a social right. For example, the second G in the Indian MGNREGA programme stands for 'Guarantee', and Brazil's conditional cash transfer programme, Bolsa Família, meaning 'Family Allowance' in Portuguese, is understood as a guaranteed minimum income (Leisering and Barrientos, 2013).

As discussed earlier, the ILO is firmly entrenched in a rights perspective on social protection. Viewing social protection as a right implies that social protection is available to all citizens, irrespective of their situation relative to others. In this sense, the rights perspective is non-relational, just like the priority view.[8] Hence, justifications for social protection in the main take a non-relational stand, which explain why distributive justice has not been a central consideration of social protection paradigms.

Nevertheless, critical analyses of social protection schemes (particularly cash transfers) have led some academics to recommend the subordination of social protection to a relational social justice paradigm as the primary reference point (Hickey, 2014). This more radical view recognises that poverty and vulnerability are rooted in economic and social institutions and structures (Sabates-Wheeler and Koehler, 2011). Relational approaches to social protection have a strong awareness of vertical (compared to total population) and horizontal (between group) inequality. They recognise that all people are born into inequality and that inequality reproduces inequality (Koehler, 2011). Inequalities are viewed as the negative outcome of skewed power dynamics (not just a natural or 'neutral' outcome of neoliberal economic policies). Power relations are identified as the root cause of the uneven distribution of rights and resources between individuals (Hickey, 2014). Power is characterised as a relational rather than an individual capability or resource (Sabates-Wheeler and Koehler, 2011). Consequently the way to achieve social justice is to tackle the systems of power that perpetuate injustice (Carroll, 2011).

Locating social protection within a relational approach to justice, some leading social protection advocates have consequently argued for a transformational dimension to social protection. In 2004, Devereux challenged the 'thin' aims of social protection policy, describing them as limited to the economic (rather than social) protection of livelihoods (Devereux and Sabates-Wheeler, 2004). In their book chapter on 'Transformative social protection: the currency of social justice', Sabates-Wheeler and Devereux (2008) re-frame the scope of social protection as a vehicle for social and economic transformation to address the unjust and exclusionary structures that underlie poverty (Tessitore, 2011). The view that social protection can be socially transformative and be a tool to empower marginalised people has been very influential in the design of some social protection initiatives. Gender inequality has, for example, been increasingly incorporated as a core concern in the design of many programmes globally. Girl child grants in India have sought to halt female foeticide. In Bangladesh, school stipends for girls have successfully aimed to close the gender gap in education enrolments (Koehler, 2011), as has Oportunidades, a conditional cash transfer in Mexico (Adato et al., 2000).

Summing up, the transformational view on social protection is, in our view, firmly entrenched in ideas of relational justice – a key aspect of distributive justice. However, its proponents position themselves primarily within the rights movement rather than distributive justice specifically, and the framework has arguably emerged from within the social development policy school and therefore remains to some extent rooted in paradigms which focus on poverty reduction, with less emphasis on the achievement of comprehensive systems of social protection that transcend poor/non-poor divides. Moreover, transformational social justice is not the dominant view among key international agencies. This is partly because transformational social justice puts strong emphasis on unequal structures as causes to poverty, which does not sit well with international actors, who are uncomfortable with downplaying the role of individuals in exiting poverty. International aid agencies also have a pragmatic approach to social protection, as we explain in the following.

Importantly, even as we argue for stronger relational justice frameworks, we also seek to retain the strengths of non-relational approaches, since these are also necessary for a full realisation of social protection for all, in the context of broad-based and inclusive social and fiscal policy. Indeed, while we advocate analytical and interventionist approaches, which tackle the implicitly relational nature of inequality, we believe that the principles of ethical individualism are important. From this perspective, individuals 'are the ultimate units of moral concern' and we should thus evaluate structures, institutions and policies 'in virtue of the causal importance that they have for individual well-being' (Robeyns, 2008: 90).

Pragmatism as a Justice Perspective

There has been a lack of a strong and broadly recognised justice-driven rationale for social protection. In practice, this has meant that ethical issues regarding the justification for social assistance have remained subordinate to the superlative aim of getting the job done (Barrientos, 2013). Thus, pragmatism has de facto become a justice perspective in its own right, generating guiding principles for social protection. In fact, one may argue that as the international agencies' social protection agendas tail many social protection programmes by national governments, international agencies are inductively building on the experiences from and lessons of existing national programmes.

International agencies, including the World Bank and the ILO, are key promoters of social protection in many developing countries. The influence of development partners is substantial, particularly in Africa where they provide 68 per cent of the funding for social protection programmes, going up to 75 per cent if middle-income countries are excluded (Monchuk, 2014: 121). The World Food Programme (WFP) and the United Nations Children's Fund (UNICEF) provide the majority of funding for food distribution schemes and children's programmes respectively, while the World Bank is increasingly becoming involved in the design of and support for cash transfer programmes. Other UN agencies and some bilateral donors also support social protection programmes, whereas the ILO primarily provides technical assistance in social security matters more broadly (Hall, 2007; Monchuk, 2014). Donor-supported programmes differ in certain respects (for instance whether benefits are in kind or in cash, and whether conditions are attached to benefits or not) but commonly social protection programmes aim to provide a minimum transfer to targeted (poor and/or vulnerable) groups.

Two outcomes can emerge from a disproportionate weight given to the how, as opposed to the why, of social protection. First, social justice concerns can in reality appear more as an add-on, rather than as a driving framework with social protection programme design as its natural outworking. For example, the Kenyan Hunger Safety Net Programme was designed with a primary aim of smoothing consumption and protecting the assets of vulnerable people in Kenya. As a way of empowering the marginalised group at which the programme was aimed, the donor-led and funded programme included a rights component consisting of civic education and a grievance mechanism. Yet, as Tessitore notes, the rights did not apply beyond the confines of the social protection programme itself. Nor were the intended beneficiaries included in the design and monitoring of the programme (Tessitore, 2011).

Second, a focus on targeting becomes an essential concern in the design of a social protection programme. Targeting involves practical budgetary considerations and the identification of beneficiaries at greatest need, in order to maximise the effectiveness of limited resources. This 'sufficiency' view is based on the philosophical intuition that as not everyone can be helped equally, social protection should focus on the worst-off in order to ensure that they have sufficient resources for survival (Barrientos, 2013). This is clearly articulated by the World Bank in the 2014 Africa report: 'given the vast extent of poverty and vulnerability in Africa, safety nets cannot reach all of the poor. They need to focus on the extremely poor and on specific vulnerable groups for maximum effect and affordability' (Monchuk, 2014: 5).

Although the sufficiency view may take a relational perspective in that focus is on those worse off – in comparison to others – the sufficiency view most generally claims the centrality of a 'basic threshold' by which focus should be on those below the threshold (Barrientos, 2013). Seen from this perspective, even the ILO with the ultimate goal of entrenching social protection as a right to all, arguably accepts a sufficiency view – the primary initial aim of the Social Protection Floor is to ensure 'effective access to at least essential health care and a basic level of income security as a matter of priority' (ILO, 2014: 5). Thus, in a context of perceived resource constraint in many developing countries, the World Bank, and even the more progressive ILO, regard targeting as a critical component of social protection programmes.

To conclude, while we recognise that any solution will have a degree of flaw and pragmatism to it as it will be an ideal principle applied in a non-ideal world, this is entirely different to applying a non-ideal principle as a motivator for an even less than non-ideal policy approach. The 'that's the best we can do' pragmatic approach to driving policy dangerously circumvents many tough decisions, ideas and debates, and can result in short-term non-transformative interventions which create, justify and perpetuate exclusionary systems.

Material and Symbolic Redistribution

We have argued, so far, that social protection is currently advocated as a mechanism for ensuring some basic income security for the poorest and most vulnerable. This implies a distribution of resources from the well-off (nations or citizens depending on funding source) to those with far fewer resources. Yet, counter-intuitively, ideas of distribution and redistribution have received very little attention in the social protection discourse (Sabates-Wheeler and Koehler, 2011).

We propose that the disregard for distributive justice perspectives within the social protection literature is at least in part due to the prominence of the 'priority' view and rights approach. While distributive justice depends on interpersonal comparisons, and an understanding of power asymmetries underlying poverty, as a foundation for determining the route towards justice, the priority view and rights approach takes a non-relational approach with an evaluation of what a person's life could and should be. Furthermore, given the prominence of the sufficiency view in practice, distribution, if considered, is a means to achieving desirable outcomes, rather than a just outcome in its own right.

Nonetheless, the critical and more radical literature on the transformative potential of social protection applies a relational perspective and is consequently open to a distributive justice interpretation, though as noted earlier this perspective in practice still often remains within the sphere of poverty alleviation policy. In fact, transformative social protection ideas have sought to move beyond a sole consideration of the distribution of material resources, towards a broader understanding of recognition and dignity as essential 'goods' without which distribution becomes meaningless. This also follows from an understanding of poverty that has not only material but also relational dimensions, as discussed earlier (Devereux and McGregor, 2014). Thus, in this new and evolving milieu of social protection, traditional concepts of distributive justice are strung between the poles of an instrumental approach to material distribution at one end and a strongly idealist view of symbolic redistribution at the other. We discuss these perspectives and their implications below.

Material Redistribution: Means or End?

Social protection programmes have been primarily concerned with the reduction of poverty, and focus has therefore been the distribution of material goods that can improve economic well-being. The prevailing attention to extreme poverty has meant that considerations of inequality have been superficial (Adesina, 2011), and that, to the extent that redistribution is considered, it plays an *instrumental* role, which acquiesces to the leading aim of poverty alleviation (Sabates-Wheeler and Koehler, 2011). Reaching across North–South wealth differentials, poverty-alleviation interventions have generally stopped short of notions of global redistribution. Instead, as the more prominent rationale for action is poverty reduction, redistribution does not have a justice identity of its own. For example, the financing of social assistance through taxes (as one option) is sometimes described as a procedural consideration rather than a redistributive principle. Similarly, in evaluations of large-scale social protection programmes, reductions in inequality are often noted as a favourable outcome, rather than as a just aim in themselves (World Bank, 2012).

In the case of the World Bank, equity concerns have not been absent, but economic growth has prevailed over considerations of justice itself as a recipe for poverty reduction. The priority given to economic growth by the World Bank is motivated by an understanding that growth drives prosperity and that prosperity reduces the need for social welfare to be so expansive. The World Bank in its documentations recognises that high levels of inequality are associated with a range of social ills such as less social cohesion and political instability (World Bank, 2013: 150; World Bank, 2004: 32). Moreover, the World Bank also acknowledges that safety net programmes (such as cash transfer schemes) have been instrumental in decreasing inequality in some countries (World Bank, 2013: 93; World Bank, 2010: 107–108). Yet the Bank does not support the promotion of public policies that could redress inequality more substantially: 'most public policies should be indirect and focused on proper regulation, because direct policy interventions can lead to unintended consequences, including large redistribution effects and distorted incentives in the private sector' (World Bank, 2013: 215). Thus, public redistributive policies should be kept at a minimum and targeted cash transfers – to the extent that they do not distort market mechanisms – are accepted as a means to alleviate extreme poverty, with the potential side effect of also reducing inequality.

Unlike the World Bank, the ILO locates social protection within a framework of human rights and social justice. Still, redistribution is primarily discussed in relation to the redistributive ability of some policies, rather than as a desirable and just end in itself. For instance, social protection is recognised as 'one of the channels through which the benefits of growth can be shared in a more equitable way' and progressive taxation is regarded as 'the principal redistribution tool available to policy-makers' (ILO, 2014: 143, 151). In the ILO 2012 Social Protection Strategy, words like 'redistribution' and 'distributive' do not feature at all (ILO, 2012). Social protection approaches such as these, then, tend to fall well short of the notions of redistribution of, for example, Nancy Fraser (1995: 73), who champions redistribution as a form of fundamental political–economic restructuring, which might include directly 'redistributing income, reorganising the division of labour, subjecting investment to democratic decision-making, or transforming other basic economic structures'.

Thus, distributive justice – or even the role of redistribution – features only marginally in the social protection discourse, as international agencies and social protection scholars are preoccupied with the challenges of addressing poverty. Interestingly, the poverty agenda is being overtaken by a new reality where the majority of poor people no longer live in low-income countries but in middle-income countries – a fact that would require a reframing of poverty alleviation to focus more on redistribution within sufficiently resourceful states (Sumner, 2013, 2012). Consequently, there are good reasons why debates around the redistribution of resources should take centre-stage. However, distributive justice is about not only material redistribution but also symbolic redistribution, which currently receives limited attention with detrimental consequences, as we will discuss in the following.

Symbolic Redistribution: Dignity as a Justice Issue

Some scholars have begun

> to ask whether justice might not require some sort of fair distribution of goods quite different from either rights or material things. Inspired, perhaps, by Rawls's intriguing suggestion that the most important primary good is 'the social basis of self-respect', some people have suggested that we need to consider the distribution of *symbolic* goods as well as political and material ones.
>
> (Fleischacker, 2004: 121)

These symbolic goods have most often been described as a form of recognition, where recognition is understood variously as, for example, the acknowledgement of the holders of rights (Leisering and Barrientos, 2013), such as older people in the case of old age pensions, a right to dignity and social inclusion in the process of resource distribution (Sabates-Wheeler and Devereux, 2008), and an institutionalised relation of social equality (Fraser, 2000).

The ILO does acknowledge the links between material and symbolic redistribution. For instance, the strategy for the extension of social security is argued to recognise 'the importance of the universality of protection, based on social solidarity, for the prevention and reduction of poverty, inequality, social exclusion and insecurity' (ILO, 2012: 8). Social exclusion is a dynamic process that 'precludes full participation in the normatively prescribed activities of a given society and denies access to information, resources, sociability, recognition, and identity, eroding self-respect and reducing capabilities to achieve personal goals' (Silver, 2007: 1, cited in Babajanian and Hagen-Zanker, 2012: 1). Engagement with this issue alludes to issues of dignity and respect, key to the concept of recognition.

Fraser's notion of recognition as institutionalised social equality is useful in that it cannot be considered as a mere add-on benefit of redistribution, but has to be consciously *integrated* with goals of redistribution as otherwise we fall short of the achievement of justice. She makes the point that redistribution on its own cannot achieve justice and that recognition on its own is essentially meaningless when meted out in a materially unequal context. Instead, Fraser argues that both are necessary to attain a just society. Recognition, in her view, is not identity-based; in other words, this is not just about the respect of group identify or cultural recognition. Rather, recognition is dignity at personal and social levels,[9] and is critically about the 'status of individual group members as full partners in social interaction'. To be

> misrecognized ... is not simply to be thought ill of, looked down upon or devalued in others' attitudes, beliefs or representations. It is rather to be denied the status of a full partner in social interaction, as a consequence of institutionalized patterns of cultural value that constitute one as comparatively unworthy of respect or esteem.
>
> (Fraser, 2000: 113–114)[10]

Drawing from Fraser's approach it is necessary to give full consideration to distributive justice as a goal of social protection. However, we argue that even if integrated redistribution and recognition are not the ultimate aims of a programme, it is a minimum requirement that a programme does not increase misrecognition or misrepresentation in communities. Unintended consequences of social protection can easily undermine particularly the recognition aspect of distributive justice. If the potential for negative social impacts is not considered, then boosting destructive power hierarchies or social exclusion, or encouraging stigmatisation or social polarisation, are possible outcomes of social protection programmes (Sabates-Wheeler and Devereux, 2008).

The consequences of targeting are often cited as particularly problematic as they are a common cause of tension for those *excluded* from programmes. Fraser's notion of misrecognition is useful here, as it describes the sense of humiliation and lack of acknowledgement that poor people often feel when they are passed over for inclusion in social protection programmes as they do not meet the targeting criteria. Concomitantly, participation can put people in a certain social category. For example, a 2008 study on the Mchinji Social Cash Transfer (MSCT) scheme in Malawi revealed that the programme resulted in resentment and heightened conflict in the community, and the authors hypothesised that this could have been in response to a targeting formula that was opaque and meaningless to people, because in this area poverty was endemic and thus there was a perception that 'we are all poor here' (Ellis, 2012; Levy and Barahona, 2002; MacAuslan and Riemenschneider, 2011). They comment that 'targeting of individual households may run counter to the perceptions of people in the targeted villages ... the distinction that some received the benefit while others did not could well have seemed arbitrary' (MacAuslan and Riemenschneider, 2011: 63). The divisions that targeting creates have caused similar tensions in schemes in many other countries, such as Indonesia, Peru, Mexico and Nicaragua (Adato and Roopnaraine, 2004; Hanlon et al., 2010; Kidd and Wylde, 2011).

Fraser could describe these experiences as misrecognition: the sense of hurt puzzlement that comes with being told you are not poor *enough* for assistance, despite your suffering, while others who don't seem any worse off than you, or only slightly worse off, are helped, is both humiliating and undignified. You are treated as having a different *status* to others (Fraser's definition of misrecognition) and therefore unworthy of esteem. Treating these consequences as falling 'outside' the programme is a disingenuous perception of the impacts of social protection.

Programme designs can have negative consequences in other ways, too, often causing tension among those *included* in programmes. While there is a large body of literature praising cash transfers as the programme of choice for much of the developing world, research on the social impacts of the Zimbabwe Emergency Cash Transfer (ZECT) (disbursed in 2009/10) revealed that the cash itself degraded inter-household relations in communities. Culturally, sharing food was acceptable and common when people were in need, but sharing cash was not socially welcomed. MacAuslan and Reimenschneider (2011: 64) comment that

> the aversion to sharing cash is a cultural practice, common throughout the world, and was in contrast to the provision of food, which had a positive impact on social relations, because food is usually shared. This raises important questions for the desirability of alternative forms of transfer.

A personal sense of dignity is sometimes undermined just via the fact of needing to receive external assistance (Adato et al., 2000; Grosh et al.,

2008). A study from Tanzania reveals that potential recipients of a community-based targeted cash transfer programme sometimes feel under pressure to present their circumstances in ways that can be viewed as degrading: sometimes they try to appear poorer and more miserable than they are to receive a support that they believe they deserve but are too scared of being disqualified for. Or they avoid revealing their own insufficiency in front of community peers, for instance, by claiming to provide their family with more than one meal a day (although, by saying this they risk not being deemed eligible for a cash transfers) (Myamba et al., forthcoming). Targeting thus carries the risk of incentivising certain behaviours that are quite rational, but which do not contribute to dignity.

While there is a strand of development literature that acknowledges that all social protection programmes must consider trade-offs between achievements in material and symbolic spheres and grapples with the issue of recognition (Eggen, 2013; Ellis, 2012; MacAuslan and Riemenschneider, 2011; Sabates-Wheeler and Devereux, 2008), the conversation is not yet mainstream. Drawing on theoretical conversations about dignity can contribute greatly to the justice outcomes in social protection programmes, because it allows the consideration of the distribution of symbolic, relational and status fairness along with material distribution.

Conclusion

This chapter has shown a broad range of implicit and explicit justifications for social protection. For the most part, existing justice perspectives on social protection are non-relational in the sense that social protection is regarded as a right owed to all citizens, irrespective of the situation of others. However, as international agencies focus more on the 'how tos' of social protection rather than a 'why' mandate, and in contexts of perceived resource constraints, the dominating rationale is to prioritise social protection for the poorest and most vulnerable, in isolation from broader social and fiscal policy. Within this context of weak justice antecedents for social protection, material distribution has had a predominantly instrumental role (in contrast with distributive justice as a goal in itself), and symbolic distribution has rarely been a guiding consideration in the design and implementation of social protection programmes.

We argue that a strong justice approach to social protection is necessary and attractive, since it offers opportunities for the achievement of more far-reaching goals than a pragmatic approach. We further argue that, in addition to non-relational justice antecedents, a relational justice approach which incorporates but also transcends poverty alleviation goals needs to be brought into the mainstream of international institutions' policy and practice. In this scenario, distributive justice takes centre-stage. The benefit of such a perspective is that it does not rebrand redistribution as a static intervention, where the 'from' and 'to' of redistribution remain unchanged in a perpetual cycle. A dynamic view of redistribution seeks to gradually transform the direction of redistribution itself by challenging the underlying structures that create inequality and the need for redistribution in the first place. Current social protection policies in many developing countries also offer a platform to consider the 'what' of redistribution and the deep interdependence between both material and symbolic redistribution.

The strength of a distributive justice focus on social protection is that the relational aspects of individuals and society are recognised, thus including dignity at the centre of social and economic policy making. This is largely ignored in the dominant social protection practice in developing countries, where a preoccupation with poverty reduction leads to a disregard for potential negative consequences of the targeting process. By recognising that social protection is a distributive practice and that redistribution has both material and symbolic effects, we have shown that targeting carries the risk of undermining potential beneficiaries' sense of recognition and dignity. Furthermore, as dignity can be undermined by targeting, new levels of social stratification may be introduced by social protection.

While we recognise that poverty alleviation is a just goal in itself and that universal access to social protection may only be a long-term goal, we suggest that a distributive justice focus enables us to critically reflect on the potential trade-offs in current social protection practice. Is targeting the poorest – even in contexts where they come to stand out from their almost-as-poor peers – always the best way to do development? Can we be satisfied in our efforts if material basic needs are met, even if a reduction in social cohesion and a sense of dignity are consequent costs? These are questions that a distributive justice perspective helps us to ask.

Notes

1 There are different understandings of what constitutes social protection. The description used here is broad and well accepted, and would include provisions such as cash transfers, food parcels or vouchers, agricultural transfers such as seed or fertiliser, subsidised housing or energy, and health, pension and other insurance schemes. Social security, social assistance (non-contributory cash transfers), social insurance (contributory income protection) and safety nets, terms we will use in this chapter, are all forms of social protection.

2 This definition of poverty is distinct from a *relative* definition of poverty (which defines poverty as being poorer relative to others) since it incorporates an absolute component (having basic needs met). However, the definition emphasises a *relational* aspect of well-being, which relates to our sense of dignity, self-worth and recognition vis-à-vis others, and draws attention to the structural and relational nature of poverty, as a result of exploitative and asymmetrical power relationships.

3 Organisations supporting this initiative are as follows: lead agencies: ILO, WHO; cooperating agencies: FAO, IMF, OHCHR, UNAIDS, UNDESA, UNDP, UNESCO, UNFPA, UN-HABITAT, UNHCR, UNICEF, UNODC, UN Regional Commissions, UNRWA, WFP, WMO, World Bank and development partners; see *Social Protection Floor Initiative, (Fact Sheet 2012)*, www.social-protection.org/gimi/gess/ShowRessource.action?ressource.ressourceId=30430 (accessed 5 June 2014).

4 See website: www.ilo.org/global/about-the-ilo/lang–en/index.htm (accessed 5 June 2014).
5 Conditional cash transfers place an obligation on the recipient (unlike unconditional transfers), usually to ensure that children attend school and/or that one visits health clinics for key vaccinations and check-ups.
6 *Social Protection Floor Initiative, (Fact Sheet 2012)*, www.social-protection.org/gimi/gess/ShowRessource.action?ressource.ressourceId=30430 (accessed 5 June 2014); italics added by authors.
7 Fleischacker (see Chapter 1 in this volume) suggests that distributive justice in its modern sense is based on the following five premises: that 'each individual … deserves respect, and … is due certain rights and protections'; 'a share of material goods sufficient to cover basic needs is … [deserved by] everyone'; 'the fact that individuals deserve this can be justified rationally'; 'the distribution of this [deserved] share of goods is practicable'; 'the state [should be the primary guarantor of] the distribution'. Fleischacker (2004: 123) exposes the relational aspects to distributive justice when he argues that because 'society is a cooperative effort that we can shape and reshape if we wish' and as we have 'obligations to respect other human beings', then we should 'remake the distribution of resources in our society so that it better helps all its members develop their capacities'.
8 We acknowledge that, theoretically, the rights approach does include distributive elements. That is, as the state is considered the primary guarantor of rights, there is an implicit assumption that the state will ensure redistribution across society in ways that ensure everyone's basic minimum rights. Yet we argue that in the application in practice of human rights approaches, these distributive elements are lost, and that the focus, particularly with regard to the role of international institutions, is non-relational.
9 Dignity is a concept widely used in different fields and disciplines. Here we use it in a secular way to mean a sense of human worth and respect.
10 Her third arm of justice is also worth noting: 'representation' to her denotes political voice, or 'inclusion in, or exclusion from, the community of those entitled to make justice claims on one another' (Fraser, 2009: 17). This has relevance for social protection programmes in relation to who makes decisions, whether community representatives genuinely represent the community and who is politically silenced in these programmes.

References

Adato, M. and Roopnaraine, T. (2004), *A Social Analysis of the Red de Protección Social (RPS) in Nicaragua, Final Report*, Washington, DC: IFPRI.

Adato, M., de la Brière, B., Mindek, D. and Quisumbing, A. (2000), *The Impact of PROGRESA on Women's Status and Intrahousehold Relations*, Washington, DC: International Food Policy Research Institute.

Adesina, J. O. (2011), 'Beyond the social protection paradigm: social policy in Africa's development', *Canadian Journal of Development Studies/Revue Canadienne D'études du Développement*, 32 (4): 454–470.

Babajanian, B. and Hagen-Zanker, J. (2012), 'Social protection and social exclusion: an analytical framework to assess the links', ODI Background Note, Overseas Development Institute.

Barrientos, A. (2013), *Social Assistance in Developing Countries*, New York: Cambridge University Press.

Carroll, K. (2011), 'Addressing inequality: framing social protection in National Development Strategies', *IDS Bulletin*, 42 (6): 89–95.

Cook, S. (2013), 'Rescuing social protection from the poverty trap: new programmes and historical lessons', in K. Bender, M. Kaltenborn and C. Pfleiderer (eds), *Social Protection in Developing Countries: Reforming Systems*, London: Routledge.

Cornwall, A. and Nyamu-Musembi, C. (2005), 'Why rights, why now? reflections on the rise of rights in international development discourse', *IDS Bulletin*, 26: 9–18.

De Haan, Arjan (2014), 'The rise of social protection in development: progress, pitfalls and politics', *European Journal of Development Research*, 26 (3): 311–321.

Devereux, S. and McGregor, A. (2014), 'Transforming social protection: human wellbeing and social justice', *European Journal of Development Research*, 26 (3): 296–310.

Devereux, S. and Sabates-Wheeler, R. (2004), *Transformative Social Protection*, IDS Working Paper 232, Brighton, UK, Institute of Development Studies.

Devereux, S., McGregor, A. and Sabates-Wheeler, R. (2011), 'Introduction: social protection for social justice', *IDS Bulletin*, 42 (6): 1–9.

Eggen, O. (2013), 'Making and shaping poor Malawians: citizenship below the poverty line', *Development Policy Review*, 31 (6): 697–716.

Ellis, F. (2012), '"We are all poor here": economic difference, social divisiveness and targeting cash transfers in sub-Saharan Africa', *Journal of Development Studies*, 48 (2): 201–214.

Fleischacker, S. (2004), *A Short History of Distributive Justice*, Boston: Harvard University Press.

Fraser, N. (1995), 'From redistribution to recognition? dilemmas of justice in a "post-socialist" age', *New Left Review*, I: 212.

Fraser, N. (2000), 'Rethinking recognition', *New Left Review*, 3 (May–June): 107–120.

Fraser, N. (2009), *Scales of Justice: Reimagining Political Space in a Globalizing World*, New York: Columbia University Press.

Grosh, M., del Ninno, C., Tesliuc, E. and Ouerghi, A. (2008), *For Protection and Promotion: The Design and Implementation of Effective Safety Nets*, Washington, DC: International Bank for Reconstruction and Development/World Bank.

Hall, A. (2007), 'Social policies in the World Bank: paradigms and challenges', *Global Social Policy*, 7 (2): 151–175.

Hanlon, J., Barrientos, A. and Hulme, D. (2010), *Just Give Money to the Poor: The Development Revolution from the Global South*, West Hartford, CT: Kumarian Press, Sterling.

Hickey, S. (2014), 'Relocating social protection within a radical project of social justice: towards a relational approach', *Economic Journal of Development Research*, 26: 322–337.

ILO (International Labour Organisation) (2001), *Social Security: Issues, Challenges and Prospects : Sixth Item on the Agenda*, Geneva: ILO.

ILO (2012), *Social Security to All: The Strategy of the International Labour Organisation : Building Social Protection Floors and Comprehensive Social Security Systems*, Geneva: ILO.

ILO (2014), *World Social Protection Report 2014/15 Building Economic Recovery, Inclusive Development and Social Justice*, Geneva: ILO.

Kidd, S. and Wylde, E. (2011), *Targeting the Poorest: An Assessment of the Proxy Means Test Methodology*, Canberra: Australian Agency for International Development (AusAID).

Koehler, G. (2011), 'Transformative social protection: reflection on South Asian Policy experiences', *IDS Bulletin*, 42 (6): 96–103.

Leisering, L. and Barrientos, A. (2013), 'Social citizenship for the global poor? the worldwide spread of social assistance', *International Journal of Social Welfare*, 22: S1–S18.

Levy, S. and Barahona, C. (2002), *2001–02 Targeted Inputs Programmeme (TIP): Main Report of the Evaluation Programme*, Lilongwe, Malawi: Logistics Unit, Ministry of Agriculture and Irrigation.

MacAuslan, I. and Riemenschneider, N. (2011), 'Richer but resented: what do cash transfers do to social relations?', *IDS Bulletin*, 42 (6): 60–66.

Mkandawire, P. T. (2004), 'Social policy in a development context: introduction', in P. T. Mkandawire (ed.), *Social Policy in a Development Context*, Houndmills, Basingstoke and New York: Palgrave Macmillan, pp. 1–33.

Monchuk, Victoria (2014), *Reducing Poverty and Investing in People: The New Role of Safety Nets in Africa*, Directions in Development, Washington, DC: World Bank.

Munro, L. (2008), 'Risks, needs and rights: compatible or contradictory bases for social protection', in A. Barrientos and D. Hulme (eds), *Social Protection for the Poor and the Poorest: Concept, Policies and Politics*, Basingstoke: Palgrave Macmillan, pp. 27–46.

Myamba, Flora, Tibandebage, Paula and Israel, Caroline (forthcoming), 'Perceptions of targeting conditional cash transfers in Tanzania', Dar es Salaam, REPOA working paper.

Parfit, C. (1991), *Equality or Priority? The Lindley Lecture*, Kansas City, MO: University Press of Kansas.

Robeyns, I. (2008), 'Sen's capability approach and feminist concerns', in S. Alkire, M. Qizilbash and F. Comim (eds), *The Capability Approach: Concepts, Measures and Applications*, Cambridge: Cambridge University Press.

Sabates-Wheeler, R. and Devereux, S. (2008), 'Transformative social protection: the currency of social justice', in A. Barrientos and D. Hulme (eds), *Social Protection for the Poor and Poorest: Concepts, Policies and Politics*, London: Palgrave MacMillan, pp. 64–84.

Sabates-Wheeler, R. and Koehler, G. (2011), '(Re)distribution and growth: what is the role of social protection?', *IDS Bulletin*, 42 (6): 86–88.

Sen, A. (1999), *Development as Freedom*, Oxford: Oxford University Press.

Sen, A. (2009), *The Idea of Justice*, London: Penguin.

Silver, H. (2007), 'The process of social exclusion: the dynamics of an evolving concept', CPRC Working Paper 95, Manchester: Chronic Poverty Research Centre.

Sumner, Andy (2012), *From Deprivation to Distribution: Is Global Poverty Becoming a Matter of National Inequality?* IDS Working Paper 394, Brighton: Institute of Development Studies.

Sumner, Andy (2013), 'Poverty, politics and aid: is a reframing of global poverty approaching?' *Third World Quarterly* 34 (3): 357–377.

Tessitore, S. (2011), 'One step beyond: from social protection recipients to citizens', *IDS Bulletin*, 42 (6): 13–20.

World Bank (1990), *Poverty, World Development Report, 1990*, New York: Oxford University Press; www.worldbank.icebox.ingenta.com/content/wb/bk50851 (accessed 11 November 2014).

World Bank (2004), *A Better Investment Climate for Everyone, World Development Report 2005*, New York: Oxford University Press.

World Bank (2010), *Development and Climate Change, World Development Report 2010*, Washington, DC: World Bank.

World Bank (2012), *Resilience, Equity and Opportunity: The World Bank's 2012–2022 Social Protection and Labor Strategy*, Washington, DC: World Bank.

World Bank (2013), *Risk and Opportunity: Managing Risk for Development, World Development Report 2014*, Washington, DC: World Bank; http://library-titles.ebrary.com/Doc?id=10776325 (accessed 10 August 2015).

11 Territory, Desert and Global Distributive Justice

Kim Angell[1]

Introduction

Over the past three centuries, one of the primary modes of justifying exclusive rights over external objects has been John Locke's *labour theory* of property rights-acquisition. Locke famously argued that a person in the state of nature may appropriate an external object by expending labour upon it. In Locke's words: 'His *labour* hath taken it out of the hands of Nature, where it was common, and belong'd equally to all its Children, and *hath* thereby *appropriated* it for himself' (Locke, 2009: paragraph 29). This mode of acquisition is unilateral, but subject to certain limits: possessions acquired through labour are justifiably held only as long as *enough and as good* is left for others to appropriate, and nothing useful is *wasted* in a person's possession (ibid.: paragraphs 27 and 31).

Locke's justification of individual property rights has recently been revisited in some prominent theories of the just distribution of *territorial rights* between states. Whether this is a felicitous visit is the theme of this chapter. My conclusion will be largely negative. The theories of territorial rights I shall discuss follow Locke in defending unilateral rights-acquisition through labour, but they crucially depart from his theory by operating with *collective*, as opposed to individual, labouring agents (cf. e.g. Nine, 2012, and Miller, 2012). I shall argue that this dis-analogy has important – and unexpected – implications for the distribution of territorial rights justified on these collectivistic Lockean theories: in short, redistribution of territorial rights will be easier to justify than what they claim.

Before we start, let us clarify the concept of territorial rights. What do they include? States as we know them claim various rights over the physical spaces they currently control. First and foremost among these rights is the jurisdictional right to make, adjudicate and enforce law across the territory. Furthermore, states claim the right to control the natural resources within their respective territories and the right to control movements of persons and goods across territorial borders (Nine, 2012: 6; Miller, 2012: 253).

Due to the extensiveness and exclusivity of territorial rights, it is clear that their distribution between states has pivotal influence on the global distribution of various significant goods between individuals belonging to different polities. If a person identifies with a group which wields territorial rights over a particular territory, this will be valuable for that person in the sense that it serves the person's interest (if it is an interest) in being a member of a politically self-determining group, rather than belonging to a permanent minority within a larger citizenry. Moreover, if the state's territory is rich in natural resources, has a favourable climate, and so on, having territorial rights over it may have decisive (beneficial) effects on the living standards of the state's citizens. So, if we can *justify* a certain distribution of territorial rights between states, this will have significant implications for the just distribution of benefits and burdens between persons globally as members of different political communities.

Given its importance for global distributive justice, it is surprising that the justification of territorial rights has been a relatively neglected issue within political philosophy. Writing in 2001, A. John Simmons noted that political philosophers 'have almost always *begun* with the idea of states as units with legitimate territorial dimensions, proceeding more or less immediately to questions about how such territorial states can be justly governed'. This is an omission, he writes, because 'there is a logically prior question to be asked: what is the nature and basis of states' claims over those territories within which each of us comes nonvoluntarily to be?' (2001: 302).

However, over the last decade or so this omission has started to be rectified, with various theories of territorial rights having been developed and being debated by political philosophers.[2] As mentioned, a collectivistic version of the Lockean labour theory of acquisition has been appealed to in some of the most prominent contributions. In what immediately follows I will elaborate on this justification, and explicate that it relies on a *desert*-based reading of Locke's theory.[3]

What we can therefore call the *Lockean Desert*-justification of territorial rights claims, in short, that: a collective may labour to create value in land, and on that basis deserve to wield territorial rights over the improved land as a fitting reward. For ease of presentation I will focus only on Cara Nine's version of this justification of territorial rights. However, I believe that the conclusions drawn from my analyses of her theory are applicable, *mutatis mutandis*, also to the prominent theory defended by David Miller.[4]

After having outlined the relevant parts of Nine's theory, I will develop two independent (combinable) arguments which show that her theory incurs a *Partial-Responsibility Problem*: the labouring collective cannot claim sole responsibility for the value added to the territory. I shall argue that this invalidates the collective's desert-based claim to *exclusive* territorial rights over a particular physical space, and that global redistribution of such rights is therefore easier to justify, all else equal, than Nine claims.

Although I am critical of Nine's Lockean Desert-argument, I do not claim that other parts of her theory will also fail. She claims that two other Lockean arguments, from efficiency and autonomy, can also be 'directly employed to explain and justify particular territorial rights' (2012: 92). I will not assess these arguments and instead focus only on showing the deficiency of her desert-argument as a justification of particular (exclusive) territorial rights.

Nine on Lockean Desert

Nine offers a desert-based reading of Locke's individualistic labour theory of property rights-acquisition:[5]

> Locke appeals to desert as a justification for particular property rights. Of goods that are useful to us, Locke attributes most (99/100) of their value to labour. When a person invests her labour in the land, the land produces valuable products. The value of those products and of the land is attributed mostly to the labour. The owner of the labour, then, deserves the product of her labour [i.e. the envalued land], because it is her labour that made the product valuable.
>
> (2012: 84)

There are several ways of objecting to Locke's labour theory when it is cast in such desert-terms. The first thing we can note is the emphasis Nine places on Locke's notorious claim (cf. 2009: paragraphs 40–43) about labour being responsible for *virtually all* of the improved land's use-value. This claim is important because the desert-argument (Locke's as well as Nine's) aims to reward the labourer with rights to control *the land itself*, not only the added value: as Nine puts it, labouring agents 'deserve rights over the things that they changed to create the value and over the value itself' (2012: 85). One might ask here why the labourer should deserve rights over more than the added value (Nozick, 1974: 175). However, if the raw materials used to create the valuable result were almost worthless prior to the labourer's actions, the desert-theorist might reply that 'appropriators gathered nothing worth mentioning when they established exclusive control over tracts of natural resources' (Cohen, 1995: 176).

As Cohen has argued, in my view convincingly, the premise about labour's contribution to the value of land,[6] and its role in the justification of appropriation, is implausible (1995: 165–194). For present purposes, however, I will set this issue aside. I will assume that the differential between the use-value of the unimproved land and the contribution of labour to the use-value of the improved land is sufficiently large to (somehow) establish a desert-based claim both to the value produced by labour *and* the raw materials used in the production – regardless of whether the added value accounts for 99/100, more or (probably much) less, of the improved land's use-value.

Another important objection to the desert-based argument centres on an indeterminacy problem: why should we regard rights over the labour's *product* as the most fitting reward? Why can we not properly reward the labourer's desert with something else? Another challenge is to explicate why one deserves a reward if one's actions only benefit oneself. Why not claim that desert-conferring actions should be supererogatory and of some sort of advantage to others? Questions such as these must at some stage be answered by any plausible Lockean Desert-based argument. However, they will not detain us here.[7]

I will instead develop a different line of criticism of the desert-based argument, what I above called the Partial-Responsibility Problem. This problem, I argue, is necessarily incurred by Nine's collectivistic Lockean Desert-justification of territorial rights, but not by Locke's own individualistic property rights-justification.

To grasp what the Partial-Responsibility Problem is about, consider this. It seems to me evident that, on the desert-based argument, a labourer deserves that (but only that) which *she herself* is responsible for having created. For argument's sake, we have just assumed that the labourer deserves rights over the raw materials she used to create the valuable product. Regardless of what the initial use-value of those materials might be, she cannot claim responsibility for it; so that is an exception to the above claim. However, there can be no other exceptions. If we universalise the claim about deserving to keep the products of one's labour, it follows that a labourer cannot deserve rights over the value, if any at all, *added by other labourers*. This claim is arguably supported by Locke's own remarks. Locke seems to reject the possibility that a person can deserve rights over any value created by others: no person has a right to 'the benefit of another's Pains' (2009: paragraph 34).

Here it is pertinent to emphasise that the desert-claim (in Nine's theory, as well as in Locke's) concerns *initial* appropriation. The labourer creates value in the state of nature (either on 'empty' land that has never been laboured on, or on land that others have 'wasted'), and thereby deserves to control the improved land. It is a further question whether objects initially acquired in that way might be legitimately *transferred* to other agents. If such transfers are justified, the agent who is, say, voluntarily given an object obtains rights over that gift. In this non-initial-appropriation sense, an agent might become *entitled* to 'the benefit of another's Pains' – although the agent cannot, of course, claim to *deserve* that entitlement based on the agent's own value-creating labour. Because Nine does not discuss the issue of transfers, I shall not consider it any further here.[8]

I will now proceed on the assumption that, in order to deserve *exclusive* control over the improved land, the labourer must be *solely* responsible for having enhanced its value, all else equal. In what follows I will argue that the collective labouring agent in Nine's theory cannot claim sole responsibility for the added use-value that the improved land holds. The Partial-Responsibility Problem is thus incurred, and Nine's Lockean Desert-theory fails to establish exclusive territorial rights for the labouring collective, all else equal.

I shall soon turn to develop the two arguments which show this failure, and also make clear why it implies that global redistribution of territorial rights will be easier to justify than Nine expects. But first we must have a closer look at Nine's theory.

Nine's Theory of Territorial Rights

There are three elements in Nine's theory which are relevant for our purposes. The first is her account of the justification of *general* territorial rights, and of which agents qualify for such rights. The second is the account of how such eligible agents can acquire *particular* territorial rights over a specific territory. The third concerns how the particular territorial rights of existing agents might have to be *redistributed* in order for the system of territorial rights to meet the general territorial rights of new emerging agents (such as ecological refugees from sinking island states), who are 'latecomers', so to speak, to the 'acquisition-game'.

Let us start with the first element. According to Nine, the territorial rights of states are in general justified because having such rights is 'essential for the provision of individual basic needs' (2012: 3). A state can use its territorial rights to solve various 'coordination problems' and thereby achieve stable provision of the goods necessary to meet the basic needs of its citizens:

> Because the jurisdictional authority over territory is a crucial means to solving important coordination problems, such as the provision of potable waters, sewers, property rights, public order, and so on, attributing the right of jurisdictional authority over territory to an agent that solves the coordination problem serves basic individual interests. This is the moral mandate of territorial rights – that the right only exists if the exercise of the right functions to meet individuals' basic needs.
>
> (Ibid.: 49)

In Nine's view, only collectives (of a certain size) can solve such coordination problems (ibid.: 46–50). So, if territorial rights are to fulfil their valuable purpose, they must be held by such *collective* agents, who are capable of acting with one, authoritative voice.

Apart from its having a certain size, to be eligible for general territorial rights a collective must meet two criteria. First, it must have demonstrated its capacity to establish state institutions which implement the rule of law in accordance with certain 'minimal' standards of justice: 'to provide secure access to the objects of basic human needs for members and to respect the basic human rights of all persons' (ibid.: 67). Second, the collective's members must 'share a common conception of justice' (ibid.). This latter criterion is related to Rawls's idea of an overlapping consensus (1996). On Nine's usage, when persons have a shared conception of justice, they 'share certain values and presumptions', including 'political conceptions regarding the just use of lands and resources within [the state's territory]' (2012: 65–66).

Let us now turn to the second main element in Nine's theory. On her view, territorial rights over a *particular* territory can be claimed by the eligible collectives on the basis of Lockean Desert for value-creation. She states her desert-principle as follows: '[o]n the Lockean principle of desert, if the value of a territory is significantly attributable to the collective, then the collective has a weak rights claim to the territory' (2012: 84).[9]

How does this rights-claim come about? Collectives can 'change the land', Nine writes, 'in similar ways as individuals, via labour' (ibid.: 82). However, the value-creation that such collective agents must perform in order to deserve territorial rights is of a special kind. On Nine's theory, collectives enhance the value of a specific territory by *creating complex state institutions which establish (minimally just) rule of law* on it: 'they labour by creating, adjudicating, and enforcing laws and by creating and maintaining social and economic institutions and norms' (ibid.).

There are various beneficial effects to be had from the collective's operation of well-functioning state institutions:

> The collective's governance of land use creates stable systems of agriculture and other forms of production that create value in land (and air and water) at any particular time and over long periods of time. Much of the value of the lands occupied by the members of a collective is due to the coordinated efforts of those members under the guidance of collective institutions. Examples are technological advances built upon group and cross-generational research and conservation efforts coordinated by communities and enforced by rule of law. These actions engender many kinds of valuable results ranging from real estate value to the fundamental value of providing food, clothing, and shelter to individuals.
>
> (Ibid.: 84)

Apart from the *instrumental* value produced by the state's '[e]nforcement of rules', which 'creates a stable environment which is crucial for individuals to reliably access the objects of their basic needs' (2012: 49), Nine also regards state governance as *intrinsically* valuable. Having 'political control over one's environment', she writes, 'is intrinsically valuable because it is an essential part of the dignity of a human being' (2012: 33).

Now, at this stage one might wonder why the collective's creation of (instrumentally and intrinsically) valuable state institutions confers *territorial* rights rather than, say, collective *property* rights (within a larger, encompassing state). Nine's answer is that the fitting reward for the collective's labour is territorial (not property) rights because granting such rights to the collective will best promote the relevant fundamental value of *providing for individual basic needs* (or what Locke, 2009: paragraph 6 would refer to as the value of preserving 'Mankind'/God's 'Property'):

> In the case of property rights, a person is entitled to control the use of, access to, and benefits from the good. We think that such entitlements are justified because, on Lockean arguments, they efficiently help to *realize relevant liberal values*. In the case of territorial rights, a collective is entitled to establish determinate jurisdiction within a region. Such entitlements are justified because, on Lockean grounds, they efficiently help to realize *the same values* through the establishment of justice.
>
> (2012: 83, my emphases)

So, the idea is that the same 'fundamental liberal concern for basic needs' (ibid.: 82) can be used to justify different entitlements: property rights for individuals, and territorial rights for collectives.

The analogy to Locke's labour theory of property rights-acquisition does not end with the account Nine gives of how collectives establish particular exclusive rights based on desert for value-creation. Like Locke, Nine also places *two limits* upon such unilateral acquisition: a collective's territorial rights over a particular territory are justified only as long as 'enough and as good' is left for other collectives to acquire, and the collective does not 'waste' its territorial holdings.

Consider first her account of the waste-limit:

> The way that collectives 'use' territory is in their provision of the rule of law.... On this understanding, a collective misuses its territory (lets it spoil) when it fails to provide legitimate institutions for those that are within the territory, when the institutions fail to provide for members' basic needs.
>
> (2012: 41)

In addition to the waste-limit, Nine also defends an 'enough and as good'-proviso. For Locke, Nine explains, individual property rights-acquisition is justified because it is necessary for the preservation of humankind: because the consent of all is impossible to obtain, no individual can survive unless the world's resources can be put to use through unilateral acquisition. But an 'enough and as good'-limit on such acquisition is justified on the same basis: without such a proviso, firstcomers could acquire all the world's resources and thereby threaten the preservation of latecomers (2012: 164–165). As she puts it: 'When the exercise of a particular exclusive right over goods severely threatens the value(s) that are used to justify the right (or system of rights of which it is a part), then the particular right should be changed so that it no longer undermines those values' (ibid.: 165).

Nine takes the reasoning behind Locke's proviso and adapts it to territorial rights. Her Lockean proviso is developed in relation to cases where certain collectives – 'ecological refugee states' – lose their territory due to rising sea levels. Recall that Nine regards territorial rights as generally justified because of their role in the provision of basic human needs.

A system of territorial rights, she writes, 'is justified because *self-determination over territory* is necessary to meet basic needs of individuals' (2012: 166, my emphasis). For the system of territorial rights to serve its justifying value, the proviso must, Nine claims, protect existing self-determining collectives, such as ecological refugee states, by making each collective a *candidate* for territorial rights over a (new) particular territory (2012: 171).

However, in practice, the upshot of the proviso will be less than egalitarian: their being 'a candidate' is not enough for the refugees to receive *exclusive* territorial rights over a new territory. The reason is that the world currently holds no unacquired land:

> Other groups also have legitimate claims to territorial rights, and currently there is *no unoccupied, viable land*. This means that any claim that an ecological refugee state might have to a territory as a result of the Lockean proviso will *compete with* another group's right to self-determination. A likely consequence of this state of affairs is that the people of Tuvalu cannot expect to gain *exclusive* territorial sovereignty over any land. However, a case can be made for an arrangement of nested self-determination, where the Tuvaluans have rights to *limited self-determination* within another state's territory. This arrangement, I believe, would resolve the conditions that trigger the Lockean proviso applied to territorial rights.
>
> (2012: 179–180, my emphases)

In practice, Nine stops short of an equalising proviso. The refugees' general right cannot be implemented without upsetting the particular territorial rights of existing states (held on behalf of the collectives they represent). Those particular rights, as we have seen, are based on desert for value-creation. When the weight of those desert-claims is taken into consideration, what is on balance justified for the refugees is merely *non-exclusive* ('limited') territorial rights.

Note that the existing states which have desert-based particular rights also have a general claim to wield territorial rights. That general claim is identical to that of the refugees. But because the existing states' general claims could in principle be satisfied by granting them territorial rights over (virtually) *any* territory – at any rate, a smaller one than they currently control – then *that* claim cannot be the one which is used to 'compete with' (and eventually outweigh) the general claim of the refugees. It must be the *desert*-claim which does that crucial job. However, if it can be shown that the existing states' desert-claims are less weighty than expected – in fact, that they are not claims to exclusive territorial rights at all – then the Lockean proviso Nine defends will be more prone to justify redistribution of exclusive territorial rights for new eligible claimants, all else equal.

I will now develop two independent arguments which show that the Partial-Responsibility Problem applies to Nine's desert-argument. If so, we can anticipate a different outcome from the balancing of claims that goes on when Nine's Lockean proviso-mechanism kicks in. All else equal, exclusive (at any rate, less 'limited') territorial rights will be justified for the ecological refugees, and other eligible claimants, even in our fully appropriated world.

Argument 1: Agency and Responsibility

Let us start by noting that, on any version of the Lockean Desert-argument, we discuss what Miller has called 'primary desert-judgments', where the bases of desert are 'performances for which the agents in question are responsible' (2003: 27). Nine has the same kind of desert-base in mind. She refers to how 'the value of the land is significantly attributable to the collective' and that the collective 'is deserving on the basis of performing [the value-creating] action' (2012: 84).

It seems uncontroversial to claim that, in order to generate such desert, one must qualify as an *agent*: one must have the capacity to (freely) choose whether to perform the relevant behaviour or not, and be able to (freely) carry out one's decision. One seems to deserve neither reward nor punishment based on types of behaviour which one could not have avoided performing. In fact, for someone's behaviour to count as 'labour' at all (from the Lockean perspective), the behaviour must arguably have been intended: the labour must have been done with a purpose; it must have been expended with a certain goal in mind (Simmons, 1992: 271–272; Becker, 1977: 52).[10]

This means that someone's capacity for agency must exist *prior to* someone's value-creating behaviour in order for that value-creation to count as labour and consequently render the (alleged) labourer deserving of a reward. If the value-creation was not rationally intended, its performer cannot claim responsibility for it in the way required in primary desert-judgements.[11]

Now, I do not mean to suggest that rational agency (and responsibility) is necessary for *any* desert-claim. Some things you might deserve 'in virtue of being a person', regardless of whether you have performed any specific action (Feldman, 1995: 69). However, as pointed out, for the category of desert-claims which are meant to be established by the Lockean labour theory, some notion of agency-capacity seems required.[12]

So, I shall proceed on the following assumption: if the relevant agent comes into existence *after* (or during) the value-creation – indeed, *as a result of* the value-creation – then the value-creation which happened before the agent's genesis cannot have been rationally intended and performed by that agent in the way required for meting out desert based on purposive value-creation. As I will now suggest, granting these arguably straightforward points will lead Nine into the Partial-Responsibility Problem.

To see why, it is instructive to consider two aspects of Nine's theory. Recall first her take on the social ontology of groups. On Nine's view, a set of persons residing in a specific territory can be a distinct collective as long as they share a common conception of justice: a 'unique set of principles and ideals arising from the unique blend of values and aspirations represented within the region' (2012: 64).

The second aspect is Nine's (ibid.: 18–19) favouring of Joseph Raz's *interest theory* of rights. On this theory, Nine writes, a collective need not be formally organised in order to be eligible for holding rights: '*rational agency* is not necessary for the *identification* of relevant collectives' (ibid.: 67, my emphases). Nine favours the interest theory exactly because of this feature. She wants to avoid having to conclude in advance that a group which qualifies as a distinct collective (due to its members sharing a common conception of justice) cannot be a potential rights-holder because of its lack of capacity for rational agency:

> [t]he people of failed states, peoples in the midst of brutal civil war, minority groups who wish to secede but their basic human and civil rights to organize politically are oppressed – each of these groups may claim that others have obligations towards them as a collective.... The interests of the individual members of this collective still justify the collective's rights-claim, even if the collective is not formally organized.
>
> (Ibid.)

However, even if we accept that a collective which lacks agency-capacity is a potential holder of territorial rights, nothing follows about whether that collective does have such rights based on desert for value-creation. To claim such rights, the collective would first have to possess the capacity for (group) agency (i.e. have a collective decision mechanism), rationally decide (through the requisite decision mechanism) to create a justice-establishing state and then carry out the requisite value-creation.

The puzzle here is that the kind of valuable result that is supposed to be created by the collective – namely, a justice-enforcing state – arguably includes the very creation of institutions that enable a set of individuals *to function as* a group agent. But if so, Nine's argument seems to implausibly imply that a group of persons which lacks the capacity for rational agency has *nonetheless acted as an agent* and created the relevant value of justice-establishing state institutions.

At this stage Nine might object that the requirement of group agency could be satisfied before state institutions in a full-blown sense have been created. That is, she might suggest that a *rudimentary* organisational structure (i.e. an agency-enabling institution) might be established on unimproved land before more complex state institutions are created. This agency-enabling institution might perhaps come about through the unstructured and uncoordinated actions of a group of persons who share a common conception of justice (but have no prior agency-capacity) or, perhaps (more probably) through the outright coercion of some of them by others (i.e. a state-building elite).[13]

This seems plausible in principle. After having acquired group agency, the collective could make a rational decision to start to create value in the form of more and more complex institutions. This (subsequent) value-creation would count as purposive labour, and the collective would become deserving owing to their having increased the value of the rudimentary institutions, by transforming them into full-blown, justice-enforcing state institutions.

However, insofar as the establishment of the rudimentary institutions constitutes an improvement of the land, the *collective agent* cannot claim more than *partial* responsibility for the enhanced use-value that the improved land now has. The persons (who may or may not be members of the collective) whose purposive actions resulted in the creation of the rudimentary institutions will have similar deserts based on their having contributed to the relevant valuable result, namely: the creation of justice-establishing state institutions.

The exact size of the contributions of these individual labourers will depend upon the size of the gap between the value of the agency-enabling institutions and that of the full-blown (minimal) justice-establishing state institutions envisaged by Nine. I will not attempt to say much about the expected size of that gap. However, whenever the relevant collectives are anything near as large as the citizenries of modern states, the institutions required for establishing and operating *well-functioning* decision-procedures among such large groups might be rather complex and perhaps approximating full-blown state institutions. If so, the relative contributions of the individual agents will be quite significant.

So, it seems safe to say that at least some (and, I expect, a significant amount) of the value of justice-establishing state institutions will have been created by other labouring agents acting prior to the agency-capable collective's genesis. The Partial-Responsibility Problem is thus incurred, and the labouring collective's Lockean Desert-based claim cannot justify *exclusive* rights to control the territory.

The upshot of this is the redistributive implications discussed in the previous section. Here one might wonder whether Nine could reply by saying that the fitting reward for the *individual* labourers' efforts is to grant them *property* rights over the land, rather than (non-exclusive) territorial rights, because the value of providing for basic human needs is best realised with *such* rights in their case. This reply will not work. For one thing, it would cause problems for Nine's definition of jurisdictional rights, on which those rights include the right to amend private property arrangements within the territory (2012: 7). If individuals have laboured to establish property rights on the territory in the state of nature – that is, prior to the establishment of the state – why are those *natural* property claims justifiably subjected to the juridical authority of that state? Unless Nine can explain why the collective is justified in amending such natural property rights-claims, the implication seems to be that what her theory justifies is merely a *policy-specific* (or 'fragmented') jurisdictional right, where the state's right to make, adjudicate and enforce laws is restricted to certain policy-areas.

More importantly, the 'property, not territory'-reply would only show that the individual labourers cannot claim desert-based (non-exclusive) territorial rights *individually*. It would not deny them the right to conjoin the improved lands which they have individually envalued (and thus acquired), and unite to form an eligible *collective* with the capacity to establish minimally just state institutions. If they can achieve this, then rewarding their deserts would seem to require granting them (non-exclusive) territorial rights.

Finally, even assuming that the individual labourers cannot unite into such a capable agent, there is no escaping the fact that *parts* of the value of the full-blown (minimally just) state institutions have nonetheless been created by *someone else* than Nine's labouring collective. To deny that conclusion we would have to implausible claim that the rudimentary institutions have no value at all.

Argument 2: Normative Individualism and Collective Interests

Even if we disregard the problems caused by Argument 1, there is another serious threat to Nine's Lockean Desert-argument. Let us assume that the collective was somehow able to function as a group agent prior to the value-creation. As I shall now argue, even in this happy scenario it need not follow that the collective is justified in wielding exclusive territorial rights based on Lockean Desert. The reason is that the *current* members of the (trans-historical) collective agent cannot claim sole responsibility for the value-creation. Why?

Let us start by recalling that Nine embraces Raz's interest theory of rights. She also endorses his *collective* conception of group rights (Nine, 2012: 18–19). According to Raz:

> a collective right exists when the following three conditions are met. First, it exists because an aspect of the interest of human beings justifies holding some person(s) to be subject to a duty. Second, the interests in question are the interests of individuals as members of a group in a public good and the right is a right to that public good because it serves their interest as members of the group. Thirdly, the interest of no single member of that group in that public good is sufficient by itself to justify holding another person to be subject to a duty.
>
> (1986: 208)

Raz's interest theory of collective rights conforms to what we can call *normative individualism*: the view that 'groups have no moral standing that is not wholly reducible to the moral status of the individual persons who make them up' (Jones, 1999: 366). In Raz's own words:

> [r]ights, even collective rights, can only be there if they serve the interests of individuals. In that sense collective interests are a mere *façon de parler*. They are a way of referring to individual interests which arise out of the individuals' membership in communities.
>
> (1986: 208)

Because she endorses Raz's theory, I will assume that normative individualism is shared by Nine.[14]

What does this mean for how we conceive of the relevant interests that the value-creating labourer can submit on Nine's desert-argument? The most obvious candidate is the interest in 'keeping the product of one's labour'. If we believe, with Nine, that desert for value-creation is a valid moral principle, we will regard that interest as morally significant. Unfortunately, however, if we hold on to normative individualism, we cannot ascribe that interest directly to the *trans-historical collective itself*. Or more precisely, the interest of such a collective is only *morally significant* when satisfying it 'serves' the interests of individuals 'as members of the group' (cf. Raz's second criterion). That is to say, the interest which is meant to ground the collective's desert-based rights cannot be *the collective's* interest in keeping the products of *its* labour. For that latter interest to ground the collective's territorial rights it must be conceived of as – or, more precisely, serve – a morally significant *individual* interest held by the group members considered severally. That (morally significant) individual interest would ground a collective right if and when cumulating/aggregating it is sufficient to justify the imposition of the requisite duties on others (cf. Raz's third criterion).

It might make good sense to say that a collective agent *exists* as a trans-historical entity, regardless of changes in its individual members. As seen, Nine favours a social ontology in which collectives ('peoples') can endure over time. However, what we are concerned with here is not such ontological claims, but rather how we can *justify* territorial rights for trans-historical collectives. And normative individualism, in conjunction with the interest theory of rights, demands that we justify the relevant rights by reference to the interests of individuals.

As alluded to, this seems to imply that, from the justificatory (as opposed to the ontological) perspective, the collective entity will lose its trans-historical character. The collective must instead be treated as the mere set of individual members who make it up at any particular moment in time. As normative individualists, we must focus on the interests of those individual members (and eventually non-members) when attempting to justify the collective's right. The collective *qua* collective is irrelevant here.

But if we focus on the interest in 'keeping the product of one's labour' from the point of view of each *current* member of the collective, that interest will not be sufficient for grounding *exclusive* territorial rights. The reason, again, is that those current group members are (normally) not solely responsible for the improved land's added use-value.

In order to appreciate the force of this point, it is instructive to consider what I take to be the normal case for a theory such as Nine's: that of a consolidated state which has existed for a century or more. The current set of individuals making up the people which collectively governs such a state cannot claim responsibility for value-creating actions done by *former* sets of group members, although all sets of members belong, or have belonged, to the same trans-historical entity. Clearly, the present individuals currently act as a group agent when maintaining (and perhaps increasing still, or so we can assume) the value of those state institutions into which they were born, and under which they live. However, in the case at hand, there is no escaping the fact that other (former) group members have also contributed to creating the value of those institutions.

Recall Locke's view, that a person has no right to 'the benefit of another's Pains'. Submitting the individual interest in 'keeping the product of *previous members'* labour', then, is of no avail for the current set of group members: that interest in 'benefiting from another's Pains' cannot be seen as morally weighty *from the point of view of Lockean Desert*.[15] So, the interest which *is* morally significant from that desert-perspective – the interest in 'keeping the products of one's own labour' – is insufficient to ground *exclusive* territorial rights for the current generations: after all, they are not solely responsible for the added value that the land now has.[16]

This implies, somewhat paradoxically, that the citizenries of consolidated states, which for a long time have performed well in (maintaining) the provision of basic needs, do not deserve exclusive territorial rights, whereas the citizenries of 'new' states, which have just started to perform satisfactorily in these respects, do deserve such rights (assuming that the state was established *within* the lifetime of its current members). This implication is, I think, counter-intuitive. Moreover, in the latter case: as soon as the first state-building generations pass away, the new generations which labour to maintain the valuable state institutions cannot claim sole responsibility for the value of those institutions. This means that it is impossible for Nine's Lockean Desert-argument to justify a temporally *stable* set of (exclusive) territorial rights. There seems to be no way indeed of avoiding the Partial-Responsibility Problem.

Could there be an easy fix to this? Perhaps shifting to a different conception of group rights could work. In fact, Nine's desert-principle seems to presuppose what Jones has called the 'corporate' conception of group rights, according to which the group is a separate entity that exists independently from its members, has a moral standing on its own and can have morally significant interests (1999: 361–364). Embracing the corporate conception of group rights would avoid the problem of letting current generations claim desert for previous group members' labour. The group itself could instead be ascribed the morally significant interest in keeping the product of *its* labour. However, this move would not be cost-free. As Jones (ibid.: 366) points out, shifting to the corporate conception, while holding on to the interest theory, would imply (controversially) rejecting normative individualism, which is a widely endorsed view.

Note that embracing the corporate conception of group rights need not imply embracing a collectivistic social *ontology*. There is an ongoing debate about whether and how we can make room for group entities within a fully individualistic social ontology. According to a prominent view, defended by List and Pettit (2011), we can. But note that, even though they claim that irreducible group entities can exist within an individualistic ontology, List and Pettit hold on to *normative* individualism: 'no approach we know suggests that group persons have morally commanding interests such that a corporate good or benefit would determine what should be done, independently of the good or benefit to individuals' (ibid.: 182).

On the other hand, if Nine wants to keep normative individualism, while still shifting to the corporate conception, she might instead have to reject the *interest theory* of rights. She could embrace the *choice theory* of rights, on which the eligibility-criterion for holding rights is an entity's capacity to control the imposition of duties (Preda, 2012: 230). If Nine's relevant collective – or, more precisely: 'corporation' – could sustain sufficient agency-capacity over the period in which it is claimed to labour, it could claim responsibility, *qua* group, for its value-creation across generations.

Shifting to the choice theory of rights would go against Nine's view that groups without agency-capacity may also be rights-holders. But that might be acceptable if the revision saves her Lockean Desert-argument from the Partial-Responsibility Problem. Unfortunately, however, the said revision will not deliver that much. It will not solve the challenge posed by Argument 1. The choice theory of rights is, after all, only a theory of rights-*eligibility*. The *justification* of territorial rights for the eligible agent would still have to be done by the Lockean Desert-principle. And as long as that principle implies that sole responsibility for value-creation is required for exclusive territorial rights, the said modifications to Nine's theory would not be sufficient to avoid the Partial-Responsibility Problem: the group agent could still not claim responsibility for having created the rudimentary, agency-enabling institutions.

Conclusion

The Partial-Responsibility Problem has shown that Nine's collectives cannot claim exclusive particular territorial rights based on Lockean Desert. When new needy agents emerge and Nine's Lockean proviso is triggered, the moral cost of satisfying their general territorial rights is smaller than expected. Toppling non-exclusive claims is arguably easier than having to outweigh exclusive ones, all else equal.

I have not taken a stand on whether the new balancing procedure will grant the new claimants exclusive territorial rights or whether they must settle for something less. However, I hope to have shown that they are, at any rate, justified in wielding *more extensive* territorial entitlements than Nine's theory appeared to grant them.

Existing states might therefore do well to start pondering how to deal with such new claimants in what may (unfortunately) appear to be the not so distant future. If those states are to live up to the demands of global distribute justice, they may have to offer the refugees quite comprehensive degrees of self-rule within their current borders, or perhaps redraw those borders altogether. In any case, the benefits and burdens persons might justifiably receive, due to their being members of different territorial polities, will be more equally distributed than initially thought.

Notes

1 I am very grateful to Camilla Boisen and Matt Murray for their many helpful comments on two earlier drafts, which have significantly improved this chapter. Thanks are also due to Robert Huseby, Sune Lægaard and Cara Nine, for instructive discussions leading me to develop several of the claims I defend here.
2 For important contributions, see e.g. Simmons, 2001; Meisels, 2009; Miller, 2012; Nine, 2012; Kolers, 2009; and Stilz, 2011.
3 Locke's text allows for several interpretations of what exactly it is about labour which establishes exclusive entitlements (2009: mainly paragraphs 25–51). For alternatives to, and strong criticisms of, the desert-interpretation, see Simmons, 1992: 236–277, and Waldron, 1988: 191–207.
4 See my 'Lockean theories of territory' (unpublished manuscript).
5 For a similar reading, see Miller, 1980: 6.
6 Nine uses her Lockean Desert-theory, as Risse (2013: 4) notes, to justify jurisdictional rights as well as natural resource rights. In her case, the claim about labour's contribution to the land's use-value thus refers not only to *surface land* but also to *natural resources* within the territory.
7 For a critique of a desert-based interpretation of Locke's labour theory, which discusses these questions, see Becker (1977: 48–56).
8 I thus leave it an open question whether Nine's theory might avoid the redistributive implications of the Partial-Responsibility Problem by giving an account of legitimate transfers. If (exclusive or non-exclusive) territorial rights based on other labourers' desert for value-creation can be legitimately transferred to Nine's relevant labouring agent – and, as a matter of descriptive fact, has been so transferred – then that agent might be entitled to exclusive territorial rights over a particular physical space, regardless of whether it has added any value to that space at all. However, as mentioned, the basis for the territorial rights of the agent would then be different from the one Nine defends: the rights would (partly) be justified by the agent's *entitlement* to *gifted* land – as explicated, or so we can assume, by the theory of legitimate transfers – not (solely) by *desert* for value-creating labour.
9 The claim is 'weak' in order to avoid rewarding colonists for their value-creation on forcibly colonised lands.
10 It has been suggested to me that this account of how to delineate 'labour' might lead into undecipherable discourse when one tries to determine what counts as a sufficient level of intent. I cannot hope to deal with this worry here, so I mention it only to set it aside.
11 The intention-based account of labour arguably implies that accidentally added value does not confer desert. However, it need not imply that what counts as rational, intentional behaviour is *objectively* defined. I might look at someone playing cricket as an irrational application of labour, although that

need not undermine their right to profit from applying it. I owe this example to Matt Murray.

12 That notion might well be thin, however. See note 12.

13 How rudimentary can the agency-enabling institutions be? According to Preda, the requirement can be quite 'limited': what is required for agency is the capacity to form intentions, and to make choices, whereas being able to reflect on (and possibly revise) those intuitions (in light of moral reasons) is not necessary (2012: 234–238). Groups satisfy these criteria if they have a 'collective decision-making procedure' which '[transforms] different individual choices into a single and irreducibly collective decision' (ibid.: 248–249), and which is 'known to the group's members' (ibid.: 247).

14 Elsewhere, Nine states: '[a]s a liberal, I believe that all rights will be derived from a concern for individual rights and well-being' (2008: 962).

15 Recall that Locke's claim does not apply to (justifiable) transfers. So, one might be *entitled* to the value created by others on bases other than Lockean Desert. Another Lockean way of (apparently) benefiting from others' labour is found in *adverse possession*-cases. Here an owner's non-use of an object which was initially acquired through desert for value-creation, a squatter's open use of it (and, we can assume, creation of value on it) and the owner's lacking attempt to eject the squatter, combine to justify redistribution of rights over the object. Could adverse possession-cases help Nine avoid the redistributive implications of the Partial-Responsibility Problem? I think not. I need not claim that a squatter has *no* desert-based claim to the object whatsoever. The crucial question is whether the squatter has a *similar* desert-based claim as the previous owner. My claim is negative. At best, she has *non-exclusive* rights over the object (based on desert), because she, as opposed to the previous owner, cannot claim sole responsibility for the value of the improved object. Clearly, if the object totally decayed, and the squatter reconstructed it from scratch, this would confer exclusive rights. However, that situation cannot arise in the case of Nine's collective labouring agent. After all, for that agent to come into existence at all, the use-valuable agency-enabling rudimentary institutions cannot per definition have decayed away.

16 As Jones (1999: 358, n. 8) points out, Raz's interest theory allows that the moral weight of interests belonging to other agents than the rights-holder might be relevant when ascribing the right. This is consistent with the view that the interests of individuals belonging to *past generations* should be taken into account. See e.g. Ridge (2003) and Mulgan (1999) for analyses of what weight we should accord to the interests of the dead. While this adds some complexity to the issue, I think my main analysis remains unscathed: the objection is not that a collective's being *entitled* to wield exclusive territorial rights cannot be justified on the basis of interests that are somehow connected to the labour and deserts of previous generations, say, *qua* gift-givers or bequeathers (or on other bases). Again (cf. note 7 above), that would be the case, for example, if we allow for transfers of desert-based claims. The point is that the collective's territorial rights would then no longer be based (solely) on Nine's Lockean Desert-argument – as that justification currently stands. Below I briefly consider whether Nine could avoid the objections I press by shifting to the *choice theory* of rights. In connection to the present point about transfers, it is interesting to note that a choice theorist must rule out a certain kind of transfers, namely *bequests*. As Hillel Steiner (1994: 249–261) has argued, on the choice theory of rights, transfers of entitlements can only happen through the exchange *inter vivos* of the necessary correlatives (rights and powers), as in gift-giving. This makes bequeathing impossible because such transfers, per definition, happen after the death of the bequeather. Steiner underlines, however, that bequests might be explicated (as I have just mentioned) in interest theory-terms.

References

Angell, Kim (n.d.) 'Lockean theories of territory', unpublished manuscript.

Becker, Lawrence. C. (1977), *Property Rights: Philosophic Foundations*, London: Routledge and Kegan Paul.

Cohen, G. A. (1995), *Self-ownership, Freedom, and Equality*, Cambridge: Cambridge University Press.

Feldman, Fred (1995), 'Desert: reconsideration of some received wisdom', *Mind*, 104 (413): 63–77.

Jones, Peter (1999), 'Group rights and group oppression', *Journal of Political Philosophy*, 7 (4): 353–377.

Kolers, Avery (2009), *Land, Conflict, and Justice*, Cambridge: Cambridge University Press.

List, Christian and Pettit, Philip (2011), *Group Agency: The Possibility, Design, and Status of Corporate Agents*, Oxford: Oxford University Press.

Locke, John (2009), *Two Treatises of Government*, edited by Peter Laslett, Cambridge: Cambridge University Press.

Meisels, Tamar (2009), *Territorial Rights*, second edn, Dordrecht: Springer.

Miller, David (1980), 'Justice and property', *Ratio*, 22: 1–14.

Miller, David (2003), 'Comparative and noncomparative desert', in Serena Olsaretti (ed.), *Desert and Justice*, Oxford: Clarendon Press.

Miller, David (2012), 'Territorial rights: concept and justification', *Political Studies*, 60 (2): 252–268.

Mulgan, Tim (1999), 'The place of the dead in liberal political philosophy', *Journal of Political Philosophy*, 7 (11): 52–70.

Nine, Cara (2008), 'Territory is not derived from property: a response to Steiner', *Political Studies*, 56 (4): 957–963.

Nine, Cara (2012), *Global Justice and Territory*, Oxford: Oxford University Press.

Nozick, Robert (1974), *Anarchy, State, and Utopia*, New York: Basic Books.

Preda, Adina (2012), 'Group rights and group agency', *Journal of Moral Philosophy*, 9 (2): 229–254.

Rawls, John (1996), *Political Liberalism, with a New Introduction and the 'Reply to Habermas'*, New York: Columbia University Press.

Raz, Joseph (1986), *The Morality of Freedom*, Oxford: Oxford University Press.

Ridge, Michael (2003), 'Giving the dead their due', *Ethics*, 114 (1): 38–59.

Risse, Mathias (2013), 'Review of Cara Nine, *Global Justice and Territory*', *Notre Dame Philosophical Reviews*, 5 (17 May).

Simmons, A. John (1992), *The Lockean Theory of Rights*, Princeton, NJ: Princeton University Press.

Simmons, A. John (2001), 'On the territorial rights of states', *Noûs*, 35 (1): 300–326.

Steiner, Hillel (1994), *An Essay on Rights*, Oxford: Blackwell.

Stilz, Anna (2011), 'Nations, states, and territory', *Ethics*, 121 (3): 572–601.

Waldron, Jeremy (1988), *The Right to Private Property*, Oxford: Oxford University Press.

12 The Global Commons and International Distributive Justice

Peri Roberts and Peter Sutch

Introduction

This chapter sets out to introduce the reader to a key contemporary debate in global distributive justice. This debate (more properly 'debates' in the plural as there is little moral or legal consistency) is located in international legal and political debate concerning the appropriate way to manage the global commons. Our goal is to demonstrate that distributive justice claims are a crucial part of these debates and to show how political theory might contribute to the forging of new and more coherent understanding of the distributive justice of global commons management. Contemporary reflections on global justice have been predominantly liberal-cosmopolitan and cosmopolitanism has been very focused on human rights rather than international law more broadly. Where the literature does broaden its scope it is usually to draw other aspects of international politics into human rights discourse. Without denying the importance of this aspect of contemporary international political theory we want to show how political theory could utilise its traditions to develop a politically urgent debate that has incredible potential to enrich or threaten human security.

As many of the chapters in this volume have demonstrated, property rights are an essential aspect of most arguments about social justice. On the international plane most (but importantly not all) regimes for the allocation of ownership rights and distributive obligations are thought to be the internal concern of sovereign states. Over time other entities such as international organisations, corporate bodies and individuals (or natural persons) have gained international personality (legal agency) but there is still considerable traction to the idea that international law has, as its primary purpose, the preservation of the sovereignty of states. This feature of global law and governance is often thought of as the central challenge to the establishment of environmentally and distributionally just global governance structures. We return to this below.

Issues of resource ownership and use only become internationalised as sovereign claims clash. Historically this was most evident during wars of conquest and colonialism and at the negotiation of peace treaties. In the history of political thought the key example of the latter is the discovery of the new world, something that prompted some of the classics of the natural law tradition. Today the scramble for resources is mediated by a positivist conception of law and particularly by the general prohibition of the use of force. This means that while appropriation by force is ruled out the role of moral theory in determining just distributions is largely thought to be *ultra vires*. However, international norms relating to resource ownership, use and distribution still come into play when a state's actions threaten or undermine the human rights of those within its jurisdiction (the human rights dimension), or if the trans-boundary effect of state policy is harmful to others (the international–environmental dimension) or, most importantly, as new 'unowned' resources are discovered (the global commons dimension). In contemporary political theory the key example of the latter is the evolution of global commons regimes which provides the basis for debate about how to manage unowned or common resources. In practice it is in debates over the global commons, even more than in debates regarding social and economic human rights, that developed questions of international distributive justice are to be found. The moral vocabularies in play are quite distinct, the resources at stake are (in the grand scheme of things) new to science and the legal and political frame for such debates is distinctively post-war.

Yet the debate may be as important to this and future generations as the debates of the sixteenth and seventeenth centuries were to peoples of the new world and the colonial powers that did not recognise their property rights. Political theory has placed significant emphasis on the cosmopolitan implications of human rights for global distributive justice. These considerations are indeed vital to contemporary debates but, we argue, we need to look at the broader importance of international human rights as part of a much wider set of arguments. Later we argue that normative power lies in the intersection of norms relating to human rights, environmental protection, peace and security and common heritage and that this interstitiality is most apparent in debates over global commons justice.

The Global Commons

We begin with an introduction to the context in which the debates emerged and are developing. There are two distinct phases to global commons debates. The first takes place in the cold war and in the context of post-colonial arguments about distributive justice. The second, we argue, is emerging as we write. The ideological, scientific and technological background to the argument has changed (even if the inequalities between the former colonial powers and the post-colonial states have not) and the normative import of human rights has increased. In order to substantiate our claim that this is the site of debate concerning distributive justice, we begin with the first negotiations of 'new' resource pools after the Second World War.

The global commons are primarily international resources pools that are not owned by (or appropriable by) a sovereign or commercial entity. This, as we shall see, is not a complete or satisfactory definition but it provides the basis for understanding two of the clearest examples of global commons resource pools. The first of these (in the order in which they were recognised as such by international treaty) is outer space and the second is the deep sea bed beyond national jurisdiction. Here new (or at least newly available) resource pools, thought to contain extraordinary riches in terms of minerals and/or hydrocarbons, were the subject of intense negotiation. The Outer Space Treaty (more properly the Treaty on Principles Governing the Activities of States in the Exploration and Use of Outer Space, including the Moon and Other Celestial Bodies, 1967) is the basis of space law and provides, in article 1, that

> The exploration and use of outer space, including the moon and other celestial bodies, shall be carried out for the benefit and in the interests of all countries, irrespective of their degree of economic or scientific development, and shall be the province of all mankind.

In article 2, we learn that this 'province of all mankind' shall not be subject to national appropriation. In article 4, we find that this space is to be used only for peaceful purposes. Such provisions are common to many global commons agreements. By the 1970s negotiations over the development of the law of the sea, the moon, information and communications technologies and, later, the environment were informed by the desire of developing (and often recently decolonised) states to establish a fairer economic order. Article 1 of the United Nations General Assembly Declaration on the Establishment of a New International Economic Order (NIEO) (1974) gives a clear statement of the intent.

> The greatest and most significant achievement during the last decades has been the independence from colonial and alien domination of a large number of peoples and nations which has enabled them to become members of the community of free peoples. Technological progress has also been made in all spheres of economic activities in the last three decades, thus providing a solid potential for improving the well-being of all peoples. However, the remaining vestiges of alien and colonial domination, foreign occupation, racial discrimination, apartheid and neo-colonialism in all its forms continue to be among the greatest obstacles to the full emancipation and progress of the developing countries and all the peoples involved. The benefits of technological progress are not shared equitably by all members of the international community. The developing countries, which constitute 70 per cent of the world's population, account for only 30 per cent of the world's income. It has proved impossible to achieve an even and balanced development of the international community under the existing international economic order. The gap between the developed and the developing countries continues to widen in a system which was

> established at a time when most of the developing countries did not even exist as independent States and which perpetuates inequality.

The campaign for a NIEO framed negotiations relating to global commons throughout the 1970s and 1980s in a way that has left an important moral question hanging over all subsequent practice. The negotiation of the United Nations Convention on the Law of the Sea (UNCLOS III) from 1973 to 1982 dealt with many issues. In particular it focused on sovereignty over the sea and rights to exclusive economic activity beyond territorial waters. The 1982 treaty set national rights to twelve nautical miles from the coastline, identified an exclusive economic zone (EEZ) to 200 miles beyond the territorial sea and designated the deep sea bed beyond this a global commons. This latter designation reflected a range of security, environmental protection and distributive justice concerns. The reasons the 'Area' (as it became known) assumed such significance can be found in a speech by Arvid Pardo, representative of Malta, in the UN General Assembly in 1967. Pardo, who was to become known as the Father of the Law of the Sea conference, argued that the existing Law of the Sea desperately needed amending in light of the increasing importance of the deep sea bed. It is worth quoting in full one paragraph of the 123 that makes up this famous speech.

> The known resources of the sea-bed and of the ocean floor are far greater than the resources known to exist on dry land. The sea-bed and the ocean floor are also of vital and increasing strategic importance. Present and clearly foreseeable technology also permits their effective exploitation for military or economic purposes. Some countries may therefore be tempted to achieve near-unbreakable dominance through predominant control over the sea-bed and ocean floor. This, even more than the search for wealth, will impel countries with the requisite technical competence to extend their jurisdiction over selected areas of the ocean floor. The process has already started and will lead to a competitive scramble for sovereign rights over the land underlying the world's seas and oceans, surpassing in magnitude and in its implications last century's colonial scramble for territory in Asia and Africa. The consequences will be very grave: at the very least a dramatic escalation of the arms race and sharply increasing world tensions, caused by the intolerable injustice that would reserve the plurality of the world's resources for the exclusive benefit of less than a handful of nations. The strong would get stronger, the rich richer, and among the rich themselves there would arise an increasing and insuperable differentiation between the two or three and the remainder. Between the very few dominant Powers, suspicions and tensions would reach unprecedented levels. Traditional activities on the high seas would be curtailed and, at the same time, the world would face the growing danger of permanent damage to the marine environment

through radio-active and other pollution: this is the virtually inevitable consequence of the present situation.

Part XI of the 1982 treaty responded to these by declaring the deep sea bed beyond national jurisdiction (or 'the Area') as global commons to be managed as the common heritage of mankind (CHM). In this case the designation of the Area as CHM sought to redress the economic imbalance between the developed and less developed world by establishing institutions (the International Seabed Authority (ISA) and the 'Enterprise') which would oversee site-banking (where an entity proposing exploitation of part of the Area would have to designate two areas of equal commercial worth, one of which would pass to the ISA (along with the scientific data that indicated its worth and the technology that made exploitation possible) and be exploited by the Enterprise for the benefit of less developed states. That this was the outcome of a decade of international negotiations is extraordinary and sets the scene for later fairness and justice arguments in trade and development law (see Franck, 1995).

The idea that the global commons should be managed for the benefit of all humanity (including future generations) is the central issue. The Moon Treaty (1979) also established a Common Heritage Regime, going beyond the Outer Space Treaty to create a similar common heritage regime (see especially article 11). But two vital contextual issues are salient here. The first is the cold war ideological battle between socialism and free-market capitalism which polarised the parties. The second is that the prospect of commercially viable exploitation of the moon or other celestial bodies or of the ocean floor was incredibly remote. This latter point (added to the fact that the USA and others were very keen on establishing an EEZ beyond territorial waters) mitigated the former to the extent that negotiations continued, something that would have been very unlikely if exploitation of what was thought to be incredible untapped wealth were imminent. Nevertheless part XI of the UNCLOS treaty was subject to renegotiation and the 1994 implementation agreement changed a number of key elements. Several developed states, led by the USA, refused to sign up to the convention. In part this was because the Reagan administration viewed the existing interpretation of CHM, which was closely allied to calls for a NIEO, as nothing short of international socialism (Koskenniemi and Lehto, 1996). Eventually an implementation agreement introduced a CHM regime founded on market principles and substantially weakening the Enterprise, particularly its funding, compulsory technology transfer and provisions relating to compensation for miners from less developed states whose land-based business might be affected by sea bed mining (Vogler, 2000: 67–68). Similarly the major space-going nations did not sign up to the Moon Treaty, preferring the weaker provisions of the earlier convention.

While the global commons regimes were developing, other resource pools and resource sinks were also being negotiated. The idea of a global commons and that such resources should be considered the 'common heritage of mankind' provided a normative vocabulary that permeated discussions in areas that did not quite fit the model of the global commons. Two examples here are the Antarctic Treaty System (ATS) and the environment. The Antarctic is not properly a global commons because several states have territorial claims in the region. These claims were put into abeyance by the 1959 treaty – something partly driven by cold-war fears that the USSR might site nuclear weapons in its bases (Buck, 1998: 57) and later by a desire to regulate the exploitation of mineral and hydrocarbon deposits in the region as well as increasing concerns about the cryosphere of the region that grew alongside a better understanding of its importance to the broader global environment. As well as suspending existing territorial claims the ATS deals with cooperative scientific research, conservation, non-military use and, by the 1980s, an attempt to regulate mineral exploration in the same vein as UNCLOS III (Vogler, 2000: 80–83). This initiative was overtaken by the Madrid Protocol that bans all mineral exploitation until 2048. What is significant and innovative about the ATS is the way it sets up a framework agreement in which scientific research can be conducted and where new understandings of the importance of the region to the common good of humanity can lead to further negotiations (Franck, 1995: 382–396). Key here is the idea that the Antarctic, while not the common heritage of mankind, was to be governed in the interest of all mankind (preamble to the 1959 treaty).

Our final example is importantly different again. Often referred to as the 'common concern of all humanity' (Vogler, 2000: 123) the atmosphere is a common sink resource rather than a common pool resource. This means it is important to all because of what we can put into it rather than what we can get out of it and because of the broad consequences of atmospheric pollution (from acidification of the seas, to an increase in extreme weather events, to global warming with all its implications). The issue area is scientifically and Politically complex. The need to restrain atmospheric pollution is set against the doctrines of Permanent Sovereignty over Natural Resources (General Assembly Resolution 1803, 1962) and the urgent need for the development in the Global South. Both of these issues speak to justice issues for post-colonial states but clash with environmental priorities. The need to restrain industrial development in the Global South, because the same process in the Global North has pushed the limits of the atmosphere to soak up carbon dioxide and other greenhouse gases, appears to be asking the poorest to pay for the richest. Even to speak about environmental priorities is to suggest a coherence that is absent. The Island peoples of the low-lying South Pacific are much more worried about marginal increases in the level of the sea than others who see the disappearing icecaps as an opportunity for strategic or economic advantage. Nevertheless, since the first UN conference on the Human Environment in Stockholm in 1972 there has been considerable work in dealing with, for example ozone-depleting gases (which included setting up a interim fund to transfer ozone-friendly technology to less developed countries).

This paper is not the place to develop any detailed analysis of climate change science or the prospect of mineral exploitation in outer space or on the deep sea bed. But we want to draw the reader's attention to some common features of these issues' areas. While there is a distinction to be drawn between global commons, international commons and sovereign territory with global importance and between resource pools that are to be governed as the common heritage of mankind, in the common interest of mankind or as the common concern of humanity there are also important normative overlaps. In particular we find that there are strong reasons given for managing these resources in the common interest (regardless of whether the pool sits in one jurisdiction or another) and, in the first iteration of international norm development that a concern for distributive justice – both between rich and poor states and between current and future generations – is a major driver of negotiation and treaty drafting. The second common feature is that these regimes are all under considerable pressure. While the prospect of exploitation of these resource pools was a distant hope rather than a realistic ambition when the regimes were negotiated, technology and demand have moved on. In 2014 the ISA began issuing the first licences for the exploration of the deep sea bed. At present 1.2 million square kilometres have been opened up under twenty-six licences (BBC, 2014). At the same time the USA (it was reported in February 2015) has recently begun to clear the way for the commercial development of the moon (Reuters, 2015; Reuters/*Guardian*, 2015), the politics of the Antarctic (while perhaps not so immediately exploitative) contains significant concern about the division of resource wealth (Brady, 2012) and the ongoing negotations around climate change policy see 2015 billed as 'time for global action for people and planet' (https://sustainable development.un.org/post2015). As the potential for exploitation of common resource pools grows nearer so interest in and compliance with common heritage/common interest mechanisms diminishes. The richer, technologically developed and powerful states have tended to redraw the boundaries of justice (or have simply chosen to underplay the far reaching nature of the principles in play). Some commentators see this as an inevitable consequences of technology bringing market forces into play. Scott Shackelford, for example, argues that,

> [P]revious competing legal and political theories fail to adequately explain the transformation of sovereignty over the commons. The only notion that has both the explanatory and predictive power is that technological progress catalyzes changing political realities and thereby governance regimes over the commons.
>
> (Shackelford, 2009: 113)

In similar vein Chukwumerije Okereke points to the deeply entrenched market-oriented neo-liberalism that dominates the international system (Okereke, 2008: 42). But there is more to say here. The fact that these resource pools are now open (or, in the case of common sinks, under threat of irreparable damage) makes the issues all the more urgent. The reasons offered for treating these resources as important to questions of global justice – the threat to peace and security, to sustainable development and environmental protection, the distributive and human rights issues as well as the potential for increased economic prosperity and resource security – are still in play. If anything, the potential for fruitful dialogue about international or global justice in the light of present developments is greater than it was in the 1970s and 1980s. In part this is because the ideological tensions of the cold war that drove a wedge between the normative frameworks of the developed and less developed world have dissipated even as the gap in wealth has grown. Thomas Franck, in his broad-ranging study of fairness discourse in international law and institutions, makes this point clearly;

> While the fairness discourse is just beginning, it *has* begun. In the 1990s efforts to link environmental management and preservation with development assistance are proving significantly more successful – in any event they receive a far more respectful and sensitive hearing – than comparable efforts in the 1970s to link trade and development assistance in the debate over the New International Economic Order. This time fairness related claims are seen as definitely and properly on the table.
>
> (Franck, 1995: 380)

The apparent socialisation of the developing world into the neo-liberal economic framework is not the only normative force in play. Key values from human rights to sustainable development are also commonly invoked. Franck is clear that we are witnessing the emergence of a system where distributional fairness claims are central to the idea of justice rather than the establishment of a system that is distributionally just. But despite 'serious missed opportunities' and failure to agree key targets the emergence of justice claims as central to international law-making makes clear that 'fairness' is a value competing with (and in some cases defeating) arguments from national security, economic efficiency and self-interest (Franck, 1995: 478).

An international political theory that takes the justice of global commons governance seriously has to confront a number of features of this debate. The debate is conducted in a positivist legal frame and that underlies two of the major challenges to normative progress – the statism of the international system and the resistance of positivism in law to moral theory. That said, the current debate is less ideologically polarised and there are clear human rights, international environmental and global commons dimensions to the debates. The human rights dimension speaks to what states owe those under their jurisdiction and to what the international community owes to those whose state is incapable or reluctant to respect or protect their international human rights (and to those without state protection). The international environmental dimension focuses on the costs of state policy both in specific trans-boundary instances but also in terms of general threats to human well-being caused by anthropogenic environmental degradation. The global commons dimension brings a further element to considerations of the just distribution of the benefits and burdens of available resources. Here the fact that global commons discourse has extended beyond the question of resources beyond national jurisdiction puts back on the table the questions of what to do with resources that are already owned but could have common interest characteristics (such as intellectual property rights in genetic resources for food and medicine or environmental resources like the Amazon rainforest) or ownership practices that raise serious questions of distributive fairness (such as the claim by Oxfam that, while more than a billion people live under the global poverty line, just eighty-five individuals have more wealth than the poorest 50 per cent of the human species (Oxfam International, 2015). The question that occupies the rest of this chapter is 'What can international political theory make of this?'

Distributive Justice and the Global Commons

The first thing that we need to be clear about is that international political theory does not speak with one voice and so there is no straightforward answer to this question. Even restricting the scope of the question to normative theory which is concerned with just distributions will elicit a multiplicity of responses delivered in many different voices. This, in itself, reflects a developing interest among political theorists in questions of 'global justice', 'international distributive justice' or the idea of a 'fair share' in a just distribution. It also reflects the vigorous nature of the debates that have developed between theorists about what international justice is and what it requires distributively. However, much of this debate has appeared to take the character of a re-run of long-standing arguments about domestic justice between liberals, libertarians and communitarians recast in this context as cosmopolitans, realists and statists. Understood in this way the debates about global justice run a significant risk of becoming as long-standing and entrenched as traditional debates about domestic justice have been. Seminal though the differences between these positions are, one possible advantage of thinking about international distribution through the lens of the global commons is that it holds out the potential for a recasting of these debates and the forging of new ones.

New debates can be forged on the ground of the global commons that may prove fruitful avenues for developing positions from across the spectrum. We think both that there could be significant payoffs here from a variety of theoretical points of view and that there is potential for developing some consensus among the 'many voices' on the usefulness of the focus on global commons management more generally. The remainder of this chapter starts to outline a possible agenda for research for international political theory, a 'call to arms' driven by two factors: first, by outlining the potential that a focus on the global commons and its management has in this relatively new debate; and second, by asserting the urgency of addressing global commons management now. This urgency follows from how, as we have seen, technological developments have made possible the increased exploitation of (e.g.) the mineral resources of the deep sea bed and from how this has coincided with a series of moves by powerful political and economic actors to challenge the regime of global commons management laid out in UNCLOS III, the Outer Space Treaty and similar regimes. These moves to unilaterally develop, or to signal an intention to unilaterally develop, resources that have been previously been subject to commons management regimes must be regarded as a retrograde step by all those concerned with the idea of a fair share. This could been regarded as an attempt to reassert the idea that resources beyond current state jurisdiction are *terra nullius*, unowned and liable to be claimed by states bringing them into sovereign jurisdiction, thus excluding others and denying their CHM status. Reasserting *terra nullius* where these resources are concerned would enable a land grab on a scale not seen since the nineteenth-century 'Scramble for Africa' (for an exploration of the contentious use of the concept of *terra nullius* see Fitzmaurice, 2007). This is the scenario that so worried Pardo when he advanced the idea of CHM in 1967, and it confronts us with even greater urgency than it did Pardo. The research agenda laid out here is, in part, an attempt to explore whether a reassertion of CHM, with the regimes of global commons resource management it entails, remains a plausible and attractive response to this attempted extension of state power.

There are good practical reasons why anyone concerned with global distributive justice and with making the idea of a fair share a meaningful part of international politics should take the global commons seriously. These reasons are based in concerns about moral accessibility and the 'purchase' or 'traction' that ideas of just distribution are capable of generating. Making radical plans for the international redistribution of wealth or of ownership of resources has often attracted criticisms of utopianism, idealism, abstraction from and irrelevance to the harsh real world of international politics. Even if some ideal theory of a just international distribution comes to be regarded as attractive, it will be persistently critically challenged about whether there is any plausible political path that leads us from here to there. This is one part of the challenge to normative progress, noted above, of the positivist resistance to the place of moral theory in discussions of international law and politics. A significant strand of recent normative theory has attempted to meet this challenge with a 'practical' turn, from Rawls's focus on the idea of a 'realistic utopia' (Rawls, 1999) to Buchanan's 'institutional moral reasoning' (Buchanan, 2004, 2013) to Beitz's recent work on a practical account of human rights (Beitz, 2009). What unites these accounts is a recognition that the positivist challenge can be met by paying closer attention to ideas and values that are already present in our international law and politics. This is something that our colleagues in international legal studies have been working on as they too reach out to questions of global justice and thus to international political theory (Franck, 1995; Ratner, 2015). Thinking about justice and injustice in context, rather than taking theoretically inventive flights from context, enables thinking to demonstrate a moral accessibility it is often derided for lacking. We think that the notions of CHM and the global commons is an 'open door' inviting a wider range of international theorists into at least partially framing their thinking in these more contextual terms. We return to this point in the final paragraphs.

Any account of international justice that has a significant redistributive element is likely to offer a critical account of the broadly state-centric international system arguing that it entrenches and institutionalises unacceptable levels of distributive inequality. Such an analysis is also likely to lead to wariness of the doctrine *of terra nullius*, both historically as a source of present unfairness and certainly of the distributive implications of any future extensions. Indeed, central to the inequality of the state system is the logic of *terra nullius*-style reasoning; resources are either already owned and so under exclusive state jurisdiction or they are as yet unowned and available for acquisition by states who can establish control over them, thus bringing them under state jurisdiction. Once a resource is under the exclusive jurisdiction of a state, all other states (and thus other people) are legitimately excluded from access to, use of or benefit from that resource. This logic entrenches inequalities as a consequence of the way it divides up the world, and international law is generally focused on defending that division. Moving directly from such a critical account to ideal theories of just distribution without an eye to moral accessibility cedes the ground of international politics to this logic. It allows that the current world is a world of unjustifiable inequality and argues that the solution is to make a new and better world. In doing so this approach lends power to charges of utopianism, abstraction and irrelevance. A focus on the 'open door' of the global commons and the language of the CHM is a refusal to cede this ground by highlighting competing norms that are already 'on the table' in international law and politics. Of course, as we have seen, these norms are widely recognised to be under pressure but this recognition actually highlights their current presence on the table. If they were not available norms in international law then they would not be in danger of being overwhelmed in a resurgence of land grab politics.

If we remind ourselves of what was actually placed on the table in the original UNCLOS III agreement (for example), this will serve to highlight both the potential moral purchase of political theories of distributive justice that at least partially focus on global commons and just how open the door is through which theorists are being invited. The Convention codified and developed the Law of the Sea 'in conformity with the principles of justice and equal rights and will promote the economic and social advancement of all peoples in the world' (UNCLOS III: Preamble). It did this, in part, by declaring that 'The Area [the deep sea bed] and its resources are the common heritage of mankind' (UNCLOS III: article 136) and so 'No State shall claim or exercise sovereignty or sovereign rights over any part of the Area or its resources, nor shall any State or natural or juridical person appropriate any part thereof', going on to state that 'No such claim or exercise of sovereignty or sovereign rights nor such appropriation shall be recognised'. Indeed, it is clear that 'all rights in the resources of the Area are vested in mankind as a whole ... [and] these resources are not subject to alienation' (UNCLOS III: article 137). The exploitation of resources in the Area is to be carefully managed by an international body and will 'be carried out for the benefit of mankind as a whole ... and taking into particular consideration the interests and needs of developing States' (UNCLOS III: article 140). In doing so, it will 'provide for the equitable sharing of financial and other economic benefits' and promote the transfer of the physical and intellectual technology of exploitation to developing States under fair and reasonable terms and conditions (UNCLOS III: articles 140 and 144). Even if this powerful set of commitments was significantly watered down in the later Implementation Agreement, this Agreement still reaffirmed 'that the seabed and ocean floor ... beyond the limits of national jurisdiction ... as well as the resources of the Area, are the common heritage of mankind' (UNCLOS III Implementation Agreement).

Despite the watering down, this highlights the availability of norms in international law that are in competition with the extension of sovereign claims. What is more, they are norms that speak directly to concerns about distributive justice and about the potential injustice of sanctioning a free-for-all in the exploitation of resources currently beyond state jurisdiction, going so far as to advocate managing their exploitation to particularly benefit developing countries. Again, despite the watering down of UNCLOS III, the language of global commons management and/or CHM has been successful enough to see it advanced as an organising norm(s) for resources that do not quite fit the usual global commons template, such as the Antarctic, the environment and the human genome (Buck, 1998), each time the argument being that a resource is identified that should be governed in the interests of all mankind. Even political theorists who have not expressly adopted a practical approach can find much to get interested in here. Highlighting the fairness discourse that is already on the table as at least part of the basis for thinking about distributive justice both draws on the relative success of the language of CHM and draws attention to the moral accessibility of the ideas. If you are critiquing the current state of the world, then you have good reason to build on relevant norms and values that are already present in international law as at least a starting point for discussion, an 'anchor in reality' to offset criticisms of utopianism and irrelevance. Rather than cede the realm of law and politics to the positivist critics of normative thinking, close attention to global commons and CHM is an open door to moral purchase through which international theorists could usefully consider going.

In addition to these practical considerations, there is also potential for some degree of theoretical consensus on the usefulness of ideas of CHM and global commons between at least some of the many voices within political theory concerned with distributive justice. We contend that when thinking about what a 'fair share' for everybody is, and how to legitimately realise it institutionally, good reasons can be given *from within* the accounts advanced of a wide variety of thinkers for engaging with consideration of the global commons. We are not claiming that each of these accounts *must* take this focus. Rather, we advance the more limited claim that each, on their own terms, *can* have good reason to consider the potential payoff from a reassertion of CHM and global commons norms. If our initially tentative thoughts outlined here are borne out by more concerted research in the future, then we could anticipate a developing 'overlapping consensus' on a commons focus in international political theory (Rawls, 1993). We have space only for an initial sketch of how this research might go and so will consider an indicative, though fairly diverse, range of approaches. Some of these approaches will be compatible with a commons focus, others might come to endorse it as an option while others may even come to mandate it. All we have space to do here is to suggest that none of the positions we consider are incompatible with such an approach and that they could have good reason to take it seriously. We start our initial sketch with Rawls's limited liberal approach.

John Rawls (1999: 105–120) argues against strong duties of international distributive justice, rejecting a cosmopolitan approach in favour of a more limited duty of assistance to burdened societies. Although he argues that this is unlikely to require large resource transfers between peoples it may require some, and Rawls does not really discuss how this assistance is to be funded. In opposing cosmopolitan redistribution he is clear that, because political culture is the prime determinant of inequality, the resources controlled by a state and its citizens are not liable to international redistribution simply in the face of inequality (1999: 117). While this argument is made in the context of a discussion of justice, and nothing suggests that these resources are not liable for use to fund assistance, there is a plausible alternative to using them even in this context. A global commons regime which identifies resources that are beyond state ownership and utilises the resources of (e.g.) the sea bed for the benefit of all mankind, with particular consideration paid to the interests and needs of developing states, is targeted in a way that is compatible with, and indeed potentially mirrors, the duty of assistance. The global commons could, therefore, fund Rawls's duty and it would do so without calling on states' present holdings.

Generally, Rawls is wary of resources that are unowned. He argues that (1999: 8) 'unless a definite agent is given responsibility for maintaining an asset and bears the responsibility and loss for not doing so, that asset tends to deteriorate'. He uses this argument to justify both property generally and a state's control over resources in its territory. It might also be used to justify the acquisition of unowned resources such as those of the deep sea bed in order to ensure that they are properly husbanded. However, Rawls's 'definite agent' need not be a state, so an international regime of commons management could fulfil this husbanding role by carefully managing exploitation, thus meeting his concerns about resource deterioration. There is, therefore, no prima facie reason to think that a global commons regime is incompatible with Rawls's Law of Peoples and some reason to think that it might fit his approach very well.

Turning to more redistributive positions we can consider Thomas Pogge's liberal cosmopolitan approach. Unlike Rawls, Pogge does regard significant international inequality as an issue of potential injustice and also identifies natural resources as a basis for a redistributive response. He argues that 'the global poor own an inalienable stake in all limited natural resources' (2002: 196). The injustice of inequality can at least partially be captured by the claim that the poor suffer the consequence of 'uncompensated exclusion from the use of natural resources' (2002: 199) while 'the better-off enjoy significant advantages in the use of a single natural resource base from whose benefits the worse-off are largely … excluded' (2002: 202).

He argues that this justifies what he calls a Global Resources Dividend, the proceeds of which 'are to be used towards ensuring that all human beings can meet their own basic needs with dignity' (2002: 197). The argument is basically that the better-off owe compensation to those who are worse off, and one ground for this is their exclusion of the poor from fair access to the planet's resources. Rather than argue that all resources be held as common property and then shared equally, his proposal is a more modest one that does not deny government's control of the natural resources in their territory. Instead, he argues that the Resource Dividend can be raised by a series of levies on resource use and pollution and that revenues raised in this way fund the compensation (2002: 204–206). A global commons regime managed for the benefit of the worst-off developing societies could be regarded as effectively a significant part of the dividend. Global commons regimes, appropriately managed and widely accepted, involve better-off developed societies forgoing natural resources benefits in the form of potentially lucrative exploitation opportunities in favour of the worse-off. In the absence of such a regime, the new land grab for the deep sea bed, for example, would deepen existing inequalities of access to natural resources and benefits that follow their exploitation. With such a regime this exploitation is carefully managed and would constitute at least partial compensation for the injustice that concerns Pogge.

Like Pogge, Hillel Steiner is concerned with fair access to natural resources and argues that this will require a Global Fund to undertake redistribution to ensure this. His left-libertarian position advances a foundational right to equal freedom that entails a right to self-ownership and a right to an equal share of natural resources (Steiner 1994, 2005: 32). The latter right has not been sufficiently met by our history of 'first come, first served' property acquisition which undermines the property entitlements that acquisition is supposed to establish. Steiner interprets the right to an equal share of natural resources as a right to an equal share of the value of land, therefore landowners owe, to all persons, an equal portion of the value of their (unimproved) property. Unless a tax is paid on land value as a cash equivalent to the sum of these shares then the landowner's property right is invalid. This tax goes into a Global Fund and is paid out equally to all (2005: 35–36).

Just as in the case of Pogge, could we not regard a widely accepted global commons regime as those (the better-off) who have drawn on more than their fair and equal share of natural resources forgoing their claim on as-yet-unowned resources in favour of those who have drawn on less than an equal share (the worse-off)? The cash realised by a carefully managed exploitation of the commons resources is a first payment into the Global Fund. In Steiner's case it may be that more than this would be required, but even if this is the case a commons approach is compatible as a first step to meeting rights and legitimating current property titles.

The last approach committed to international redistribution that we will sketch reflects some recent growth in interest in ideas of common ownership more generally, reviving ideas common in seventeenth-century writers such as Grotius (Armstrong, 2012, 2013; Risse, 2009, 2012). This approach takes as central the idea that 'the earth originally belongs to humankind collectively' generating a 'symmetrical claim' in all humans to the earth's resources (Risse, 2009: 285, 2012: 109). Mathias Risse cashes this out as the claim that 'all co-owners ought to have an equal opportunity to satisfy basic needs to the extent that this turns on collectively owned resources' (2012: 111). Chris Armstrong agrees that common ownership makes all 'entitled to sufficient shares of any natural resources that are necessary for them to meet their basic human rights' (2013: 341). For Risse, this opportunity to satisfy basic needs expresses a notion of at least minimum human solidarity as recognition that we all share an earth together that cannot be overridden even if no rights are violated in so doing (2012: 117). In the world that we actually share this means that the international system of states that has divided the world between them 'needs to be reconciled with Common Ownership' (Risse, 2009: 289). The notion of CHM and a global commons fits naturally with this notion of common ownership of the earth. What more appropriate way to recognise the entitlement of all to meet their basic needs from their share of an originally owned stock of planetary resources than to build on a global commons regime that recognises both collective ownership and the injunction to ensure that its proceeds are managed with particular consideration for the worst-off? Indeed, Armstrong explicitly picks out the ideas of CHM and global commons as a resonance in contemporary global politics and international law of the idea of common ownership (2012: 154–155). Here support for a focus on the commons may be mandated by this approach to global justice, not just compatible with it. Even if the link is not as strong as this, Armstrong draws our attention to the strategic advantage of a focus on this idea of a share of natural resources as an 'entry point' for any global egalitarianism (2013: 339–340, 345). In fact, this chimes with what we have seen in our brief consideration of Rawls, Pogge and Steiner. A focus on global commons regimes could be a first step towards justice.

The final sketch is more surprising, as it is of Robert Nozick's non-redistributive libertarianism. Nozick defends a set of strong libertarian property rights against violation by individual or state (1974: ix). These property rights are understood to absolutely disallow redistribution of legitimately obtained wealth for any purpose. However, it is often noted that the weight of the edifice of property entitlements is borne by his account of original acquisition, the process by which previously unowned property becomes owned. Original acquisition is legitimated, to the extent that Nozick ever settles this question, by a modified version of Locke's proviso that acquisitions leave behind 'enough and as good left in common for others' (1974: 175). Nozick's proviso states that an acquisition of property is legitimate only if it does not worsen the situation of others no longer at liberty to use the item without compensation (1974: 178). Nozick argues that a market system of libertarian property rights will satisfy this proviso as no one is likely to be worse off than they would have been in a state of nature given the compensations of living in a stable free-market society where rights are protected (1974: 182). However, it is very difficult to demonstrate the legitimacy of specific entitlements in his historical entitlement account, as any property right will have injustice somewhere in its history and this could invalidate the present-day title. More generally, it is not at all easy to show that the proviso is satisfied as the counterfactual, that people may be better off without libertarian appropriation, is difficult to disprove. Nozick acknowledges these concerns, accepting that we may need some temporary redistribution to legitimate property rights (1974: 230–231). What Nozick is most keenly interested in protecting is currently existing property rights from violation by the state in the name of justice. However, he acknowledges that these rights may be historically tarnished and illegitimate. Surprisingly, accepting the global commons as the resources that are 'enough and as good' left for others, managed and exploited for the benefit of those most likely to have been the people whose position has most probably been worsened by acquisition (the worst-off), may satisfy Locke's (and Nozick's) proviso. Distributing the proceeds of global commons regimes with particular consideration for developing countries is most likely to ensure that anyone whose position is sufficiently worsened is compensated for it. If a global commons focus does so then this performs two roles of vital interest to a Nozickian approach. First, it legitimates property rights generally by ensuring that the proviso is satisfied. Second, it does so without undermining the strong property rights that Nozick argues are already in existence.

Towards a Political Theory of the Global Commons: An Emerging Research Agenda

What we have sketched, relatively briefly, is a series of tentative arguments from a range of emblematic liberals, cosmopolitans, left and right libertarians that a global commons focus could be supported on the basis of reasons *from within* each of these positions. Of course, some of these positions will treat the commons as a pragmatic focus for raising the revenue needed for a duty of assistance or justice while others may treat the commons norms more clearly as a plausible expression of their attitude towards resources generally, while still others may regard a commons focus as required. Some may argue that this focus would be sufficient to meet the requirements of duty while others might see it as a first step towards a more radical set of redistributive conclusions. Some may see commons norms applied to the sea bed as transferable to genetic heritage, the environment and atmosphere and the rainforest, while others accept a more restricted approach. Attitudes to each of these issues and others will be varied. However, if each is able to find their own good reasons to adopt this focus for some central issues such as the deep sea bed then an overlapping consensus on global commons norms is possible and maybe even plausible. When we factor in support on a set of broadly prudential grounds that Pardo originally advanced, a security concern to avoid global powers embroiled in a scramble for resources, then the range of international theory positions that could be on board is broader than we might have expected.

There is a further possibility, one that speaks not just to an emerging debate but to a long overdue rapprochement between scholarship in international politics and international law. The practical turn in international political thought, found most explicitly in the recent work of Buchanan and Beitz, does not simply direct our attention to existing laws and institutions. It is instead an argument about the benefits and method of doing moral and political theory in context. Buchanan, who does spend some time reflecting on global commons regimes, offers what he terms a progressive conservatism by which he means

> that the theory should build upon, or at least not squarely contradict, the more morally acceptable principles of the existing international legal system. The most obvious reason for this requirement is that satisfying it will generally contribute to the accessibility of the theory's proposals.... But there is another reason: Where possible the theorist should build upon the moral strengths of the existing system, because it would be irresponsible to advocate, unnecessarily, a disregard for whatever progress has already been achieved in the system.
>
> (Buchanan, 2004: 63)

In later work, particularly in *The Heart of Human Rights* (2013), Buchanan argues forcefully that recognising the institutional and legal character of norms requires a distinct approach to political theory. There is something (morally) important about the fact that human rights law or common heritage regimes are institutionalised legal principles. Buchanan's practice-based approach to questions of international law and justice is intended to offer a critical understanding of our highly legalised and institutionalised moral lives. He does not deny that there are independent moral principles (he refers to his basic moral commitment to a natural duty of justice) but argues that morality has to accept the constraint of moral accessibility, something

> that signals that nonideal theory should make a case that the corresponding ideal theory's principles can be satisfied or at least seriously approximated through a process that begins with the institutions and culture we now have and that does not involve unacceptable moral wrongdoing in the process of transition.
>
> (Buchanan, 2004: 62)

Other scholars, such as Andrew Hurrell writing in the English School tradition in international relations theory, talk about moral accessibility as providing a deliberative purchase for the moral argument (Hurrell, 2007: 303). A focus on the commons as they appear in international law provides a stable starting point for moral deliberation because it begins with normative ideas already in play. Not only can international political theory elaborate and critically explore the moral sense and institutional implications of these ideas in the context of the legal regimes in question, but it is also the case that, while paying careful attention to the internal logic of international law (Reus-Smit, 2004: 38; Ratner, 2013: 2), international political theory brings a more holistic or systematic (Buchanan, 2004) moral view to the analysis.

Here we find another, theoretically vital, emerging debate that offers to recast the way we think about the relationship between morality, justice and law. Drawing us away from the rather unhelpful view that any moral position must be treated warily as an example of a residual naturalism has real potential. It is unlikely to alter the plurality of positions outlined above but it does have the potential to create common ground in that the debate shifts to the justice of an existing system rather than the competition between arguments from first principles. The research agenda of the current authors explores this space, arguing that the interstitial nature of the moral and legal norms in question (the overlap between human rights, environmental protection, distributive justice and peace and security as well as the overlap between moral and legal reasoning) offers to break new ground in theory and in practice (Roberts and Sutch, 2015).

The ideas of CHM and of global commons regimes open a door to potentially linking the sorts of egalitarian liberal approaches we have just sketched out to a progressive conservative attitude towards international law and international norms. Each of the egalitarian approaches is given reason in their own terms to focus on something that already has normative expression in international conventions, to anchor themselves to progressive aspects of the current system that are already 'on the table' of international politics. Different positions can be developed in ways that will be more or less challenging to the statism of that politics but they can be understood as expressing progressive elements of the international system, and deploying them to challenge regressive attempts to reassert a nineteenth-century approach of first come, first served exploitation. A global commons focus will protect the common interest against this regressive interpretation, whether supported for everyone's prudential reasons of 'limiting exploitation against their interests' or on the basis of the fairness norms highlighted by Franck enabling exploitation 'for the benefit of mankind as a whole' (UNCLOS III: Article 140). Indeed, it may be useful to regard the series of egalitarian approaches sketched out above as offering competing interpretations of what it would be to manage at least some resources 'for the benefit of mankind as a whole', a series of competing attempts to flesh out the idea with substantive content.

Finally, carrying out this sort of work on the neglected global commons dimension of debates on distributive justice could take on a broader significance. In addition to giving this dimension some much deserved attention there are clear possibilities that a focus on global commons will enable something substantial and enlightening to be said about the other dimensions of this debate, the environmental and human rights dimensions, in a more systematically unified manner. We have already seen that the language of CHM and global commons has been appropriated by some to be applied to environmental concerns about managing atmospheric pollution in terms of fair use of the common atmospheric sink and to the environmental importance and genetic diversity of the rainforests. Just as plausibly we have seen how global commons regimes could have significant redistributive implications, supporting and securing human security and the human rights that protect it. Placing global commons considerations at the heart of our thinking offers us the opportunity to develop each of these dimensions in all of our interests.

The alternative, the undermining of global commons regimes and the reassertion of a logic of *terra nullius* that has served only to undermine any notion of distributive justice, is also likely to be damaging to the environment if its track record is any guide. It also has a mixed record on the protection of human rights (to be charitable). It is exactly this alternative that appears to be being re-established as global commons regimes are threatened by developed countries' recent history and signalled intentions to unilaterally exploit in commons areas. We argue that an appropriate response to these intentions, from anyone interested in promoting 'fair shares', is to actively seek to build on and reinforce the common heritage norms already on the table of the international system rather than to ignore them or to quietly acquiesce to their destruction.

References

Armstrong, C. (2012), *Global Distributive Justice: An Introduction*, Cambridge: Cambridge University Press.

Armstrong, C. (2013), 'Natural resources: the demands of equality', *Journal of Social Philosophy*, 44 (4): 331–347.

BBC (2014), *Deep Sea Mining Licenses Issued*, www.bbc.co.uk/news/science-environment-28442640 (accessed 20 April 2015).

Beitz, C. (2009), *The Idea of Human Rights*, Oxford: Oxford University Press.

Brady, A.-M. (2012), *The Emerging Politics of Antarctica*, London: Routledge.

Buchanan, A. (2004), *Justice, Legitimacy and Self Determination: Moral Foundations for International Law*, Oxford: Oxford University Press.

Buchanan, A. (2013), *The Heart of Human Rights*, Oxford: Oxford University Press.

Buck, S. J. (1998), *The Global Commons: An Introduction*, Washington, DC: Island Press.

Egede, E. and Sutch, P. (2013), *The Politics of International Law and International Justice*, Edinburgh: Edinburgh University Press.

Fitzmaurice, A. (2007), 'The genealogy of Terra Nullius', *Australian Historical Studies*, 129: 1–15.

Franck, T. (1995), *Fairness in International Law and Institutions*, Oxford: Oxford University Press.

Hurrell, A. (2007), *On Global Order: The Constitution of International Society*, Oxford: Oxford University Press.

Koskenniemi, M. and Lehto, M. (1996), 'The privilege of universality: international law, economic ideology and seabed resources', *Nordic Journal of International Law*, 65: 533–555.

Nozick, R. (1974), *Anarchy, State, and Utopia*, Oxford: Blackwell.

Okereke, C. (2008), *Global Justice and Neoliberal Environmental Governance*, London: Routledge.

Oxfam International (2015), 'Richest 1 per cent will own more than all the rest by 2016', www.oxfam.org/en/pressroom/pressreleases/2015-01-19/richest-1-will-own-more-all-rest-2016 (accessed 8 June 2015).

Pogge, T. (2002), *World Poverty and Human Rights: Cosmopolitan Responsibilities and Reforms*, Cambridge: Polity Press.

Ratner, S. (2013), 'Ethics and international law: integrating the global justice project(s)', *International Theory*, 5 (1): 1–34.

Ratner, S. (2015), *The Thin Justice of International Law: A Moral Reckoning of the Law of Nations*, Oxford: Oxford University Press.

Rawls, J. (1993), *Political Liberalism*, New York: Columbia University Press.

Rawls, J. (1999), *The Law of Peoples: With 'The Idea of Public Reason Revisited'*, Cambridge, MA: Harvard University Press.

Reus-Smit, C. (2004), *The Politics of International Law*, Cambridge: Cambridge University Press.

Reuters (2015), *The FAA: Regulating Business on the Moon* (3 February), www.reuters.com/article/2015/02/03/us-usa-moon-business-idUSKBN0L715F20150203 (accessed 20 April 2015).

Reuters/*Guardian* (2015), 'Federal Aviation Administration pens letter stating intention to allow commercial activities on the moon to be conducted "on a non-interference basis"' (3 February), at www.theguardian.com/science/2015/feb/03/faa-moon-land-rights-commercial-development (accessed 20 April 2015).

Risse, M. (2009), 'Common ownership of the earth as a non-parochial standpoint: a contingent derivation of human rights', *European Journal of Philosophy*, 17 (2): 277–304.

Risse, M. (2012), *On Global Justice*, Princeton: Princeton University Press.

Roberts, P. and Sutch, P. (2015), 'The common heritage of humankind and global (distributive) justice', working paper presented at the University of the Witwatersrand, South Africa.

Shackelford, S. (2009), 'The tragedy of the common heritage of mankind', *Stanford Journal of Environmental Law*, 28: 109–167.

Steiner, H. (1994), *An Essay on Rights*, Oxford: Blackwell.

Steiner, H. (2005), 'Territorial justice and global redistribution', in G. Brock and H. Brighouse (eds), *The Political Philosophy of Cosmopolitanism*, Cambridge: Cambridge University Press, pp. 28–38.

Vogler, J. (2000), *The Global Commons: Environmental and Technological Governance*, second edn, Chichester: Wiley.

Official Documents Cited

UN GA Resolution 1803, 1962, *Permanent Sovereignty over Natural Resources*, http://daccess-dds-ny.un.org/doc/RESOLUTION/GEN/NR0/193/11/PDF/NR019311.pdf?OpenElement (accessed 20 April 2015).

Pardo, A., Speech to the General Assembly, Official Record of the UN GA first committee, 1967, www.un.org/depts/los/convention_agreements/texts/pardo_ga1967.pdf (accessed 20 April 2015).

Outer Space Treaty, 1967, https://treaties.un.org/doc/Publication/UNTS/Volume%20610/volume-610-I-8843-English.pdf (accessed 20 April 2015).

UN GA Resolution 3201, 1974, *Declaration on the Establishment of a New International Economic Order*, www.un-documents.net/s6r3201.htm (accessed 20 April 2015).

Moon Treaty, 1979, www.unoosa.org/oosa/en/SpaceLaw/gares/html/gares_34_0068.html (accessed 20 April 2015).

UNCLOS III, 1982, www.un.org/depts/los/convention_agreements/texts/unclos/unclos_e.pdf (accessed 20 April 2015).

Conclusion

Finding a Fair Share

Camilla Boisen and Matthew C. Murray

In this volume, we have approached some of the challenges, promise of and under-represented aspects of distributive justice and the debates that surround it. As a point of focus, we have spent time specifically looking at the under-representation of aspects of the global and African experience and how these have been shaped. These are presented as examples, and not the sole existing ones in our world, to frame how arguments of philosophic and theoretical justification can shape our development. However, the specific focus that was part of the last section serves as an example of a larger argument, which deserves slightly more inspection.

Even the most avid political academic or observer may be unaware of the breadth and complications of African politics, economics and society. It is a narrative with few heroes, great turmoil, immense human and natural suffering. It is a narrative punctuated with some of the most heinous violence the world has ever seen. To this day, Africa is ravaged by wars and conflicts simmering along lines created by colonial powers (some known, some far more covert) geographically, culturally, even linguistically dividing the continent. There are cultural, religious and ethnic tensions that extend beyond the contemporary and modern-era influences which have drawn increasing scrutiny for their roles in perpetuating the issues that plague the continent. It is a continent so vast and geographically unique in the issues that face it that it has created its own genres of regional inspection and study, making it a difficult region on which to make broader impacts. Consider, for example, the most recent events in Kenya, Somalia, and Nigeria and the humanitarian crimes committed there against civilians by Islamic militarist groups such as Boko Haram, ISIS and Al-Shabab; or inter-state conflicts and civil wars in countries like Sierra Leone, Angola, the Democratic Republic of Congo, the Central African Republic and Rwanda, having led to some of the most horrific mass killings and genocides since the end of the Second World War. This is to say nothing of the economic, human health and inequalities of the peoples and places of the continent that are as troubling as any gun or tank. The recent Ebola outbreak in West Africa illustrated the unequal distribution of medical care as infected Western health care and aid workers were rushed back to hospitals for treatment in Europe and the United States and given preferential access to (experimental) vaccines, with no such recourse for affected Africans. If anything, this reminds us of the moral arbitrariness of state borders.

Yet it is also a story of hope, resiliency, reclamation, human fellowship and empowerment. There are examples of triumph, cooperation, success, development and perseverance, all of the aforementioned largely, though not exclusively, happening outside of the eyes of mainstream observation if not consideration. The African experience is a continuing example of how the fascination of humanity with power can lead to amazing triumphs in change and creation, but equally can be the vehicle of great destruction and loss: a cautionary tale, not just for the protagonists who call the continent home, but for the many states of the world who used or continue to use the continent as a theatre for expansion, ideological conflict, cultural hegemony and as an exploitative frontier for resources.

Yet despite the abundance of behaviours that are soundly treated as abhorrent, they all came from theories that justified them and made them 'the right thing to do'. It is a harsh reality that warlords, dictators and Western/Eastern interventions large and small do not act because they believe their cause to be wrong, but rather because they believe it to be right. Legitimacy of actions comes from the ideas that motivate them. These ideas can be a powerful tool for emancipation and equality, but equally can be the tool of segregation and oppression. Even South African apartheid, perhaps one of the best known examples of illegitimate African inequality enforced under the threat of imprisonment, death and economic deprivation, was rigorously justified by those who applied it in spite of its blatantly racist practice and ideas. These ideas matter if we are to engage with the practice and outcomes we often focus on as important.

It could be easy in light of this to do as many political practitioners have done and say that theory and philosophies of politics are not the answer to the problems of the world but the cause of them, that theory serves as only an irresolvable device to justify actions and does not speak to the content of these actions in any kind of positive way. Equally, on the other side, a political theorist might say that those who practise politics, including lawmakers, civil servants, elected officials, governmental heads and so on, do not analyse and critique their deeply held theoretical understandings in ways needed to ask better questions and find better administrative answers to the problems of our world. It is in this polarisation that the reader of this book must look beyond simply what has been presented and look more deeply, perhaps even uncomfortably and critically, into their role in identifying, changing and understanding what is needed to move forward.

Circumstances, when they are witnessed, can change how we approach our world and what is required not just to realise justice through policy but to understand its nature. Understanding the complexity of this nature and the conflicts in how it is perceived is necessary in ensuring these policies are as good and as dynamic as they can be, as much if not more than studying charts or measurables can be. They are sides of the same coin. The ability to ask a better question is a prerequisite to being able to find a better answer. Finding a better path has to be a practice studied on both ends, repeatedly, perpetually and rigorously. This may ultimately be the lesson from our collective failures of political, social, economic and perhaps even personal enterprise. Our challenge is to observe our world and to try to grasp what it tells us about our meaning and being so that we might better articulate justice. And equally, to avoid, correct or comprehensively understand these problems, a discussion of what motivated their existence is primary, not just tertiary, to realising palpable change. The harsh reality is that being good people with good observational research skills is not an element on its own which is enough to make a good world or good policy. There is a space where these worlds collide. This intersectionality is equally important a field of study in a contemporary and historical sense, but likely the area in which the rubber meets the road in driving our shared future carved by the policies that touch us all and the ideas that motivate them.

There are many aspects here where a reader of this volume can postulate development through new ideas or perspectives from authors given here, or how they relate to a given reader's interests, or even in direct opposition to an idea presented here. However, let us for now approach the constraints of the field of study itself as a practice where the ideas meet the method of action and dissemination in academia and learning. It is important to expose the fact that the dichotomy between theory and practice, which is causing or at least exacerbating many political problems large and small in pretty much any political context one could name, is paralleled in the institution tasked with understanding political conflicts.

There are many failings which led to this deeper problem which we witness in separating theory and practice, the ideal and non-ideal, the applied and the theoretical or analytical. We see today an academic industry that is increasingly fragmented, internally politicised and now the playground of schools of thought which encourage vocational apprenticeship to derivative idolisation that seeks only to buttress an existing form of thought or indeed, intellectual individual or cadre. In seeking to solidify the legacy of their impact, these actions can be understood sympathetically in that we want our voices and ideas to have space and scope. They are important to the researcher and we seek to make impacts that are lasting and valued. Yet this academic propriety can in fact undermine the subjects of their study in that it potentially constrains the narrative of the study and the values others can see in it. It undermines further the potential validity of their lasting impact as *how* we approach issues of justice, distributive or otherwise, rather than the specific content of an approach that they toiled to cast. Perhaps we ought to be charged with passing the torch rather than fanning the flame. The best and brightest are trapped so deeply in the footprints of imposed giants that they cannot see their way out of their own assumptions; after assumptions nor do they want to, as being a philosopher or political theorist is secondary or even harmful to being an academic specialist or professional.

This phenomenon may be acutely visualised in today's academia, but in reality it is an old practice of winners and losers in philosophy forming a canon of influence. We can see, time and time again, individuals staking out their fiefdom of thought and defending it with zealotry, ardour and even, on occasion, malice. The competitive nature of resources within academia is also leading to a veritable turf war between the sub-genres of politics and sadly is resulting in stark deficiencies in how the discipline is passed to the next generation at many institutions. As we have hopefully shown here, this process, separation of study, separation of discipline and specialisation itself, has wildly impoverished elements of the theoretical argument which have undoubtedly harmed the thought and subsequent policies that have derived from this thought. The practice of the field in what it values in its proprietors, how it instructs them, the outputs it prizes from them, must be modified to avoid this perpetuation even if these practices and those who undertake them feel they are 'right' for doing so. If the gap is to be bridged, the primary audience of this very volume must look in the mirror and at least resolve not to be part of the problem, and to acknowledge that the deficiencies of the study rival the deficiencies of the practice of politics. Our collective abilities to bring these convergences of politics and thought, study and practice back to the fore will likely determine how bright or dark our future as a global society will be. The ivory tower casts a shadow we must acknowledge before we can illuminate those who stand in the shade it casts. These are phenomena we must face as ambassadors of thought if we are to represent the importance of ideas to those who clearly need to be exposed to them.

The narrowing and splintering of politics into approaches and fields, genres and specialisations is one that has another effect. Through the dialogue of the volume, the narrative underlines how important it is for our conversations about theory and philosophy, but equally about practice and policy, to be aware of and translatable to each other. This again mirrors many of the problems we also see in distributive justice debates. Access to the narrative and inclusion within it will not ensure that the narrative will not be dominated, and hence the study of it dominated, by those who seek to protect their 'share' of it. We have to work to include each other's perspectives by valuing their distinct languages, challenges and narratives that ultimately enrich the broader and encompassing one.

There are few if any who will look at distributions in the present tense, conceptually or literally, as perfect. Regardless of whether this is an eternal condition of our human existence, we still must try to work conceptually and will always be tasked with acting in distributive ways. We then must ensure that our arguments about all aspects of a subject, distributive justice being the focus here, are not incomplete. This would imply the difficult and ongoing task of identifying and transcending our parochial baggage of conceptual structure even when doing so is hard, uncomfortable and may require profound change within the 'academy'. Having all of these voices across disciplines at the table requires that we accept specific paradigmatic particularisms critically and sympathetically, inclusive of our research, teaching and modes of discourse. It is the only way for us to avoid handing down broken tools of inquiry. Deficient discussions that result from deficient tools are, in some fundamental way, our collective fault.

We must acknowledge that something is really at stake, not just in what we talk about in terms of distributive justice, but in how we talk about it and who we let talk about it. Finding a fair share is about how we come to understand the expansive nature of distributive justice as much as what that understanding ultimately is or could be. It is to ask what, how and who is needed to talk about fairness, justice and distribution in a coherent way. We increasingly recognise the limitations of our expectations, terminologies and approaches to distributive issues in our world. These recognitions ought to cast a light equally on how we approach the production and dissemination of knowledge.

This inclusion has to happen in governments (at international, State and local levels) and at the grassroots level, certainly, but equally it must happen between the academic professionals who, in spite of academic competition, must realise their duty to heightening and informing these arguments in which they may hold strong perspectives and inclinations on which are the most interesting or valuable. The perspectives in this volume are indicative of what the value of broadening our pursuit of knowledge of these areas can be. If we are to teach, research and facilitate the learning of others about justice (distributive or otherwise), we must collectively work to practise what we preach, not simply through our content but in how we approach each other and our fields. We must be aware that our practices and actions in how we present and research our topics can actively or passively perpetuate our own impoverishment. Furthermore, that impoverishment has very real consequences. This is to ask hard questions about our practices of learning and discourse that include how we elevate luminaries, accept consolidations of thought, assess the troubling aspects of patronage and overproduction present in publication, the troubling hiring practices and increasing reliance on non-continuing labour in the profession as a whole, the subjugation of political thought as a fourth- or fifth-order priority in many institutions curriculums, just to name a few.

We ask you, the reader, to engage with the specific ideas, problems and perspectives this volume has presented. Equally, we ask you to recognise the way in which the volume has presented these arguments, as parts of a much larger dialogue we must foster, and that our structures of thought, learning, practice and observation are, in key ways, tied. Their advancement is in many ways shaped as much by what these ideas and perspectives say as by how they say it to each other. It is to recognise that our perspectives are artificially separated when we look at encompassing issues, and that the only way to rectify this is to seek them out, value them and engage with them on their terms. Such is the case with distributive justice. In finding a fair share, we challenge the reader to act critically and fraternally towards others in matters of study and practice, to seek out conceptually and practically the many challenges that face our study, understandings and applications of distributive justice.

Index

www.ingramcontent.com/pod-product-compliance
Ingram Content Group UK Ltd.
Pitfield, Milton Keynes, MK11 3LW, UK
UKHW022116190926
475702UK00013B/1480

* 9 7 8 0 8 1 5 3 7 0 5 0 5 *